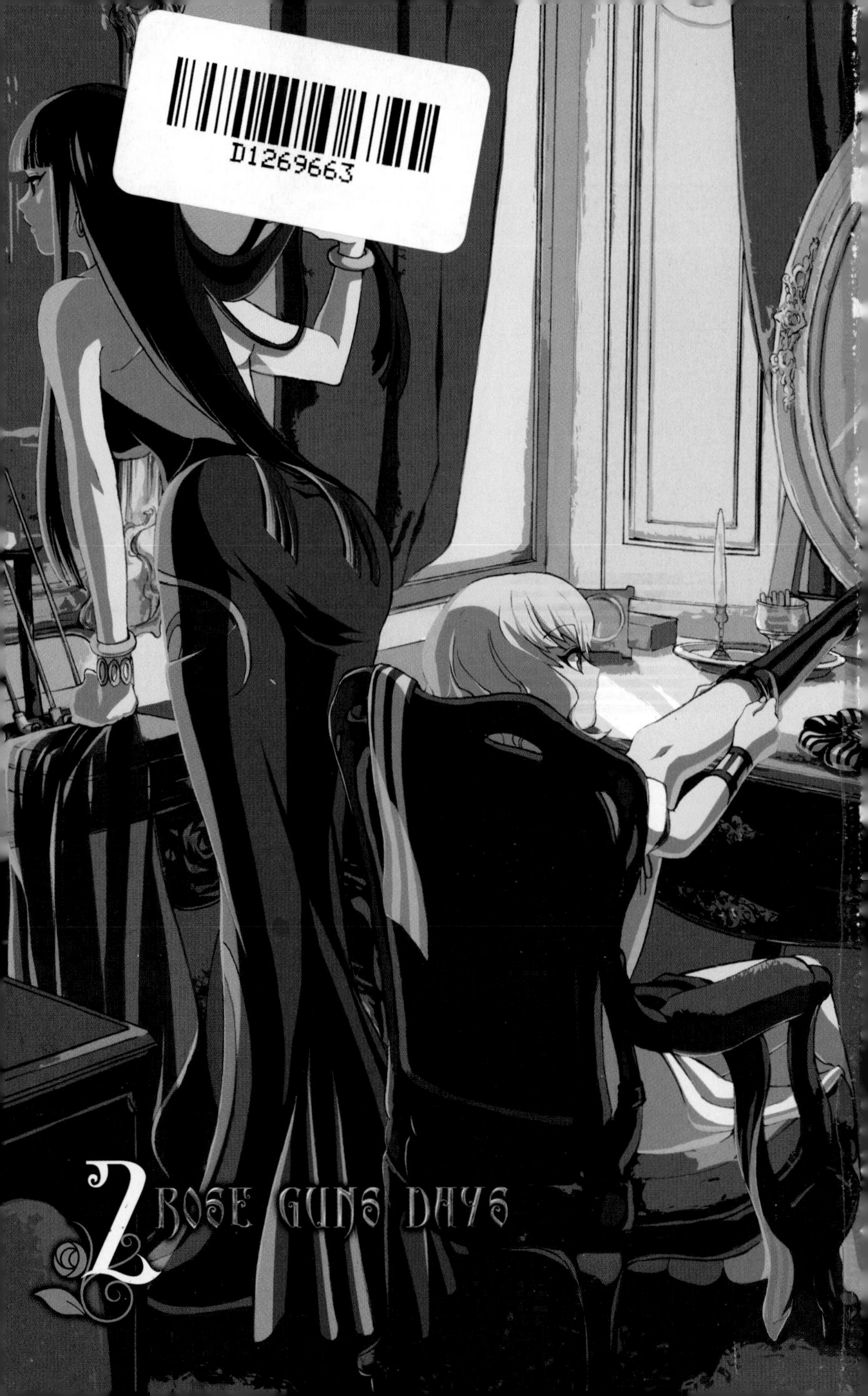
2
ROSE GUNS DAYS

Contents

ROSE GUNS DAYS

Scene: 05

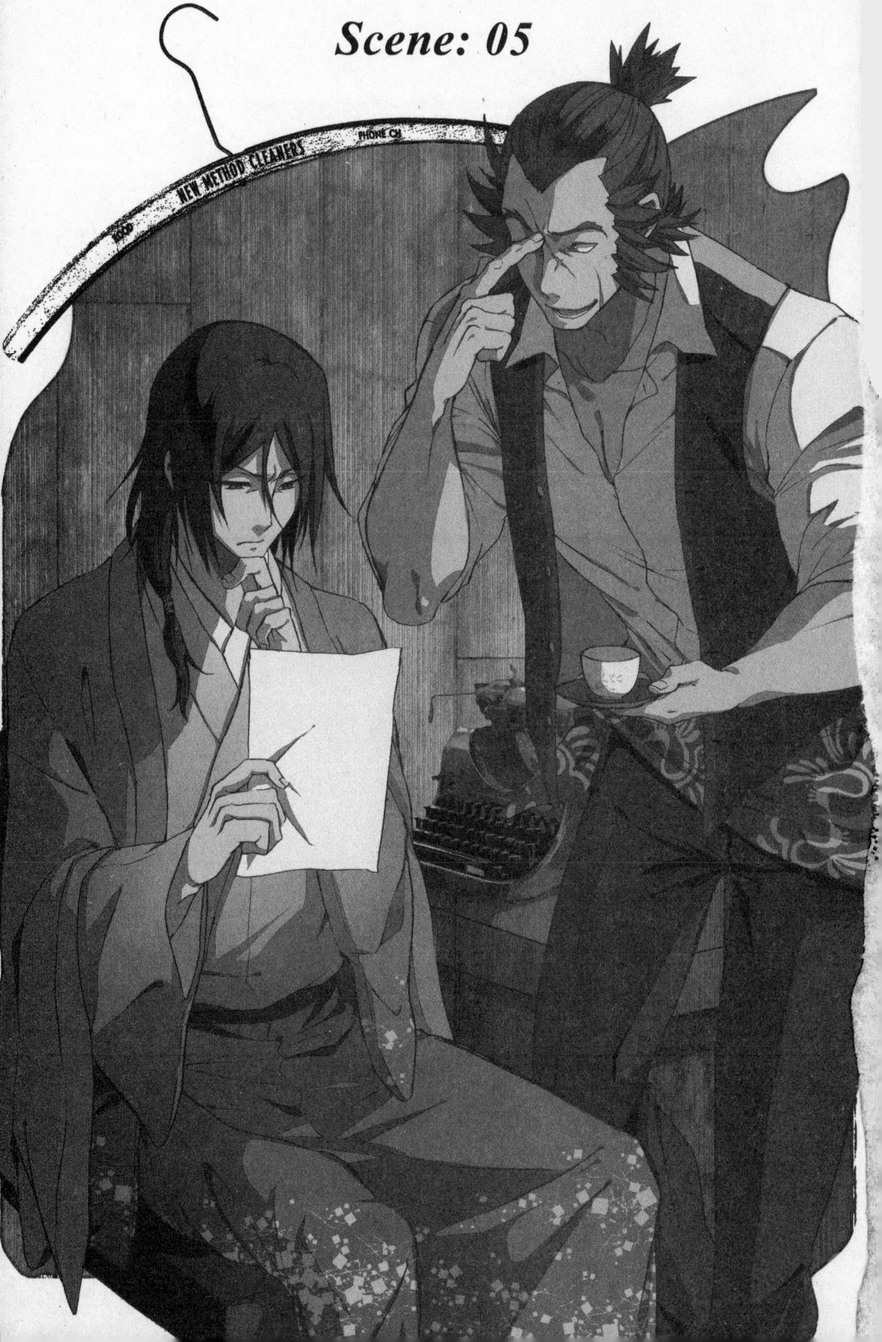
NEW METHOD CLEANERS
PHONE CH

ROSE GUNS DAYS

Season 1

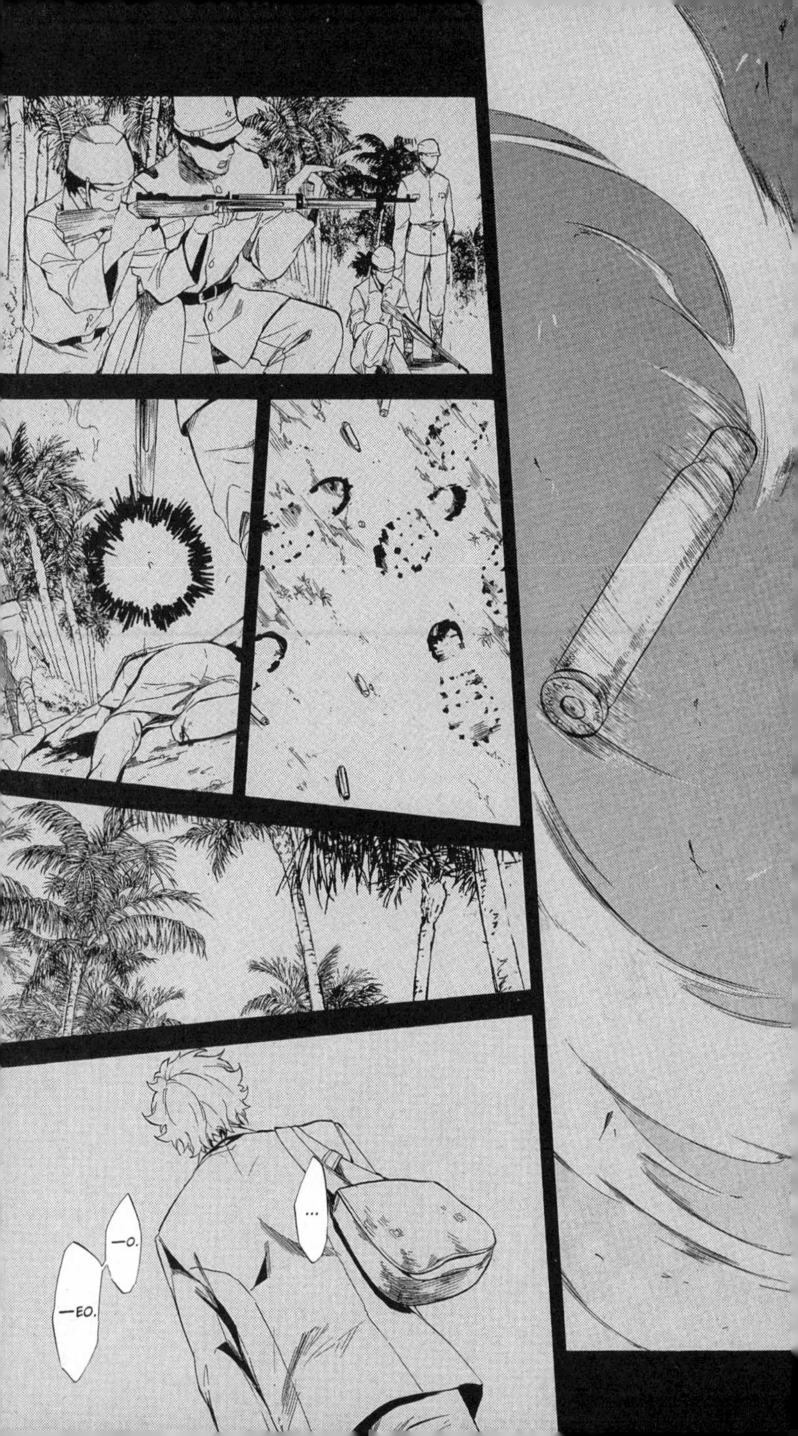
...
—O.
—EO.

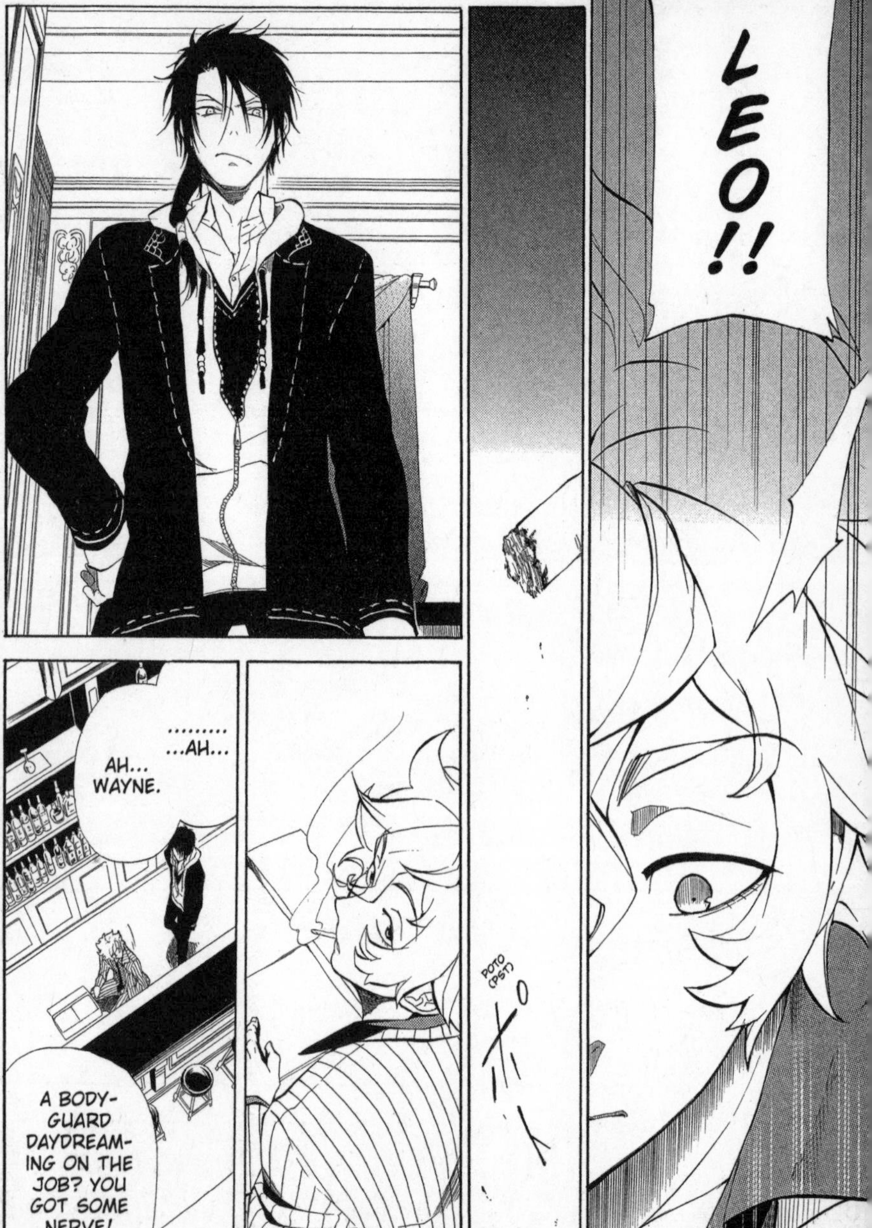
LEO!!
POTO (PST)
....
...AH...
AH...
WAYNE.
A BODY-
GUARD
DAYDREAM-
ING ON THE
JOB? YOU
GOT SOME
NERVE!

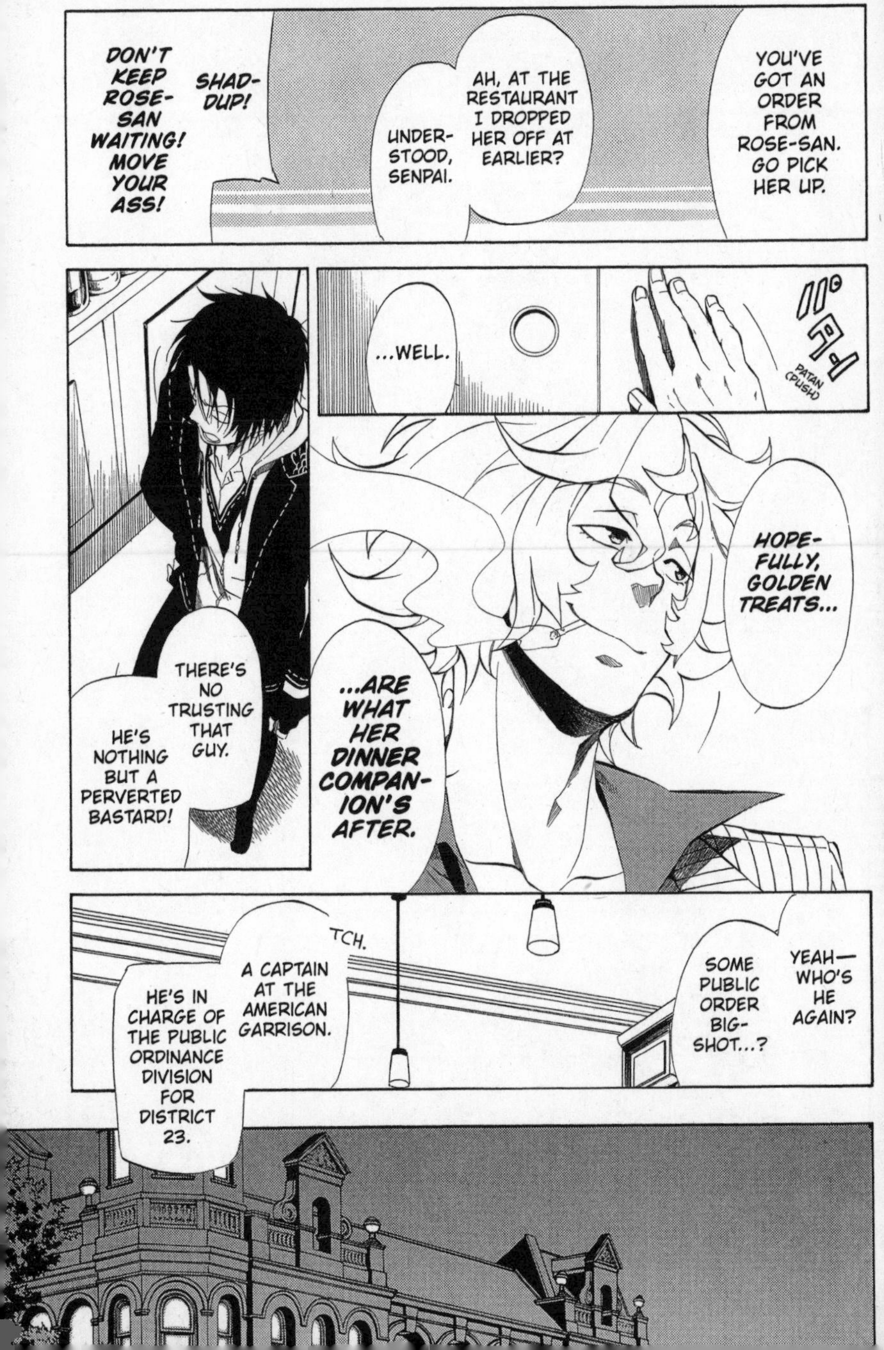
YOU'VE GOT AN ORDER FROM ROSE-SAN. GO PICK HER UP.
AH, AT THE RESTAURANT I DROPPED HER OFF AT EARLIER?
UNDER-STOOD, SENPAI.
SHAD-DUP!
DON'T KEEP ROSE-SAN WAITING! MOVE YOUR ASS!
PATAN (PUSH)
...WELL.
HOPE-FULLY, GOLDEN TREATS...
...ARE WHAT HER DINNER COMPAN-ION'S AFTER.
THERE'S NO TRUSTING THAT GUY.
HE'S NOTHING BUT A PERVERTED BASTARD!
YEAH— WHO'S HE AGAIN?
SOME PUBLIC ORDER BIG-SHOT...?
TCH.
A CAPTAIN AT THE AMERICAN GARRISON.
HE'S IN CHARGE OF THE PUBLIC ORDINANCE DIVISION FOR DISTRICT 23.

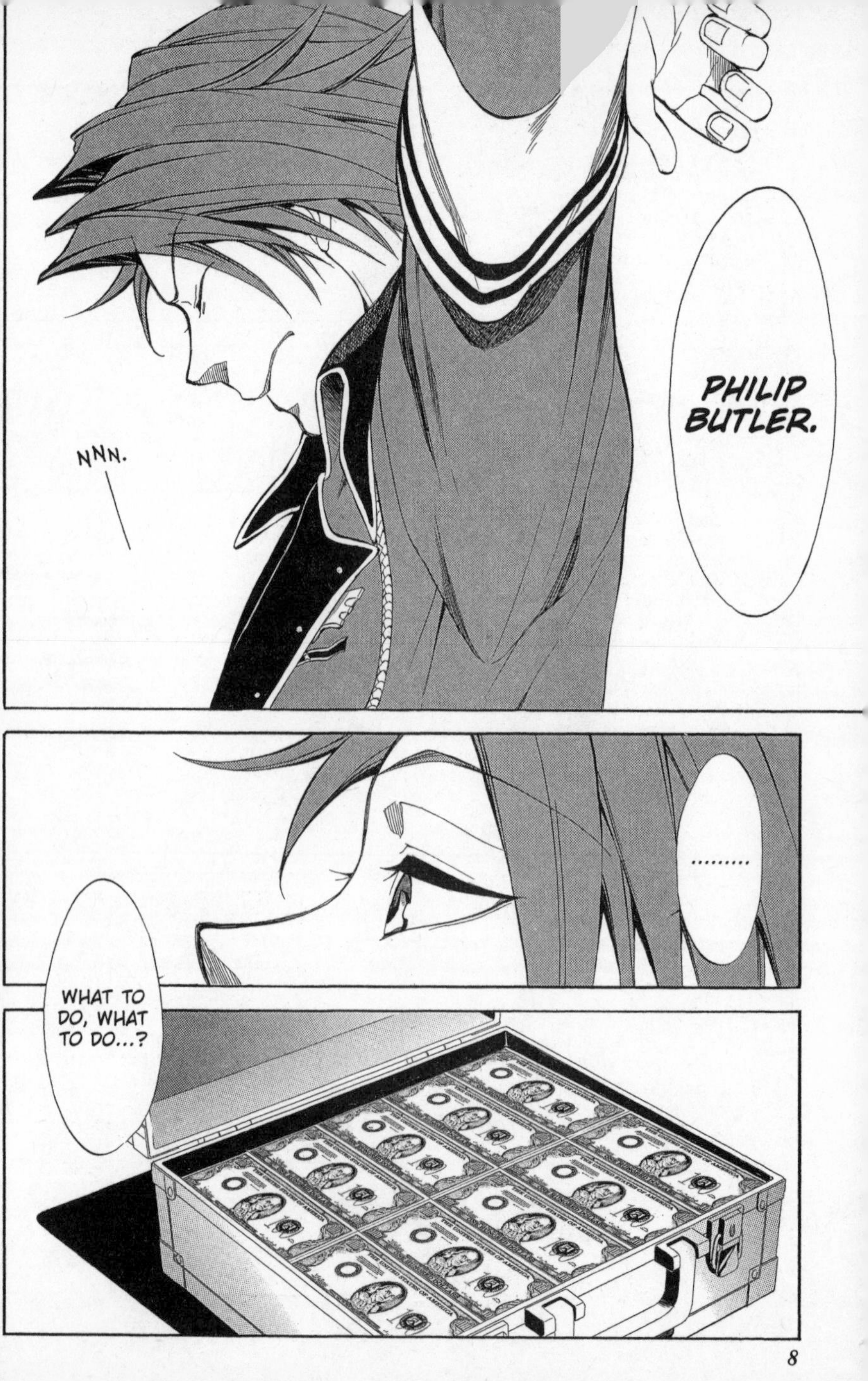
PHILIP BUTLER.
NNN.
....
WHAT TO DO, WHAT TO DO...?

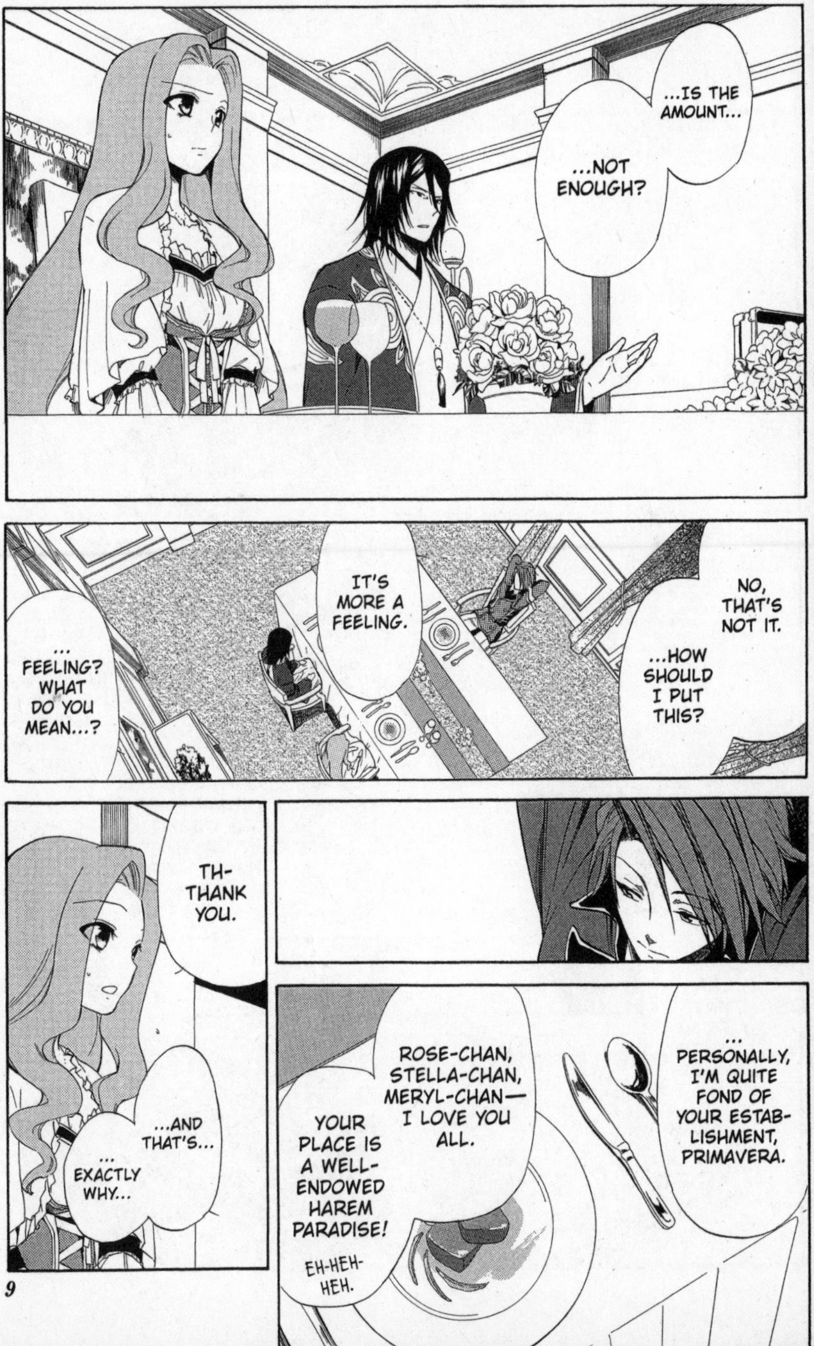
...IS THE AMOUNT...
...NOT ENOUGH?
NO, THAT'S NOT IT.
...HOW SHOULD I PUT THIS?
IT'S MORE A FEELING.
... FEELING? WHAT DO YOU MEAN...?
... PERSONALLY, I'M QUITE FOND OF YOUR ESTABLISHMENT, PRIMAVERA.
ROSE-CHAN, STELLA-CHAN, MERYL-CHAN— I LOVE YOU ALL.
YOUR PLACE IS A WELL-ENDOWED HAREM PARADISE!
EH-HEH-HEH.
TH-THANK YOU.
...AND THAT'S...
... EXACTLY WHY...

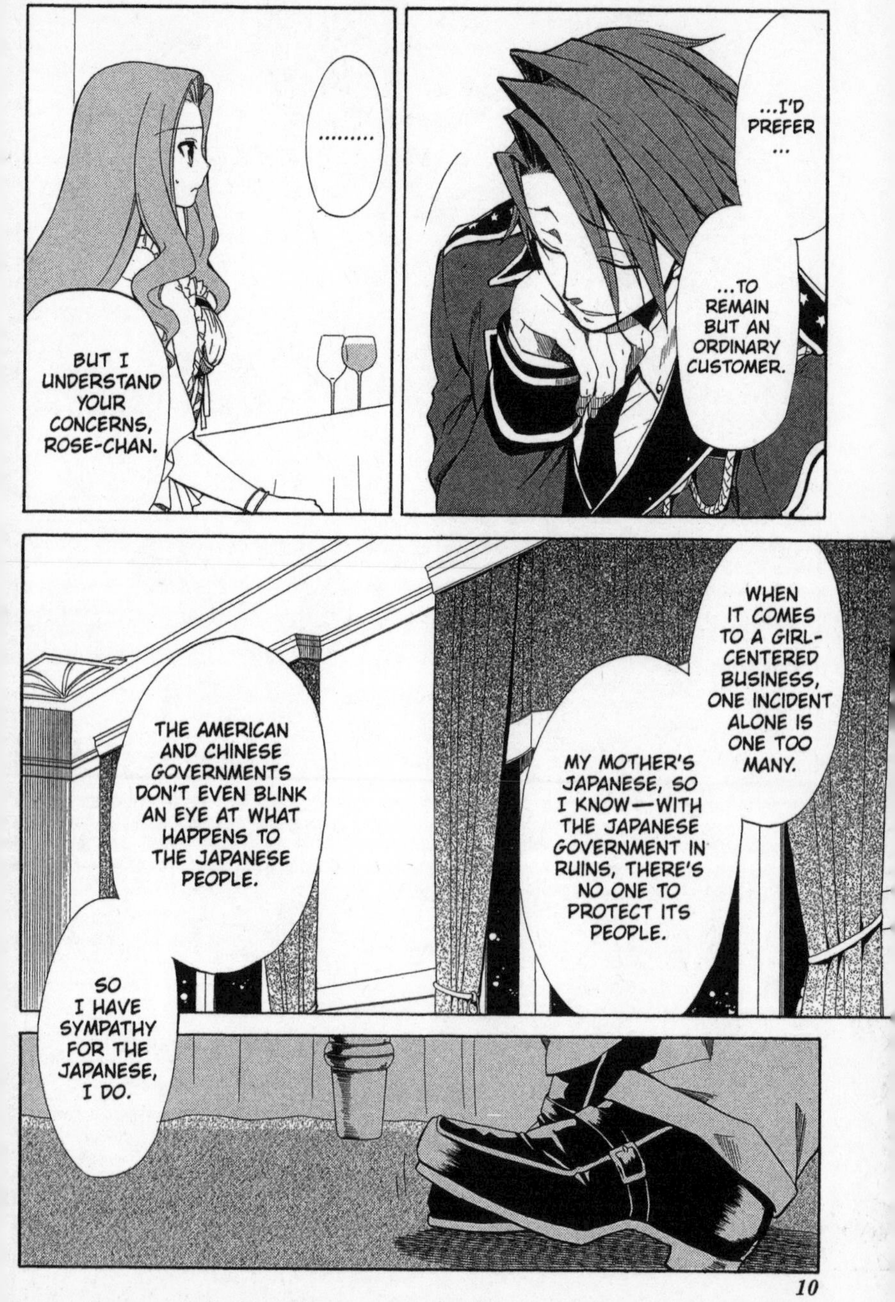
...I'D PREFER ...
...TO REMAIN BUT AN ORDINARY CUSTOMER.
....
BUT I UNDERSTAND YOUR CONCERNS, ROSE-CHAN.
WHEN IT COMES TO A GIRL-CENTERED BUSINESS, ONE INCIDENT ALONE IS ONE TOO MANY.
MY MOTHER'S JAPANESE, SO I KNOW—WITH THE JAPANESE GOVERNMENT IN RUINS, THERE'S NO ONE TO PROTECT ITS PEOPLE.
THE AMERICAN AND CHINESE GOVERNMENTS DON'T EVEN BLINK AN EYE AT WHAT HAPPENS TO THE JAPANESE PEOPLE.
SO I HAVE SYMPATHY FOR THE JAPANESE, I DO.

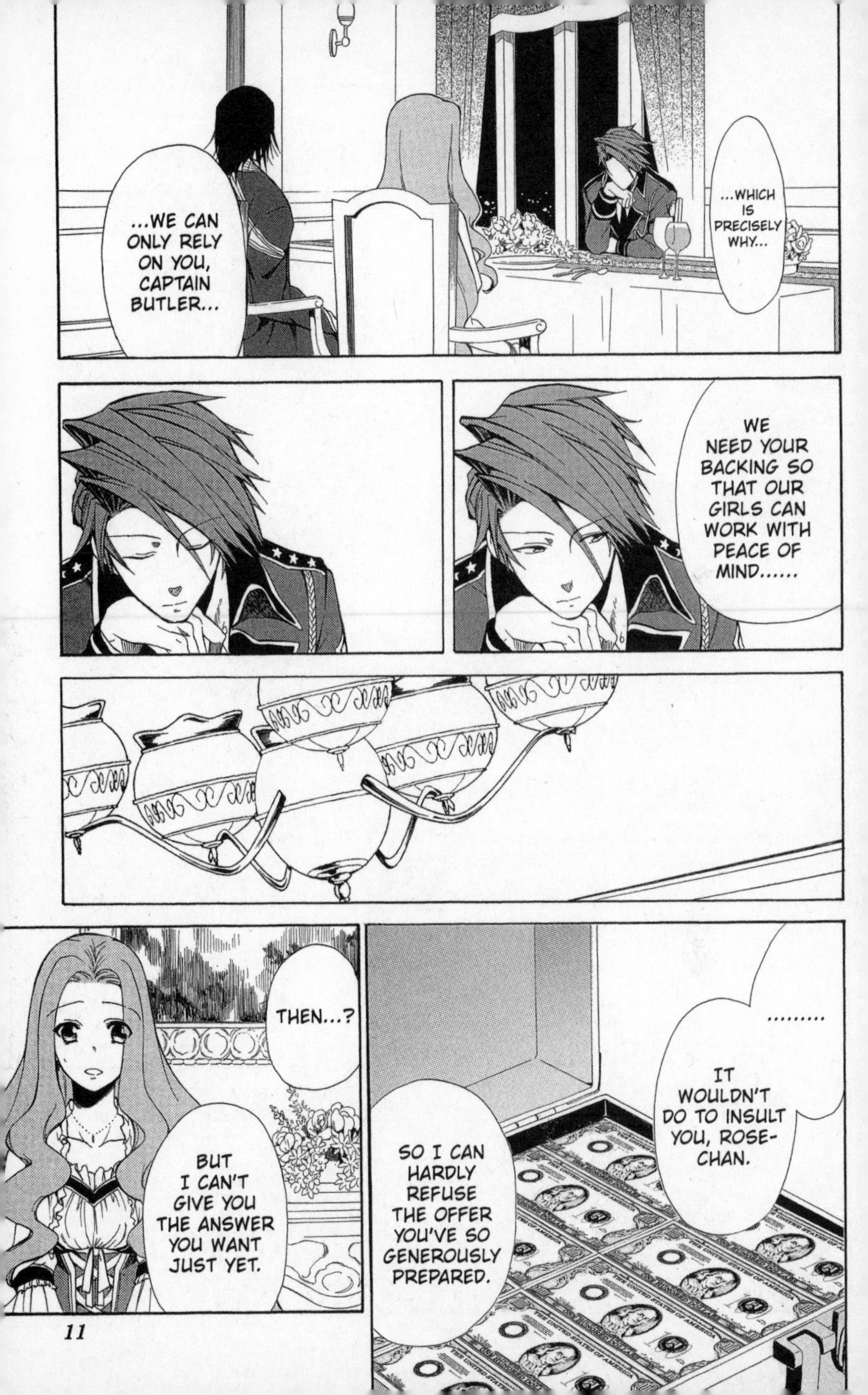
...WHICH IS PRECISELY WHY...
...WE CAN ONLY RELY ON YOU, CAPTAIN BUTLER...
WE NEED YOUR BACKING SO THAT OUR GIRLS CAN WORK WITH PEACE OF MIND......
....
IT WOULDN'T DO TO INSULT YOU, ROSE-CHAN.
SO I CAN HARDLY REFUSE THE OFFER YOU'VE SO GENEROUSLY PREPARED.
THEN...?
BUT I CAN'T GIVE YOU THE ANSWER YOU WANT JUST YET.

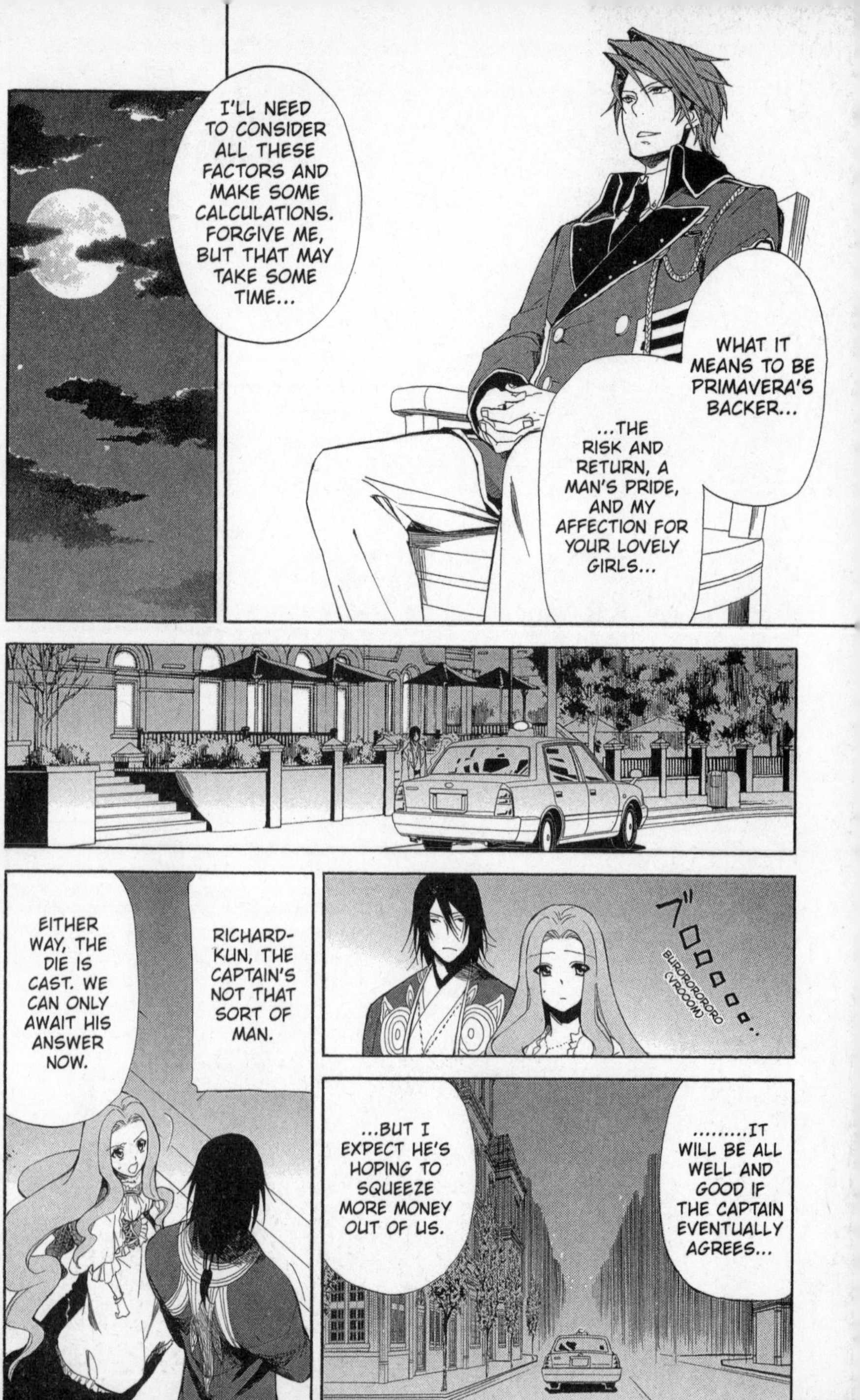
WHAT IT MEANS TO BE PRIMAVERA'S BACKER...
...THE RISK AND RETURN, A MAN'S PRIDE, AND MY AFFECTION FOR YOUR LOVELY GIRLS...
I'LL NEED TO CONSIDER ALL THESE FACTORS AND MAKE SOME CALCULATIONS. FORGIVE ME, BUT THAT MAY TAKE SOME TIME...
ブロロロロ...
BURORORORO (VROOOM)
.........IT WILL BE ALL WELL AND GOOD IF THE CAPTAIN EVENTUALLY AGREES...
...BUT I EXPECT HE'S HOPING TO SQUEEZE MORE MONEY OUT OF US.
RICHARD-KUN, THE CAPTAIN'S NOT THAT SORT OF MAN.
EITHER WAY, THE DIE IS CAST. WE CAN ONLY AWAIT HIS ANSWER NOW.

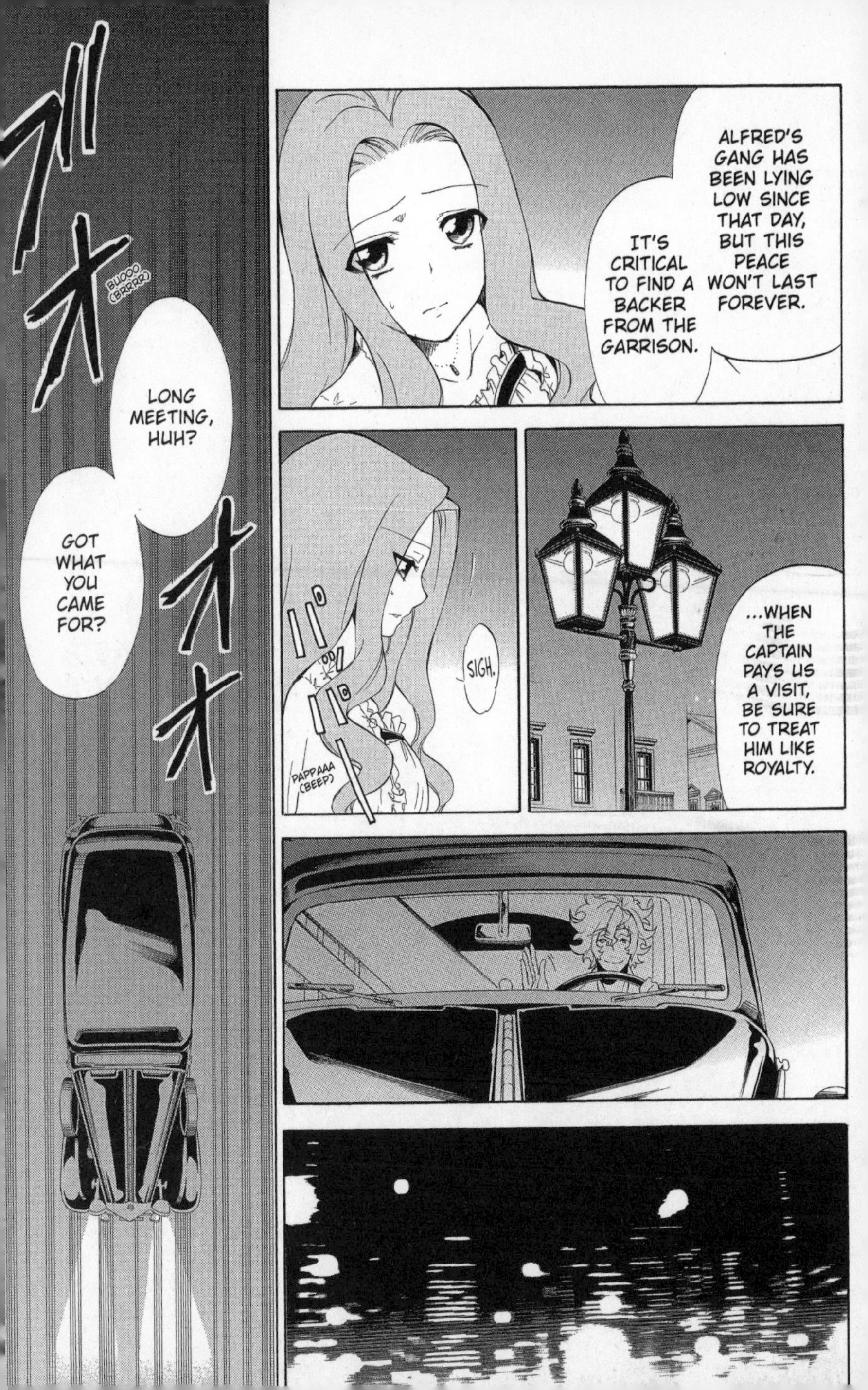
ALFRED'S GANG HAS BEEN LYING LOW SINCE THAT DAY, BUT THIS PEACE WON'T LAST FOREVER.
IT'S CRITICAL TO FIND A BACKER FROM THE GARRISON.
...WHEN THE CAPTAIN PAYS US A VISIT, BE SURE TO TREAT HIM LIKE ROYALTY.
SIGH.
PAPPAAA (BEEP)
BUOOO (BRRRR)
LONG MEETING, HUH?
GOT WHAT YOU CAME FOR?

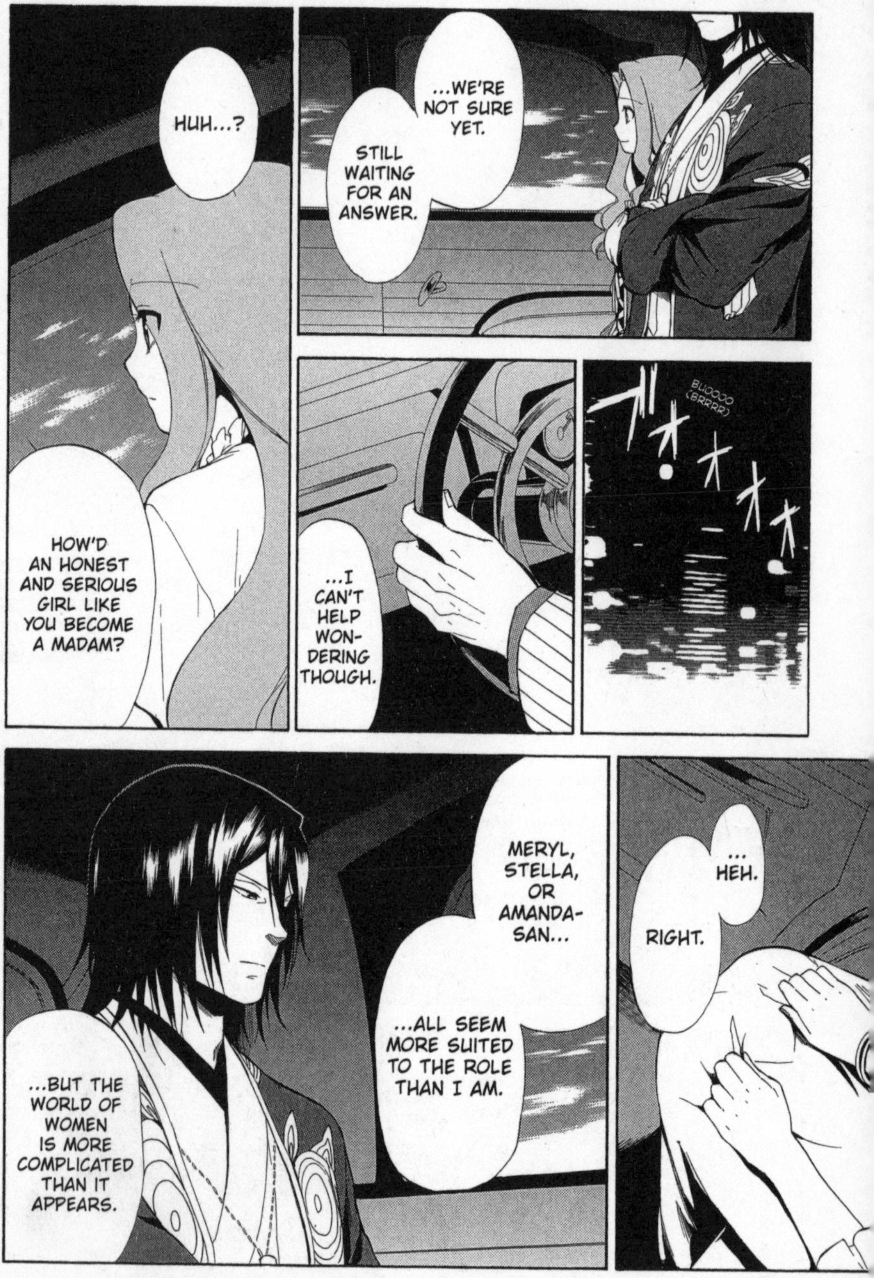
...WE'RE NOT SURE YET.
STILL WAITING FOR AN ANSWER.
BUOOOO (BRRRR)
...I CAN'T HELP WON-DERING THOUGH.
HUH...?
HOW'D AN HONEST AND SERIOUS GIRL LIKE YOU BECOME A MADAM?
... HEH.
RIGHT.
MERYL, STELLA, OR AMANDA-SAN...
...ALL SEEM MORE SUITED TO THE ROLE THAN I AM.
...BUT THE WORLD OF WOMEN IS MORE COMPLICATED THAN IT APPEARS.

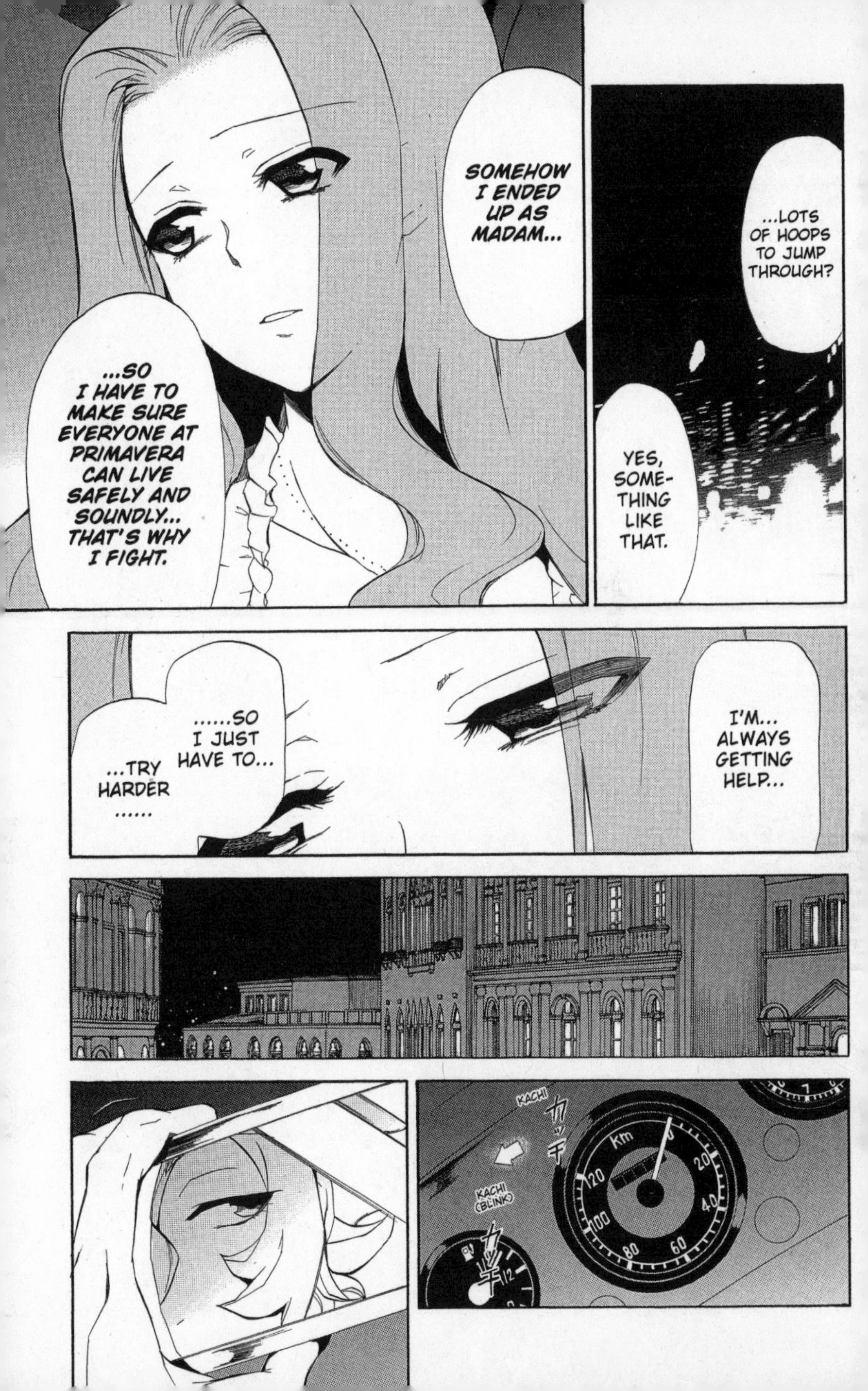
...LOTS OF HOOPS TO JUMP THROUGH?
YES, SOME-THING LIKE THAT.
SOMEHOW I ENDED UP AS MADAM...
...SO I HAVE TO MAKE SURE EVERYONE AT PRIMAVERA CAN LIVE SAFELY AND SOUNDLY... THAT'S WHY I FIGHT.
I'M... ALWAYS GETTING HELP...
......SO I JUST HAVE TO...
...TRY HARDER ......
KACHI
KACHI (BLINK)

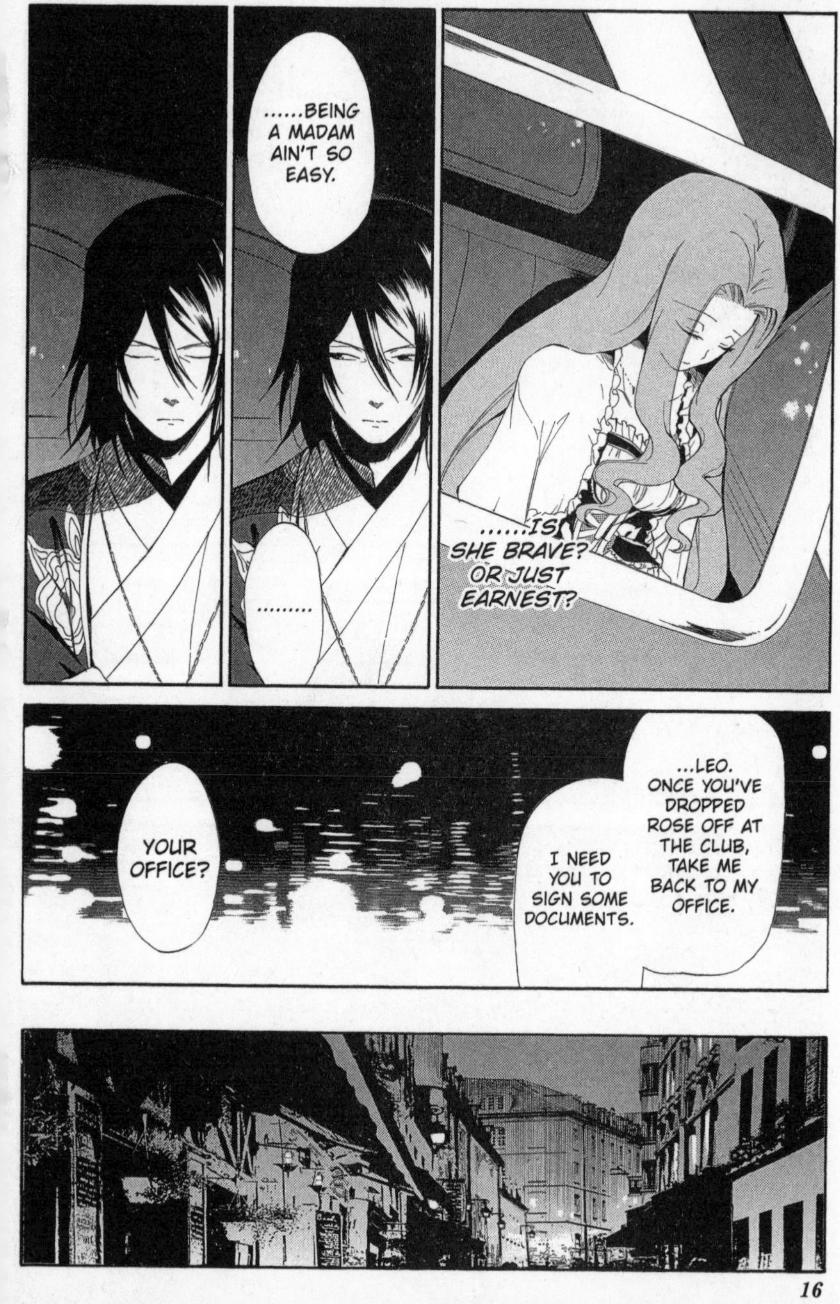
......IS SHE BRAVE? OR JUST EARNEST?
......BEING A MADAM AIN'T SO EASY.
....
...LEO. ONCE YOU'VE DROPPED ROSE OFF AT THE CLUB, TAKE ME BACK TO MY OFFICE.
I NEED YOU TO SIGN SOME DOCUMENTS.
YOUR OFFICE?

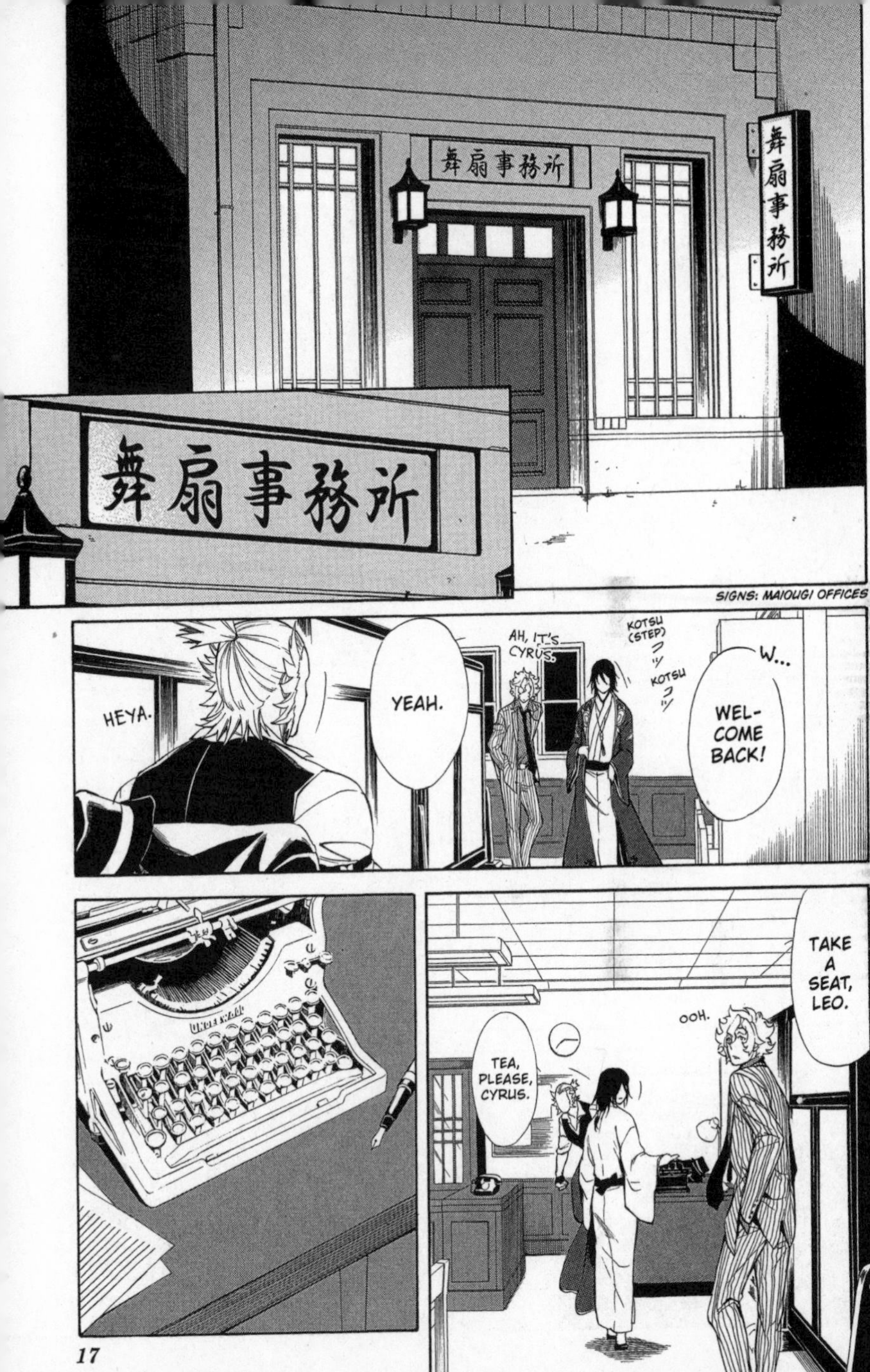
舞扇事務所
舞扇事務所
舞扇事務所
SIGNS: MAIOUGI OFFICES
W... WELCOME BACK!
KOTSU (STEP)
コツ
KOTSU
コツ
AH, IT'S CYRUS.
YEAH.
HEYA.
TAKE A SEAT, LEO.
OOH.
TEA, PLEASE, CYRUS.

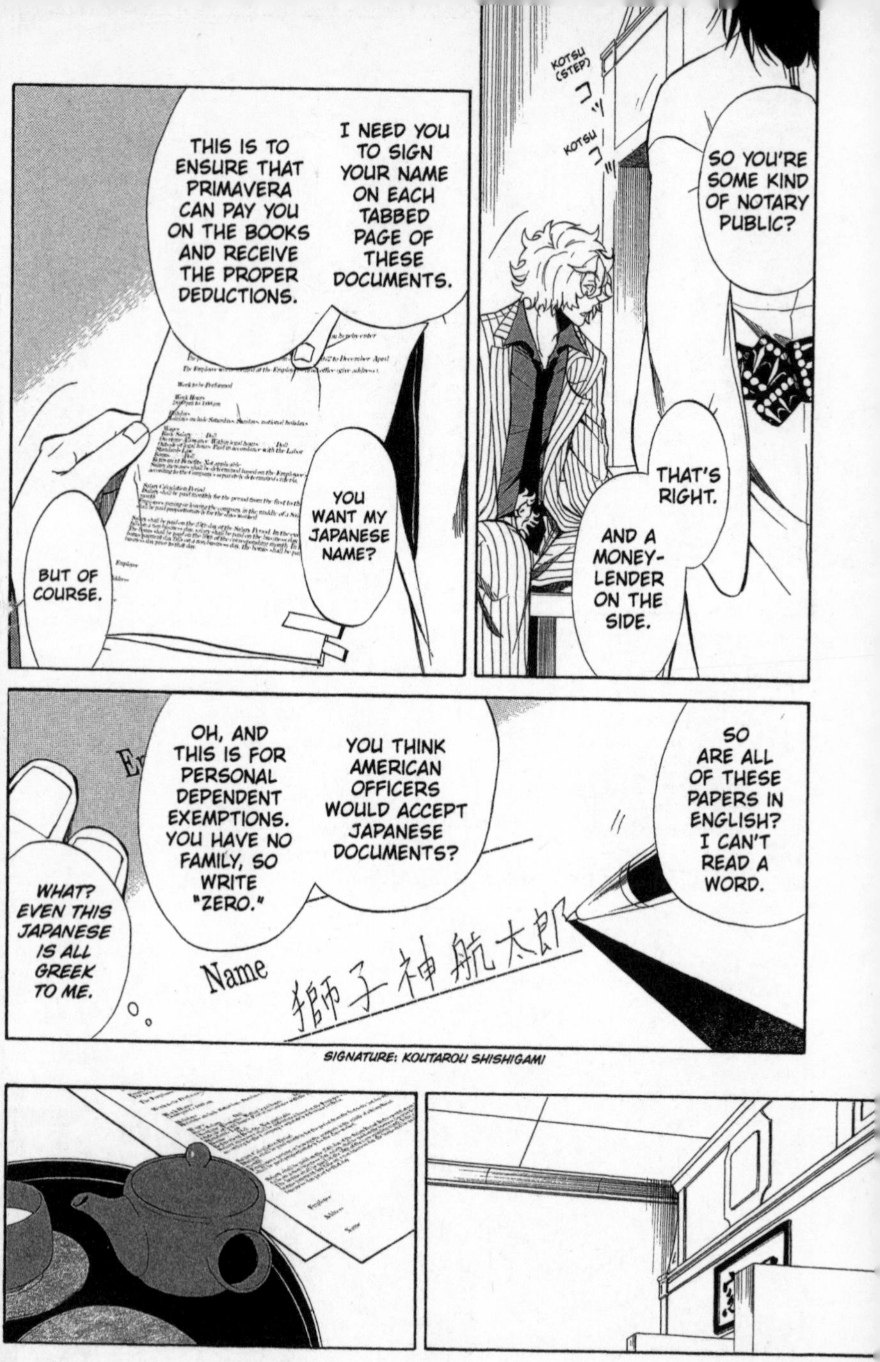
KOTSU (STEP)
KOTSU
SO YOU'RE SOME KIND OF NOTARY PUBLIC?
THAT'S RIGHT.
AND A MONEY-LENDER ON THE SIDE.
I NEED YOU TO SIGN YOUR NAME ON EACH TABBED PAGE OF THESE DOCUMENTS.
THIS IS TO ENSURE THAT PRIMAVERA CAN PAY YOU ON THE BOOKS AND RECEIVE THE PROPER DEDUCTIONS.
YOU WANT MY JAPANESE NAME?
BUT OF COURSE.
SO ARE ALL OF THESE PAPERS IN ENGLISH? I CAN'T READ A WORD.
YOU THINK AMERICAN OFFICERS WOULD ACCEPT JAPANESE DOCUMENTS?
OH, AND THIS IS FOR PERSONAL DEPENDENT EXEMPTIONS. YOU HAVE NO FAMILY, SO WRITE "ZERO."
WHAT? EVEN THIS JAPANESE IS ALL GREEK TO ME.
Name
獅子神航太郎
SIGNATURE: KOUTAROU SHISHIGAMI

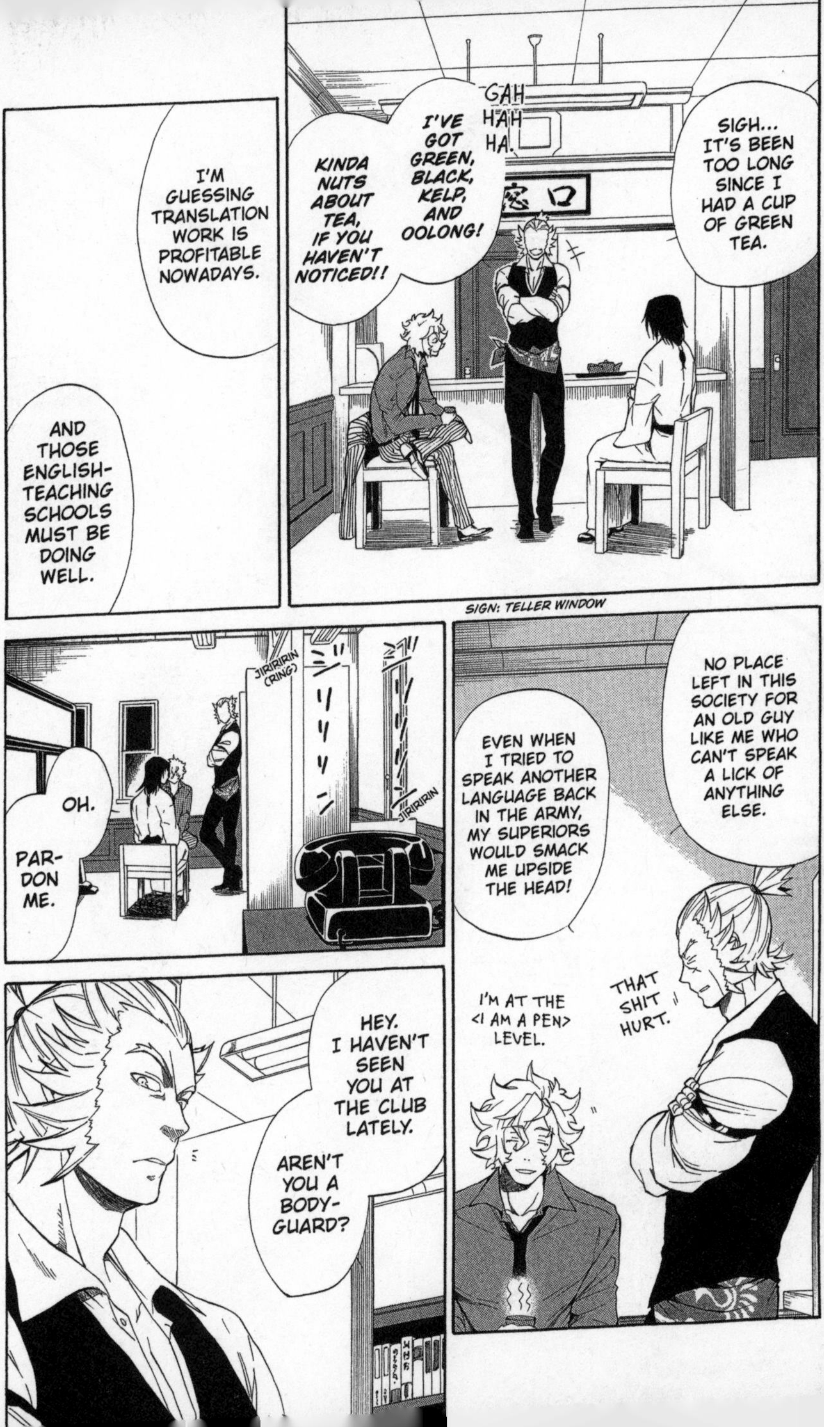
SIGH... IT'S BEEN TOO LONG SINCE I HAD A CUP OF GREEN TEA.
GAH HAH HA.
I'VE GOT GREEN, BLACK, KELP, AND OOLONG!
KINDA NUTS ABOUT TEA, IF YOU HAVEN'T NOTICED!!
I'M GUESSING TRANSLATION WORK IS PROFITABLE NOWADAYS.
AND THOSE ENGLISH-TEACHING SCHOOLS MUST BE DOING WELL.
SIGN: TELLER WINDOW
NO PLACE LEFT IN THIS SOCIETY FOR AN OLD GUY LIKE ME WHO CAN'T SPEAK A LICK OF ANYTHING ELSE.
EVEN WHEN I TRIED TO SPEAK ANOTHER LANGUAGE BACK IN THE ARMY, MY SUPERIORS WOULD SMACK ME UPSIDE THE HEAD!
THAT SHIT HURT.
I'M AT THE <I AM A PEN> LEVEL.
JIRIRIRIN (RING)
JIRIRIRIN
OH.
PARDON ME.
HEY. I HAVEN'T SEEN YOU AT THE CLUB LATELY.
AREN'T YOU A BODYGUARD?

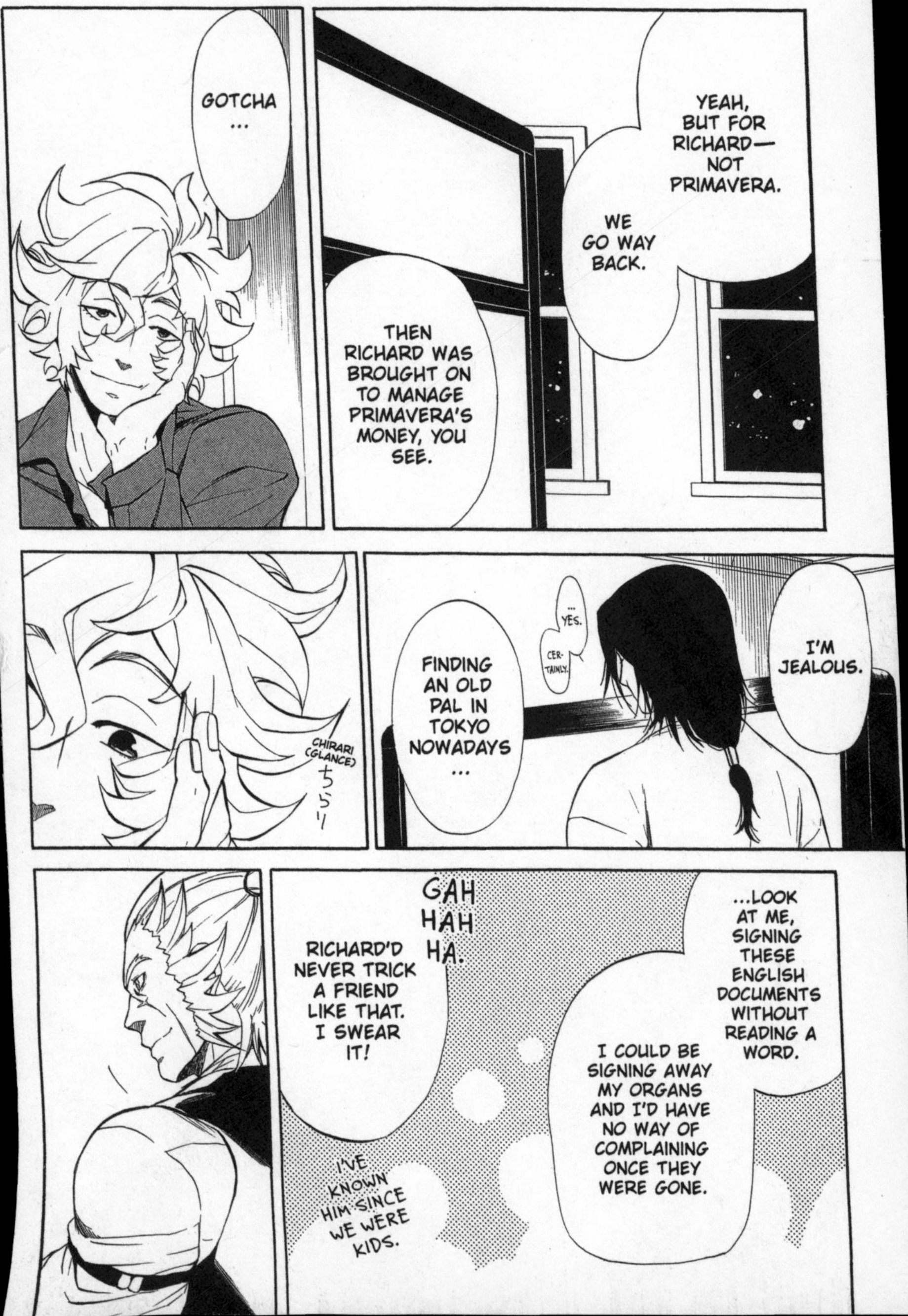
YEAH, BUT FOR RICHARD— NOT PRIMAVERA.
WE GO WAY BACK.
THEN RICHARD WAS BROUGHT ON TO MANAGE PRIMAVERA'S MONEY, YOU SEE.
GOTCHA ...
I'M JEALOUS.
... YES.
CER-TAINLY.
FINDING AN OLD PAL IN TOKYO NOWADAYS ...
CHIRARI (GLANCE)
ちらり
...LOOK AT ME, SIGNING THESE ENGLISH DOCUMENTS WITHOUT READING A WORD.
I COULD BE SIGNING AWAY MY ORGANS AND I'D HAVE NO WAY OF COMPLAINING ONCE THEY WERE GONE.
GAH HAH HA.
RICHARD'D NEVER TRICK A FRIEND LIKE THAT. I SWEAR IT!
I'VE KNOWN HIM SINCE WE WERE KIDS.

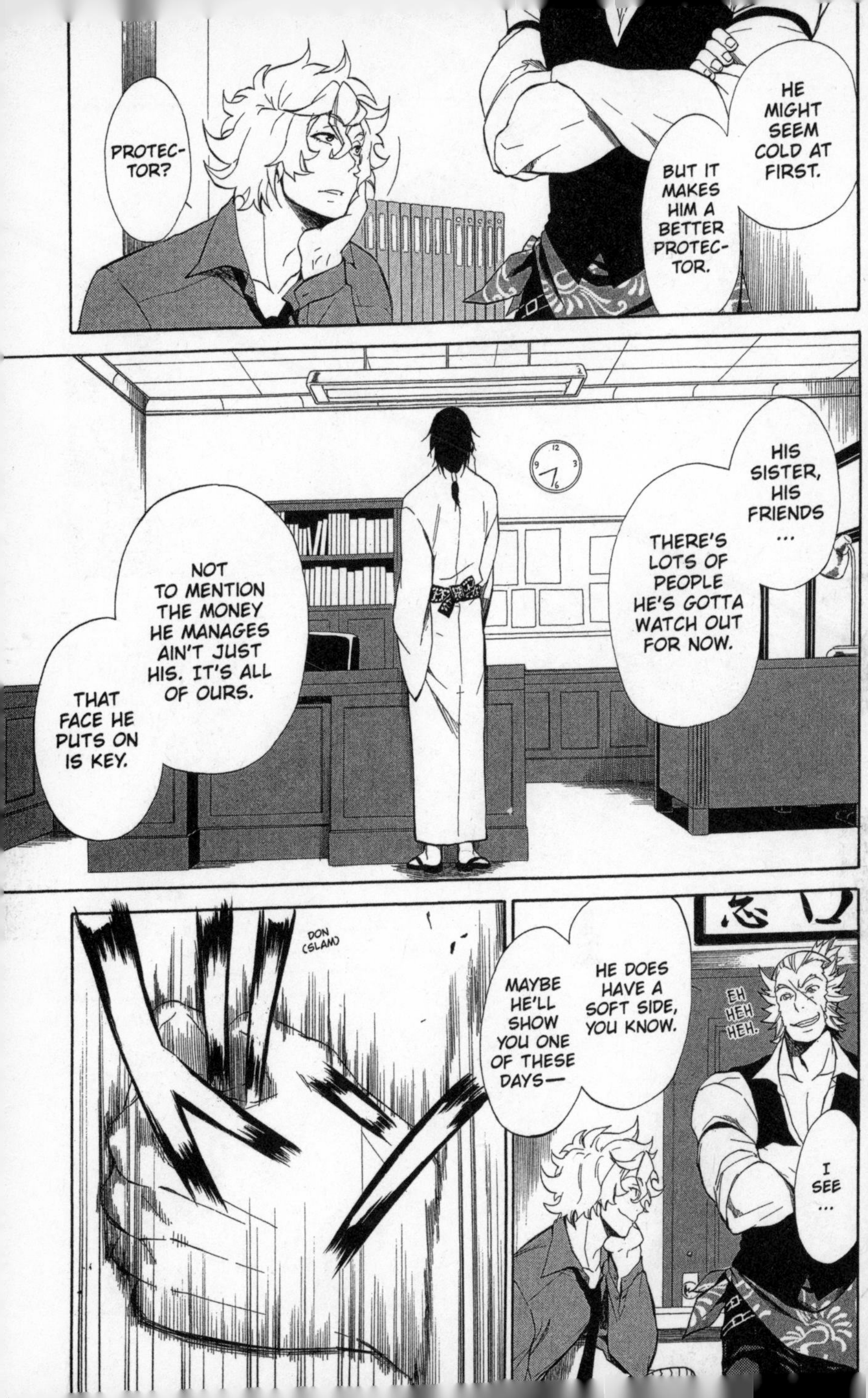
HE MIGHT SEEM COLD AT FIRST.
BUT IT MAKES HIM A BETTER PROTECTOR.
PROTECTOR?
HIS SISTER, HIS FRIENDS...
THERE'S LOTS OF PEOPLE HE'S GOTTA WATCH OUT FOR NOW.
NOT TO MENTION THE MONEY HE MANAGES AIN'T JUST HIS. IT'S ALL OF OURS.
THAT FACE HE PUTS ON IS KEY.
HE DOES HAVE A SOFT SIDE, YOU KNOW.
EH HEH HEH.
MAYBE HE'LL SHOW YOU ONE OF THESE DAYS—
I SEE...
DON (SLAM)

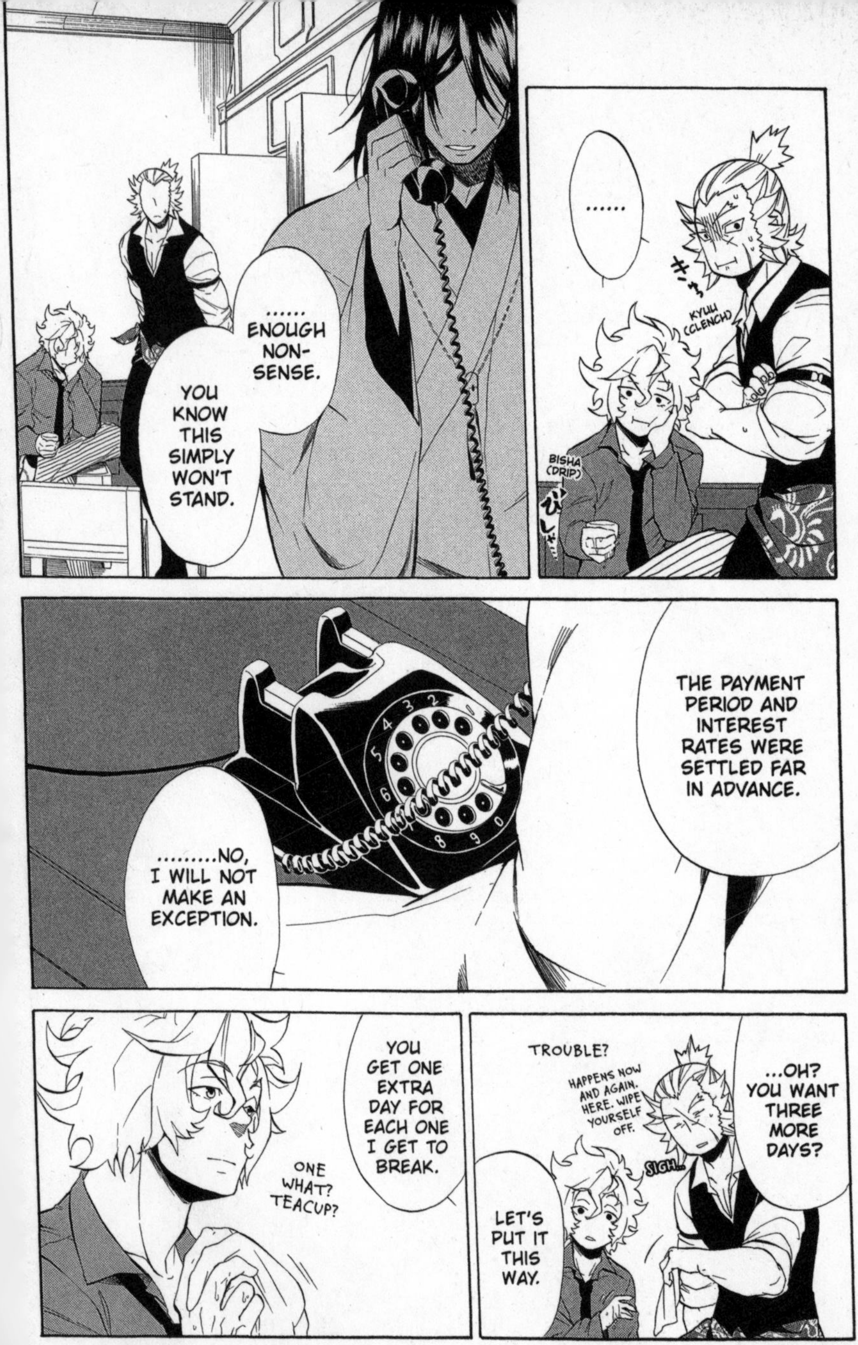
......
KYUU (CLENCH)
BISHA (DRIP)
......ENOUGH NON-SENSE.
YOU KNOW THIS SIMPLY WON'T STAND.
THE PAYMENT PERIOD AND INTEREST RATES WERE SETTLED FAR IN ADVANCE.
.........NO, I WILL NOT MAKE AN EXCEPTION.
...OH? YOU WANT THREE MORE DAYS?
TROUBLE?
HAPPENS NOW AND AGAIN. HERE. WIPE YOURSELF OFF.
SIGH...
LET'S PUT IT THIS WAY.
YOU GET ONE EXTRA DAY FOR EACH ONE I GET TO BREAK.
ONE WHAT? TEACUP?

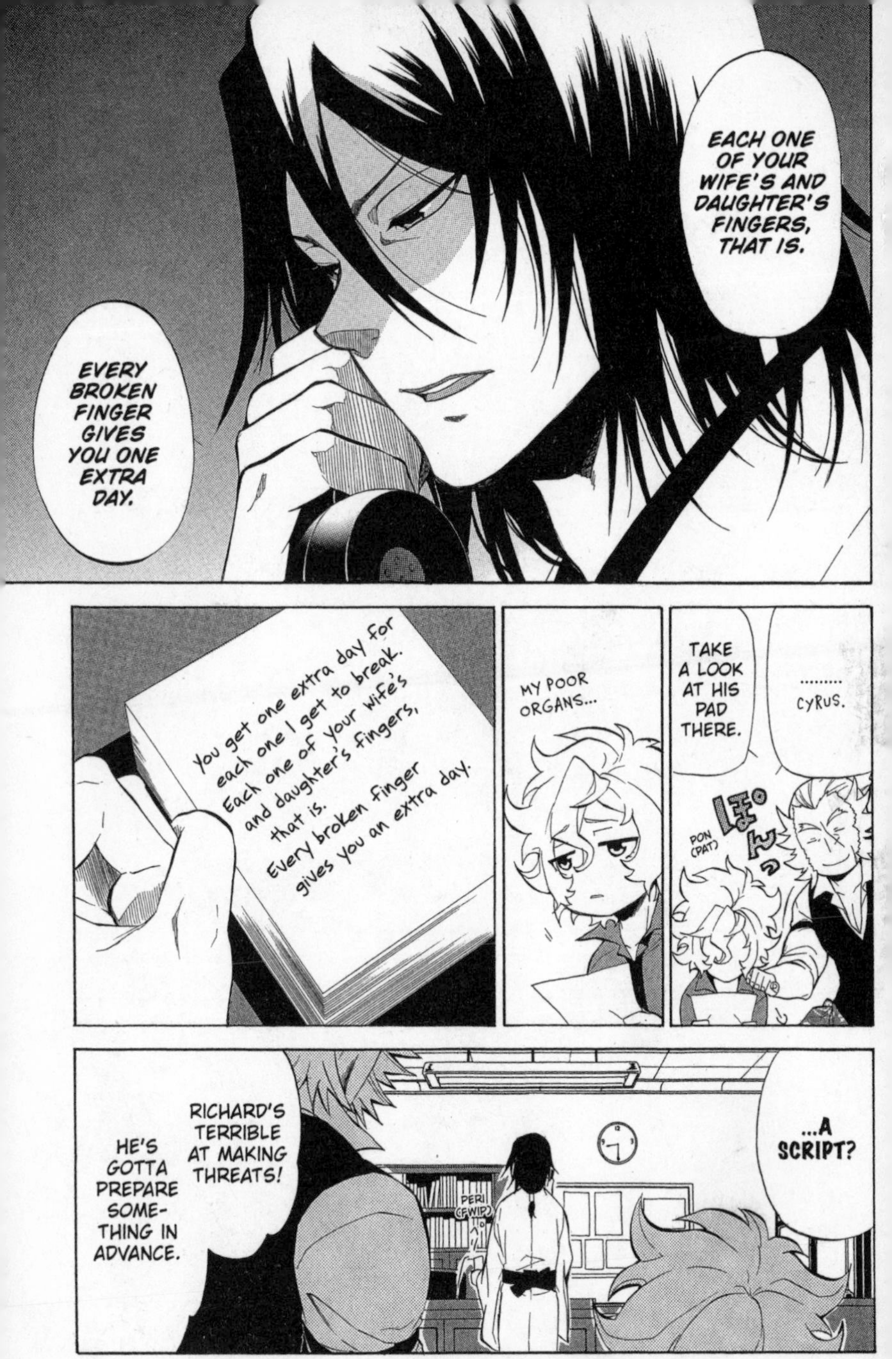
EACH ONE OF YOUR WIFE'S AND DAUGHTER'S FINGERS, THAT IS.
EVERY BROKEN FINGER GIVES YOU ONE EXTRA DAY.
.... CYRUS.
TAKE A LOOK AT HIS PAD THERE.
PON (PAT)
MY POOR ORGANS...
You get one extra day for each one I get to break. Each one of your wife's and daughter's fingers, that is. Every broken finger gives you an extra day.
...A SCRIPT?
RICHARD'S TERRIBLE AT MAKING THREATS!
HE'S GOTTA PREPARE SOME-THING IN ADVANCE.
PERI (FWIP)

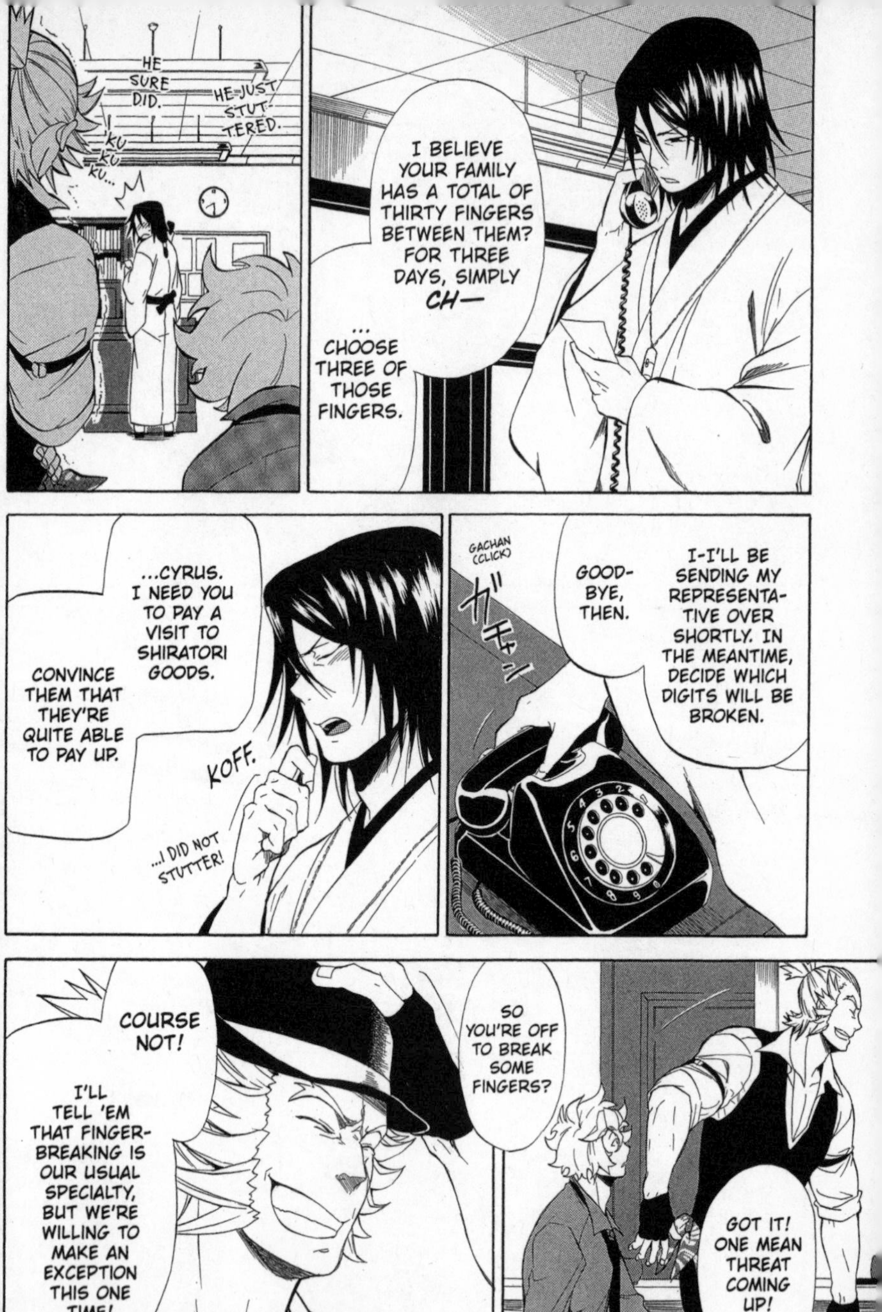
I BELIEVE YOUR FAMILY HAS A TOTAL OF THIRTY FINGERS BETWEEN THEM? FOR THREE DAYS, SIMPLY CH—
... CHOOSE THREE OF THOSE FINGERS.
HE JUST STUTTERED.
HE SURE DID.
KU KU KU...
I-I'LL BE SENDING MY REPRESENTATIVE OVER SHORTLY. IN THE MEANTIME, DECIDE WHICH DIGITS WILL BE BROKEN.
GOOD-BYE, THEN.
GACHAN (CLICK)
...CYRUS. I NEED YOU TO PAY A VISIT TO SHIRATORI GOODS.
CONVINCE THEM THAT THEY'RE QUITE ABLE TO PAY UP.
KOFF.
...I DID NOT STUTTER!
SO YOU'RE OFF TO BREAK SOME FINGERS?
GOT IT! ONE MEAN THREAT COMING UP!
COURSE NOT!
I'LL TELL 'EM THAT FINGER-BREAKING IS OUR USUAL SPECIALTY, BUT WE'RE WILLING TO MAKE AN EXCEPTION THIS ONE TIME!

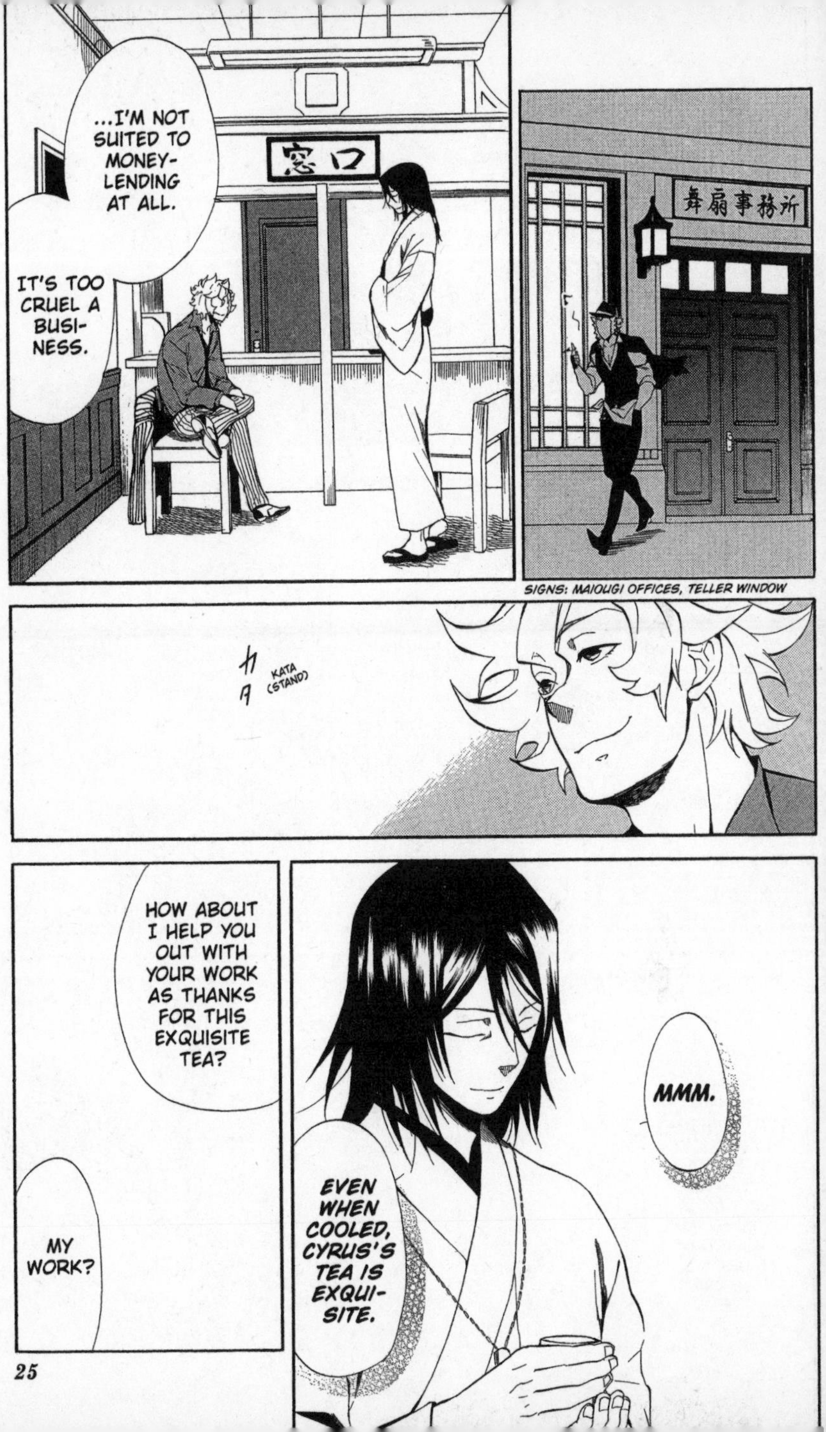
舞扇事務所
窓口
...I'M NOT SUITED TO MONEY-LENDING AT ALL.
IT'S TOO CRUEL A BUSINESS.
SIGNS: MAIOUGI OFFICES, TELLER WINDOW
カタ
KATA (STAND)
MMM.
EVEN WHEN COOLED, CYRUS'S TEA IS EXQUISITE.
HOW ABOUT I HELP YOU OUT WITH YOUR WORK AS THANKS FOR THIS EXQUISITE TEA?
MY WORK?

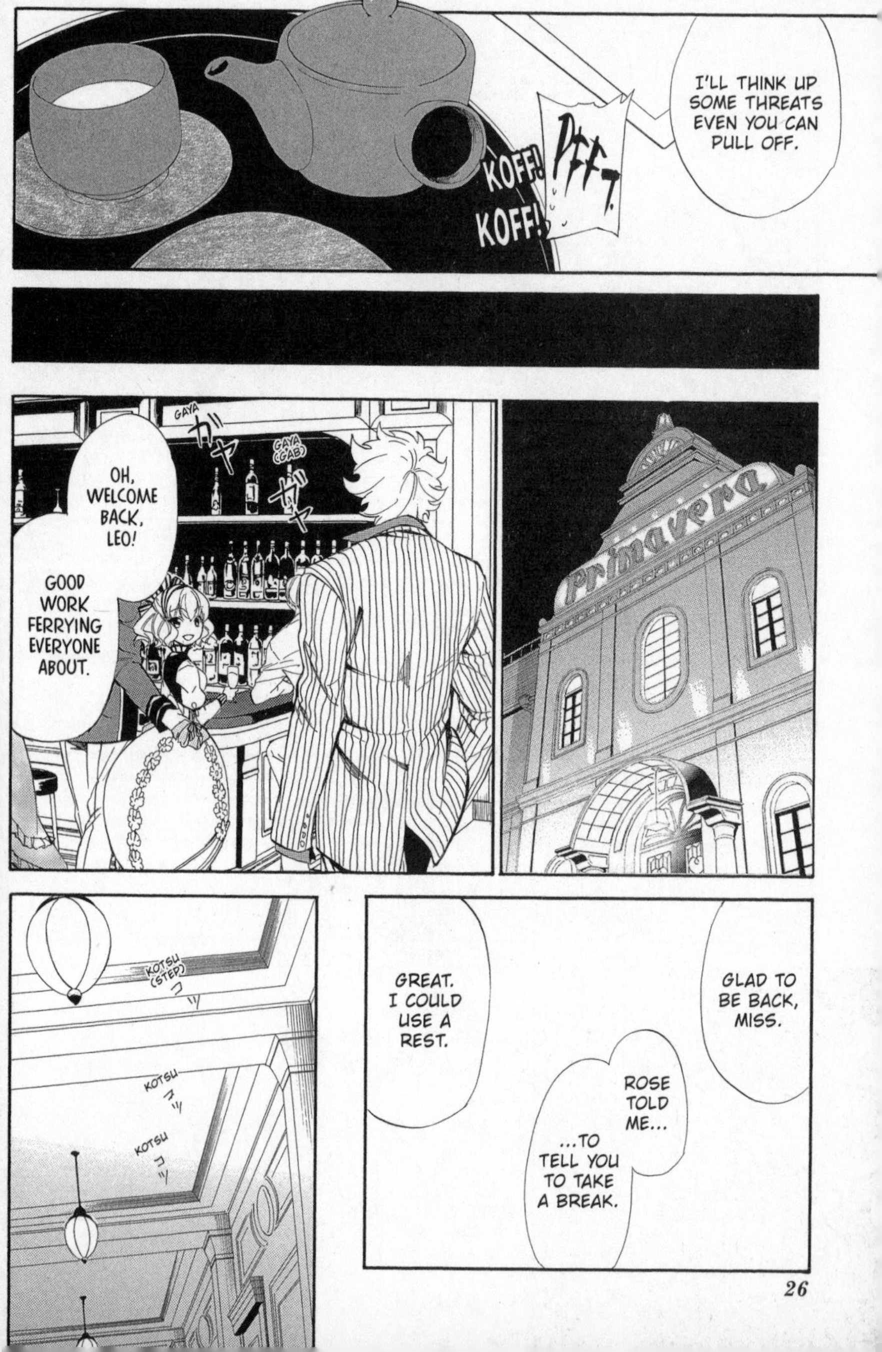
I'LL THINK UP SOME THREATS EVEN YOU CAN PULL OFF.
PFFT.
KOFF! KOFF!
Primavera
GAYA
GAYA (GAB)
OH, WELCOME BACK, LEO!
GOOD WORK FERRYING EVERYONE ABOUT.
GLAD TO BE BACK, MISS.
ROSE TOLD ME...
...TO TELL YOU TO TAKE A BREAK.
GREAT. I COULD USE A REST.
KOTSU (STEP)
KOTSU
KOTSU

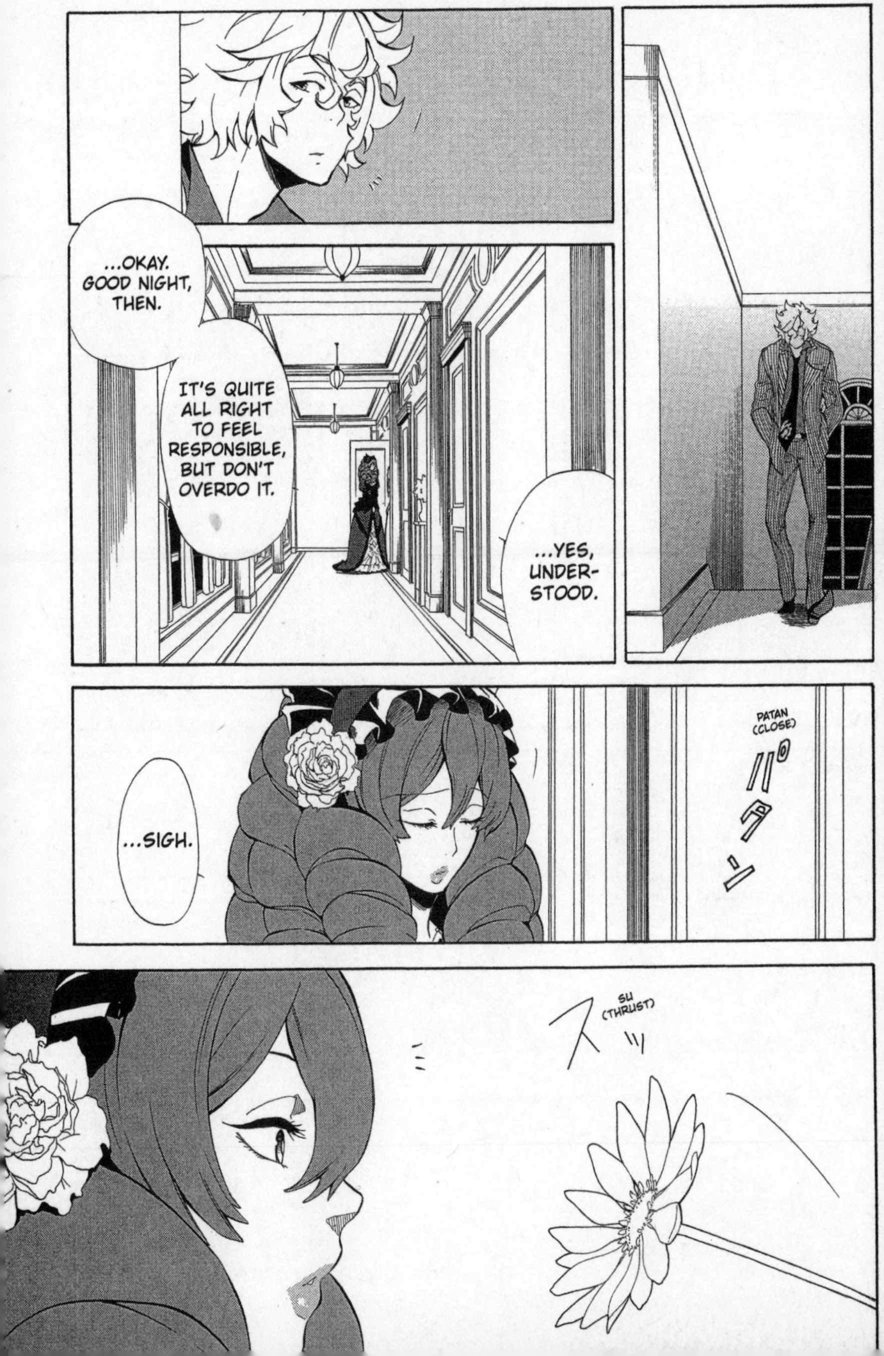
...OKAY. GOOD NIGHT, THEN.
IT'S QUITE ALL RIGHT TO FEEL RESPONSIBLE, BUT DON'T OVERDO IT.
...YES, UNDER-STOOD.
PATAN (CLOSE)
...SIGH.
SU (THRUST)

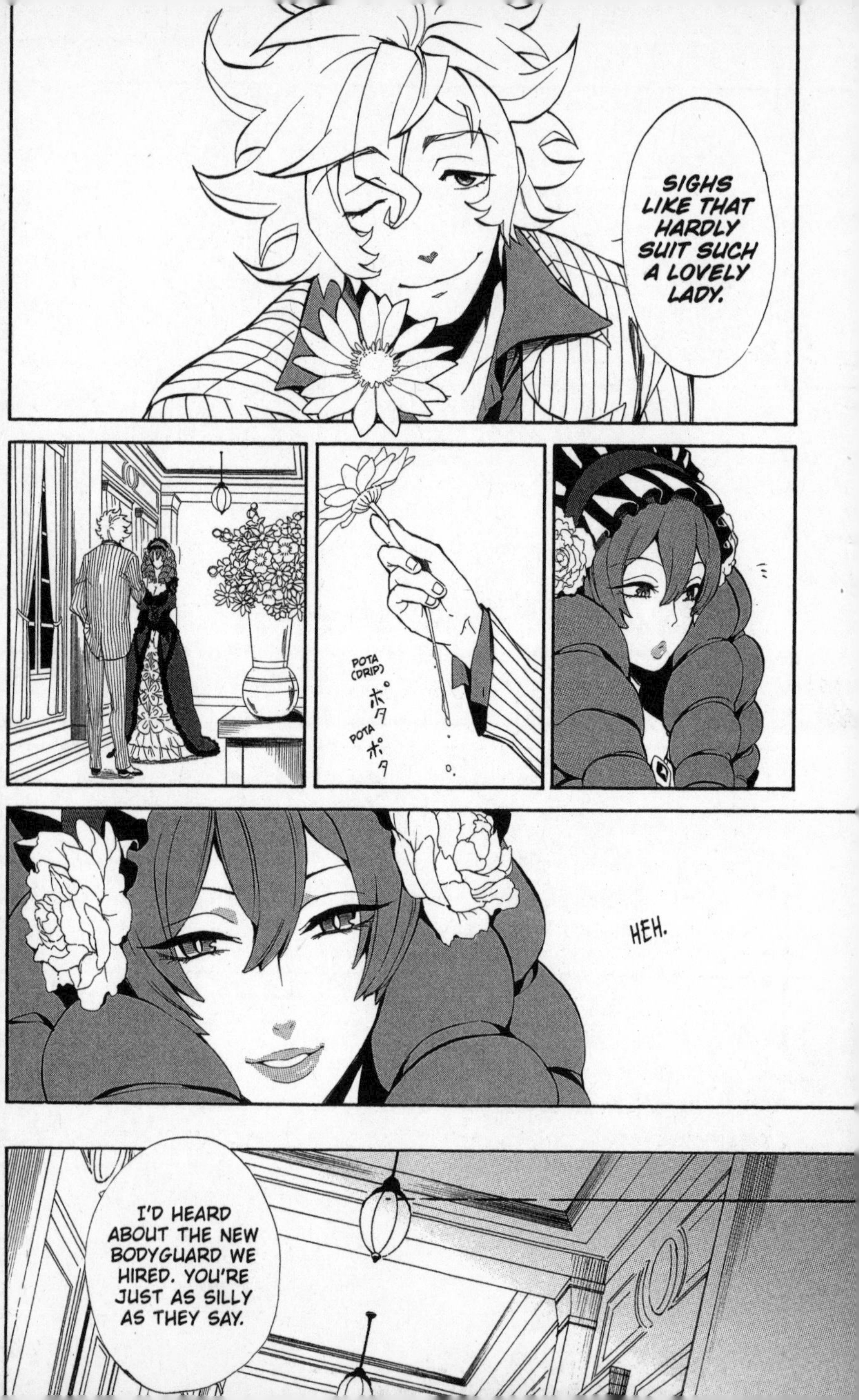
SIGHS LIKE THAT HARDLY SUIT SUCH A LOVELY LADY.
POTA (DRIP)
ポタ
POTA
ポタ
HEH.
I'D HEARD ABOUT THE NEW BODYGUARD WE HIRED. YOU'RE JUST AS SILLY AS THEY SAY.

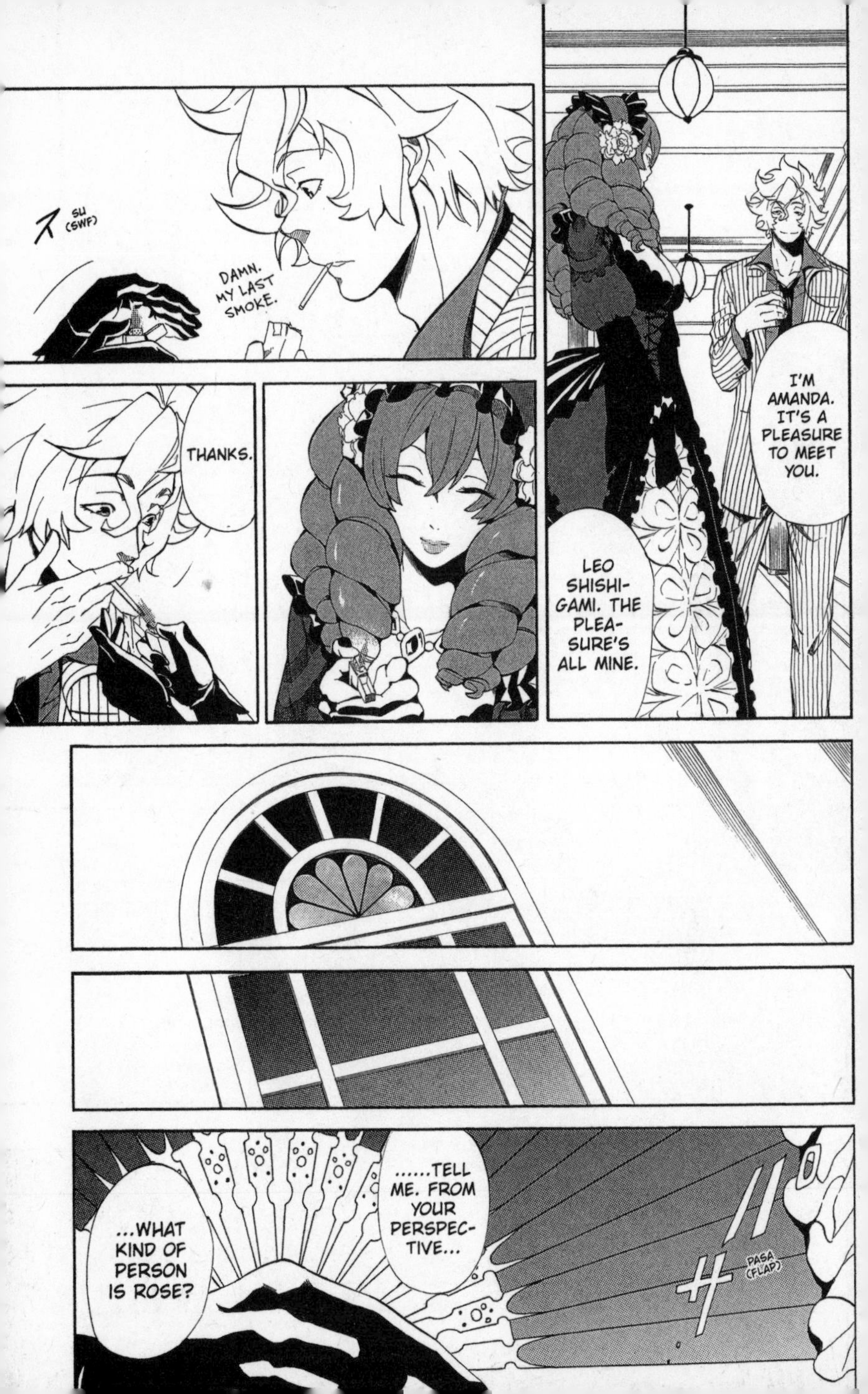
I'M AMANDA. IT'S A PLEASURE TO MEET YOU.
LEO SHISHIGAMI. THE PLEA-SURE'S ALL MINE.
DAMN. MY LAST SMOKE.
SU (SWF)
THANKS.
PASA (FLAP)
......TELL ME. FROM YOUR PERSPEC-TIVE...
...WHAT KIND OF PERSON IS ROSE?

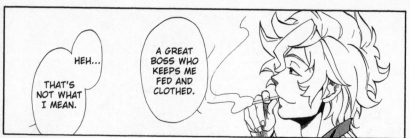

A GREAT BOSS WHO KEEPS ME FED AND CLOTHED.
HEH... THAT'S NOT WHAT I MEAN.
...WHY DID ROSE BECOME MADAM HERE?
...PUBLIC ORDER TOOK A HIT WHEN SOLDIERS STARTED REPATRIAT-ING.
AND THE ONLY THING THAT COULD STAND UP TO THE VIOLENCE OF MEN WAS THE VIOLENCE OF MORE MEN.

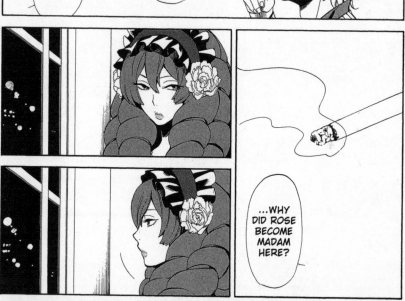

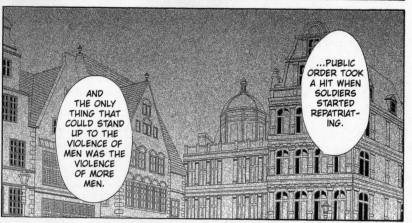

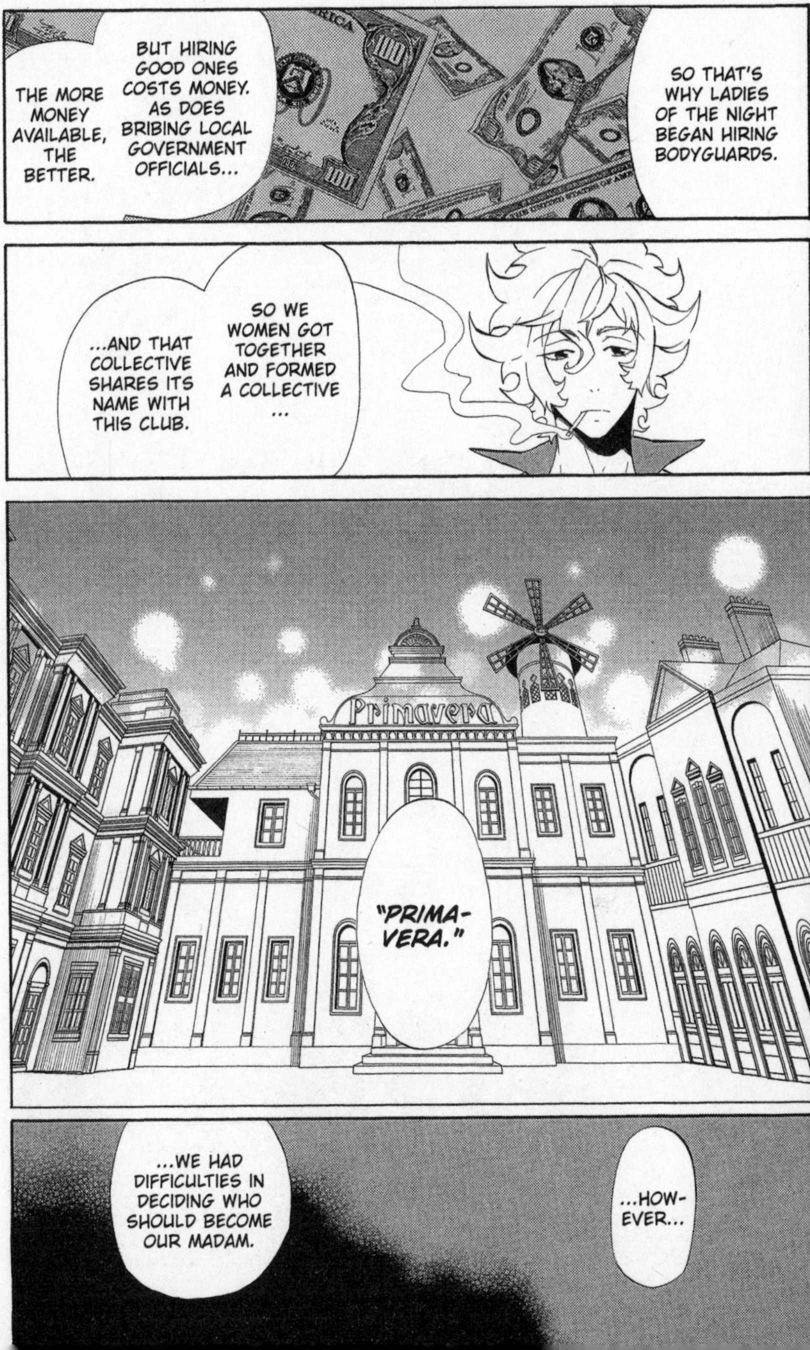
SO THAT'S WHY LADIES OF THE NIGHT BEGAN HIRING BODYGUARDS.
BUT HIRING GOOD ONES COSTS MONEY. AS DOES BRIBING LOCAL GOVERNMENT OFFICIALS...
THE MORE MONEY AVAILABLE, THE BETTER.
SO WE WOMEN GOT TOGETHER AND FORMED A COLLECTIVE ...
...AND THAT COLLECTIVE SHARES ITS NAME WITH THIS CLUB.
Primavera
"PRIMA-VERA."
...HOW-EVER...
...WE HAD DIFFICULTIES IN DECIDING WHO SHOULD BECOME OUR MADAM.

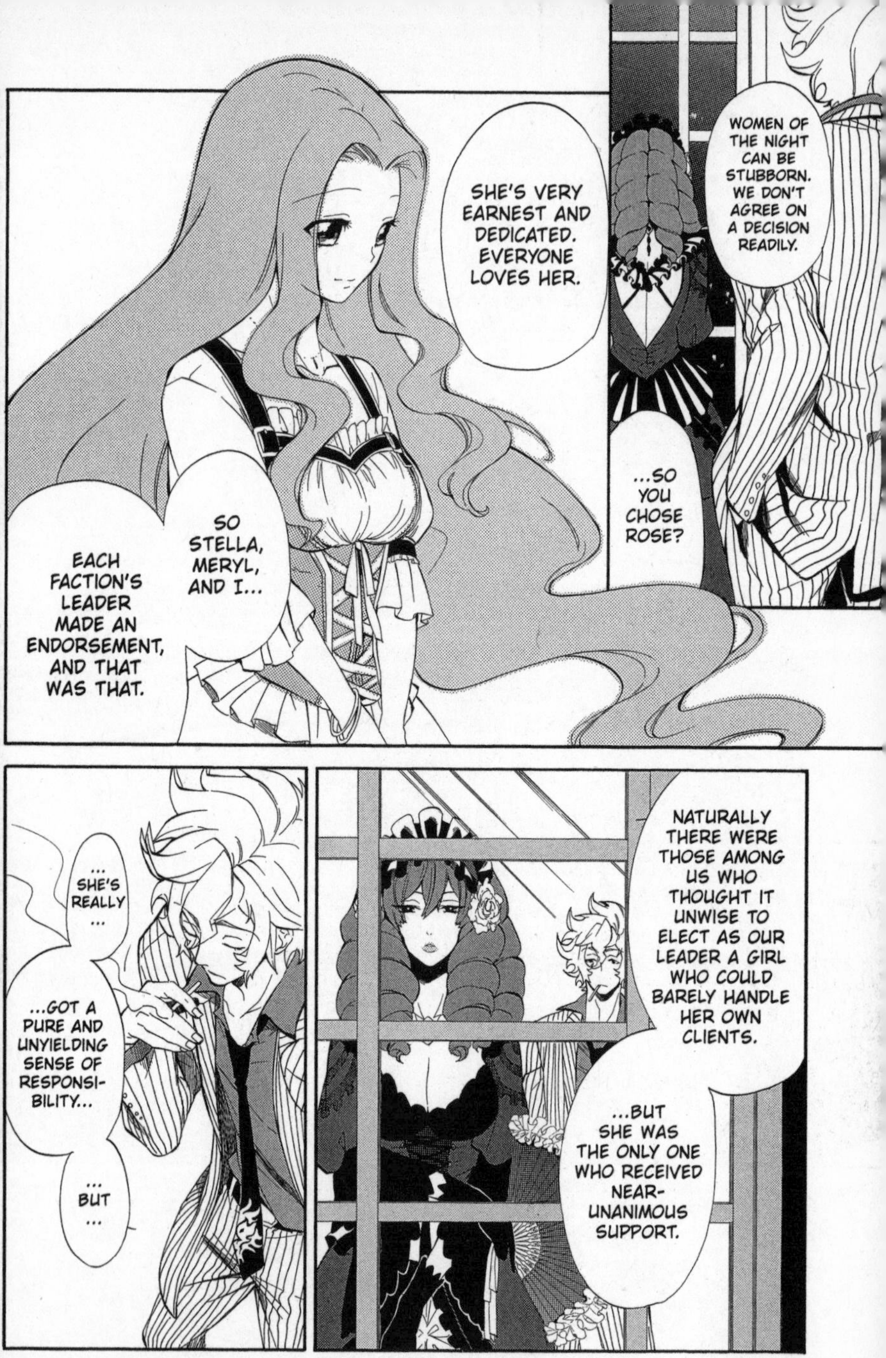
WOMEN OF THE NIGHT CAN BE STUBBORN. WE DON'T AGREE ON A DECISION READILY.
...SO YOU CHOSE ROSE?
SHE'S VERY EARNEST AND DEDICATED. EVERYONE LOVES HER.
SO STELLA, MERYL, AND I...
EACH FACTION'S LEADER MADE AN ENDORSEMENT, AND THAT WAS THAT.
NATURALLY THERE WERE THOSE AMONG US WHO THOUGHT IT UNWISE TO ELECT AS OUR LEADER A GIRL WHO COULD BARELY HANDLE HER OWN CLIENTS.
...BUT SHE WAS THE ONLY ONE WHO RECEIVED NEAR-UNANIMOUS SUPPORT.
...SHE'S REALLY...
...GOT A PURE AND UNYIELDING SENSE OF RESPONSIBILITY...
...BUT...

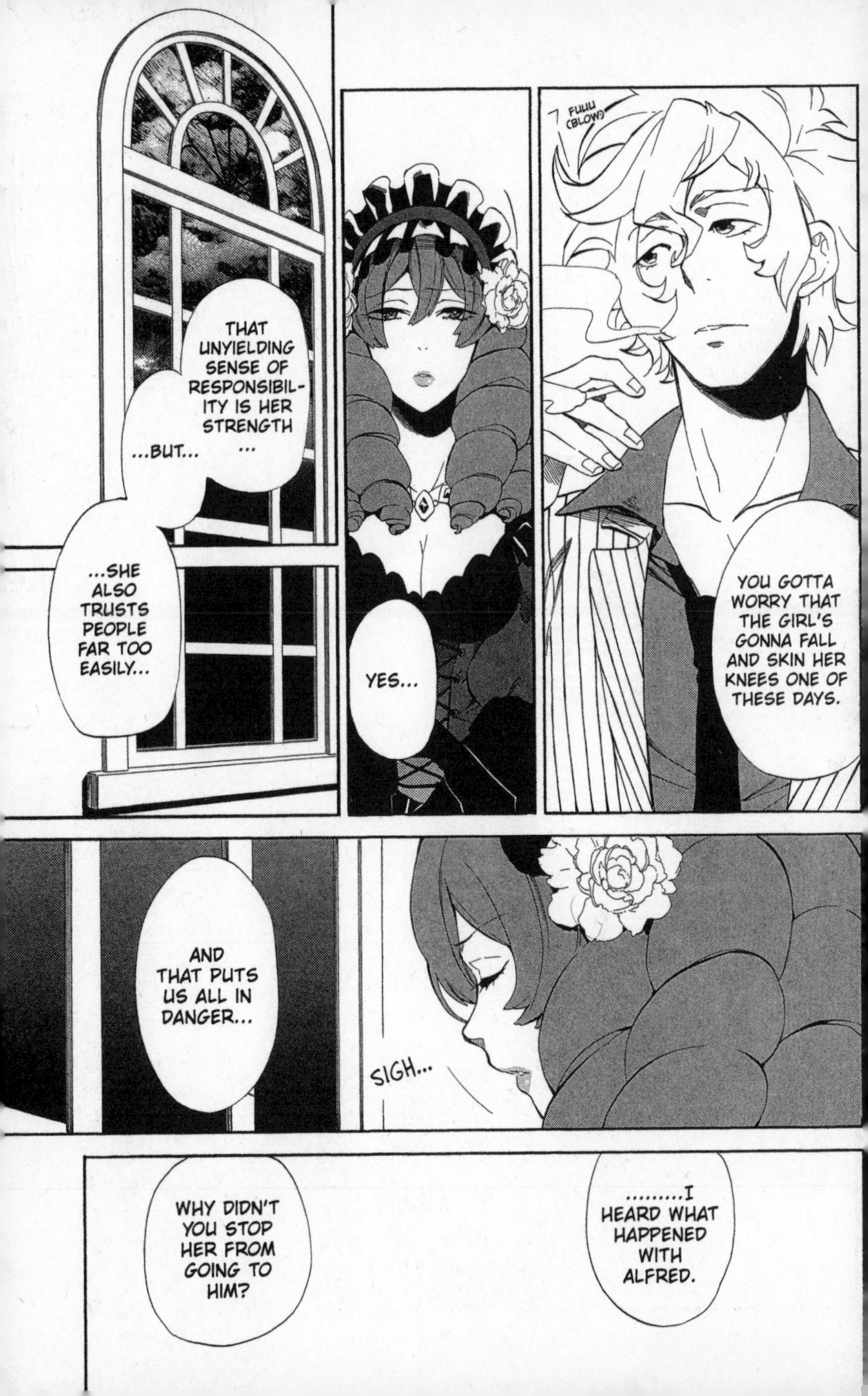
FUUU (BLOW)
YOU GOTTA WORRY THAT THE GIRL'S GONNA FALL AND SKIN HER KNEES ONE OF THESE DAYS.
YES...
THAT UNYIELDING SENSE OF RESPONSIBIL-ITY IS HER STRENGTH...
...BUT...
...SHE ALSO TRUSTS PEOPLE FAR TOO EASILY...
SIGH...
AND THAT PUTS US ALL IN DANGER...
..........I HEARD WHAT HAPPENED WITH ALFRED.
WHY DIDN'T YOU STOP HER FROM GOING TO HIM?

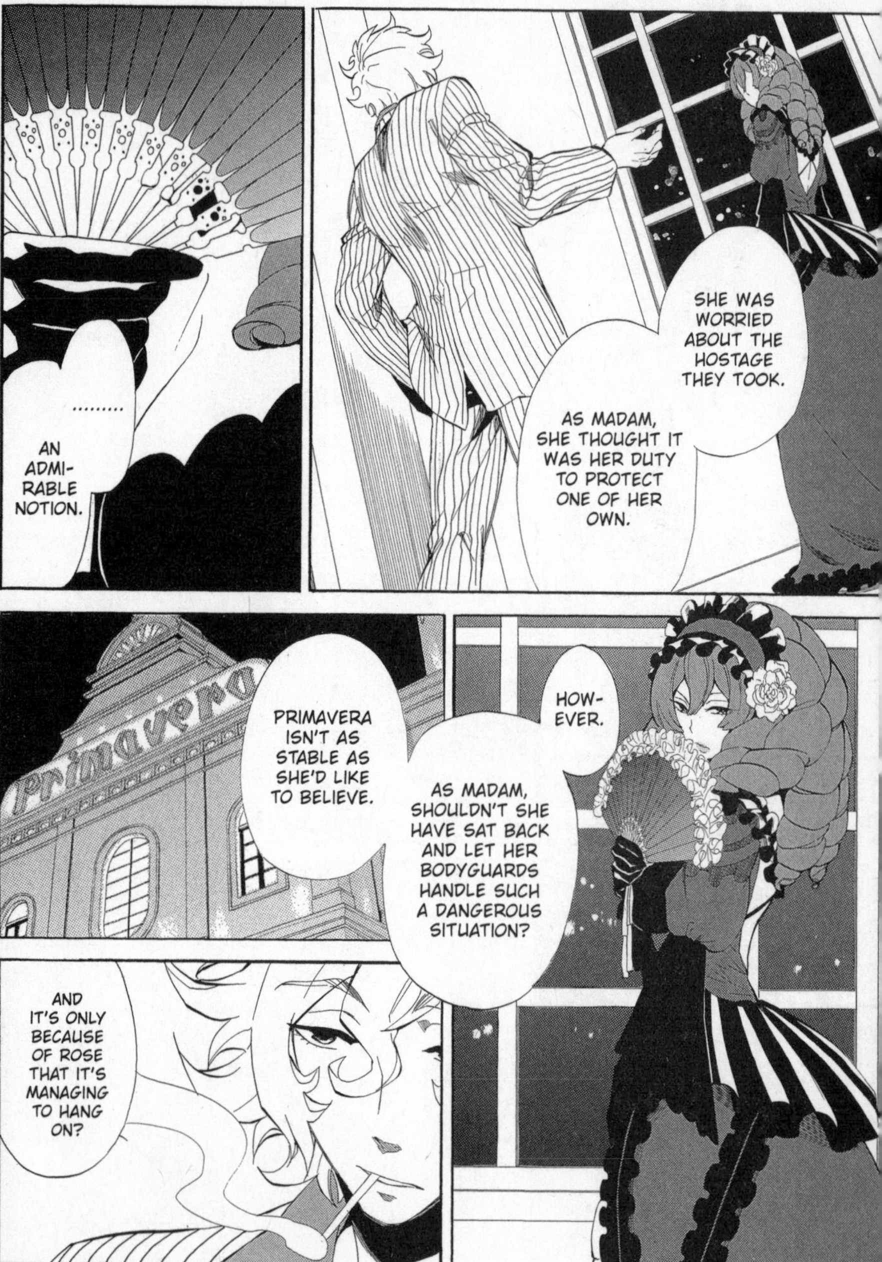
SHE WAS WORRIED ABOUT THE HOSTAGE THEY TOOK.
AS MADAM, SHE THOUGHT IT WAS HER DUTY TO PROTECT ONE OF HER OWN.
....
AN ADMIRABLE NOTION.
HOW-EVER.
AS MADAM, SHOULDN'T SHE HAVE SAT BACK AND LET HER BODYGUARDS HANDLE SUCH A DANGEROUS SITUATION?
Primavera
PRIMAVERA ISN'T AS STABLE AS SHE'D LIKE TO BELIEVE.
AND IT'S ONLY BECAUSE OF ROSE THAT IT'S MANAGING TO HANG ON?

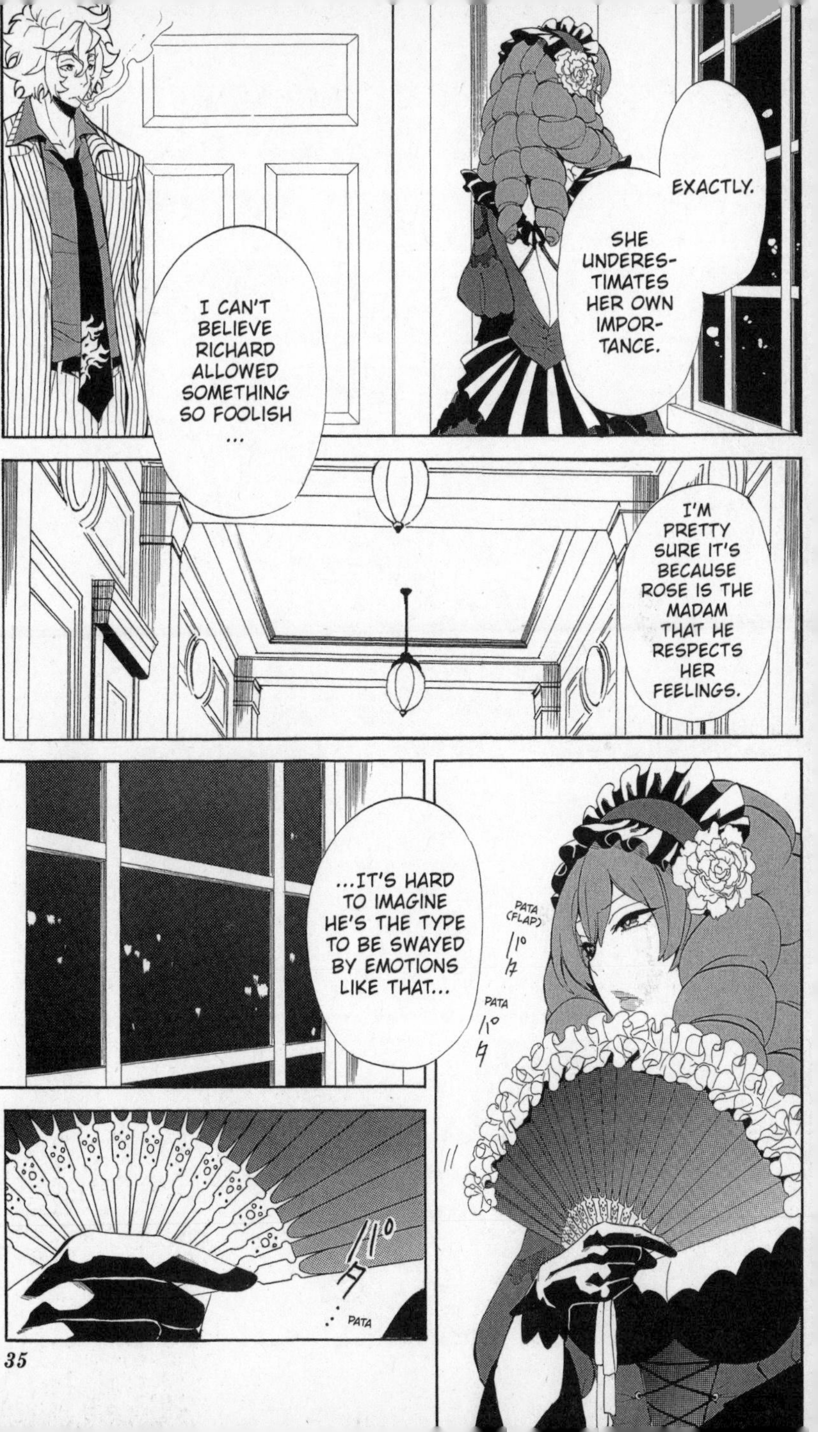
EXACTLY.
SHE UNDERES-TIMATES HER OWN IMPOR-TANCE.
I CAN'T BELIEVE RICHARD ALLOWED SOMETHING SO FOOLISH ...
I'M PRETTY SURE IT'S BECAUSE ROSE IS THE MADAM THAT HE RESPECTS HER FEELINGS.
PATA (FLAP)
PATA
...IT'S HARD TO IMAGINE HE'S THE TYPE TO BE SWAYED BY EMOTIONS LIKE THAT...
PATA

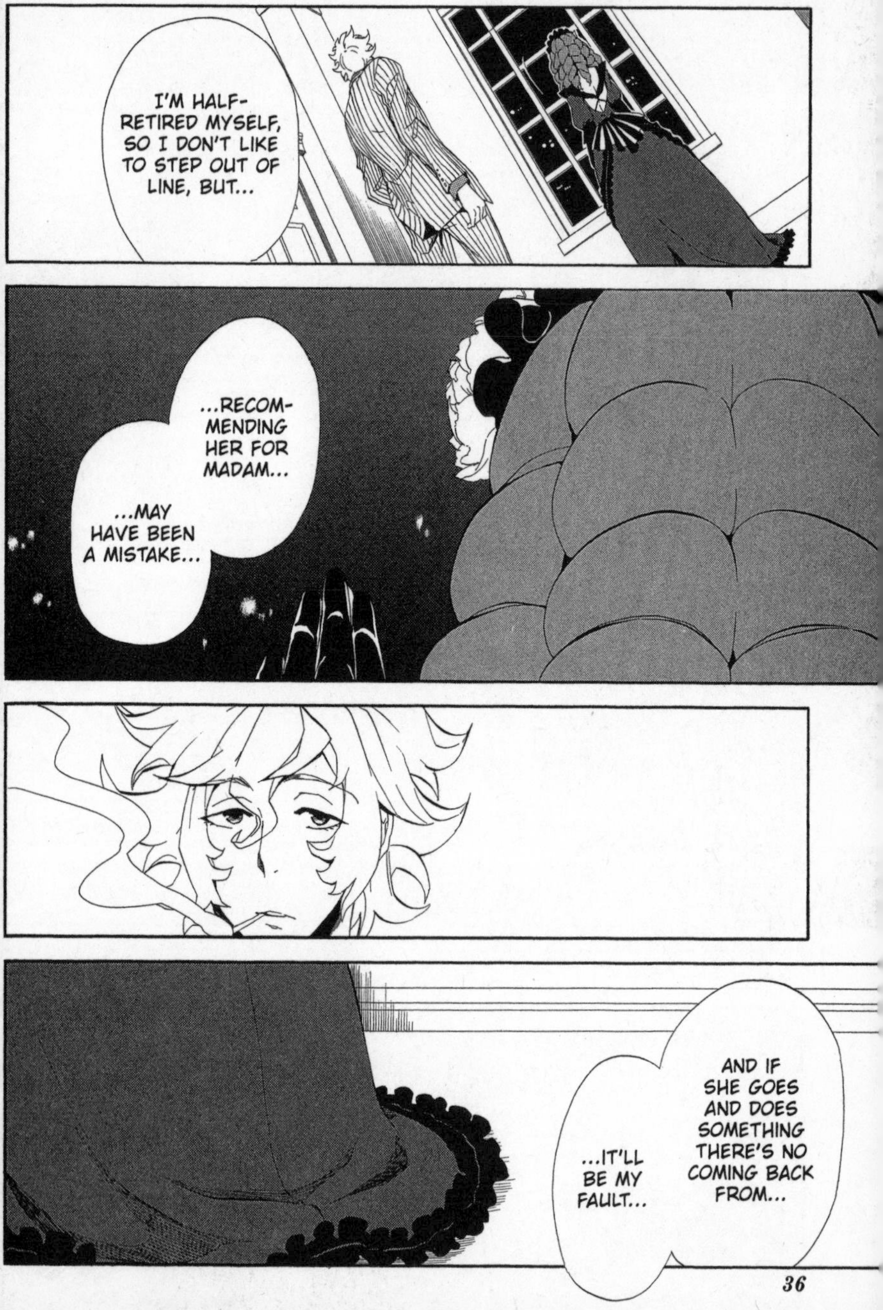
I'M HALF-RETIRED MYSELF, SO I DON'T LIKE TO STEP OUT OF LINE, BUT...
...RECOMMENDING HER FOR MADAM...
...MAY HAVE BEEN A MISTAKE...
AND IF SHE GOES AND DOES SOMETHING THERE'S NO COMING BACK FROM...
...IT'LL BE MY FAULT...

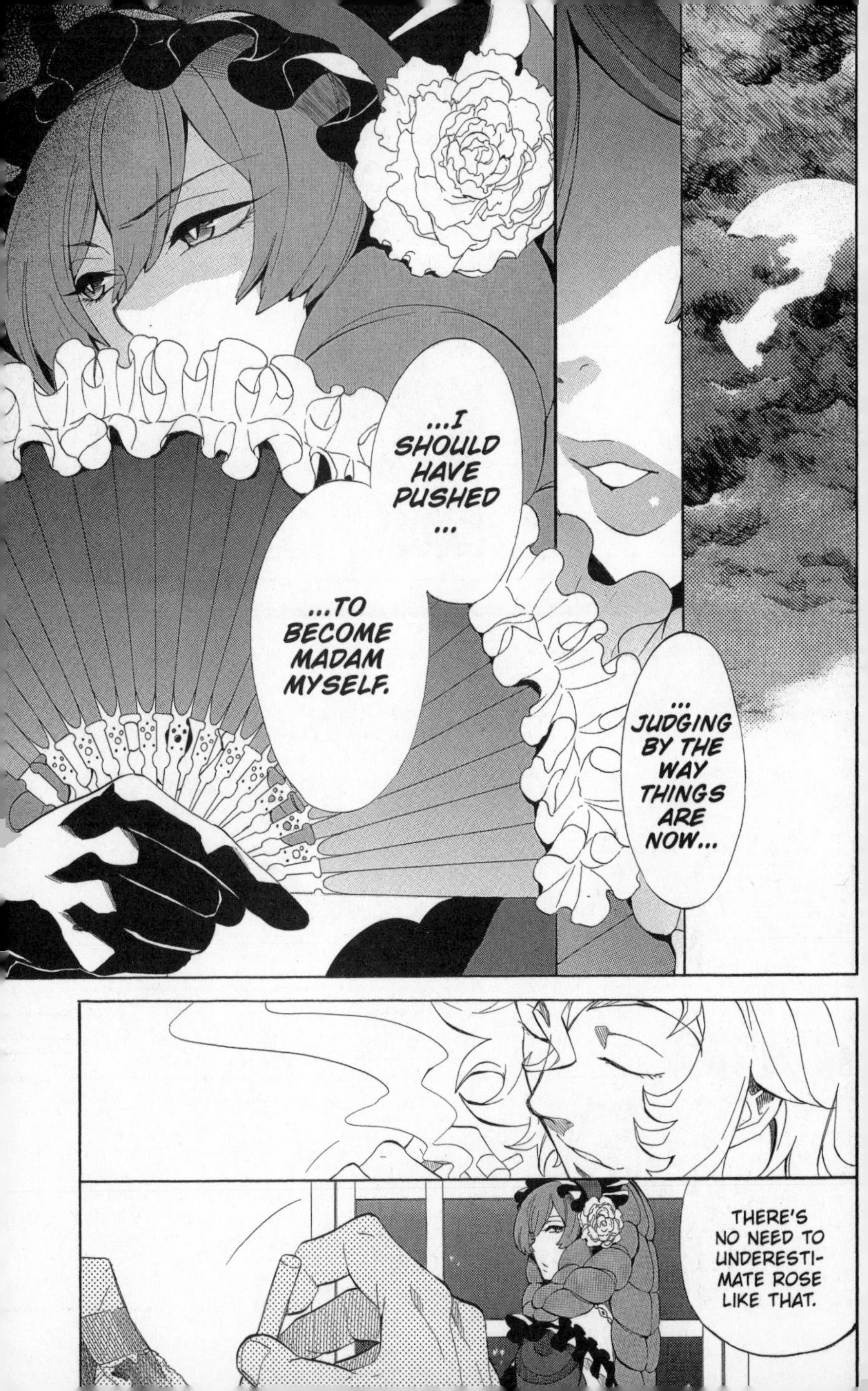
...JUDGING BY THE WAY THINGS ARE NOW...
...I SHOULD HAVE PUSHED...
...TO BECOME MADAM MYSELF.
THERE'S NO NEED TO UNDERESTI-MATE ROSE LIKE THAT.

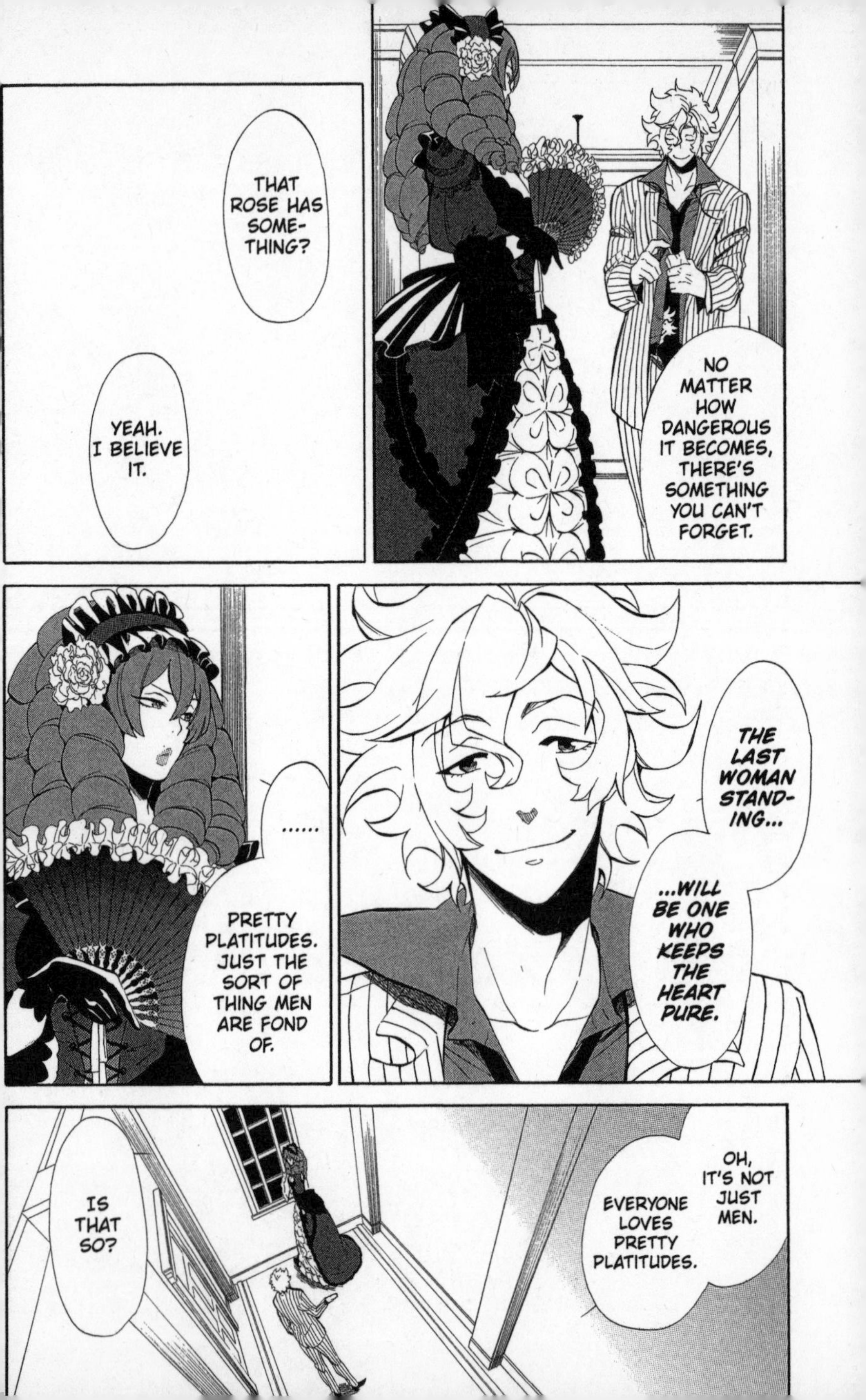
NO MATTER HOW DANGEROUS IT BECOMES, THERE'S SOMETHING YOU CAN'T FORGET.
THAT ROSE HAS SOME-THING?
YEAH. I BELIEVE IT.
THE LAST WOMAN STAND-ING...
...WILL BE ONE WHO KEEPS THE HEART PURE.
......
PRETTY PLATITUDES. JUST THE SORT OF THING MEN ARE FOND OF.
OH, IT'S NOT JUST MEN.
EVERYONE LOVES PRETTY PLATITUDES.
IS THAT SO?

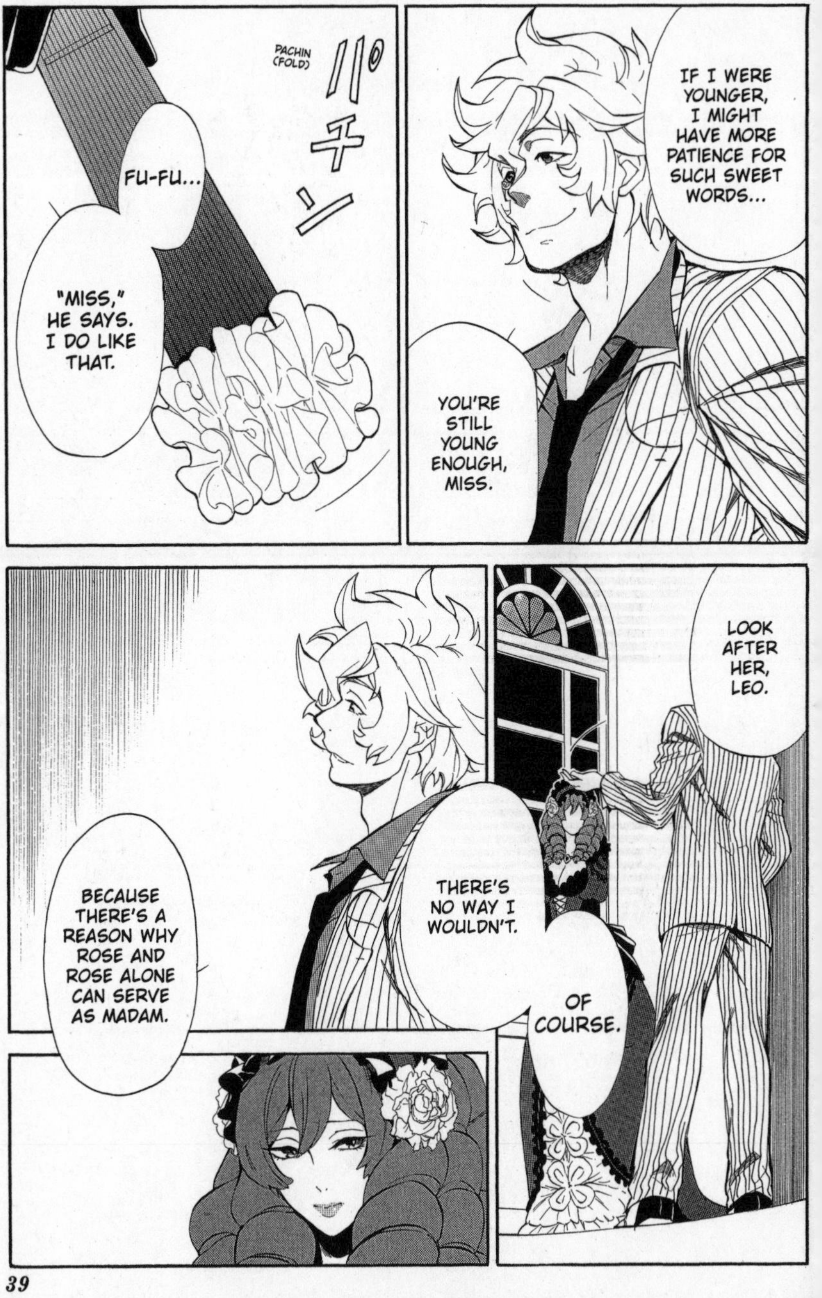
IF I WERE YOUNGER, I MIGHT HAVE MORE PATIENCE FOR SUCH SWEET WORDS...
YOU'RE STILL YOUNG ENOUGH, MISS.
PACHIN (FOLD)
FU-FU...
"MISS," HE SAYS. I DO LIKE THAT.
LOOK AFTER HER, LEO.
OF COURSE.
THERE'S NO WAY I WOULDN'T.
BECAUSE THERE'S A REASON WHY ROSE AND ROSE ALONE CAN SERVE AS MADAM.

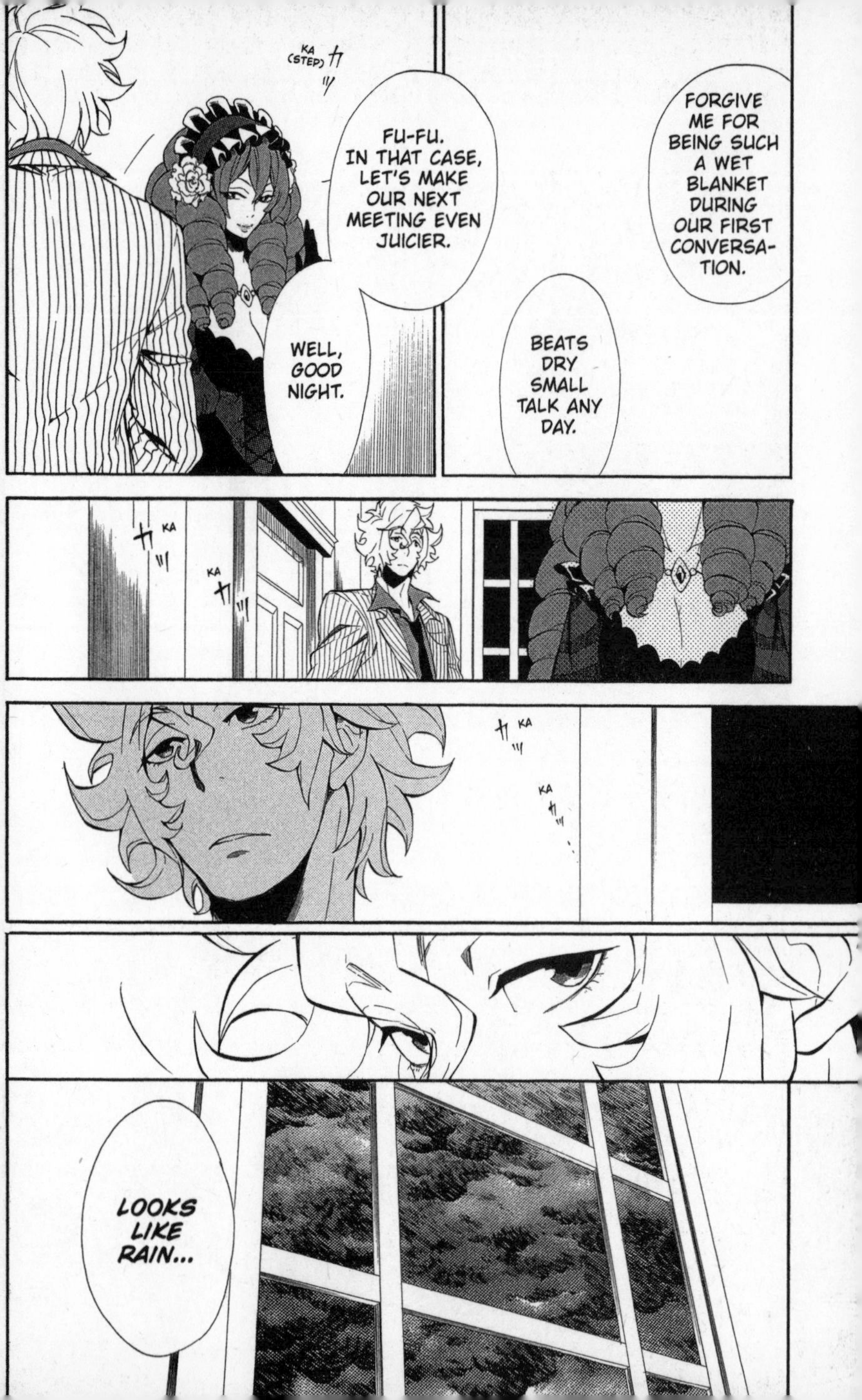
FORGIVE ME FOR BEING SUCH A WET BLANKET DURING OUR FIRST CONVERSA-TION.
BEATS DRY SMALL TALK ANY DAY.
KA (STEP)
FU-FU. IN THAT CASE, LET'S MAKE OUR NEXT MEETING EVEN JUICIER.
WELL, GOOD NIGHT.
KA
KA
KA
KA
LOOKS LIKE RAIN...

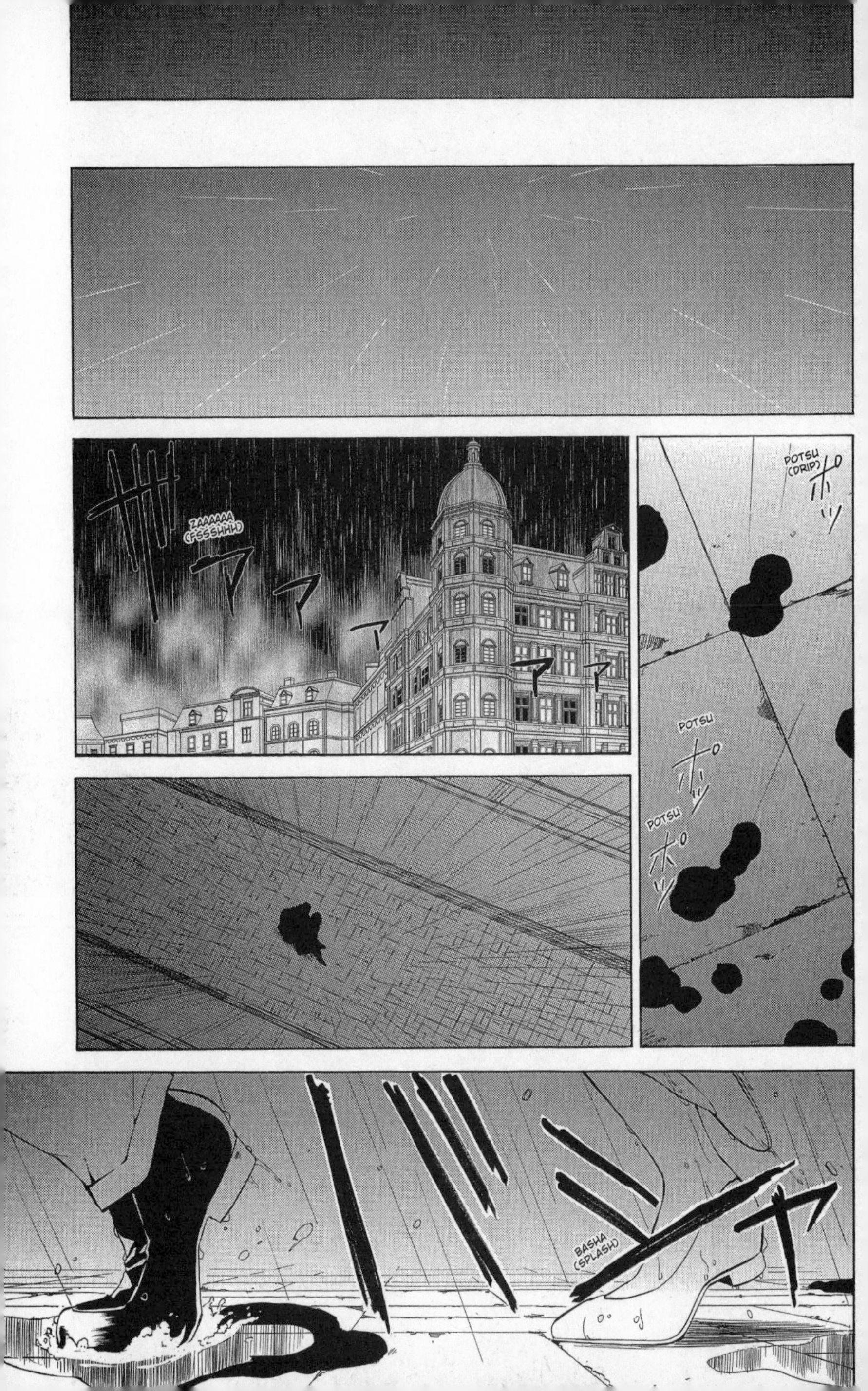
POTSU (DRIP)
POTSU
POTSU
ZAAAAAA (FSSSHHH)
BASHA (SPLASH)

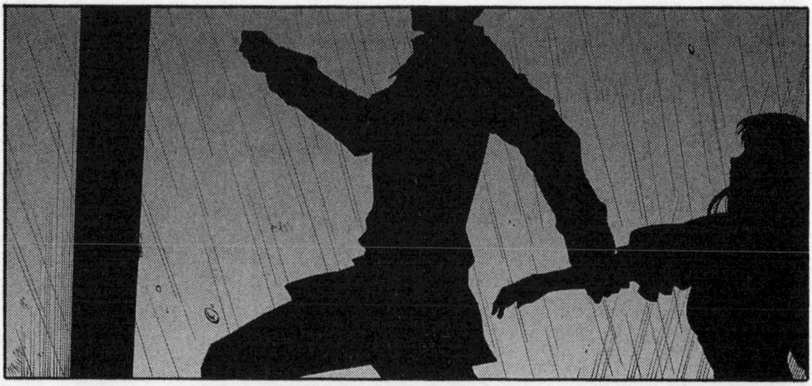

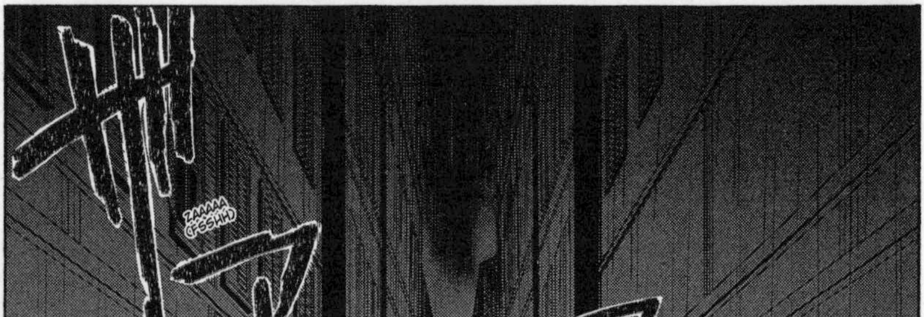
ザァァァァ
ZAAAAA (FSSHH)

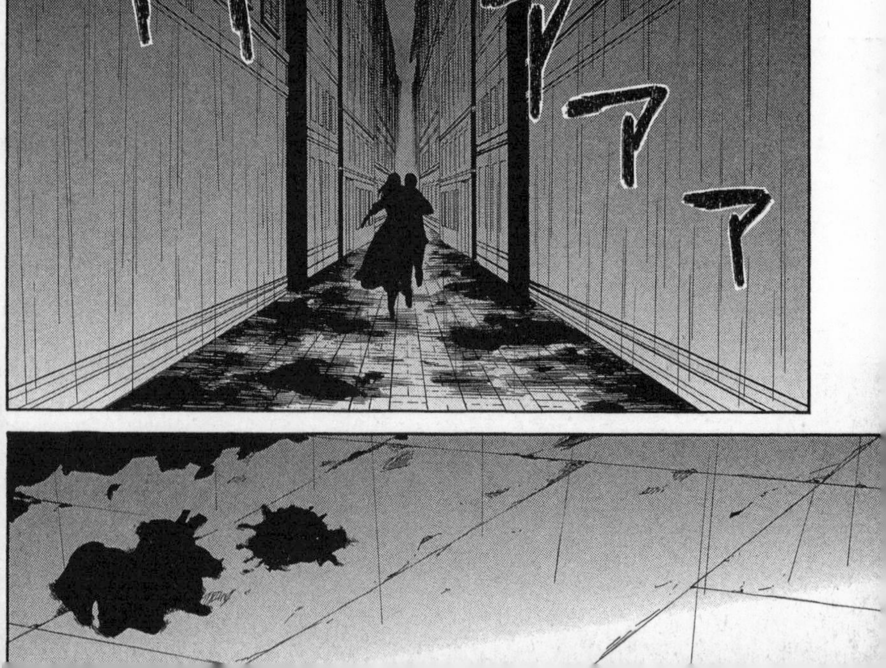

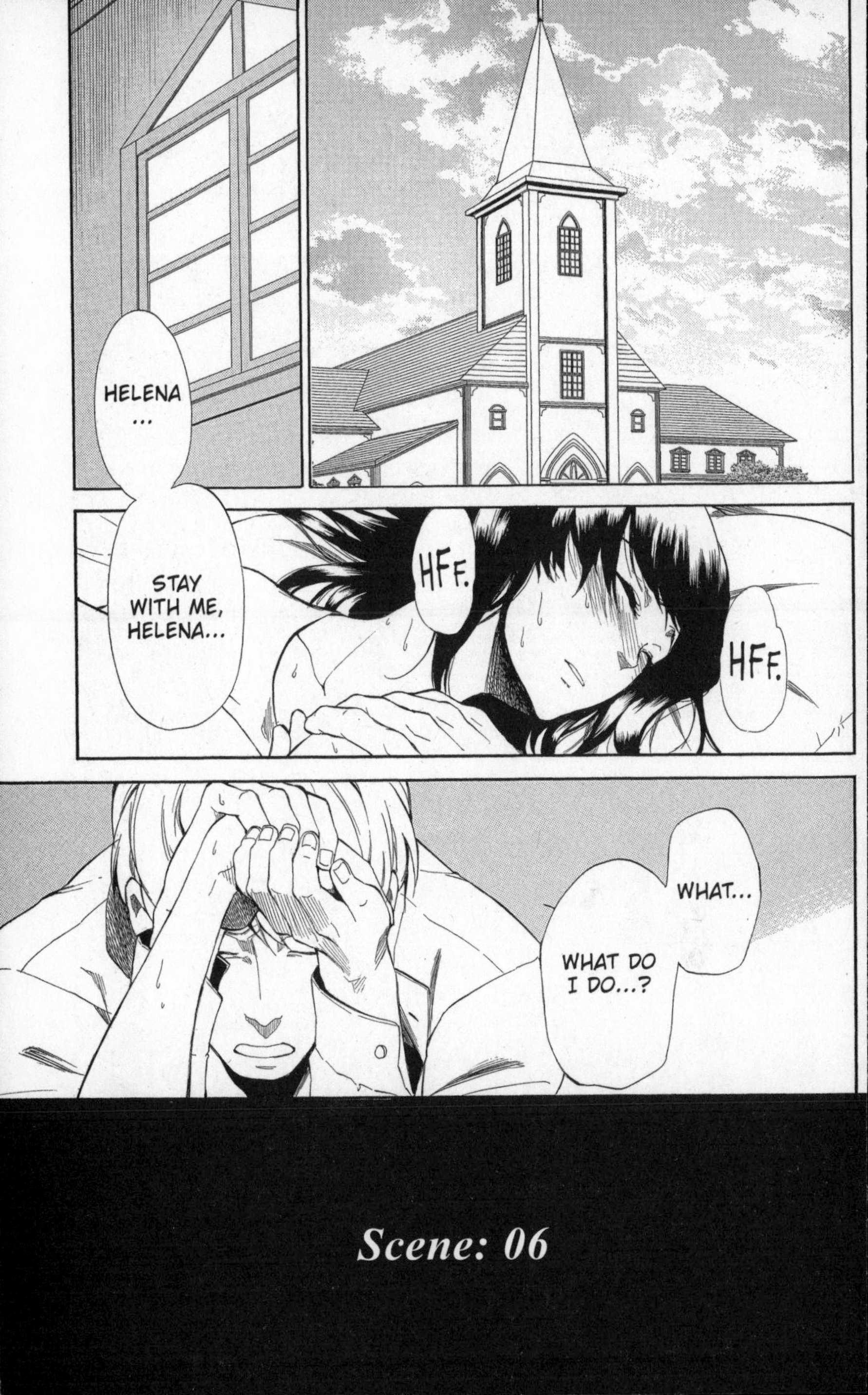
HELENA ...
STAY WITH ME, HELENA...
HFF.
HFF.
WHAT...
WHAT DO I DO...?

Scene: 06

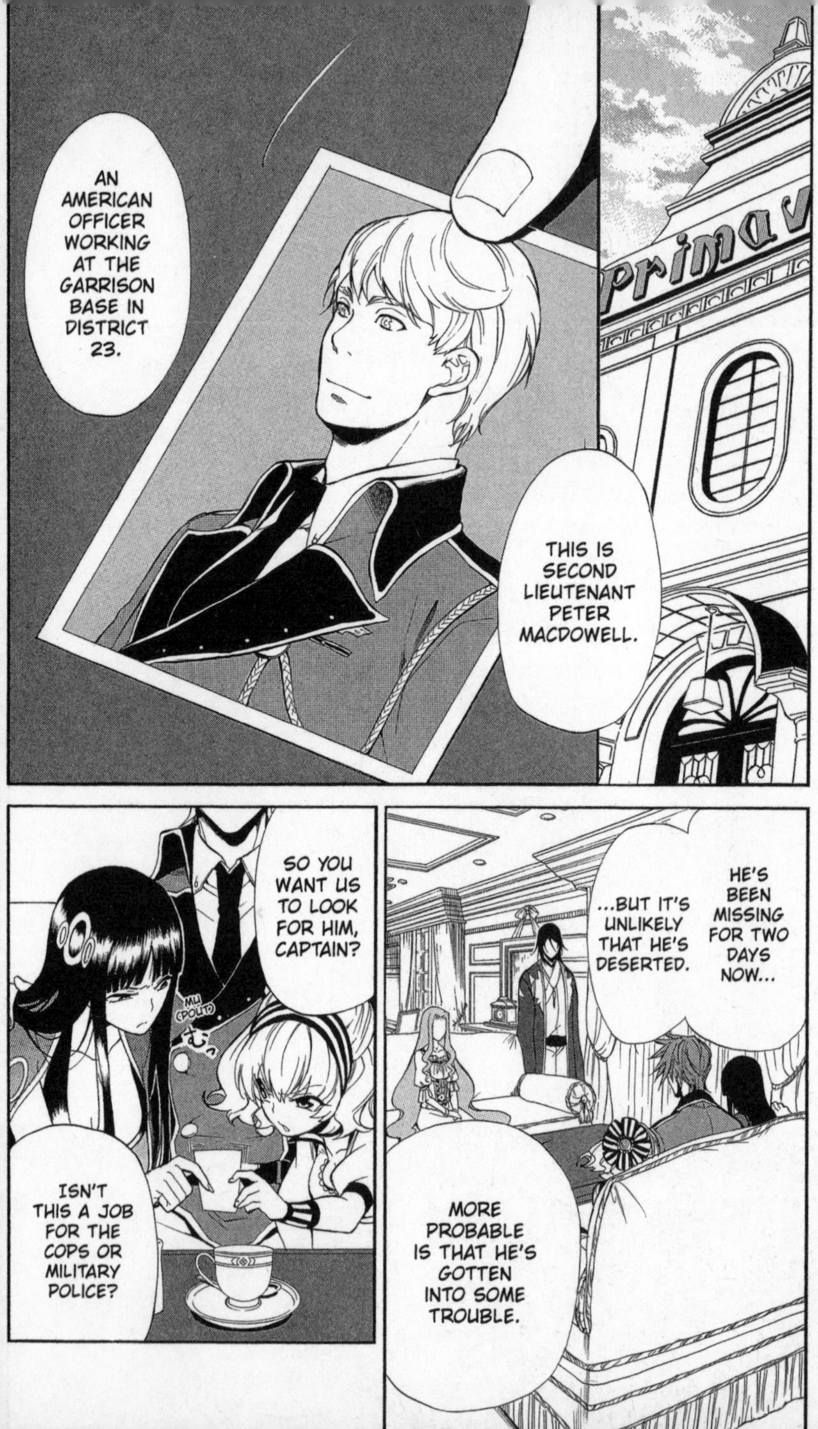
THIS IS SECOND LIEUTENANT PETER MACDOWELL.
AN AMERICAN OFFICER WORKING AT THE GARRISON BASE IN DISTRICT 23.
HE'S BEEN MISSING FOR TWO DAYS NOW...
...BUT IT'S UNLIKELY THAT HE'S DESERTED.
MORE PROBABLE IS THAT HE'S GOTTEN INTO SOME TROUBLE.
SO YOU WANT US TO LOOK FOR HIM, CAPTAIN?
MU (POUT)
むっ
ISN'T THIS A JOB FOR THE COPS OR MILITARY POLICE?

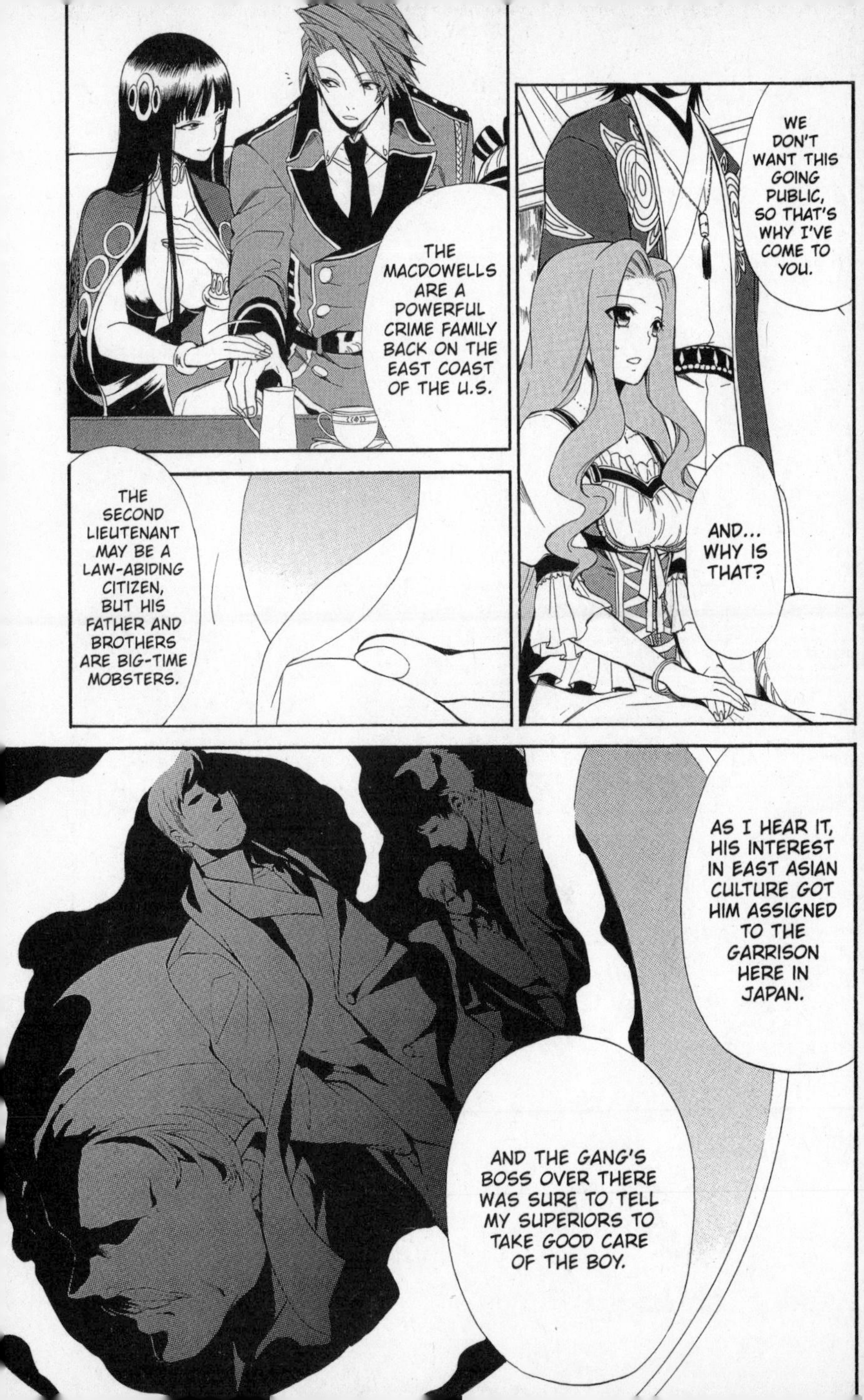
WE DON'T WANT THIS GOING PUBLIC, SO THAT'S WHY I'VE COME TO YOU.
AND... WHY IS THAT?
THE MACDOWELLS ARE A POWERFUL CRIME FAMILY BACK ON THE EAST COAST OF THE U.S.
THE SECOND LIEUTENANT MAY BE A LAW-ABIDING CITIZEN, BUT HIS FATHER AND BROTHERS ARE BIG-TIME MOBSTERS.
AS I HEAR IT, HIS INTEREST IN EAST ASIAN CULTURE GOT HIM ASSIGNED TO THE GARRISON HERE IN JAPAN.
AND THE GANG'S BOSS OVER THERE WAS SURE TO TELL MY SUPERIORS TO TAKE GOOD CARE OF THE BOY.

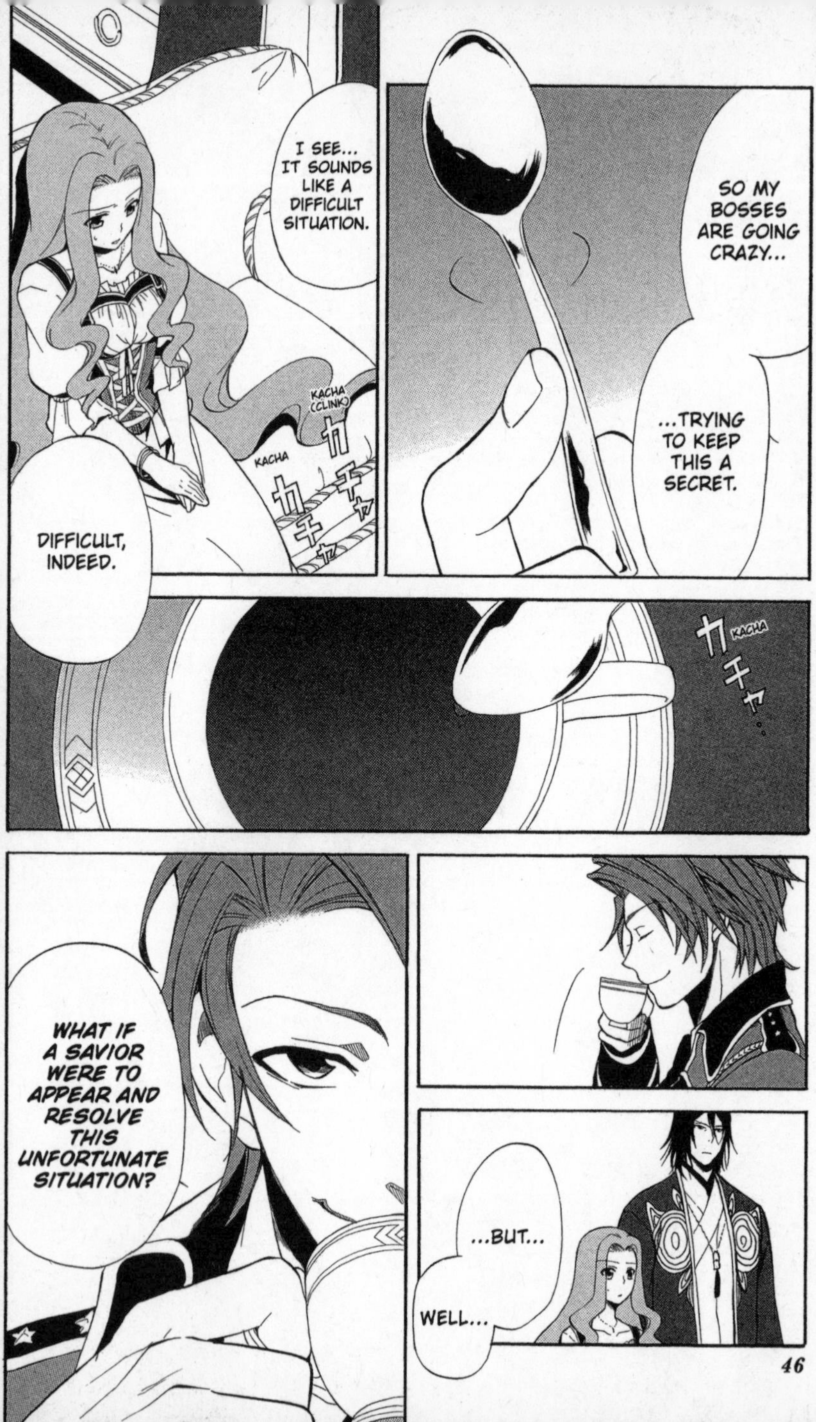
SO MY BOSSES ARE GOING CRAZY...
...TRYING TO KEEP THIS A SECRET.
I SEE... IT SOUNDS LIKE A DIFFICULT SITUATION.
KACHA (CLINK)
カチャ
KACHA
カチャ
DIFFICULT, INDEED.
カチャ..
KACHA
...BUT...
WELL...
WHAT IF A SAVIOR WERE TO APPEAR AND RESOLVE THIS UNFORTUNATE SITUATION?

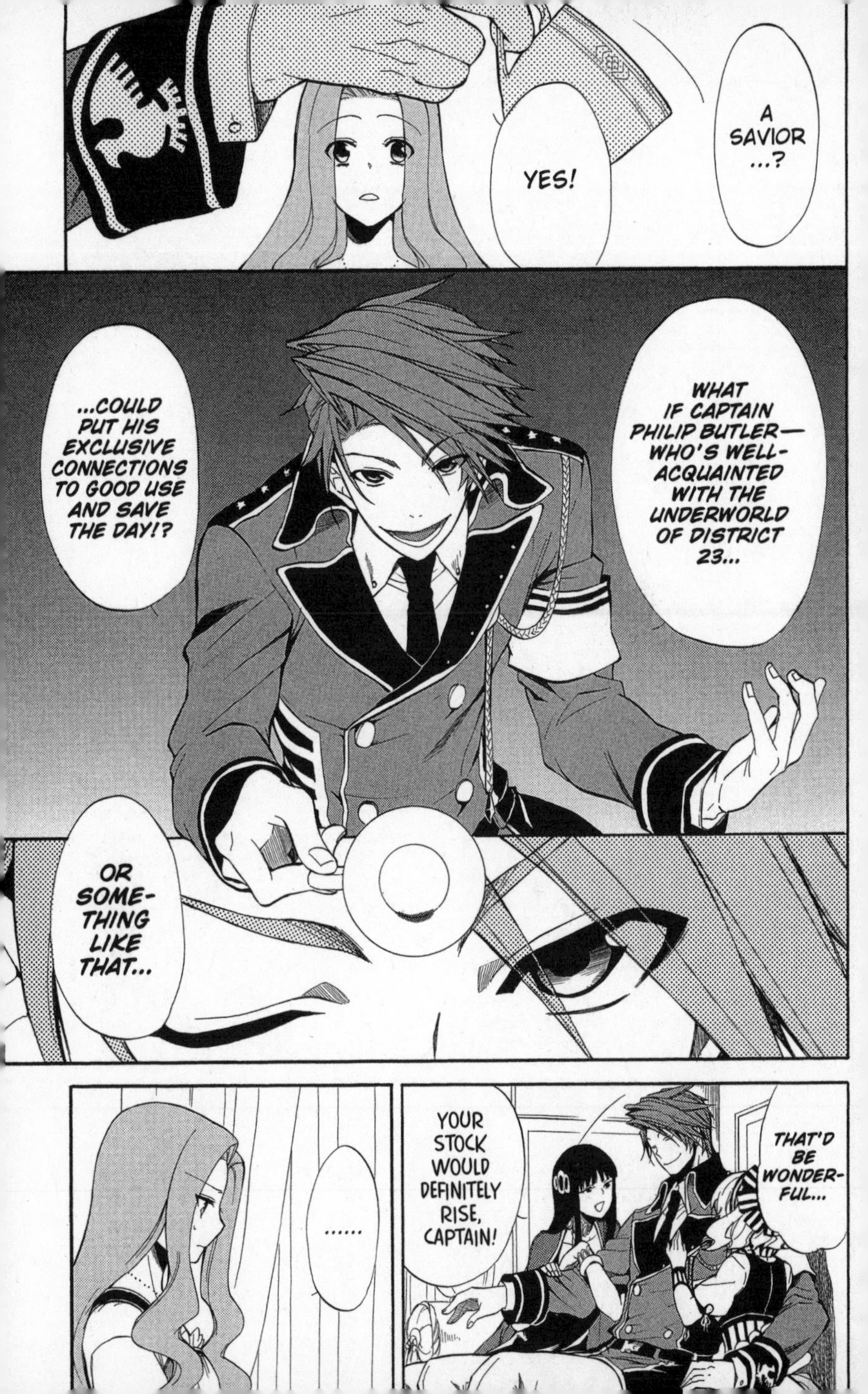
A SAVIOR ...?
YES!
WHAT IF CAPTAIN PHILIP BUTLER—WHO'S WELL-ACQUAINTED WITH THE UNDERWORLD OF DISTRICT 23...
...COULD PUT HIS EXCLUSIVE CONNECTIONS TO GOOD USE AND SAVE THE DAY!?
OR SOME-THING LIKE THAT...
THAT'D BE WONDER-FUL...
YOUR STOCK WOULD DEFINITELY RISE, CAPTAIN!
......

ROSE-CHAN, AS YOU WELL KNOW, I'M RESPONSIBLE FOR PUBLIC ORDER HERE IN DISTRICT 23.

BUT AT THE END OF THE DAY, IT'S STILL MIDDLE MANAGEMENT.

I DON'T HAVE THE POWER TO DO ANYTHING HERE, NOT ALONE.

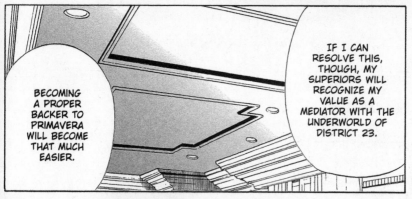

IF I CAN RESOLVE THIS, THOUGH, MY SUPERIORS WILL RECOGNIZE MY VALUE AS A MEDIATOR WITH THE UNDERWORLD OF DISTRICT 23.

BECOMING A PROPER BACKER TO PRIMAVERA WILL BECOME THAT MUCH EASIER.

...SO YOU'RE TESTING US, THEN?

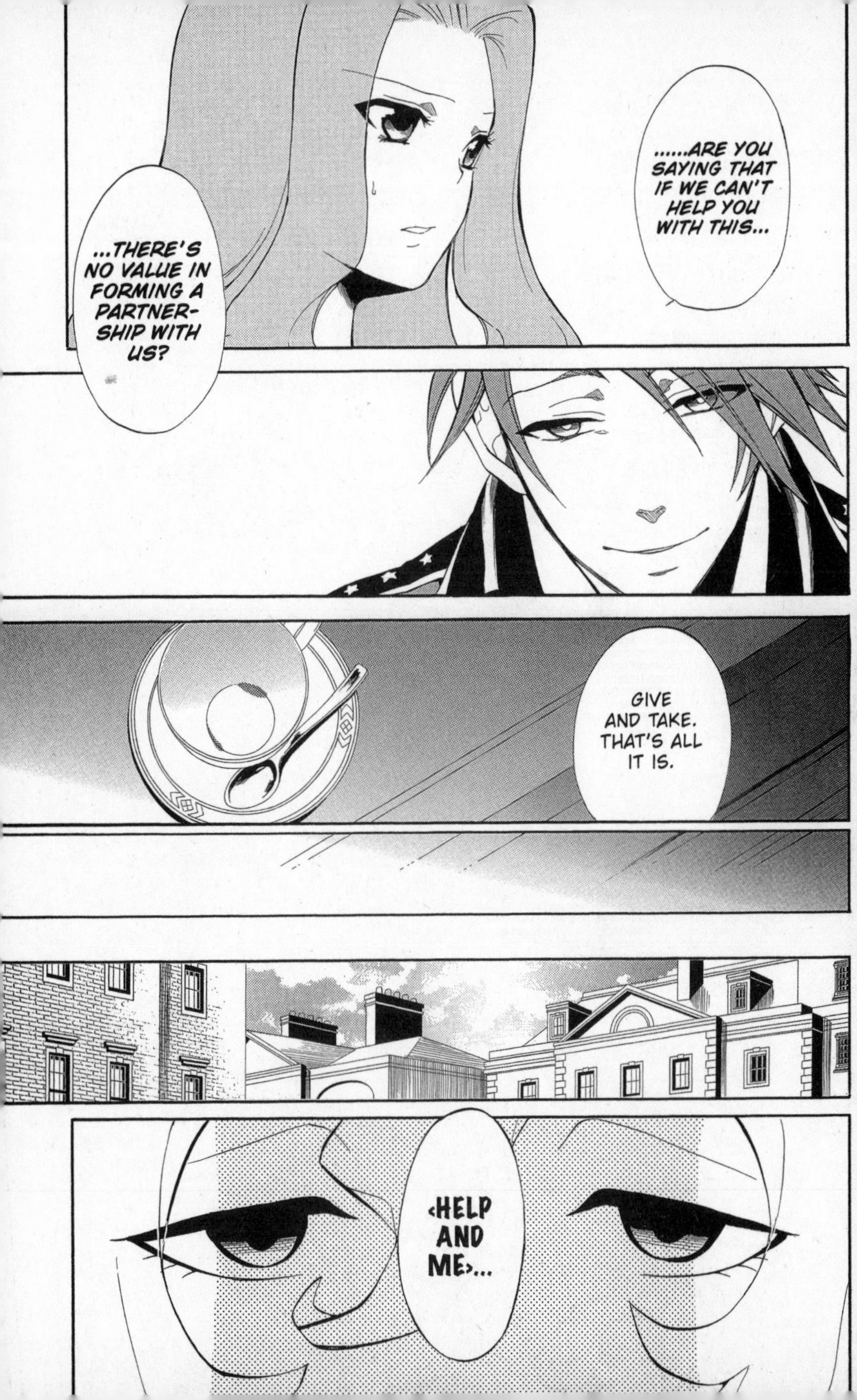
......ARE YOU SAYING THAT IF WE CAN'T HELP YOU WITH THIS...
...THERE'S NO VALUE IN FORMING A PARTNER-SHIP WITH US?
GIVE AND TAKE. THAT'S ALL IT IS.
‹HELP AND ME›...

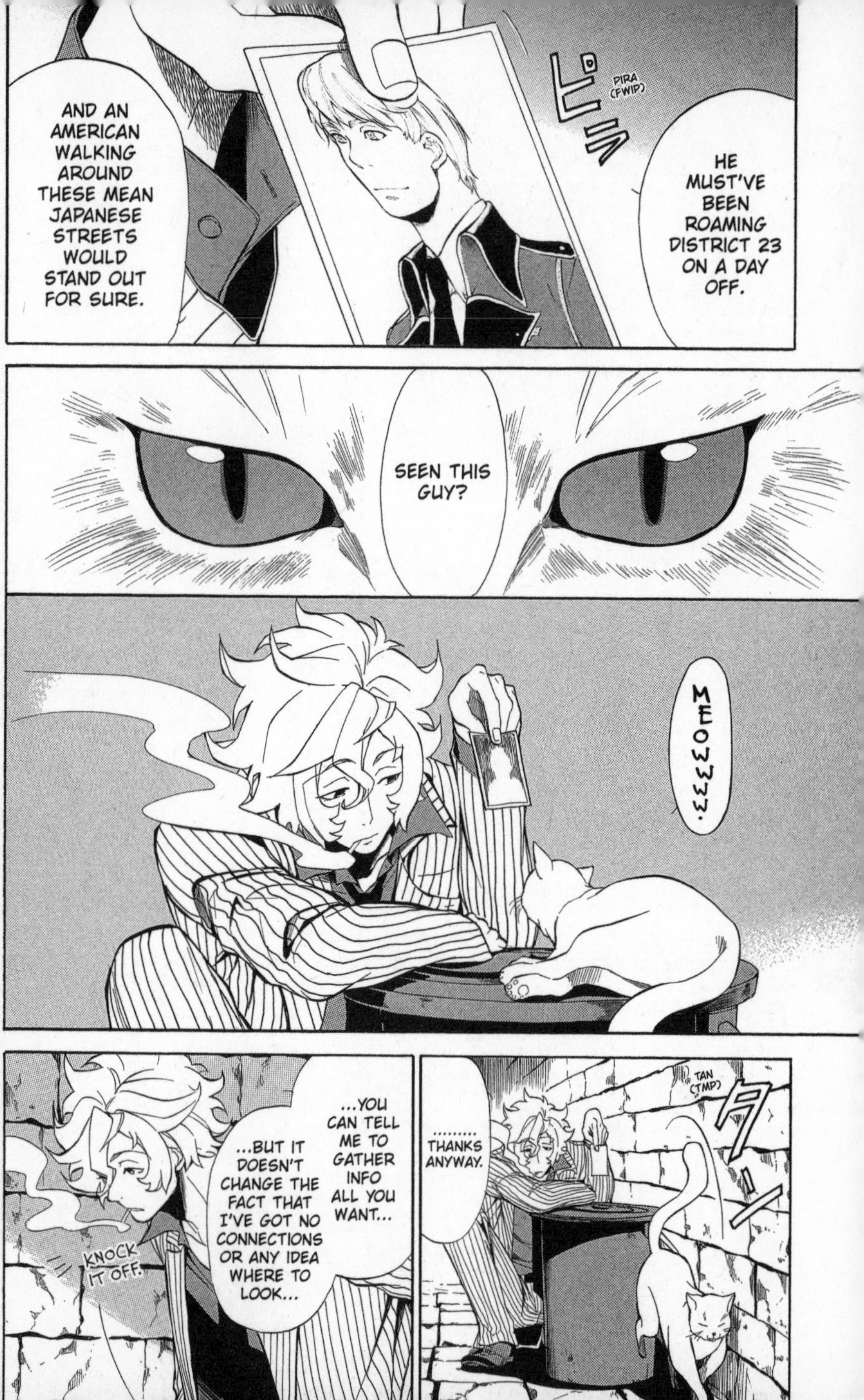
PIRA (FWIP)
HE MUST'VE BEEN ROAMING DISTRICT 23 ON A DAY OFF.
AND AN AMERICAN WALKING AROUND THESE MEAN JAPANESE STREETS WOULD STAND OUT FOR SURE.
SEEN THIS GUY?
MEOWWWW.
TAN (TMP)
.... THANKS ANYWAY.
...YOU CAN TELL ME TO GATHER INFO ALL YOU WANT...
...BUT IT DOESN'T CHANGE THE FACT THAT I'VE GOT NO CONNECTIONS OR ANY IDEA WHERE TO LOOK...
KNOCK IT OFF.

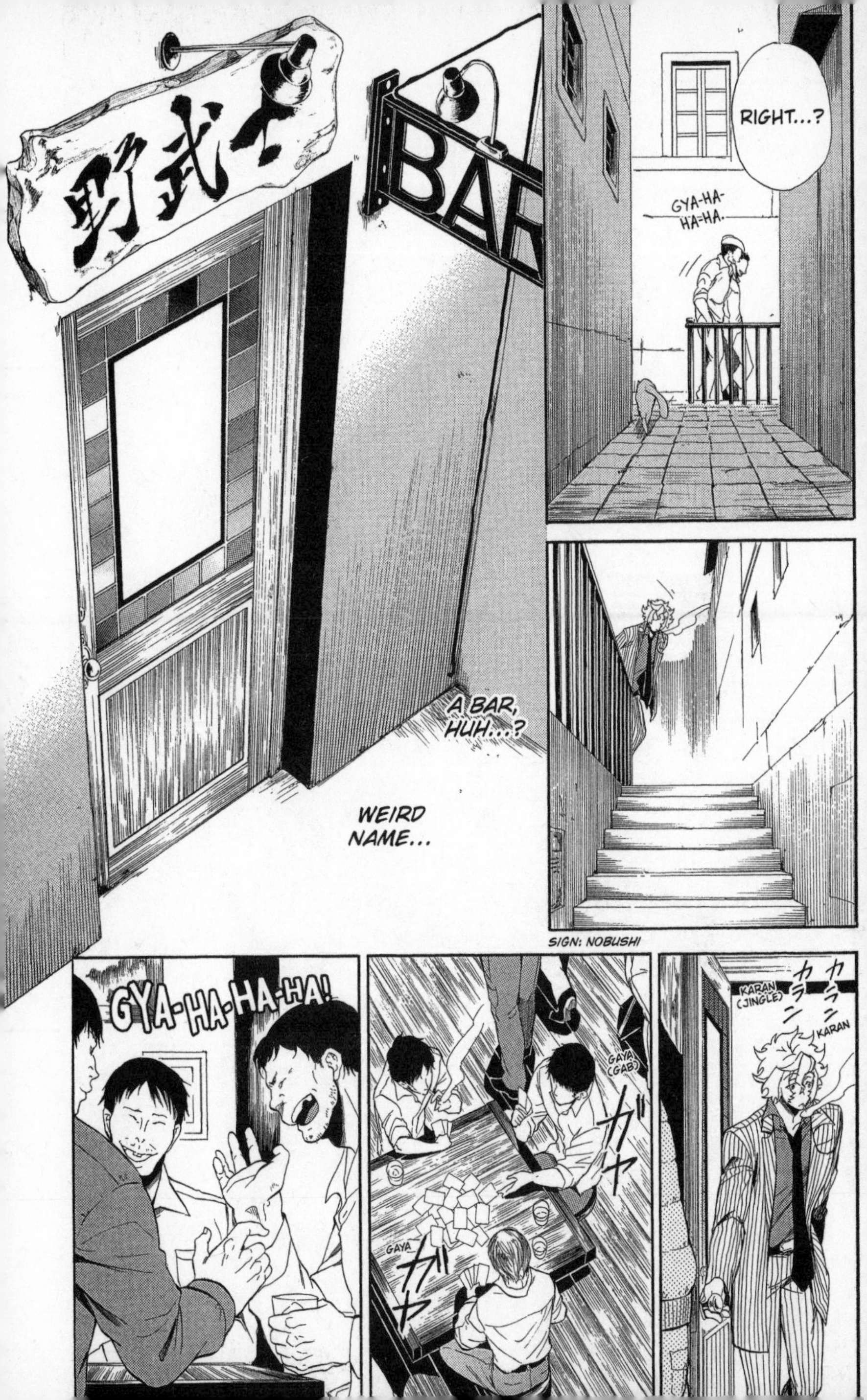
RIGHT...?
GYA-HA-HA-HA.
BAR
野武士
A BAR, HUH...?
WEIRD NAME...
SIGN: NOBUSHI
カラン
KARAN (JINGLE)
カラン
KARAN
ガヤ
GAYA (GAB)
ガヤ
GAYA
GYA-HA-HA-HA!

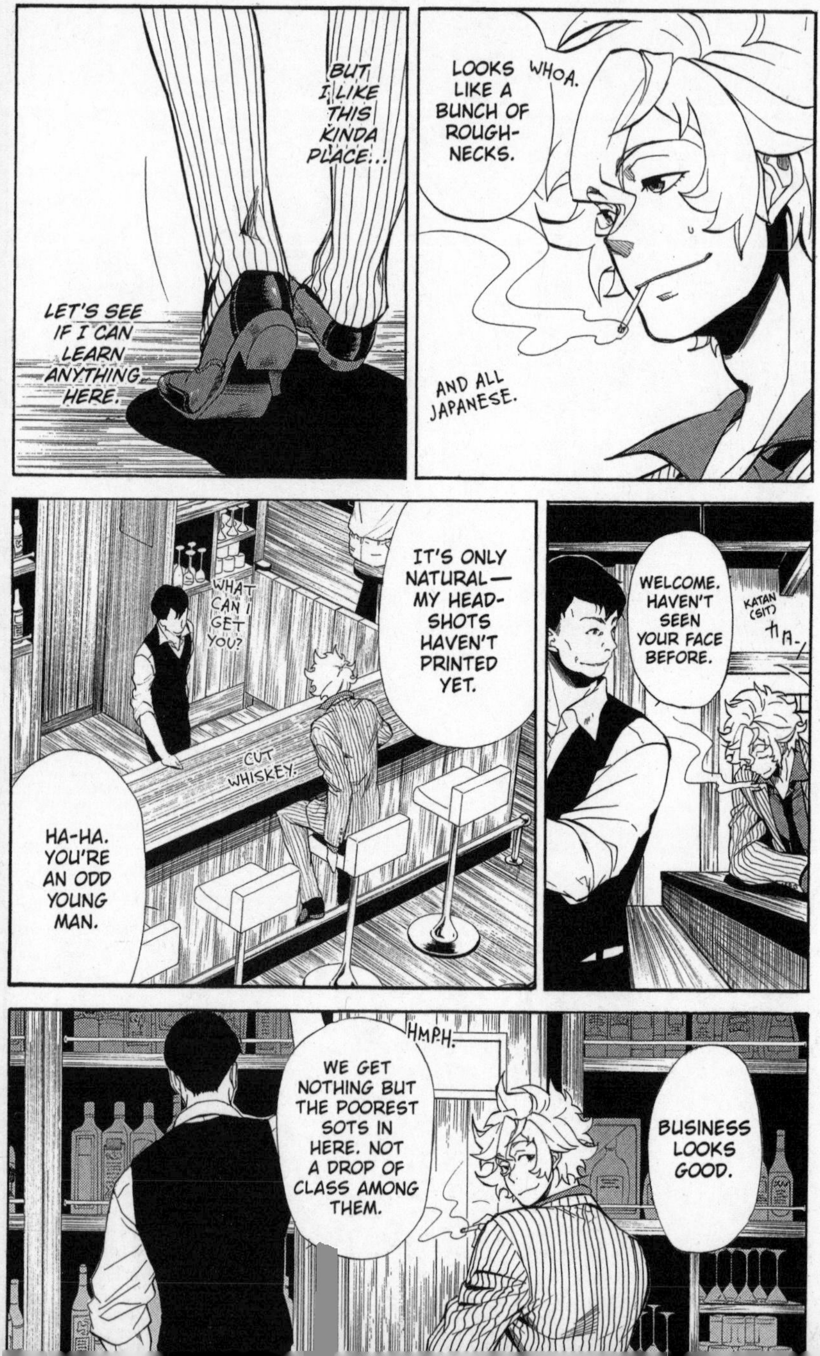
WHOA.
LOOKS LIKE A BUNCH OF ROUGHNECKS.
AND ALL JAPANESE.
BUT I LIKE THIS KINDA PLACE...
LET'S SEE IF I CAN LEARN ANYTHING HERE.
KATAN (SIT)
WELCOME. HAVEN'T SEEN YOUR FACE BEFORE.
IT'S ONLY NATURAL— MY HEADSHOTS HAVEN'T PRINTED YET.
WHAT CAN I GET YOU?
CUT WHISKEY.
HA-HA. YOU'RE AN ODD YOUNG MAN.
BUSINESS LOOKS GOOD.
HMPH.
WE GET NOTHING BUT THE POOREST SOTS IN HERE. NOT A DROP OF CLASS AMONG THEM.

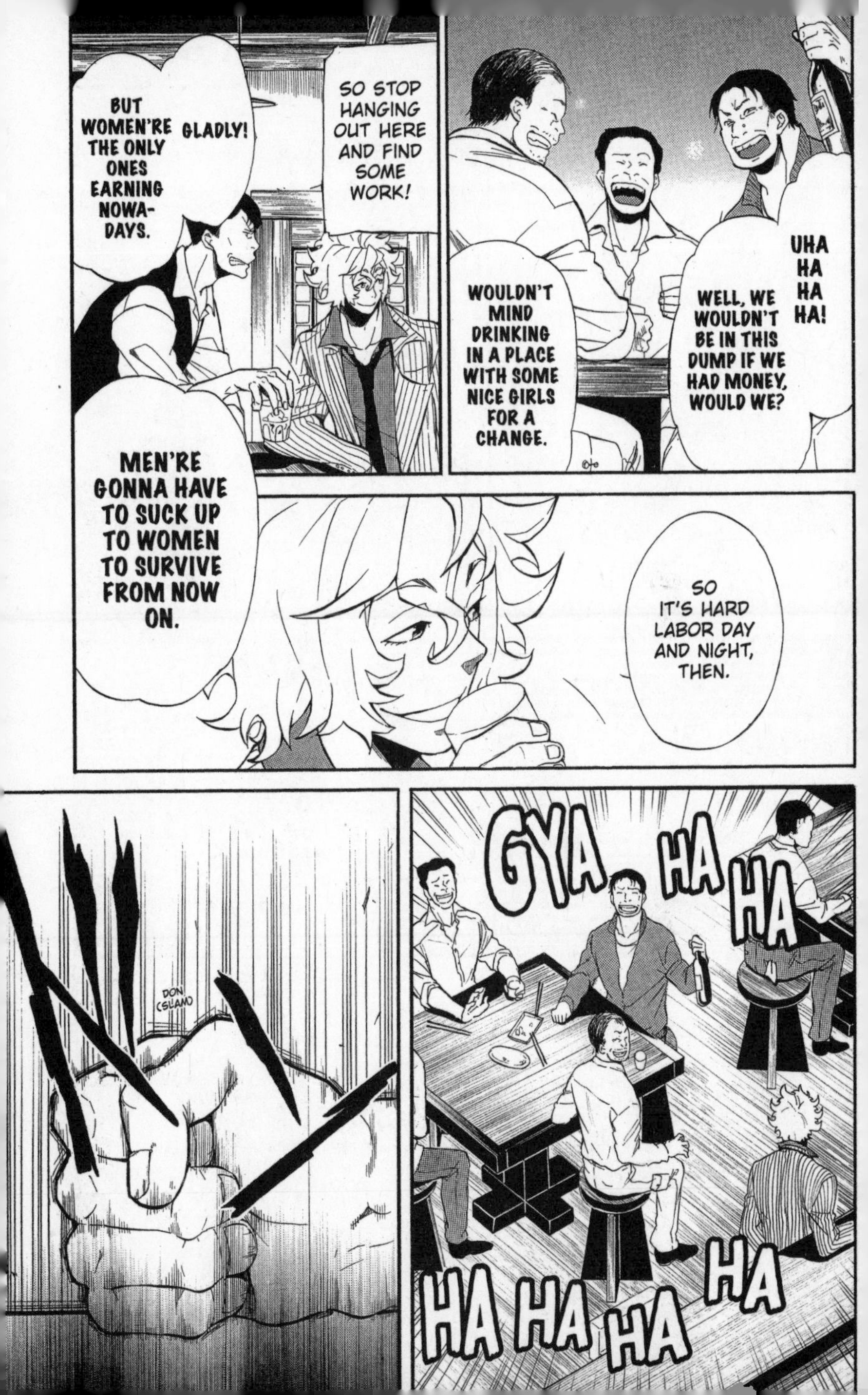
UHA HA HA HA!
WELL, WE WOULDN'T BE IN THIS DUMP IF WE HAD MONEY, WOULD WE?
WOULDN'T MIND DRINKING IN A PLACE WITH SOME NICE GIRLS FOR A CHANGE.
SO STOP HANGING OUT HERE AND FIND SOME WORK!
GLADLY!
BUT WOMEN'RE THE ONLY ONES EARNING NOWA-DAYS.
MEN'RE GONNA HAVE TO SUCK UP TO WOMEN TO SURVIVE FROM NOW ON.
SO IT'S HARD LABOR DAY AND NIGHT, THEN.
GYA HA HA
HA HA HA HA HA
DON (SLAM)

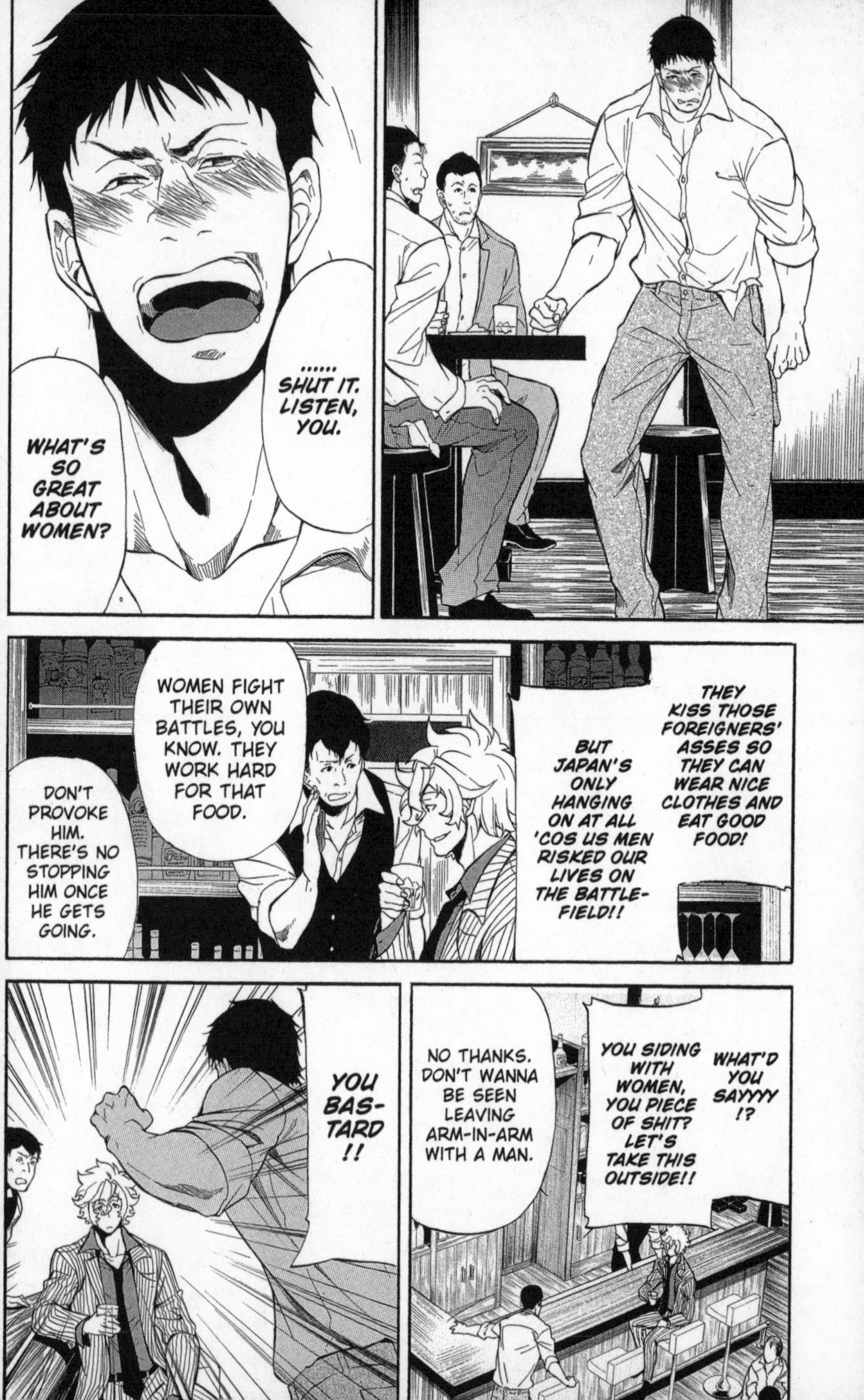
......SHUT IT. LISTEN, YOU.
WHAT'S SO GREAT ABOUT WOMEN?
THEY KISS THOSE FOREIGNERS' ASSES SO THEY CAN WEAR NICE CLOTHES AND EAT GOOD FOOD!
BUT JAPAN'S ONLY HANGING ON AT ALL 'COS US MEN RISKED OUR LIVES ON THE BATTLE-FIELD!!
WOMEN FIGHT THEIR OWN BATTLES, YOU KNOW. THEY WORK HARD FOR THAT FOOD.
DON'T PROVOKE HIM. THERE'S NO STOPPING HIM ONCE HE GETS GOING.
WHAT'D YOU SAYYYY !?
YOU SIDING WITH WOMEN, YOU PIECE OF SHIT? LET'S TAKE THIS OUTSIDE!!
NO THANKS. DON'T WANNA BE SEEN LEAVING ARM-IN-ARM WITH A MAN.
YOU BAS-TARD !!

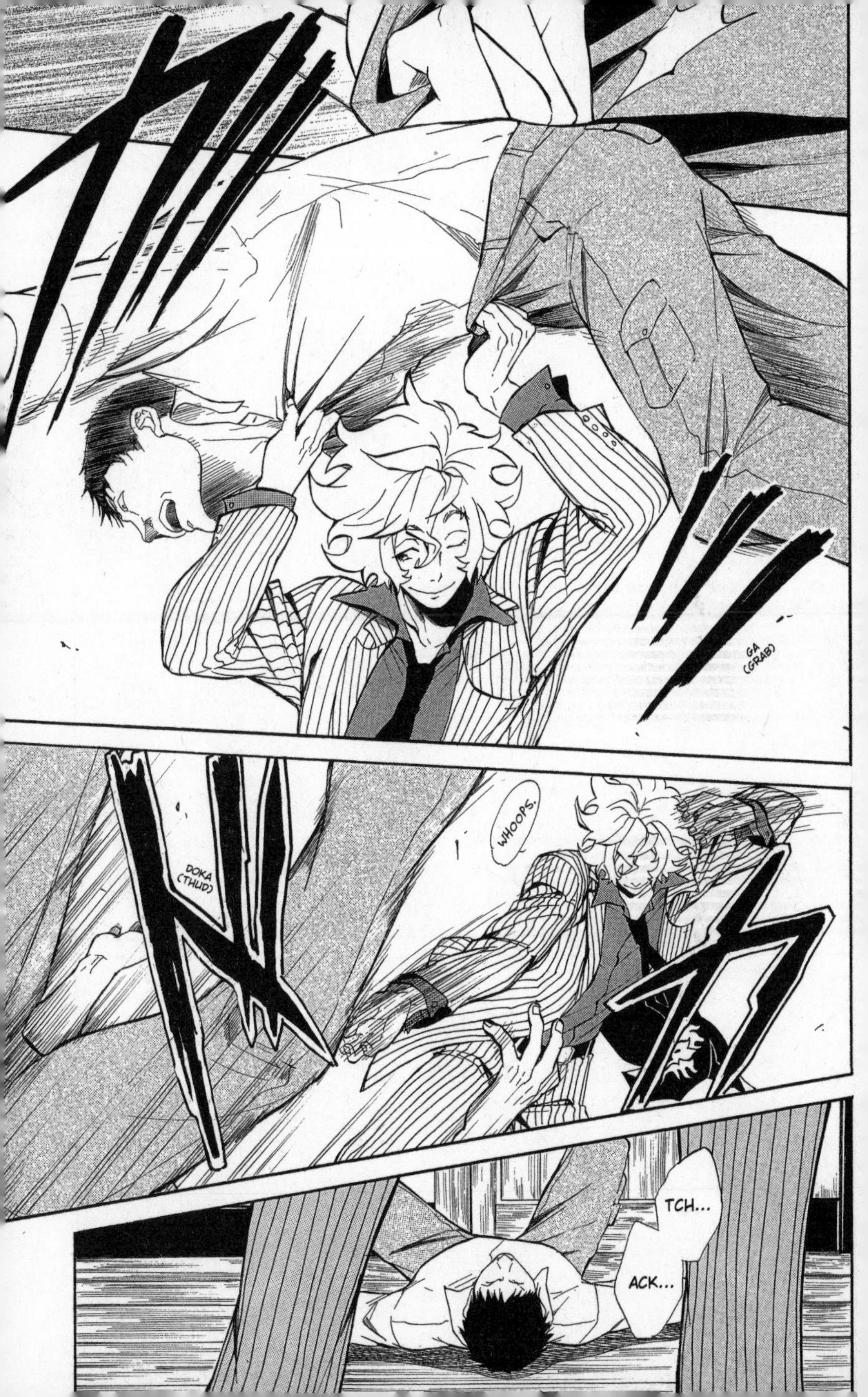
GA (GRAB)
WHOOPS.
DOKA (THUD)
TCH...
ACK...

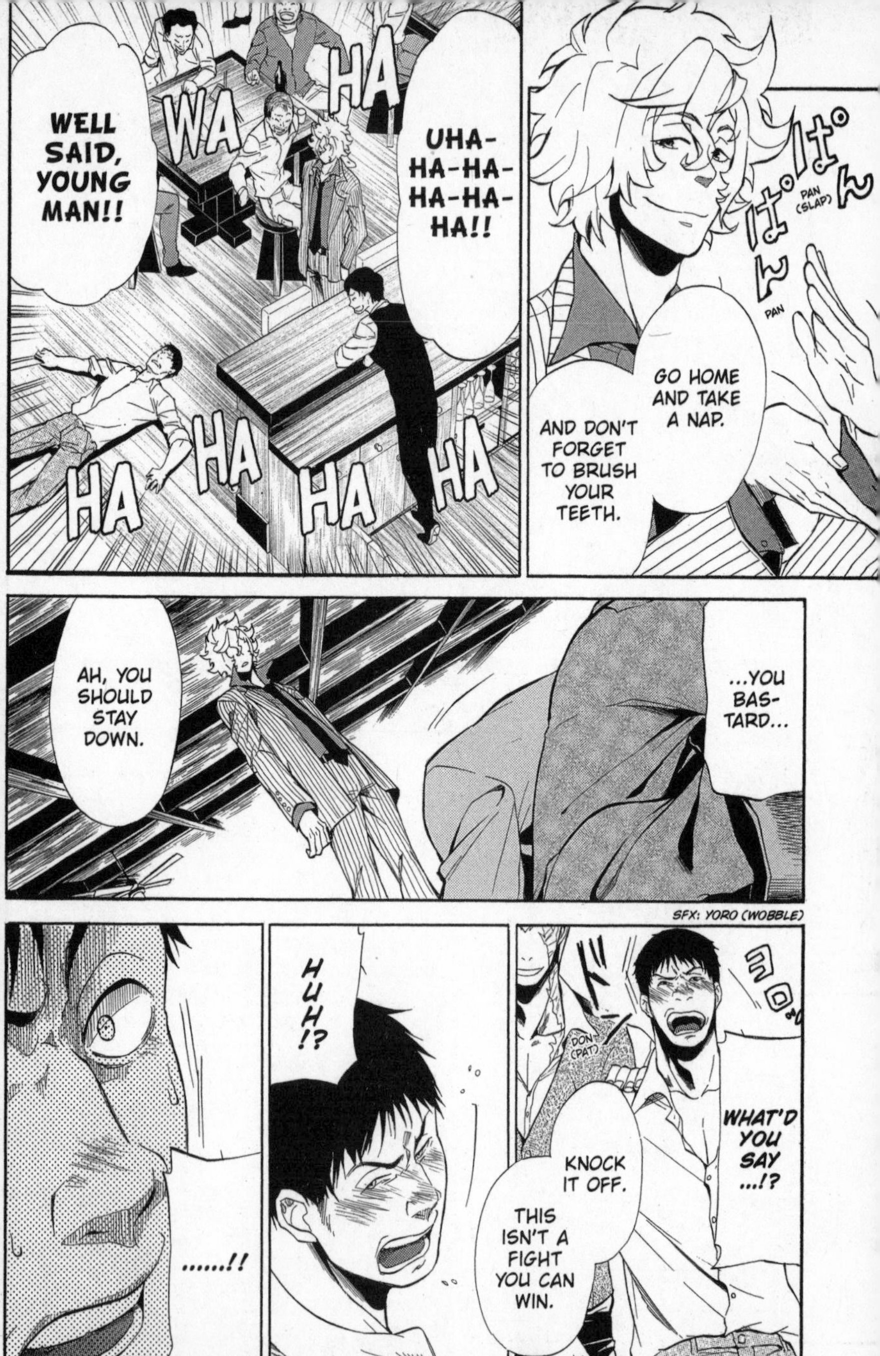
ぱんぱん
PAN (SLAP)
PAN
GO HOME AND TAKE A NAP.
AND DON'T FORGET TO BRUSH YOUR TEETH.
HA
UHA-HA-HA-HA-HA-HA!!
WA
WELL SAID, YOUNG MAN!!
HA HA HA HA
...YOU BASTARD...
AH, YOU SHOULD STAY DOWN.
SFX: YORO (WOBBLE)
ヨロ
ド
DON (PAT)
WHAT'D YOU SAY ...!?
KNOCK IT OFF.
THIS ISN'T A FIGHT YOU CAN WIN.
HUH!?
......!!

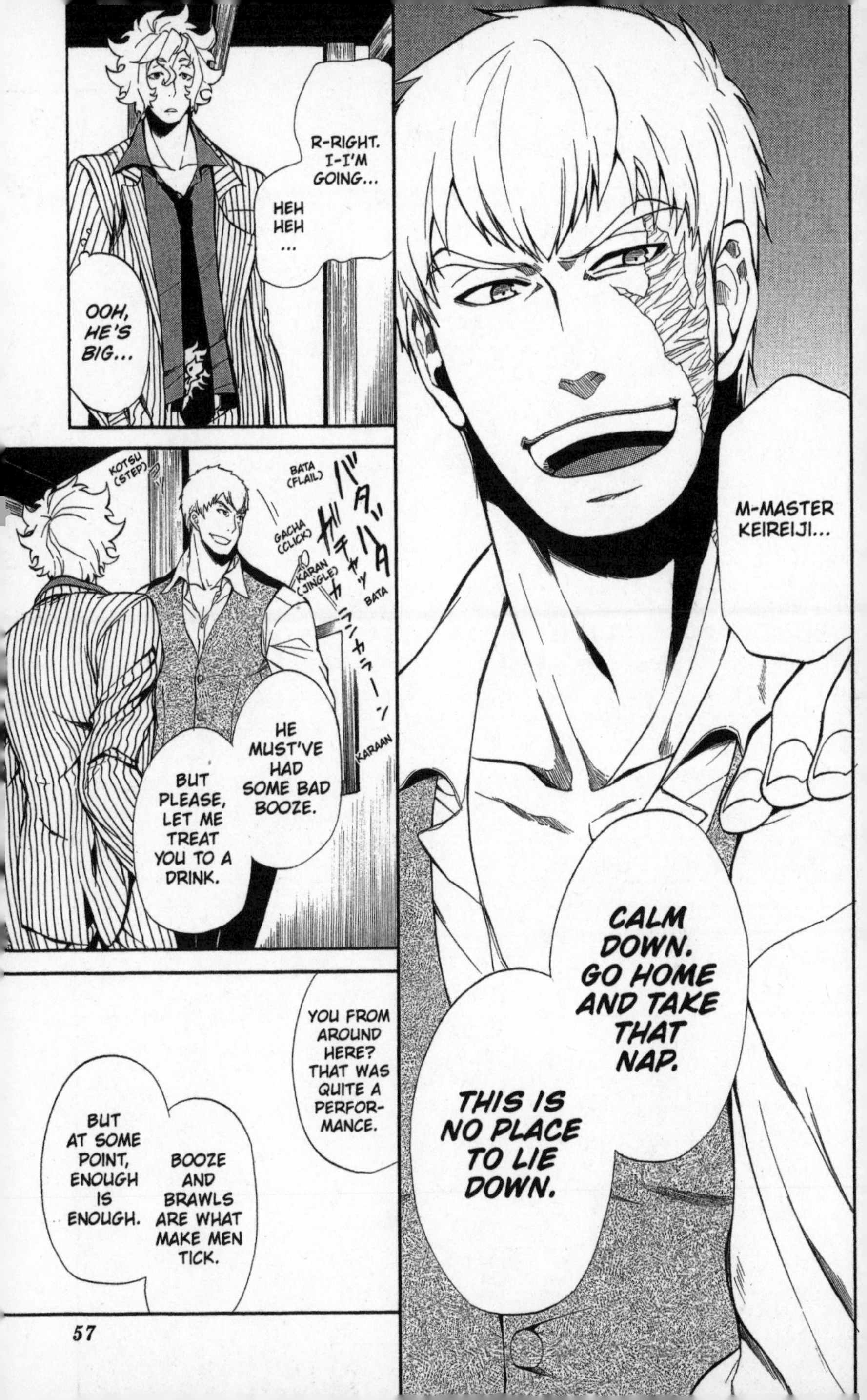

M-MASTER KEIREIJI...
CALM DOWN. GO HOME AND TAKE THAT NAP.
THIS IS NO PLACE TO LIE DOWN.
R-RIGHT. I-I'M GOING...
HEH HEH ...
OOH, HE'S BIG...
BATA (FLAIL)
バタバタ
BATA
GACHA (CLICK)
ガチャッ
KARAN (JINGLE)
カランカラーン
KARAAN
KOTSU (STEP)
HE MUST'VE HAD SOME BAD BOOZE.
BUT PLEASE, LET ME TREAT YOU TO A DRINK.
YOU FROM AROUND HERE? THAT WAS QUITE A PERFORMANCE.
BOOZE AND BRAWLS ARE WHAT MAKE MEN TICK.
BUT AT SOME POINT, ENOUGH IS ENOUGH.

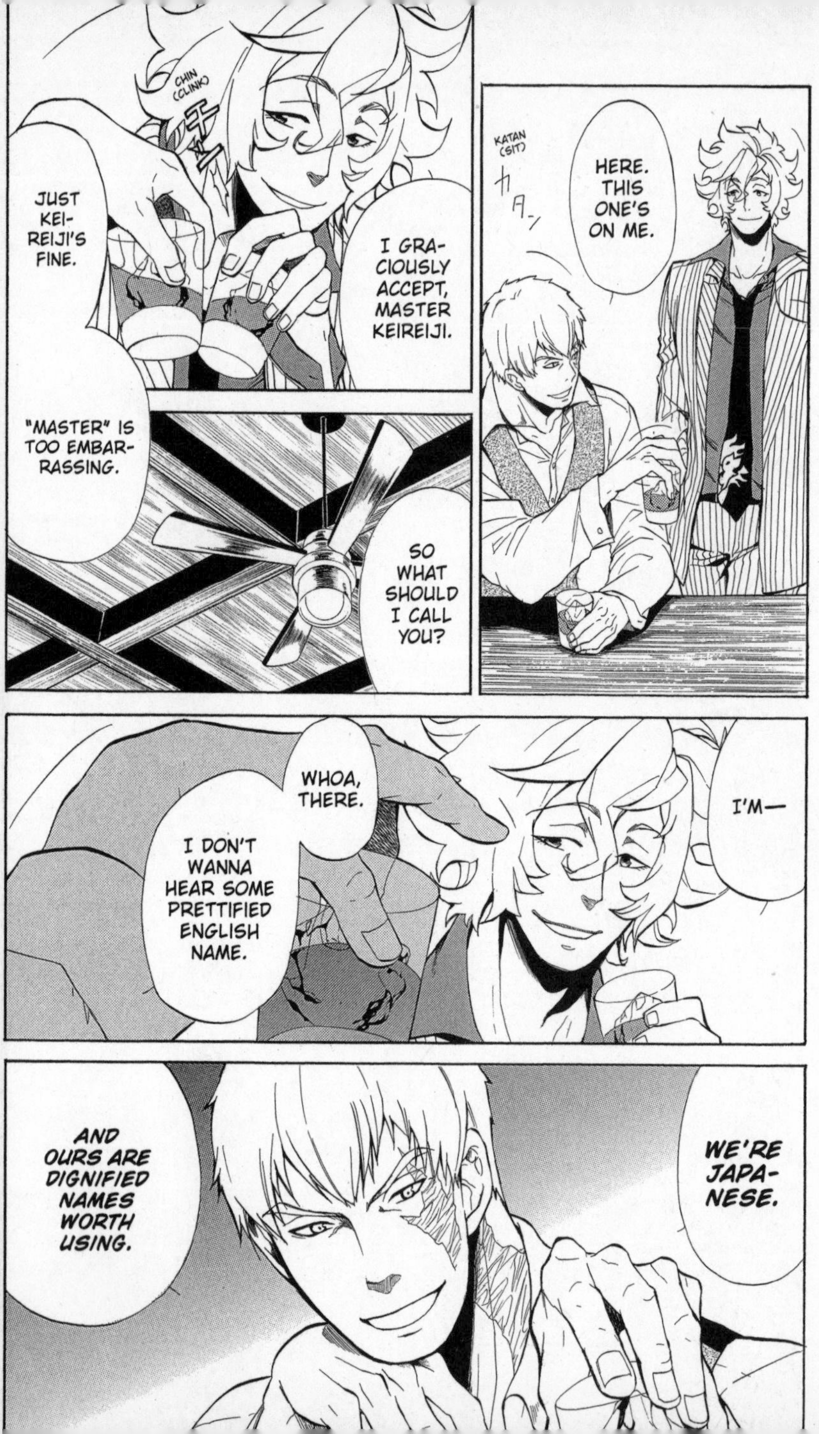
KATAN (SIT)
HERE. THIS ONE'S ON ME.
CHIN (CLINK)
I GRACIOUSLY ACCEPT, MASTER KEIREIJI.
JUST KEIREIJI'S FINE.
"MASTER" IS TOO EMBARRASSING.
SO WHAT SHOULD I CALL YOU?
I'M—
WHOA, THERE.
I DON'T WANNA HEAR SOME PRETTIFIED ENGLISH NAME.
WE'RE JAPANESE.
AND OURS ARE DIGNIFIED NAMES WORTH USING.

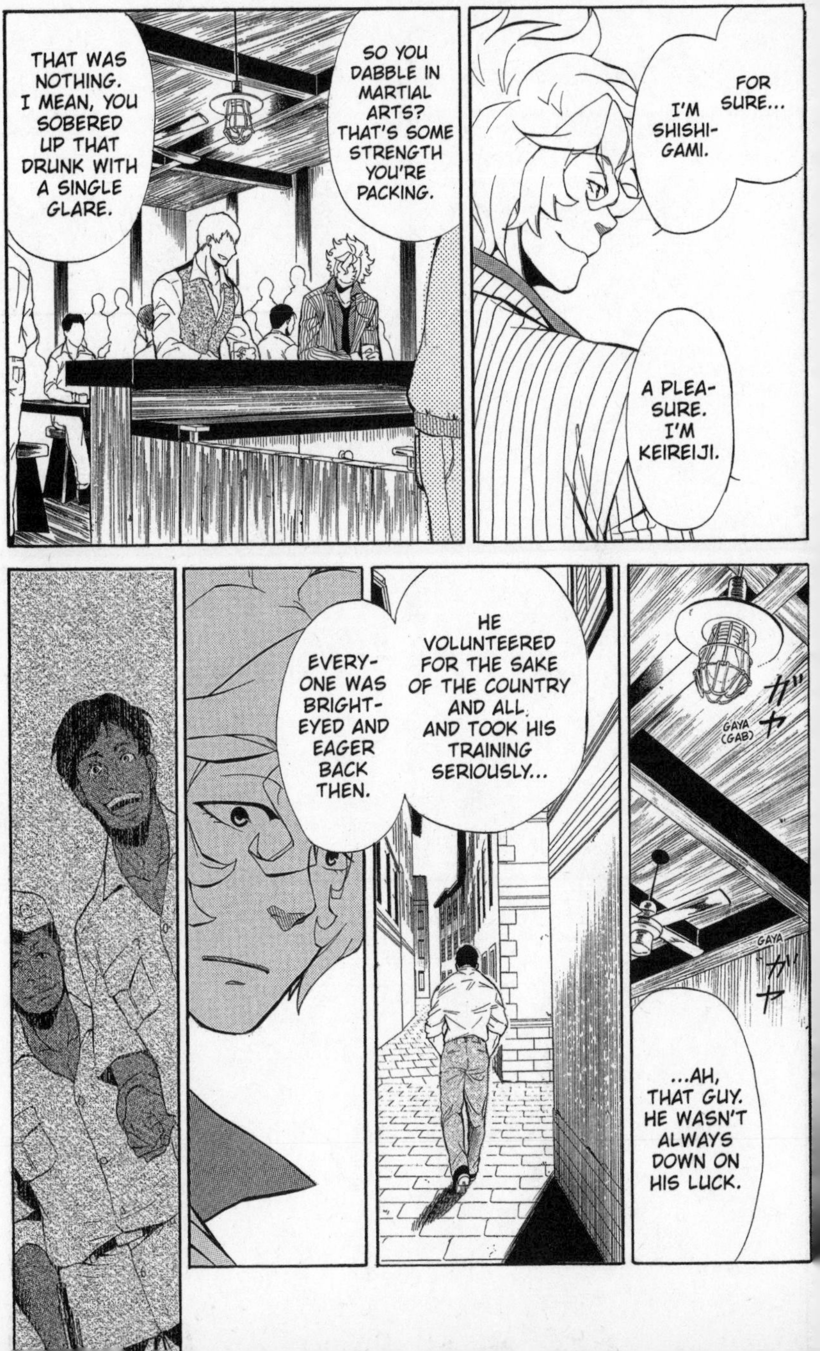
FOR SURE...
I'M SHISHIGAMI.
A PLEASURE. I'M KEIREIJI.
SO YOU DABBLE IN MARTIAL ARTS? THAT'S SOME STRENGTH YOU'RE PACKING.
THAT WAS NOTHING. I MEAN, YOU SOBERED UP THAT DRUNK WITH A SINGLE GLARE.
ガヤ
GAYA (GAB)
ガヤ
GAYA
...AH, THAT GUY. HE WASN'T ALWAYS DOWN ON HIS LUCK.
HE VOLUNTEERED FOR THE SAKE OF THE COUNTRY AND ALL AND TOOK HIS TRAINING SERIOUSLY...
EVERYONE WAS BRIGHT-EYED AND EAGER BACK THEN.

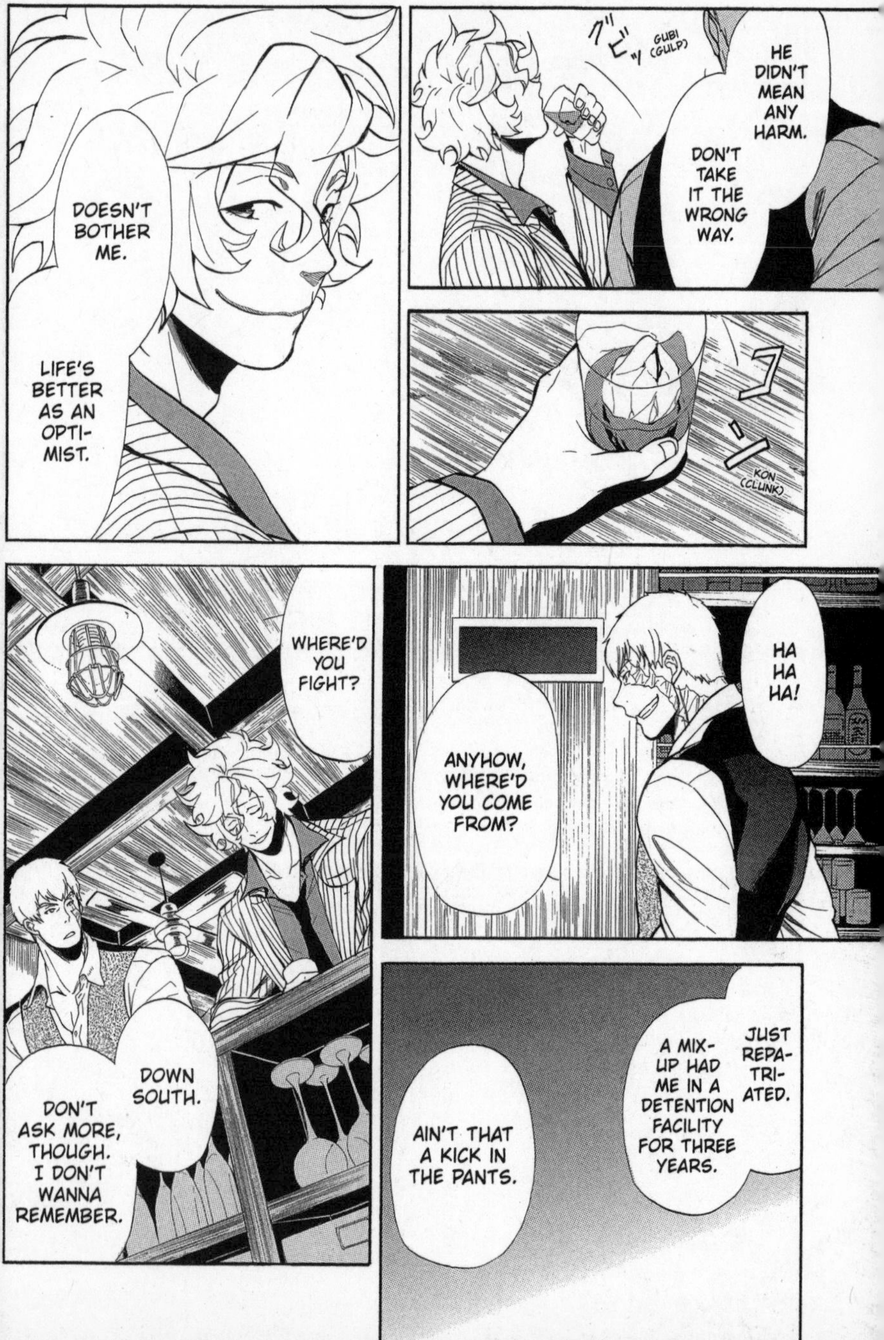
HE DIDN'T MEAN ANY HARM.
DON'T TAKE IT THE WRONG WAY.
グビッ
GUBI (GULP)
コン
KON (CLUNK)
DOESN'T BOTHER ME.
LIFE'S BETTER AS AN OPTIMIST.
HA HA HA!
ANYHOW, WHERE'D YOU COME FROM?
JUST REPATRIATED.
A MIX-UP HAD ME IN A DETENTION FACILITY FOR THREE YEARS.
AIN'T THAT A KICK IN THE PANTS.
WHERE'D YOU FIGHT?
DOWN SOUTH.
DON'T ASK MORE, THOUGH. I DON'T WANNA REMEMBER.

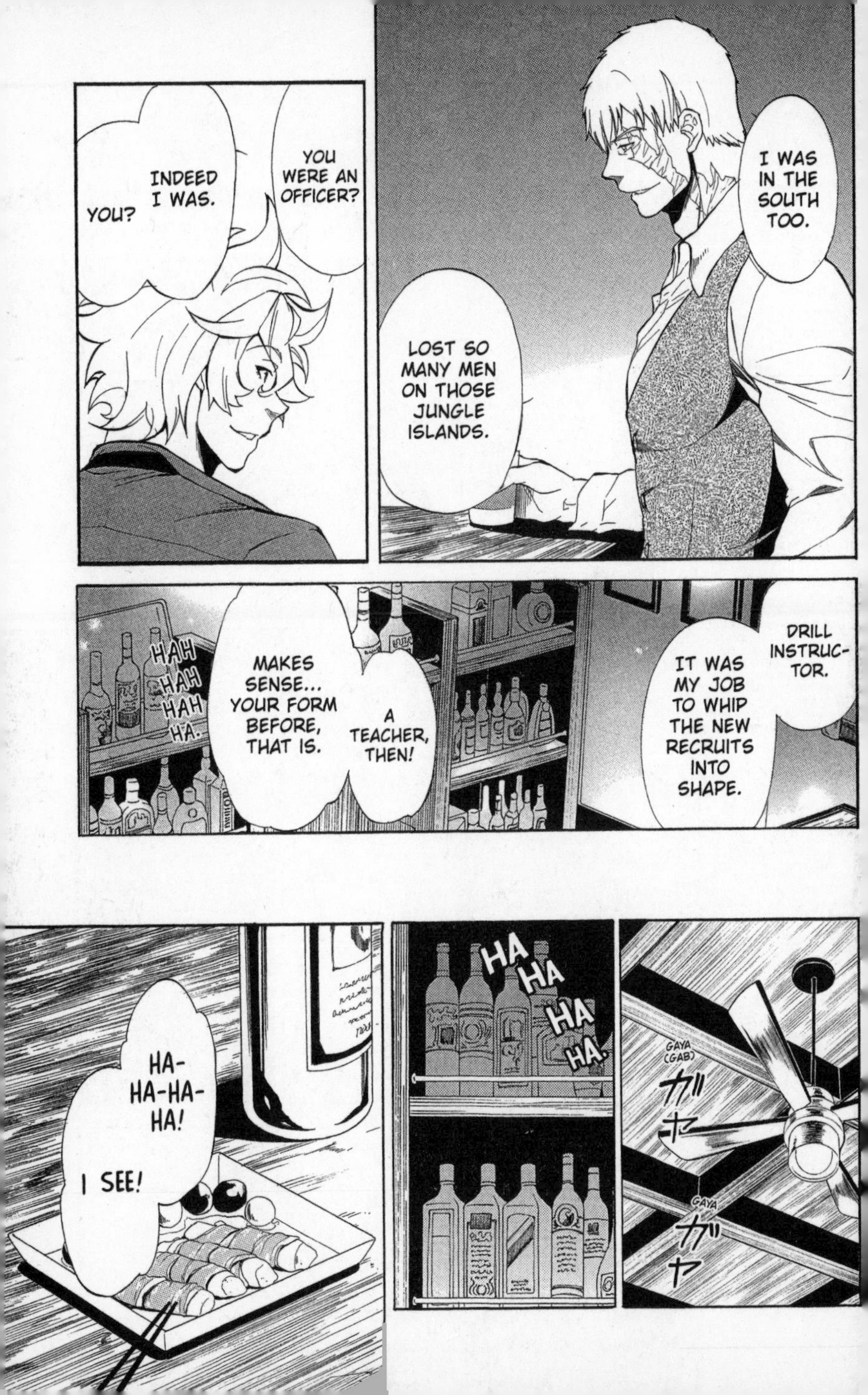
I WAS IN THE SOUTH TOO.
LOST SO MANY MEN ON THOSE JUNGLE ISLANDS.
YOU WERE AN OFFICER?
INDEED I WAS.
YOU?
DRILL INSTRUCTOR.
IT WAS MY JOB TO WHIP THE NEW RECRUITS INTO SHAPE.
A TEACHER, THEN!
MAKES SENSE... YOUR FORM BEFORE, THAT IS.
HAH HAH HAH HA.
GAYA (GAB)
ガヤ
GAYA
ガヤ
HA HA HA HA.
HA-HA-HA-HA!
I SEE!

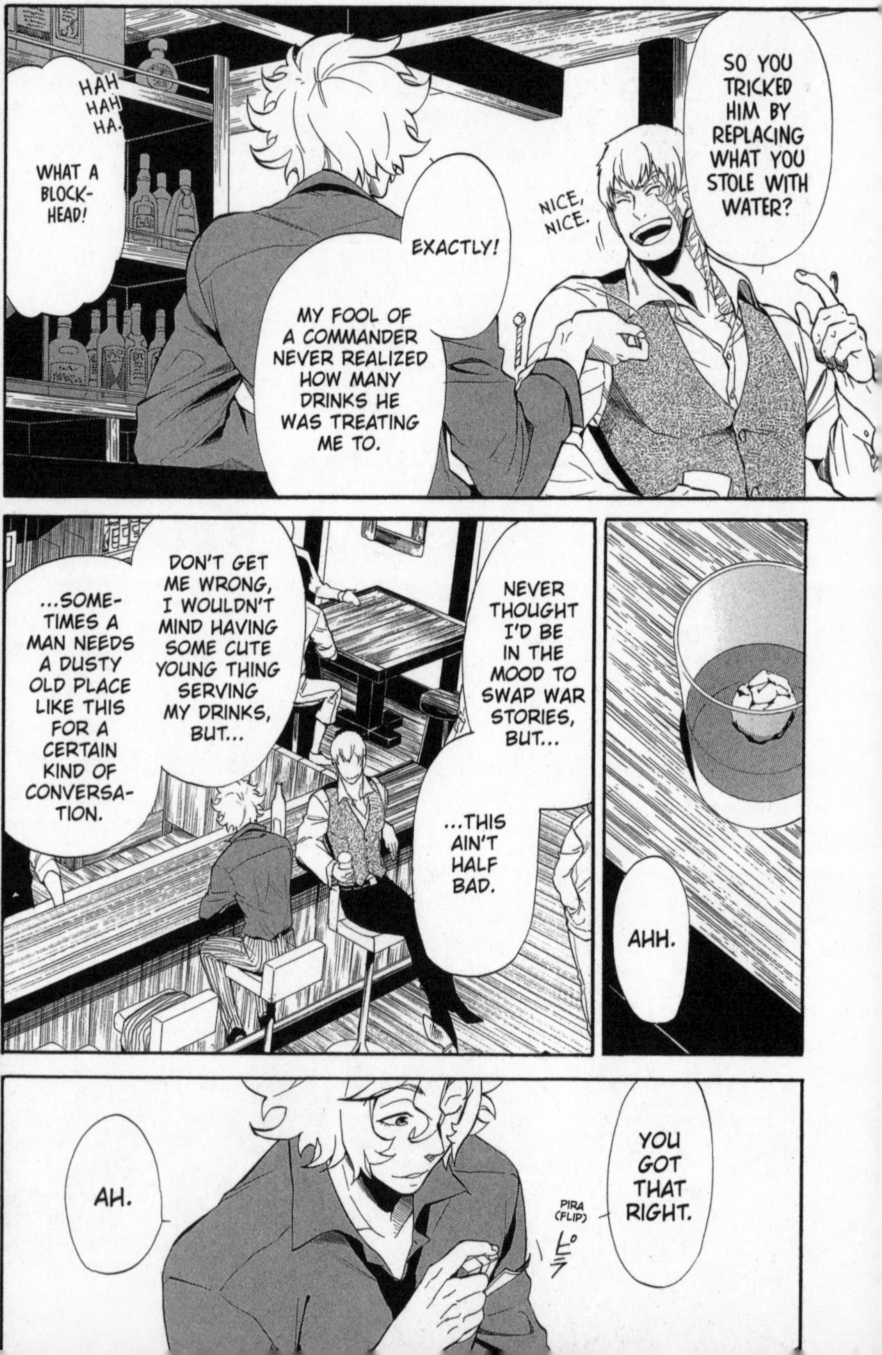
SO YOU TRICKED HIM BY REPLACING WHAT YOU STOLE WITH WATER?
NICE, NICE.
EXACTLY!
MY FOOL OF A COMMANDER NEVER REALIZED HOW MANY DRINKS HE WAS TREATING ME TO.
HAH HAH HA.
WHAT A BLOCK-HEAD!
AHH.
NEVER THOUGHT I'D BE IN THE MOOD TO SWAP WAR STORIES, BUT...
...THIS AIN'T HALF BAD.
DON'T GET ME WRONG, I WOULDN'T MIND HAVING SOME CUTE YOUNG THING SERVING MY DRINKS, BUT...
...SOME-TIMES A MAN NEEDS A DUSTY OLD PLACE LIKE THIS FOR A CERTAIN KIND OF CONVERSA-TION.
YOU GOT THAT RIGHT.
PIRA (FLIP)
AH.

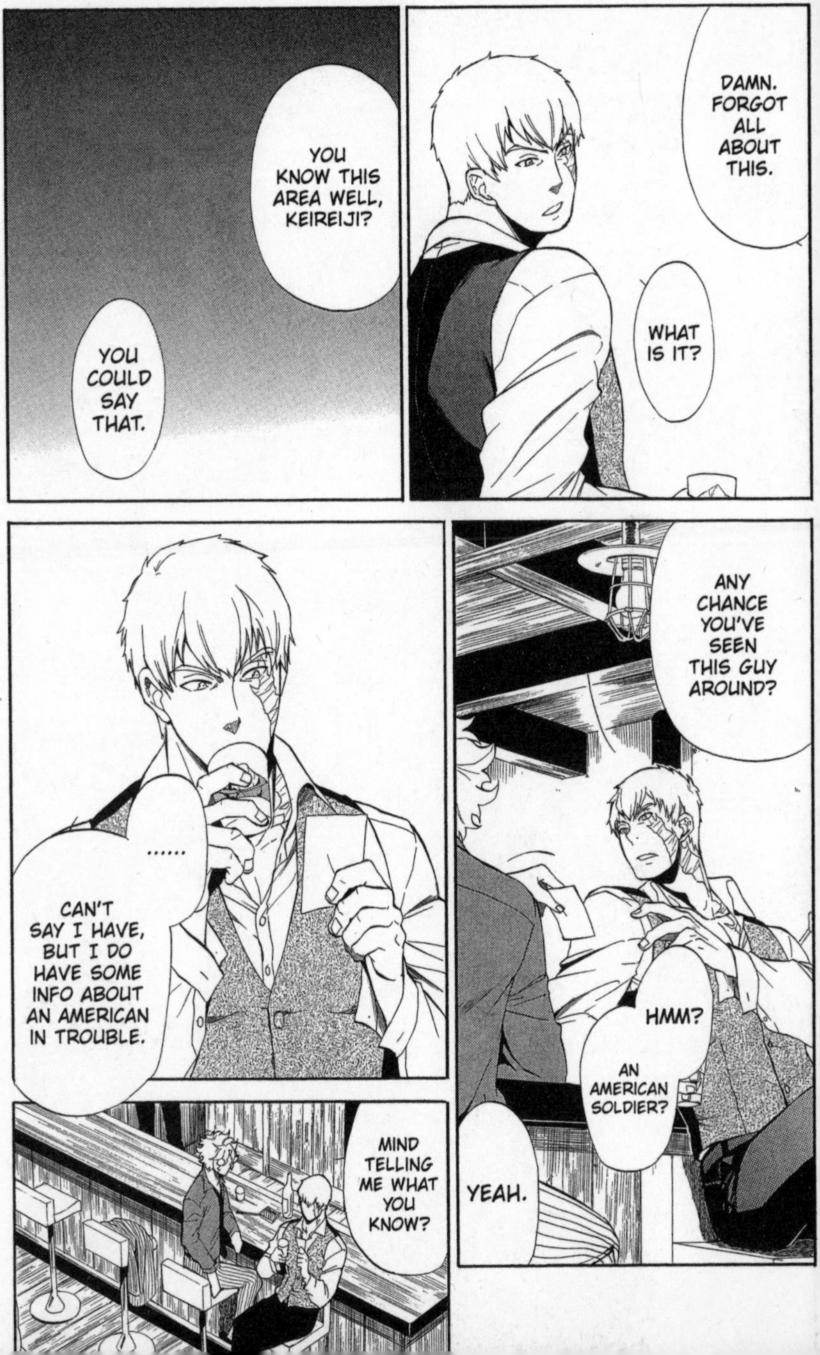
DAMN. FORGOT ALL ABOUT THIS.
WHAT IS IT?
YOU KNOW THIS AREA WELL, KEIREIJI?
YOU COULD SAY THAT.
ANY CHANCE YOU'VE SEEN THIS GUY AROUND?
HMM?
AN AMERICAN SOLDIER?
YEAH.
......
CAN'T SAY I HAVE, BUT I DO HAVE SOME INFO ABOUT AN AMERICAN IN TROUBLE.
MIND TELLING ME WHAT YOU KNOW?

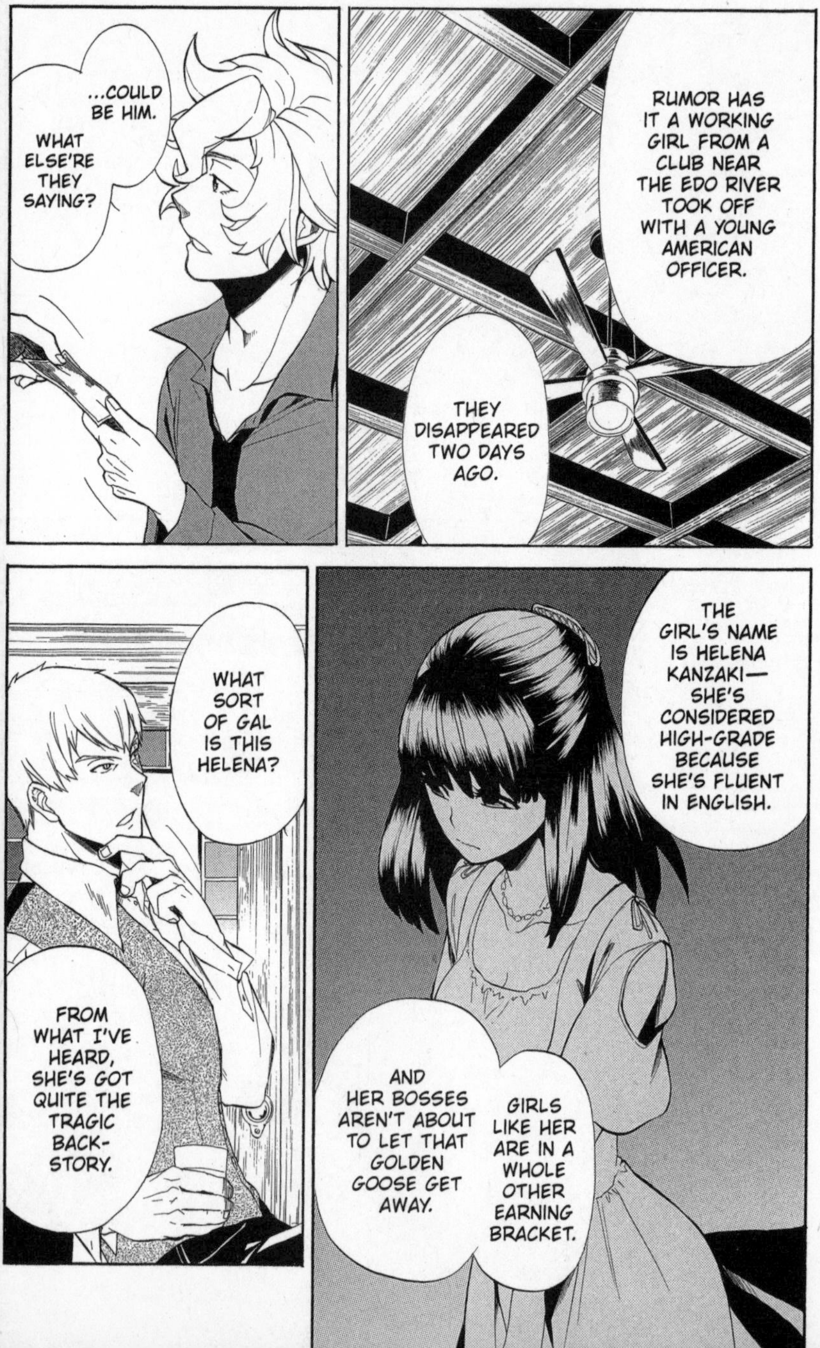
RUMOR HAS IT A WORKING GIRL FROM A CLUB NEAR THE EDO RIVER TOOK OFF WITH A YOUNG AMERICAN OFFICER.
THEY DISAPPEARED TWO DAYS AGO.
...COULD BE HIM.
WHAT ELSE'RE THEY SAYING?
THE GIRL'S NAME IS HELENA KANZAKI— SHE'S CONSIDERED HIGH-GRADE BECAUSE SHE'S FLUENT IN ENGLISH.
GIRLS LIKE HER ARE IN A WHOLE OTHER EARNING BRACKET.
AND HER BOSSES AREN'T ABOUT TO LET THAT GOLDEN GOOSE GET AWAY.
WHAT SORT OF GAL IS THIS HELENA?
FROM WHAT I'VE HEARD, SHE'S GOT QUITE THE TRAGIC BACK-STORY.

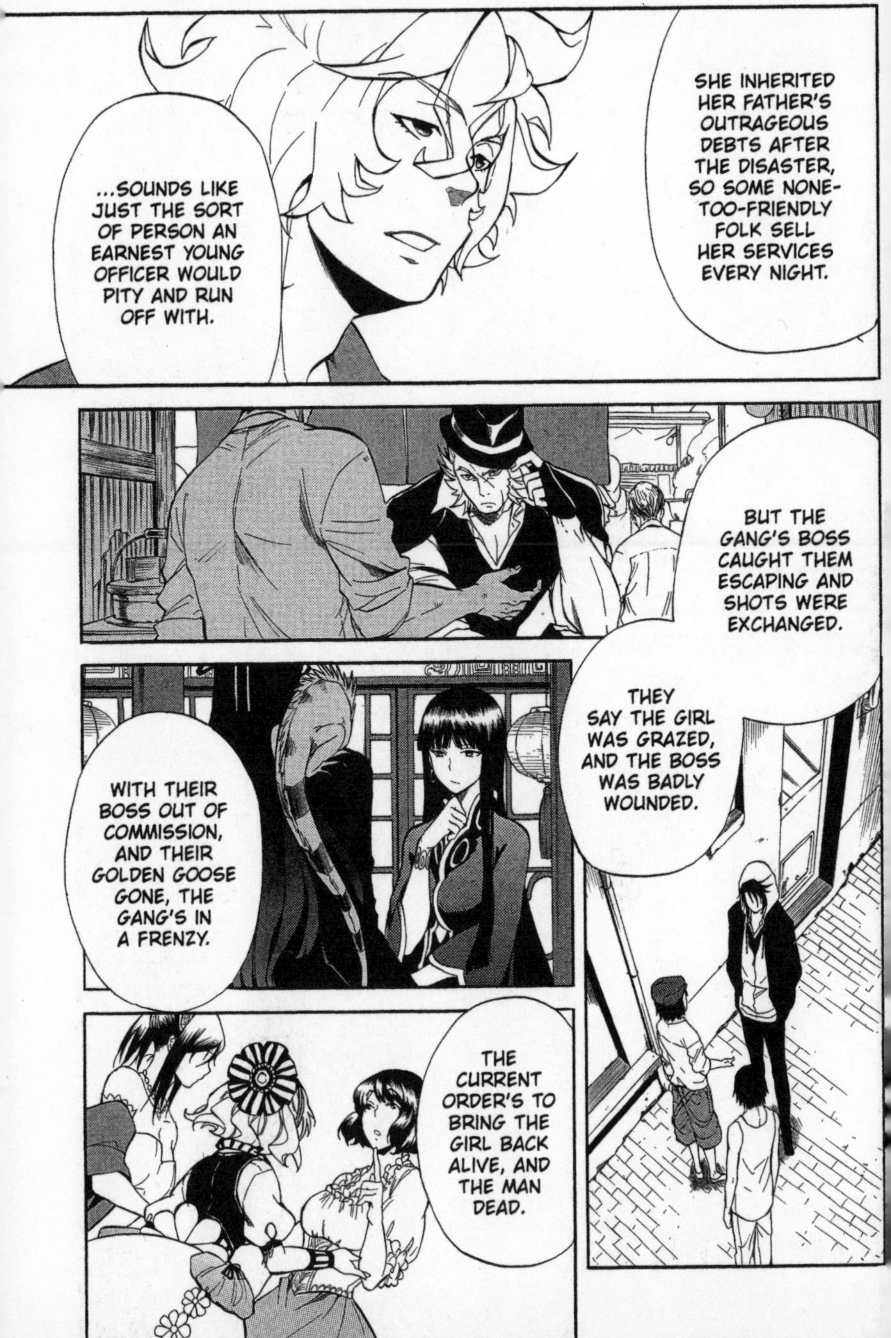
SHE INHERITED HER FATHER'S OUTRAGEOUS DEBTS AFTER THE DISASTER, SO SOME NONE-TOO-FRIENDLY FOLK SELL HER SERVICES EVERY NIGHT.
...SOUNDS LIKE JUST THE SORT OF PERSON AN EARNEST YOUNG OFFICER WOULD PITY AND RUN OFF WITH.
BUT THE GANG'S BOSS CAUGHT THEM ESCAPING AND SHOTS WERE EXCHANGED.
THEY SAY THE GIRL WAS GRAZED, AND THE BOSS WAS BADLY WOUNDED.
WITH THEIR BOSS OUT OF COMMISSION, AND THEIR GOLDEN GOOSE GONE, THE GANG'S IN A FRENZY.
THE CURRENT ORDER'S TO BRING THE GIRL BACK ALIVE, AND THE MAN DEAD.

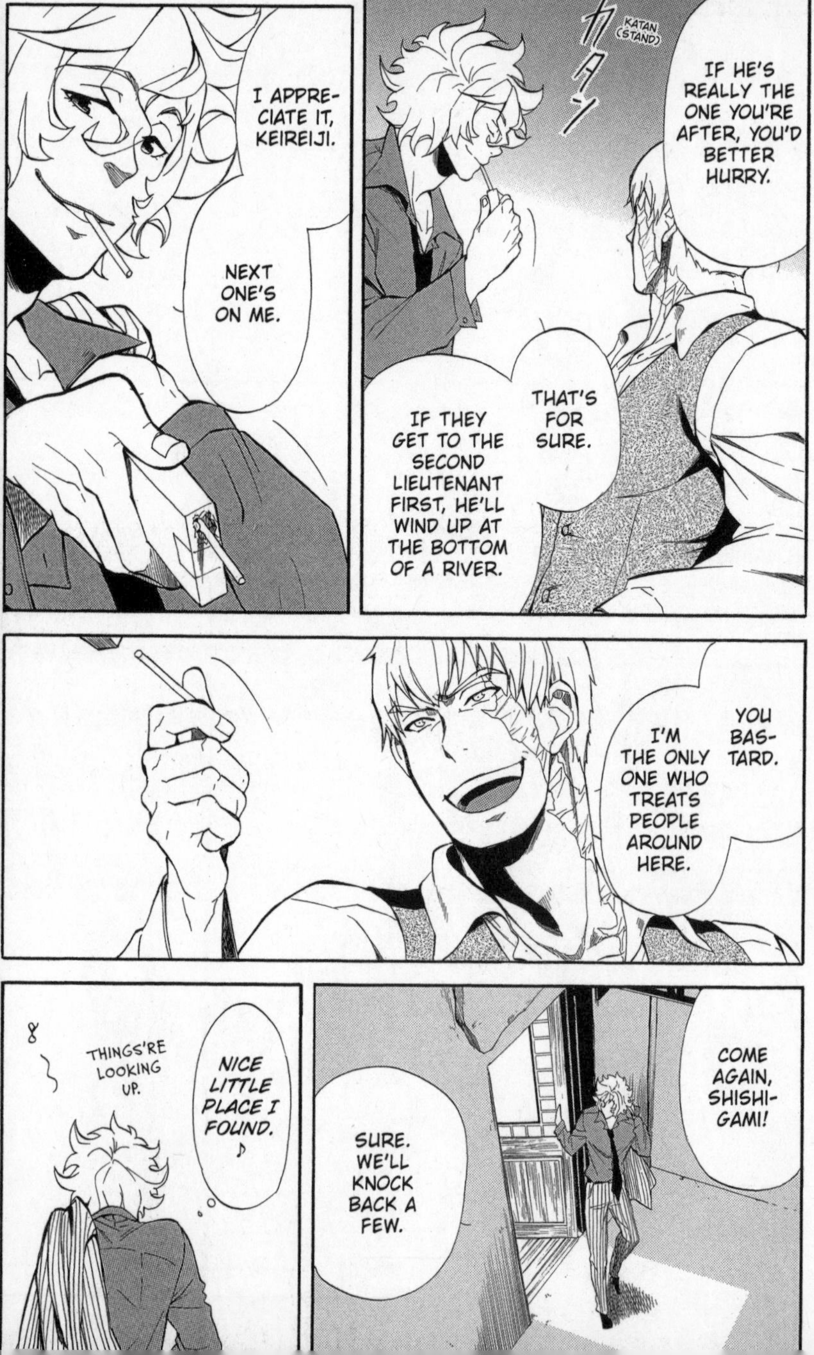
カタン
KATAN (STAND)
IF HE'S REALLY THE ONE YOU'RE AFTER, YOU'D BETTER HURRY.
THAT'S FOR SURE.
IF THEY GET TO THE SECOND LIEUTENANT FIRST, HE'LL WIND UP AT THE BOTTOM OF A RIVER.
I APPRE-CIATE IT, KEIREIJI.
NEXT ONE'S ON ME.
YOU BAS-TARD.
I'M THE ONLY ONE WHO TREATS PEOPLE AROUND HERE.
COME AGAIN, SHISHI-GAMI!
SURE. WE'LL KNOCK BACK A FEW.
NICE LITTLE PLACE I FOUND. ♪
THINGS'RE LOOKING UP.

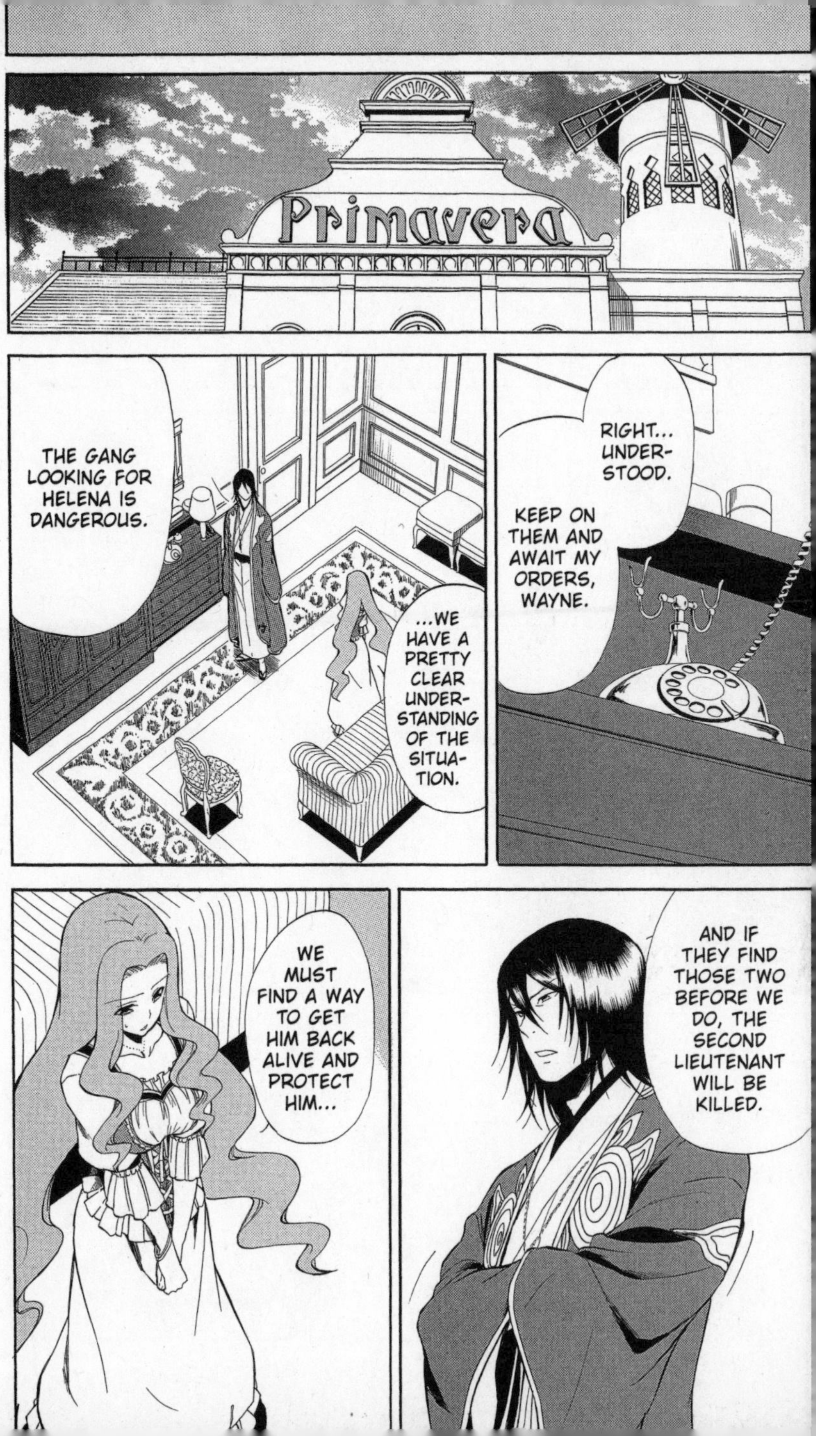
Primavera
RIGHT... UNDER-STOOD.
KEEP ON THEM AND AWAIT MY ORDERS, WAYNE.
...WE HAVE A PRETTY CLEAR UNDER-STANDING OF THE SITUA-TION.
THE GANG LOOKING FOR HELENA IS DANGEROUS.
AND IF THEY FIND THOSE TWO BEFORE WE DO, THE SECOND LIEUTENANT WILL BE KILLED.
WE MUST FIND A WAY TO GET HIM BACK ALIVE AND PROTECT HIM...

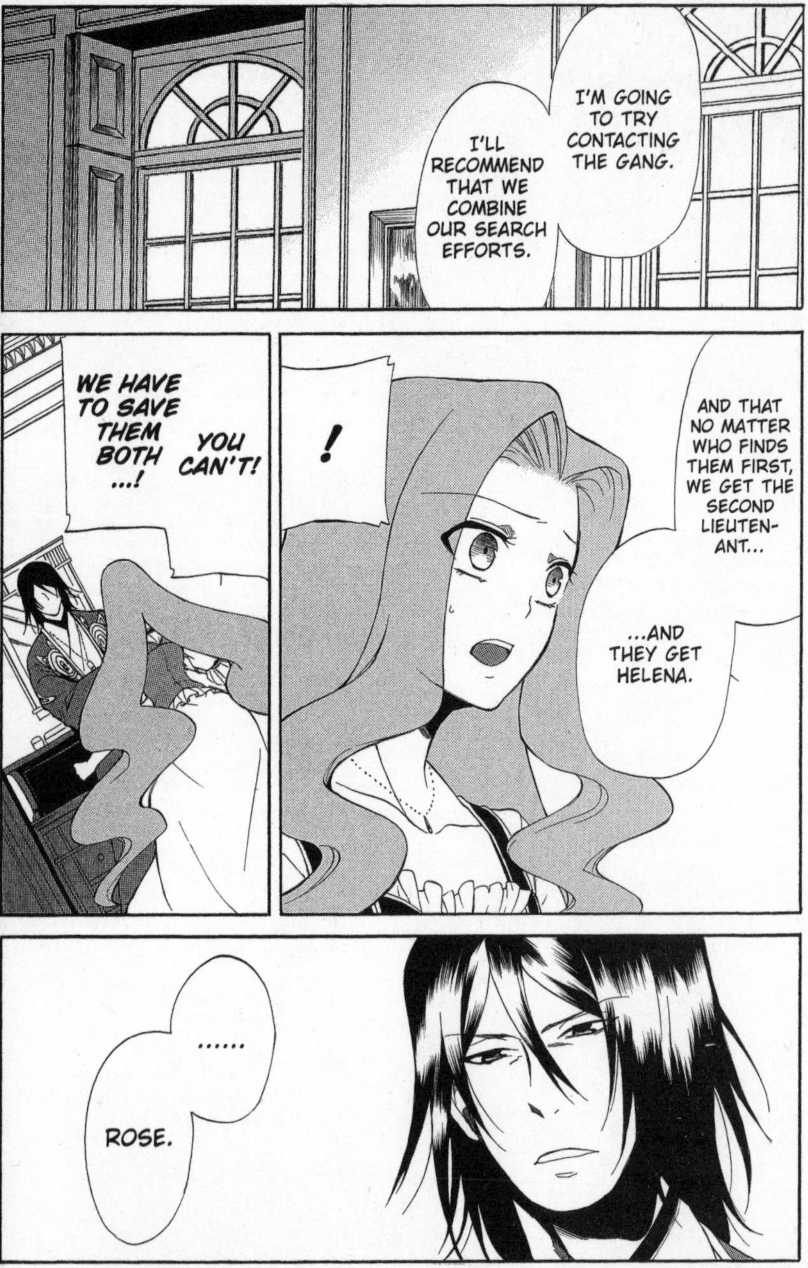
I'M GOING TO TRY CONTACTING THE GANG.
I'LL RECOMMEND THAT WE COMBINE OUR SEARCH EFFORTS.
AND THAT NO MATTER WHO FINDS THEM FIRST, WE GET THE SECOND LIEUTEN-ANT...
...AND THEY GET HELENA.
!
YOU CAN'T!
WE HAVE TO SAVE THEM BOTH ...!
...... ROSE.

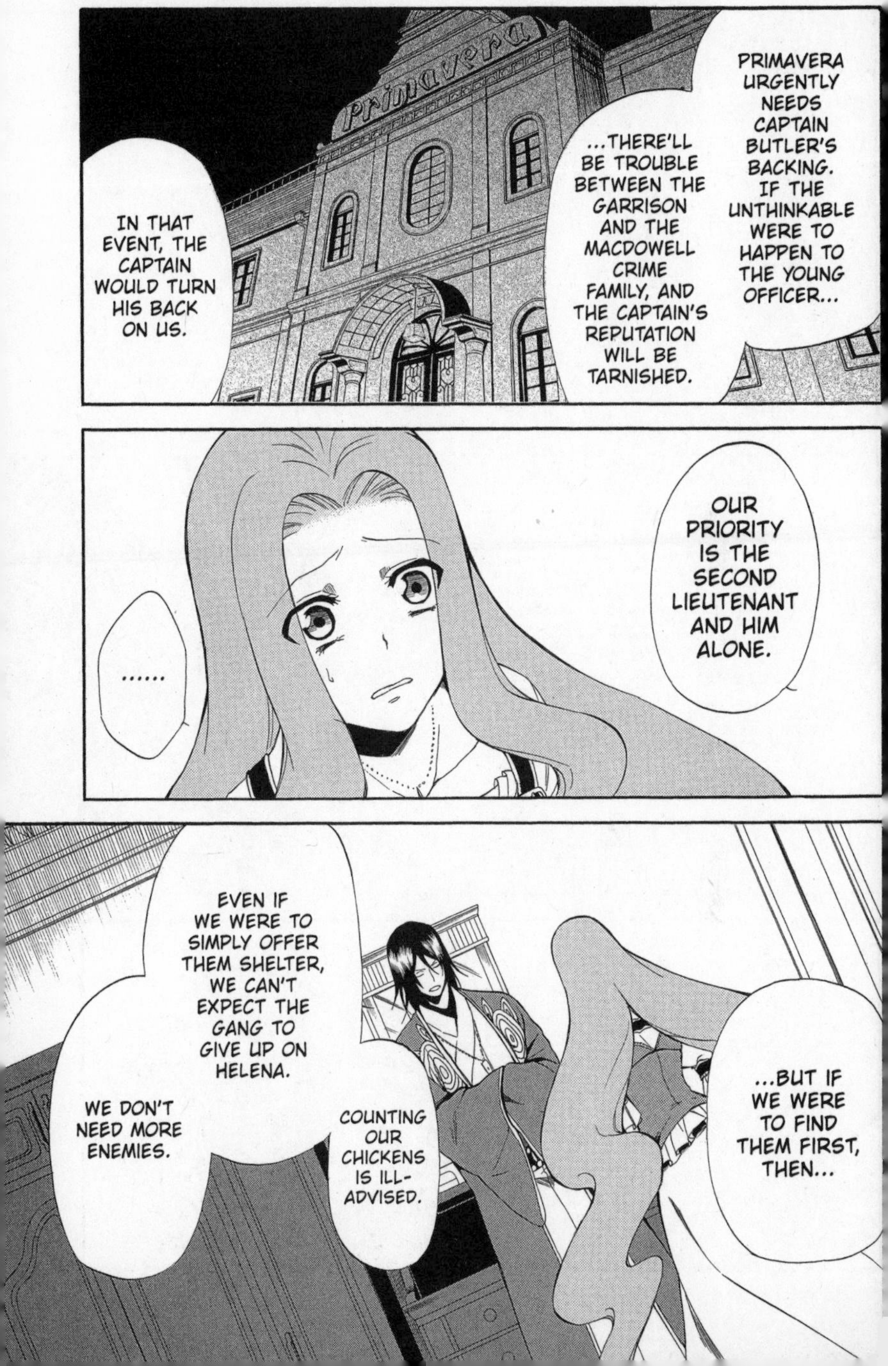
Primavera
PRIMAVERA URGENTLY NEEDS CAPTAIN BUTLER'S BACKING. IF THE UNTHINKABLE WERE TO HAPPEN TO THE YOUNG OFFICER...
...THERE'LL BE TROUBLE BETWEEN THE GARRISON AND THE MACDOWELL CRIME FAMILY, AND THE CAPTAIN'S REPUTATION WILL BE TARNISHED.
IN THAT EVENT, THE CAPTAIN WOULD TURN HIS BACK ON US.
OUR PRIORITY IS THE SECOND LIEUTENANT AND HIM ALONE.
......
...BUT IF WE WERE TO FIND THEM FIRST, THEN...
EVEN IF WE WERE TO SIMPLY OFFER THEM SHELTER, WE CAN'T EXPECT THE GANG TO GIVE UP ON HELENA.
COUNTING OUR CHICKENS IS ILL-ADVISED.
WE DON'T NEED MORE ENEMIES.

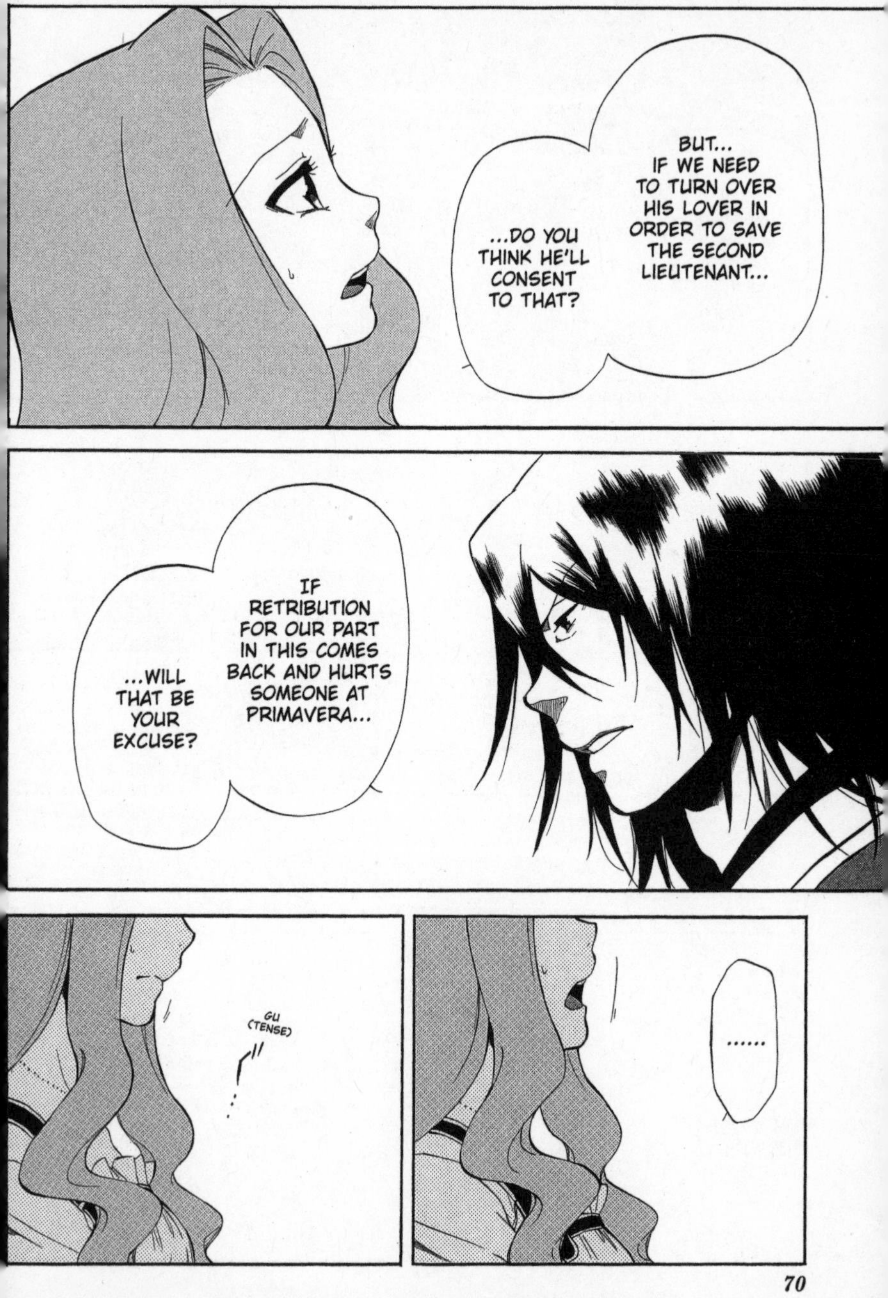
BUT... IF WE NEED TO TURN OVER HIS LOVER IN ORDER TO SAVE THE SECOND LIEUTENANT...
...DO YOU THINK HE'LL CONSENT TO THAT?
IF RETRIBUTION FOR OUR PART IN THIS COMES BACK AND HURTS SOMEONE AT PRIMAVERA...
...WILL THAT BE YOUR EXCUSE?
......
GU (TENSE)

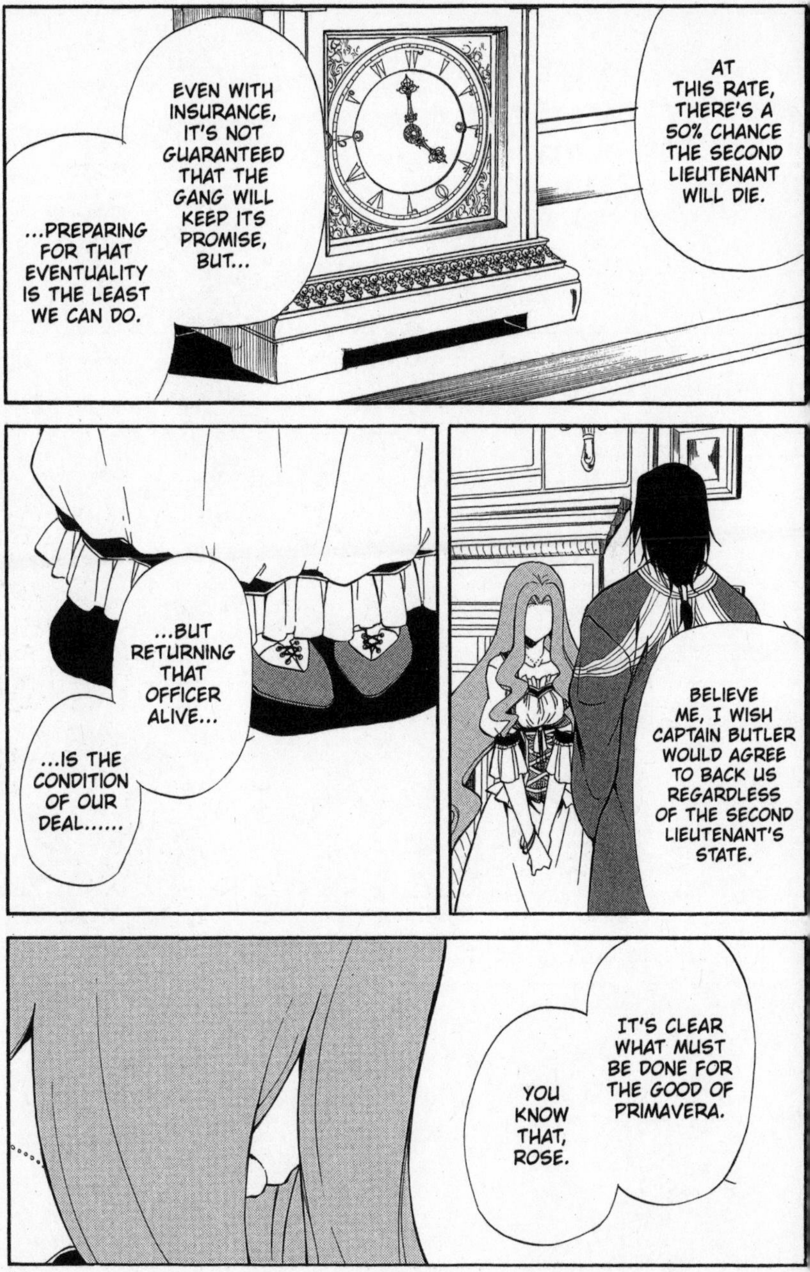
AT THIS RATE, THERE'S A 50% CHANCE THE SECOND LIEUTENANT WILL DIE.
EVEN WITH INSURANCE, IT'S NOT GUARANTEED THAT THE GANG WILL KEEP ITS PROMISE, BUT...
...PREPARING FOR THAT EVENTUALITY IS THE LEAST WE CAN DO.
BELIEVE ME, I WISH CAPTAIN BUTLER WOULD AGREE TO BACK US REGARDLESS OF THE SECOND LIEUTENANT'S STATE.
...BUT RETURNING THAT OFFICER ALIVE...
...IS THE CONDITION OF OUR DEAL......
IT'S CLEAR WHAT MUST BE DONE FOR THE GOOD OF PRIMAVERA.
YOU KNOW THAT, ROSE.

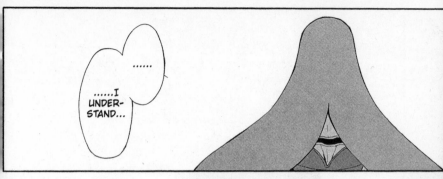

......
......I UNDER-STAND...
RICHARD-KUN... PLEASE CONTACT THEM...
I'LL... TELL EVERYONE ELSE TO CONTINUE SEARCHING.
UNDER-STOOD.
KA (STEP)
KA
KA
KACHA (CLICK)
PATAN (CLOSE)
GU (CLENCH)

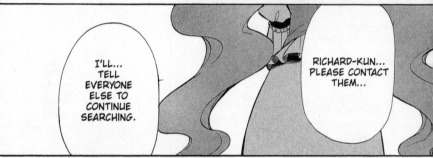

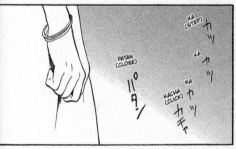

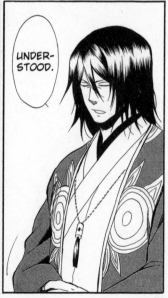

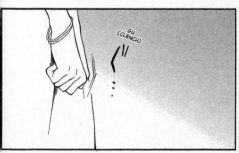

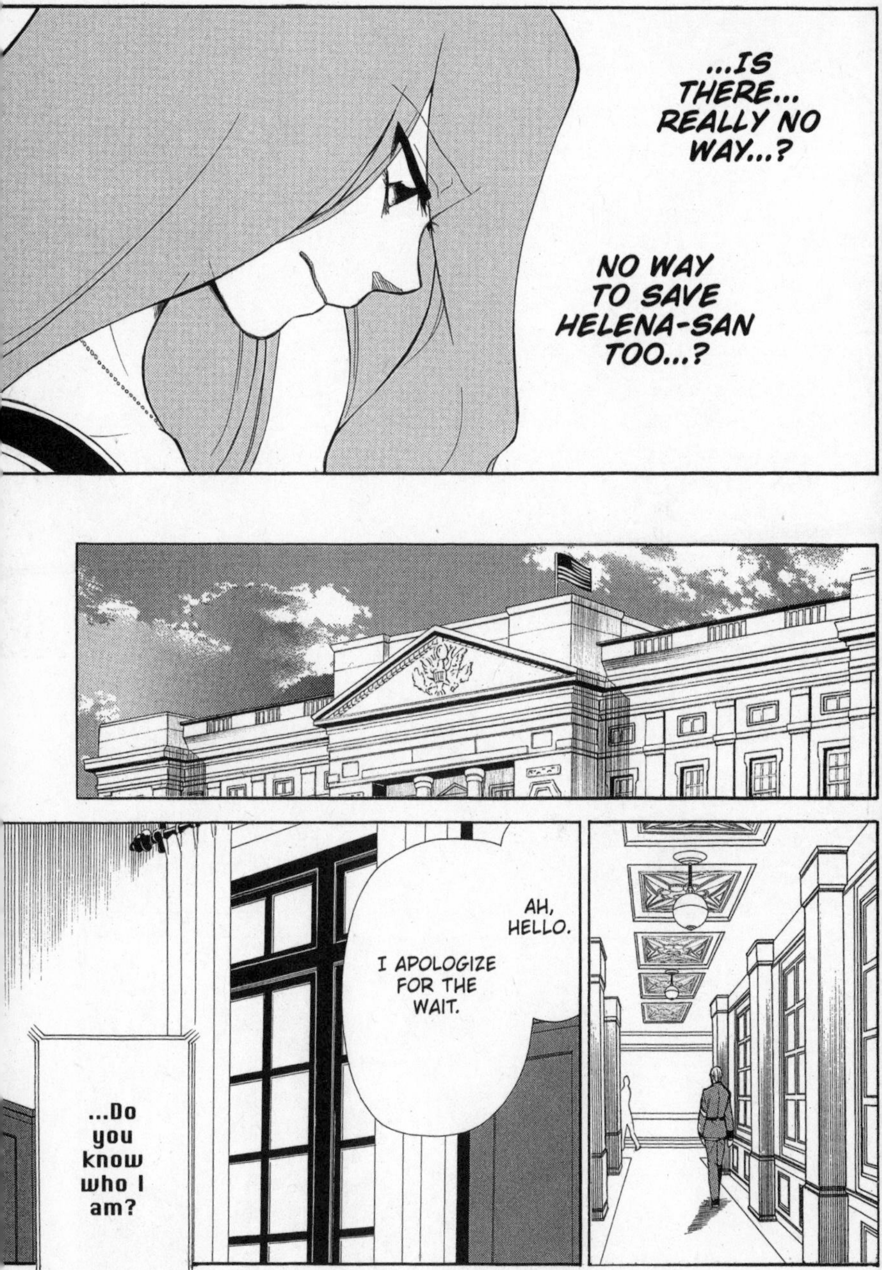
...IS THERE... REALLY NO WAY...?
NO WAY TO SAVE HELENA-SAN TOO...?
AH, HELLO.
I APOLOGIZE FOR THE WAIT.
...Do you know who I am?

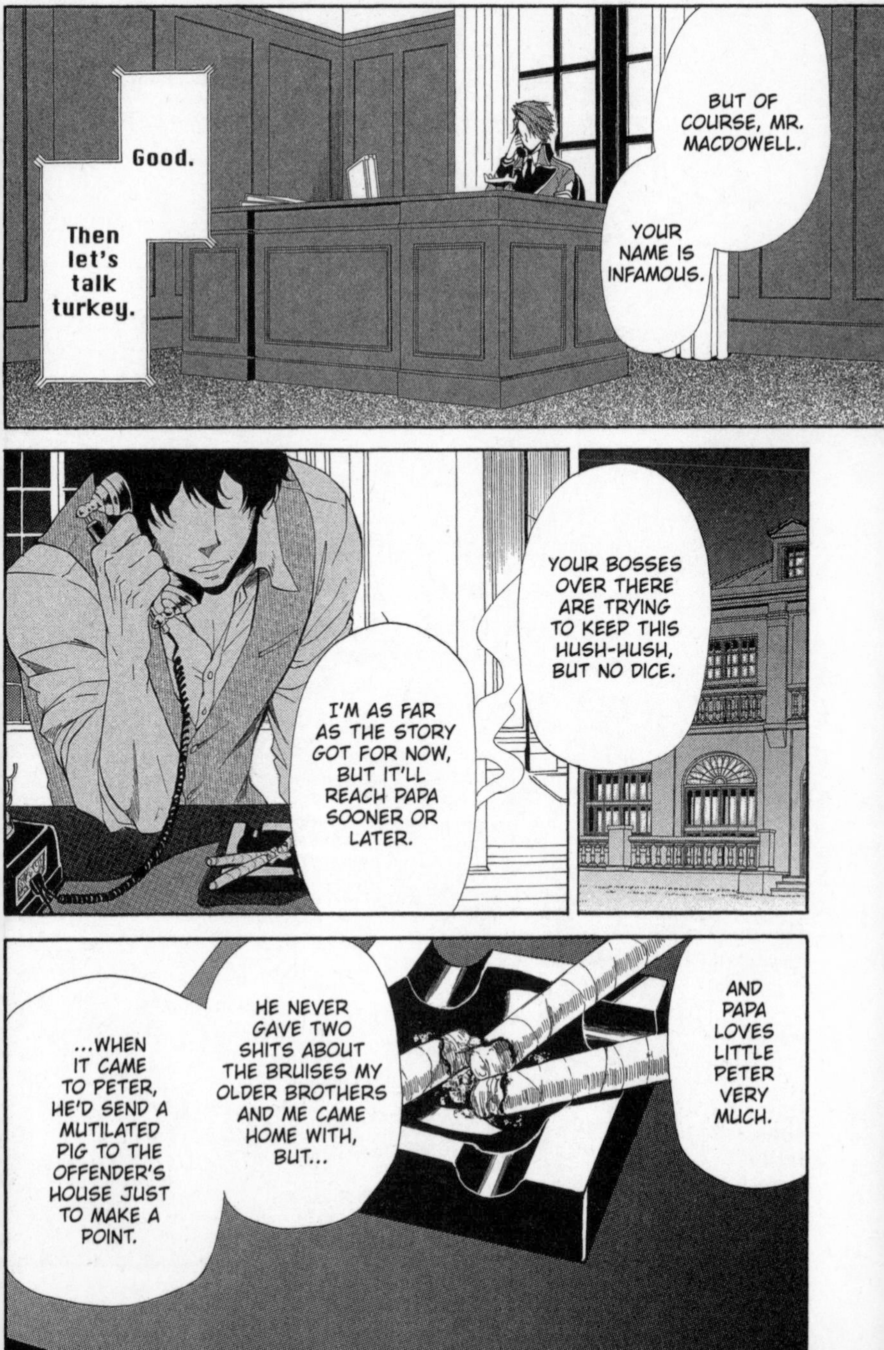
BUT OF COURSE, MR. MACDOWELL.
YOUR NAME IS INFAMOUS.
Good.
Then let's talk turkey.
YOUR BOSSES OVER THERE ARE TRYING TO KEEP THIS HUSH-HUSH, BUT NO DICE.
I'M AS FAR AS THE STORY GOT FOR NOW, BUT IT'LL REACH PAPA SOONER OR LATER.
AND PAPA LOVES LITTLE PETER VERY MUCH.
HE NEVER GAVE TWO SHITS ABOUT THE BRUISES MY OLDER BROTHERS AND ME CAME HOME WITH, BUT...
...WHEN IT CAME TO PETER, HE'D SEND A MUTILATED PIG TO THE OFFENDER'S HOUSE JUST TO MAKE A POINT.

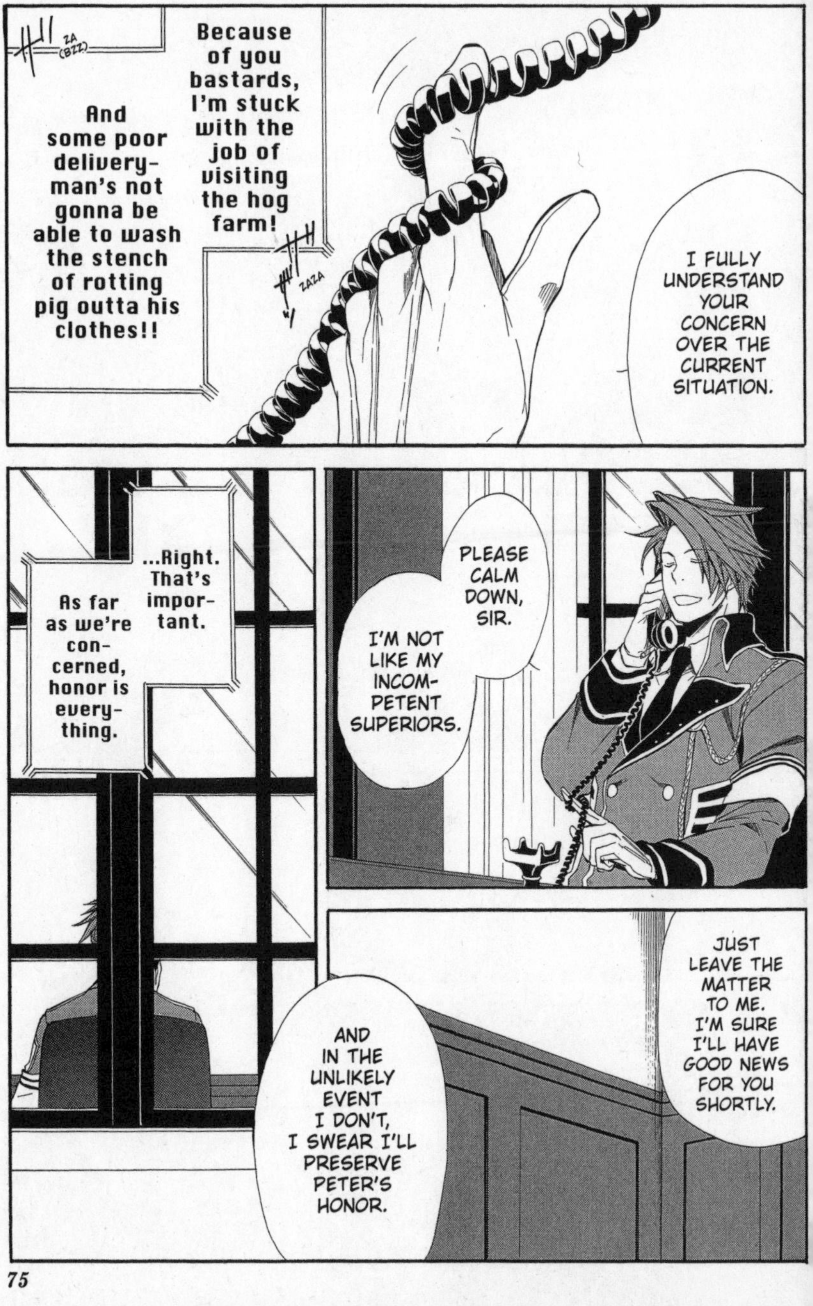

ZA (BZZ)
Because of you bastards, I'm stuck with the job of visiting the hog farm!
And some poor delivery-man's not gonna be able to wash the stench of rotting pig outta his clothes!!
ZAZA
I FULLY UNDERSTAND YOUR CONCERN OVER THE CURRENT SITUATION.
PLEASE CALM DOWN, SIR.
I'M NOT LIKE MY INCOMPETENT SUPERIORS.
JUST LEAVE THE MATTER TO ME. I'M SURE I'LL HAVE GOOD NEWS FOR YOU SHORTLY.
AND IN THE UNLIKELY EVENT I DON'T, I SWEAR I'LL PRESERVE PETER'S HONOR.
...Right. That's important.
As far as we're concerned, honor is everything.

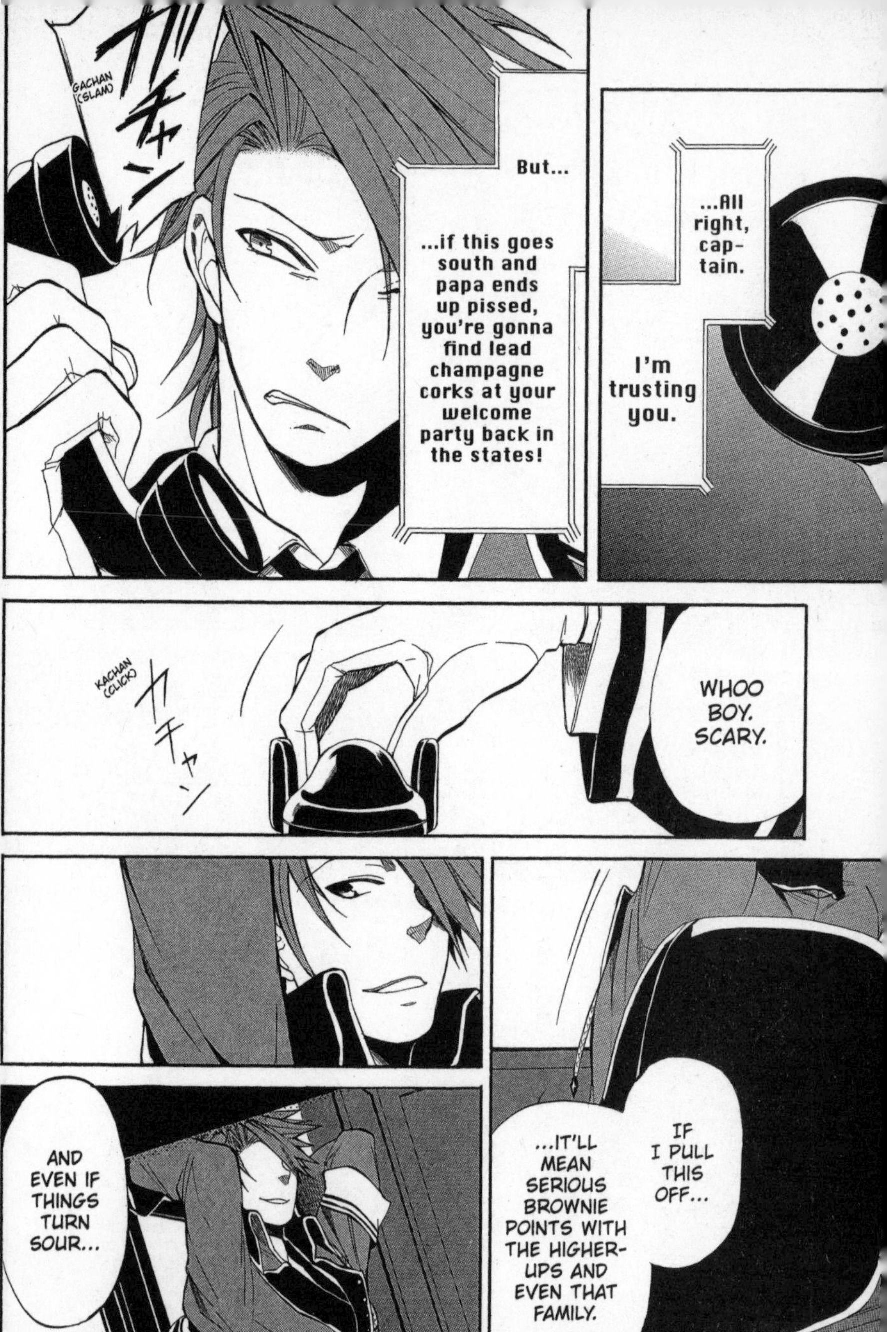
...All right, captain.
I'm trusting you.
But...
...if this goes south and papa ends up pissed, you're gonna find lead champagne corks at your welcome party back in the states!
GACHAN (SLAM)
WHOO BOY. SCARY.
KACHAN (CLICK)
IF I PULL THIS OFF...
...IT'LL MEAN SERIOUS BROWNIE POINTS WITH THE HIGHER-UPS AND EVEN THAT FAMILY.
AND EVEN IF THINGS TURN SOUR...

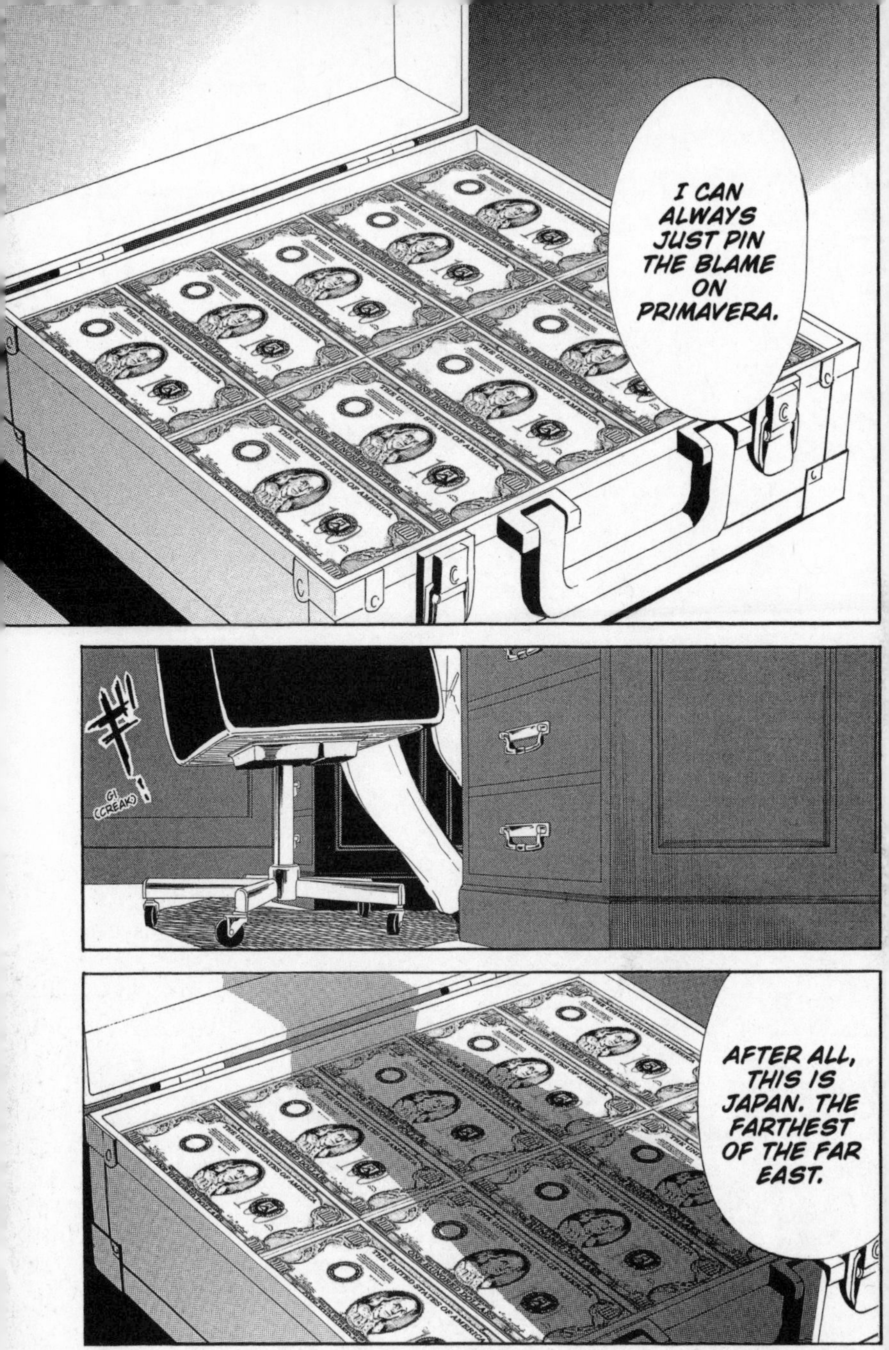
I CAN ALWAYS JUST PIN THE BLAME ON PRIMAVERA.
GI (CREAK)
AFTER ALL, THIS IS JAPAN. THE FARTHEST OF THE FAR EAST.

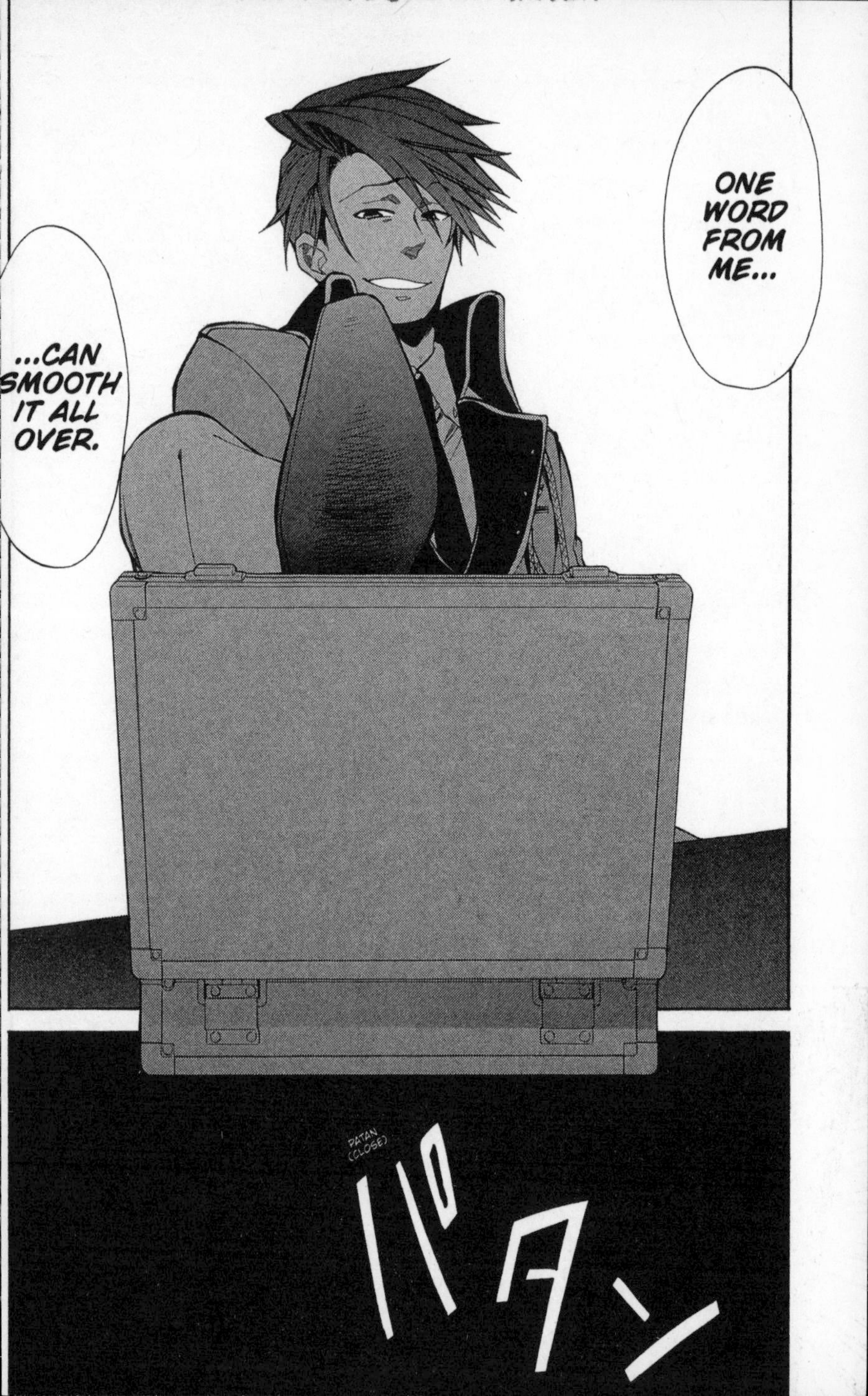
ONE WORD FROM ME...
...CAN SMOOTH IT ALL OVER.
PATAN (CLOSE)
パタン

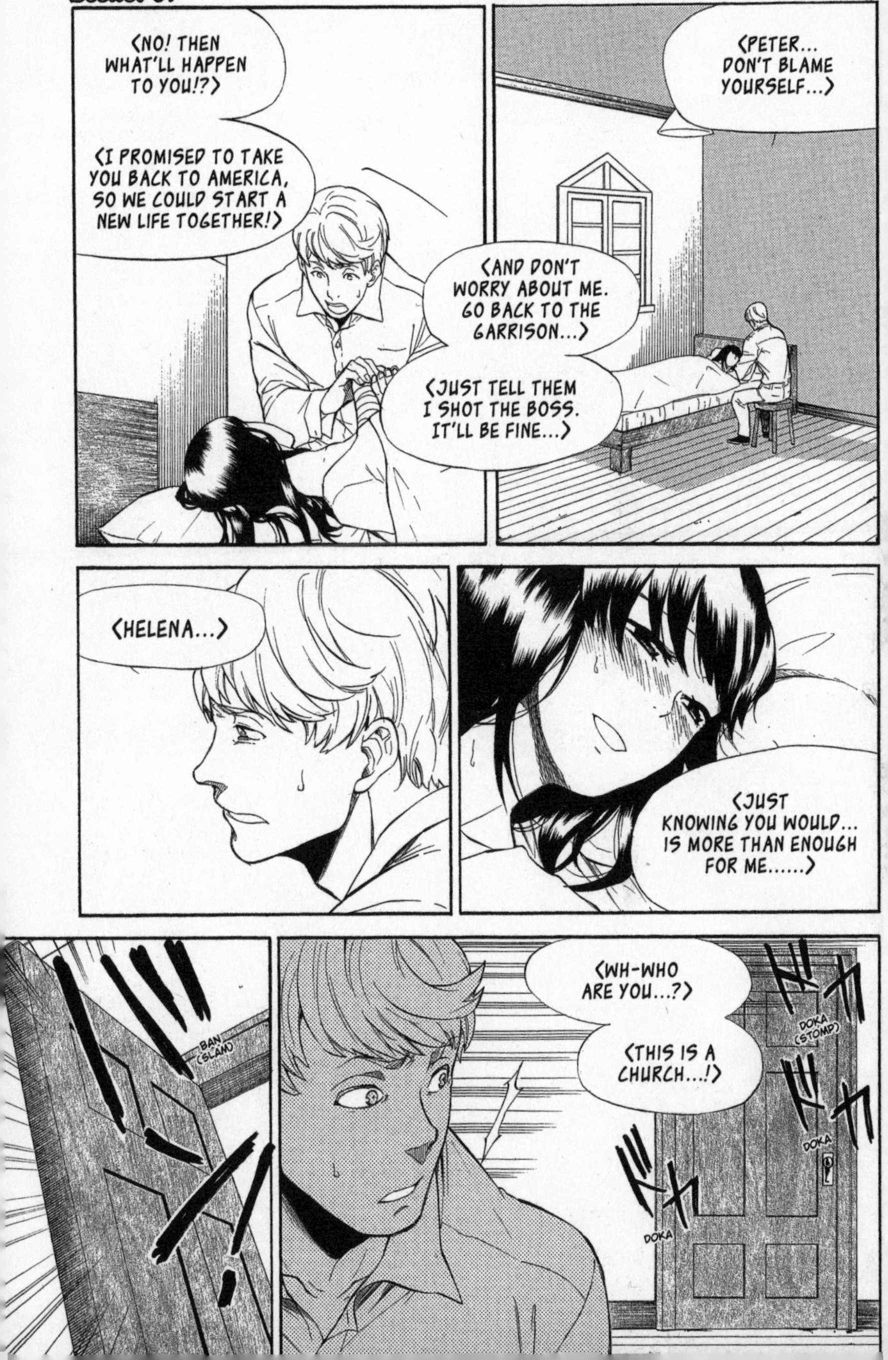
<PETER... DON'T BLAME YOURSELF...>
<AND DON'T WORRY ABOUT ME. GO BACK TO THE GARRISON...>
<JUST TELL THEM I SHOT THE BOSS. IT'LL BE FINE...>
<NO! THEN WHAT'LL HAPPEN TO YOU!?>
<I PROMISED TO TAKE YOU BACK TO AMERICA, SO WE COULD START A NEW LIFE TOGETHER!>
<JUST KNOWING YOU WOULD... IS MORE THAN ENOUGH FOR ME......>
<HELENA...>
DOKA (STOMP)
<WH-WHO ARE YOU...?>
<THIS IS A CHURCH...!>
DOKA
DOKA
BAN (SLAM)

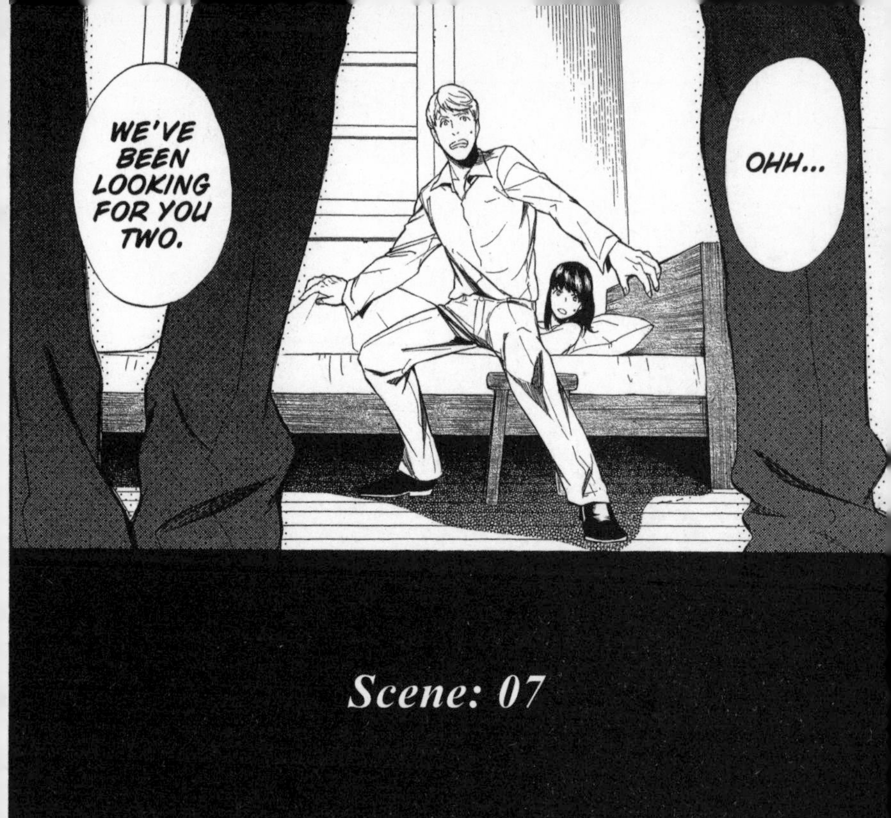
OHH...
WE'VE BEEN LOOKING FOR YOU TWO.

Scene: 07

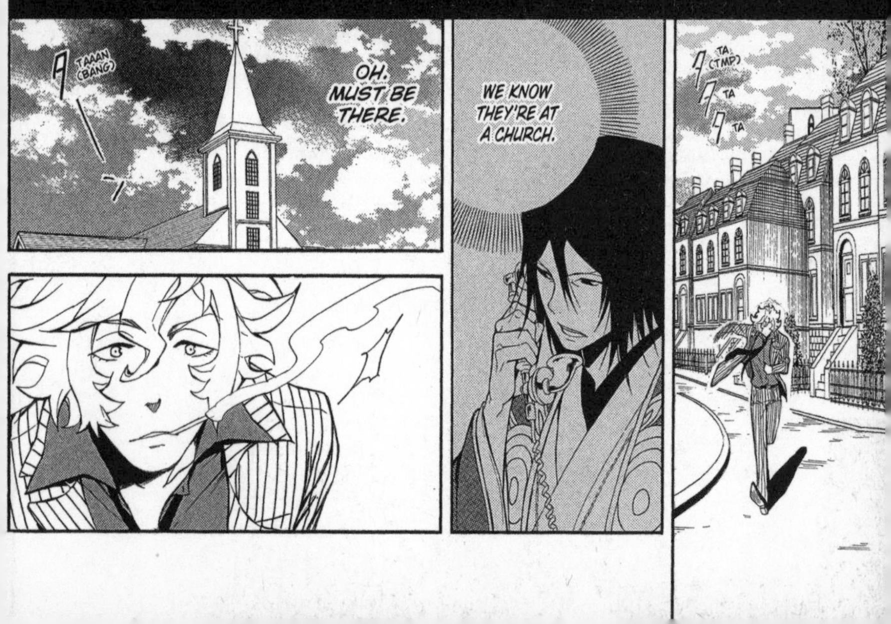
TA (TMP) TA TA TA
WE KNOW THEY'RE AT A CHURCH.
TAAAN (BANG)
OH. MUST BE THERE.

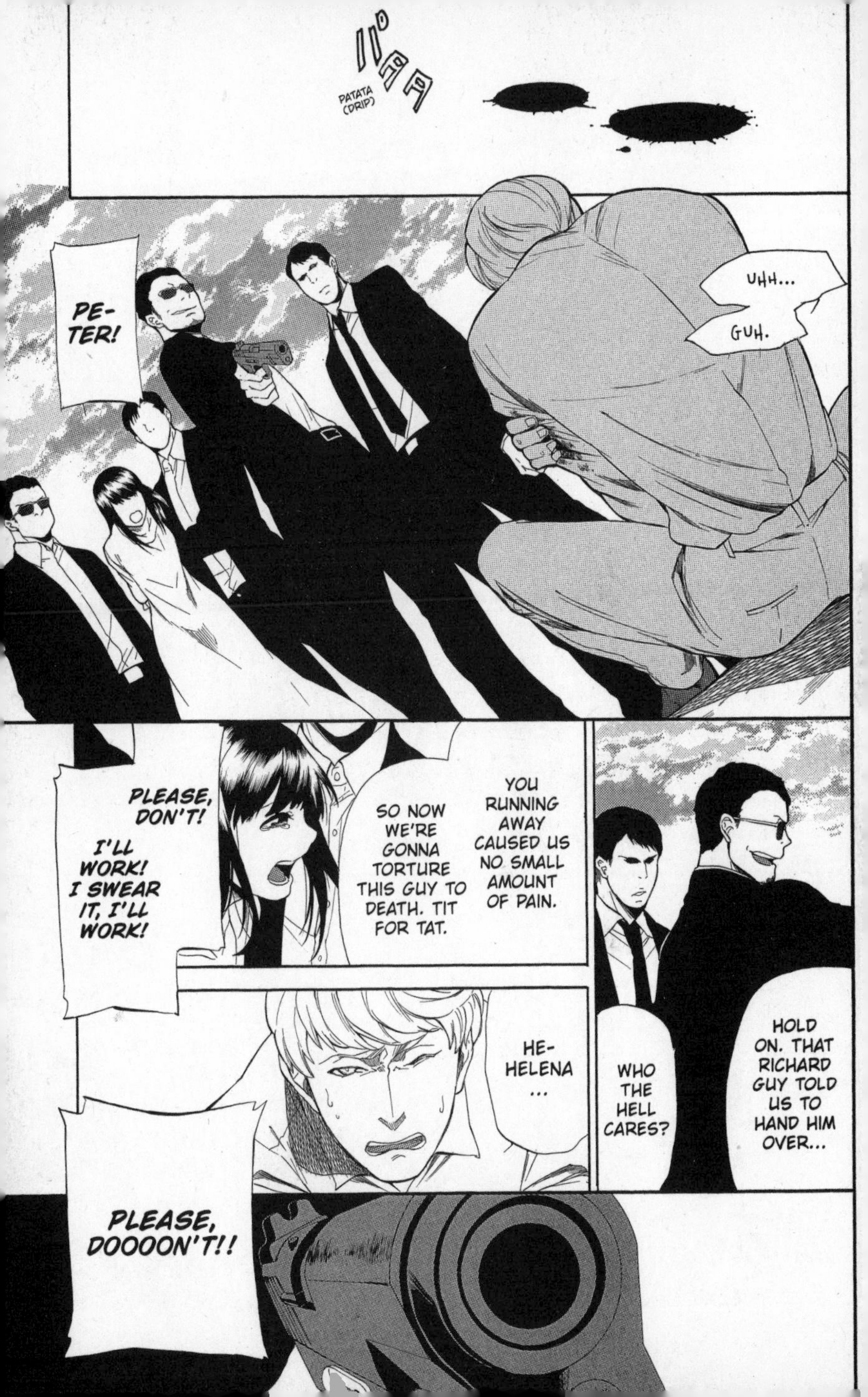
パタタ
PATATA (DRIP)
UHH...
GUH.
PE-TER!
HOLD ON. THAT RICHARD GUY TOLD US TO HAND HIM OVER...
WHO THE HELL CARES?
YOU RUNNING AWAY CAUSED US NO SMALL AMOUNT OF PAIN.
SO NOW WE'RE GONNA TORTURE THIS GUY TO DEATH. TIT FOR TAT.
PLEASE, DON'T!
I'LL WORK! I SWEAR IT, I'LL WORK!
HE-HELENA...
PLEASE, DOOOON'T!!

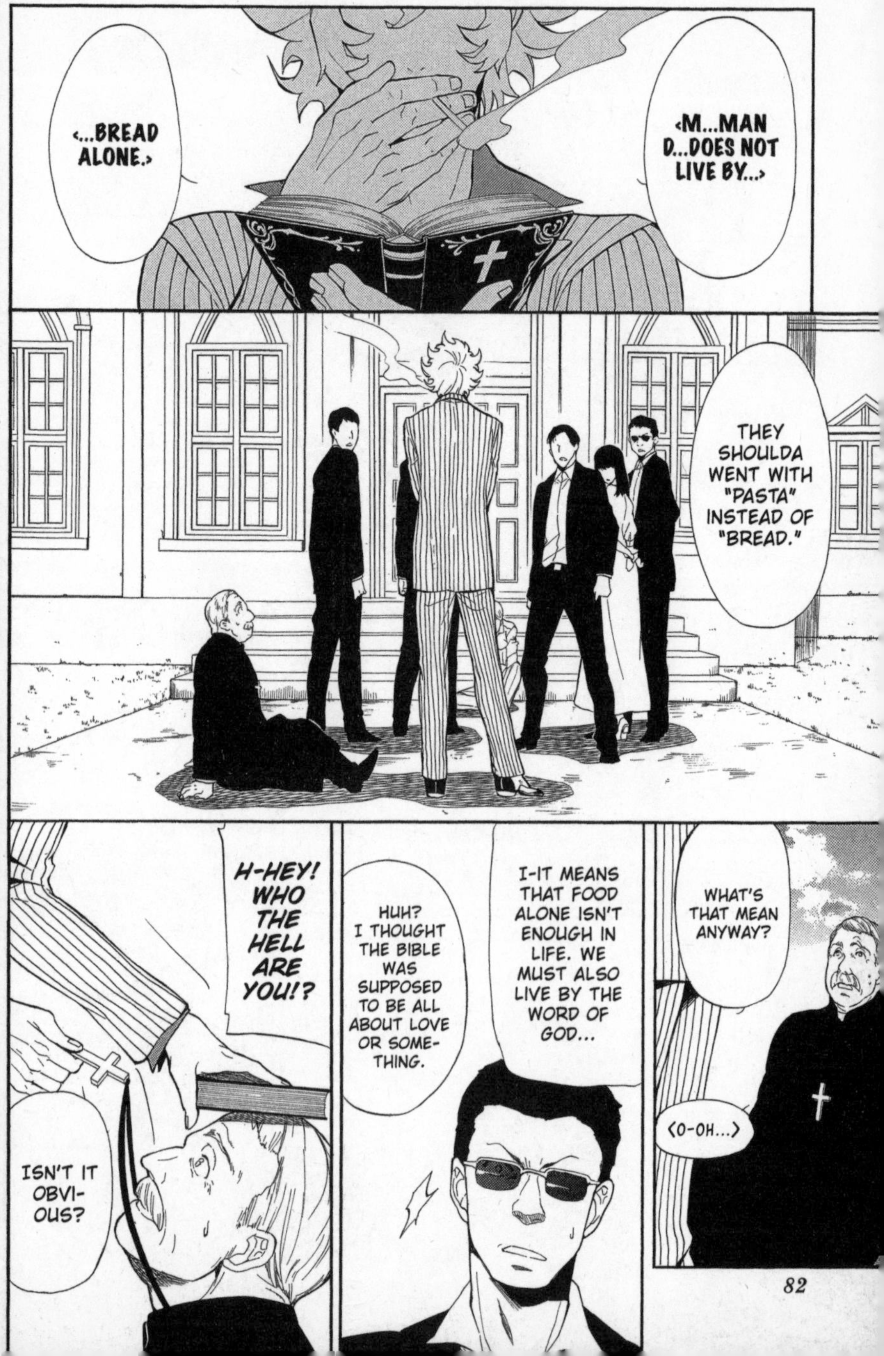
‹M...MAN D...DOES NOT LIVE BY...›
‹...BREAD ALONE.›
THEY SHOULDA WENT WITH "PASTA" INSTEAD OF "BREAD."
WHAT'S THAT MEAN ANYWAY?
‹O-OH...›
I-IT MEANS THAT FOOD ALONE ISN'T ENOUGH IN LIFE. WE MUST ALSO LIVE BY THE WORD OF GOD...
HUH? I THOUGHT THE BIBLE WAS SUPPOSED TO BE ALL ABOUT LOVE OR SOME-THING.
H-HEY! WHO THE HELL ARE YOU!?
ISN'T IT OBVI-OUS?

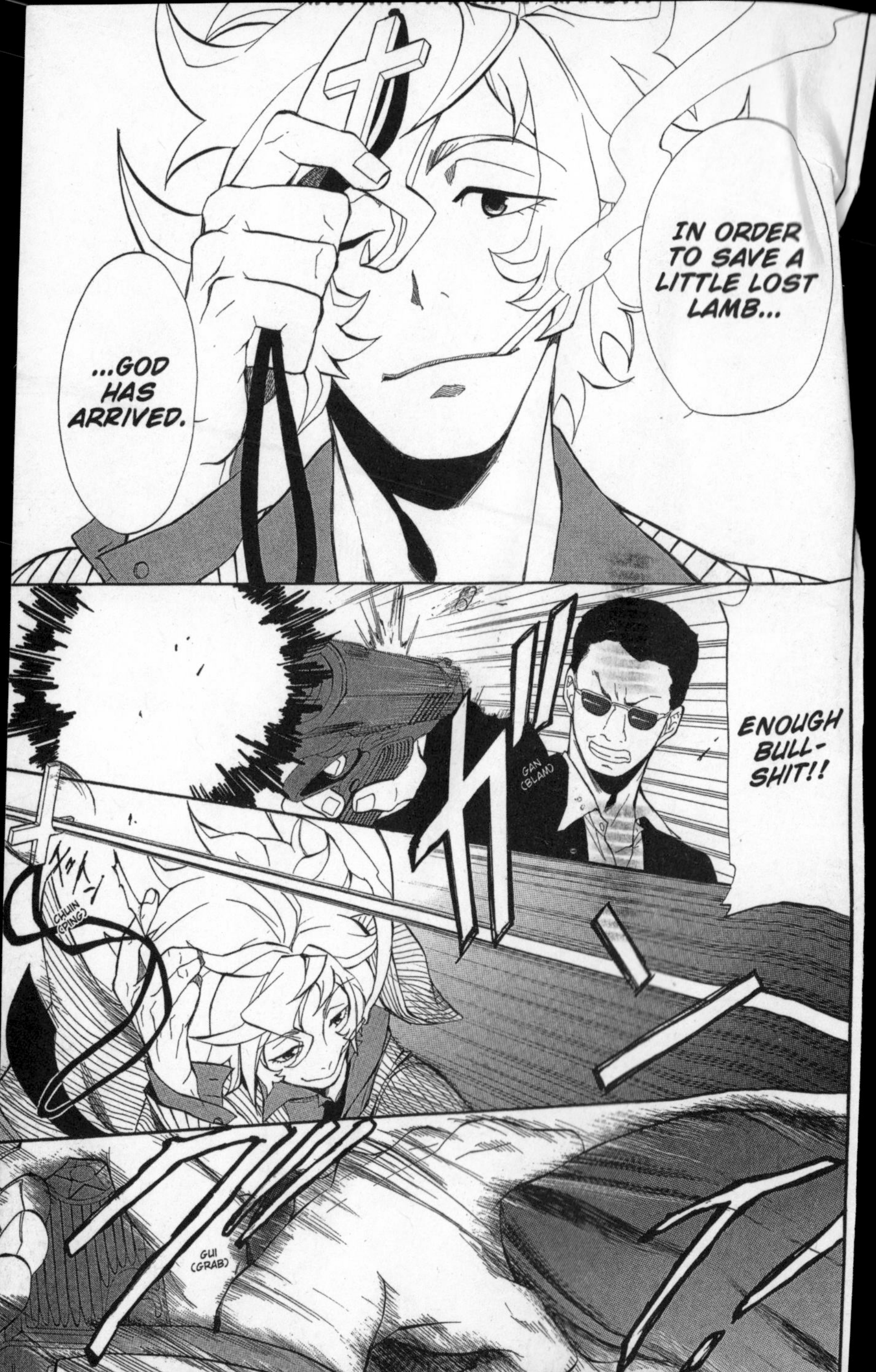
IN ORDER TO SAVE A LITTLE LOST LAMB...
...GOD HAS ARRIVED.
ENOUGH BULL-SHIT!!
GAN (BLAM)
CHUIN (PING)
GUI (GRAB)

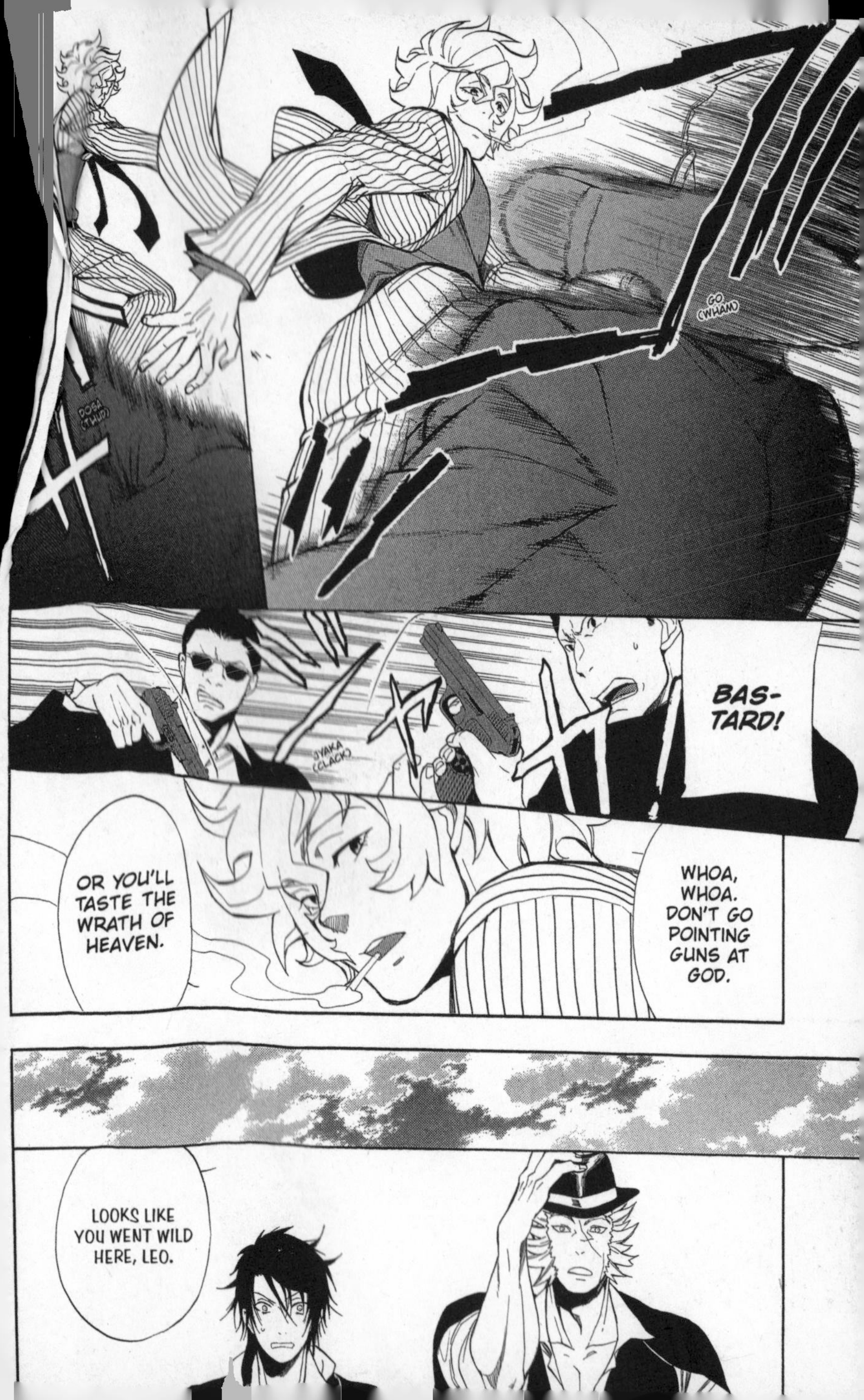
GO (WHAM)
DOGA (THUD)
BAS-TARD!
JYAKA (CLACK)
WHOA, WHOA. DON'T GO POINTING GUNS AT GOD.
OR YOU'LL TASTE THE WRATH OF HEAVEN.
LOOKS LIKE YOU WENT WILD HERE, LEO.

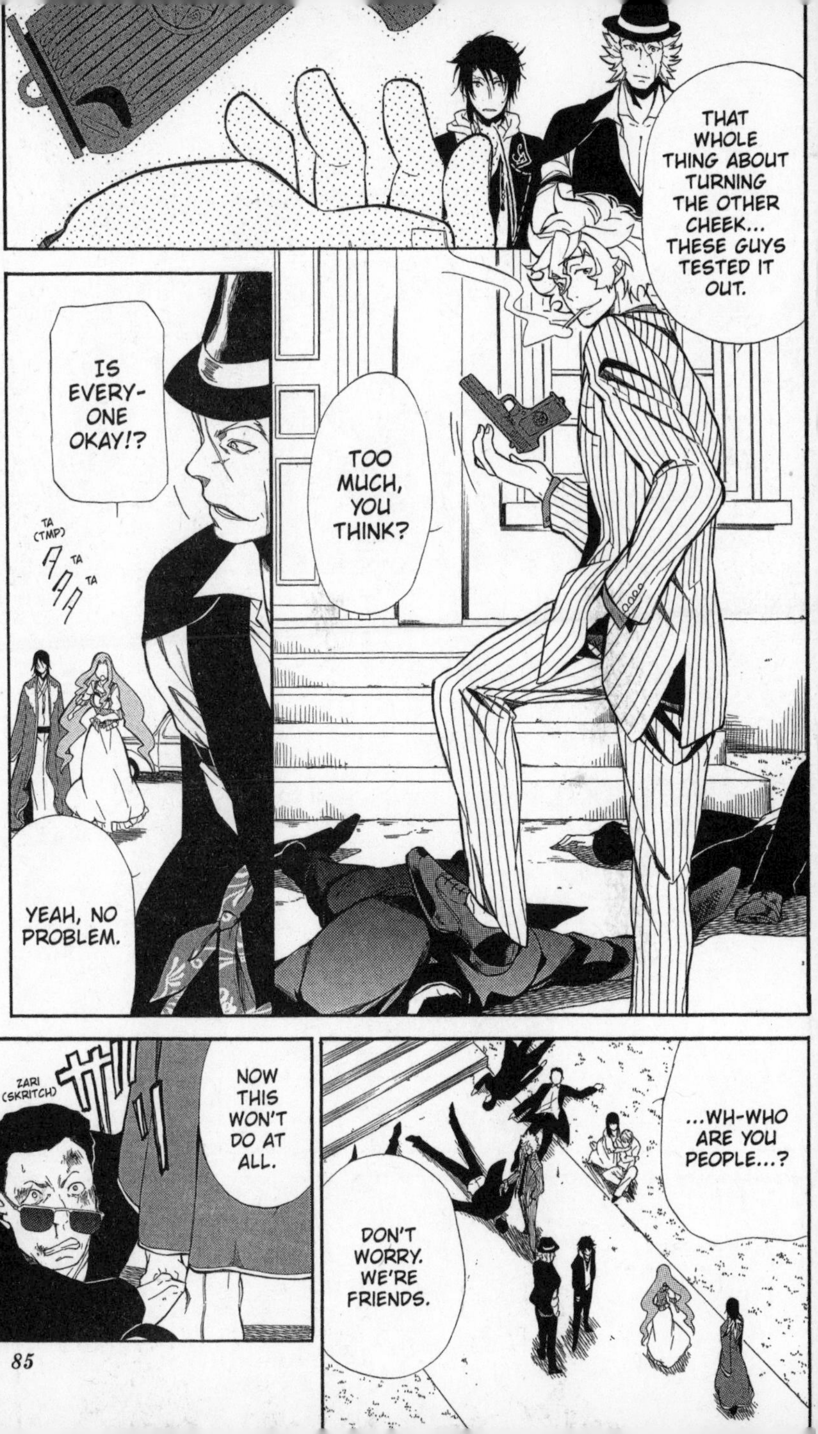
THAT WHOLE THING ABOUT TURNING THE OTHER CHEEK... THESE GUYS TESTED IT OUT.
TOO MUCH, YOU THINK?
IS EVERY-ONE OKAY!?
TA (TMP) TA TA
YEAH, NO PROBLEM.
...WH-WHO ARE YOU PEOPLE...?
DON'T WORRY. WE'RE FRIENDS.
ZARI (SKRITCH)
NOW THIS WON'T DO AT ALL.

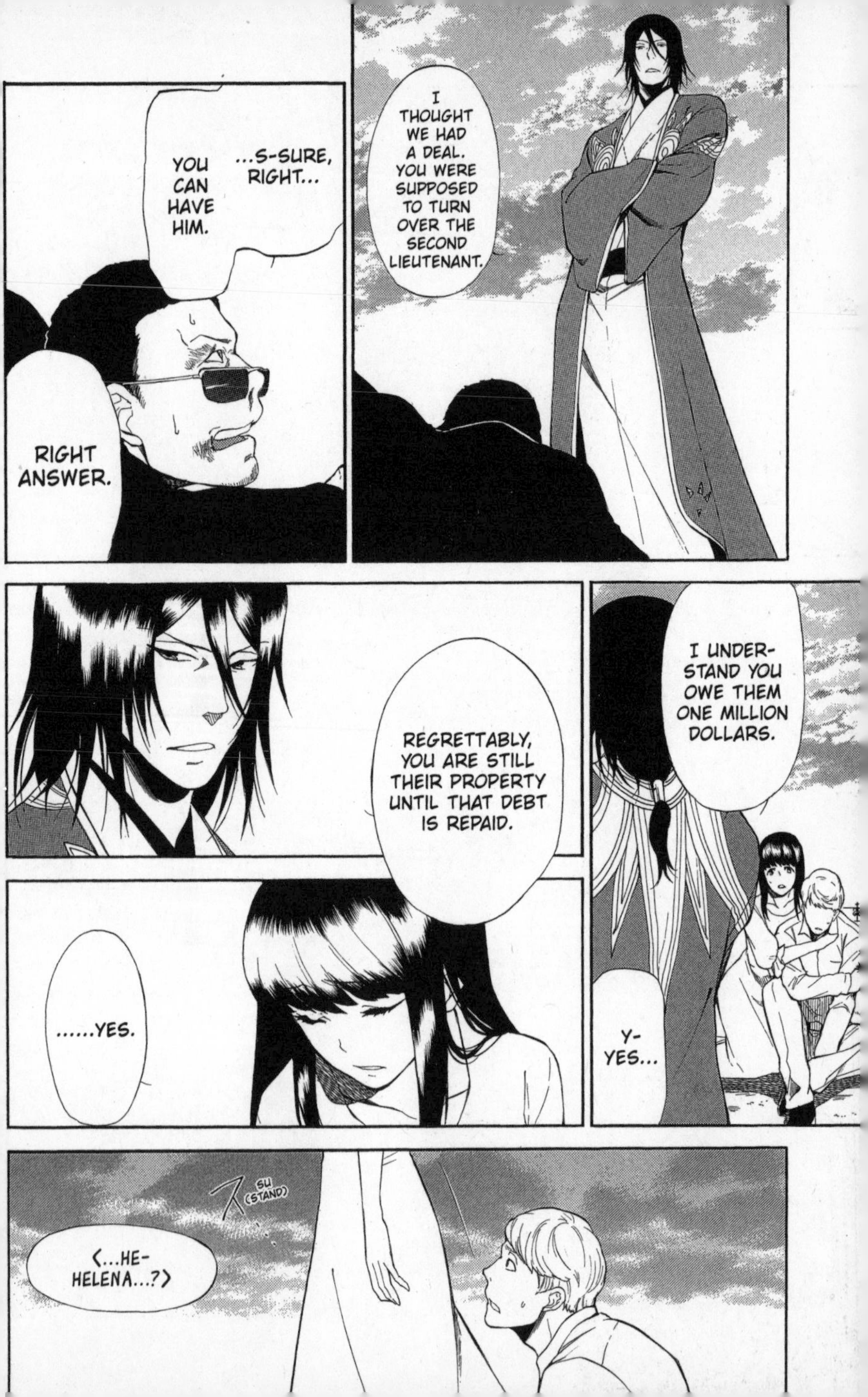
I THOUGHT WE HAD A DEAL. YOU WERE SUPPOSED TO TURN OVER THE SECOND LIEUTENANT.
...S-SURE, RIGHT...
YOU CAN HAVE HIM.
RIGHT ANSWER.
I UNDER-STAND YOU OWE THEM ONE MILLION DOLLARS.
Y-YES...
REGRETTABLY, YOU ARE STILL THEIR PROPERTY UNTIL THAT DEBT IS REPAID.
......YES.
ス
SU (STAND)
<...HE-HELENA...?>

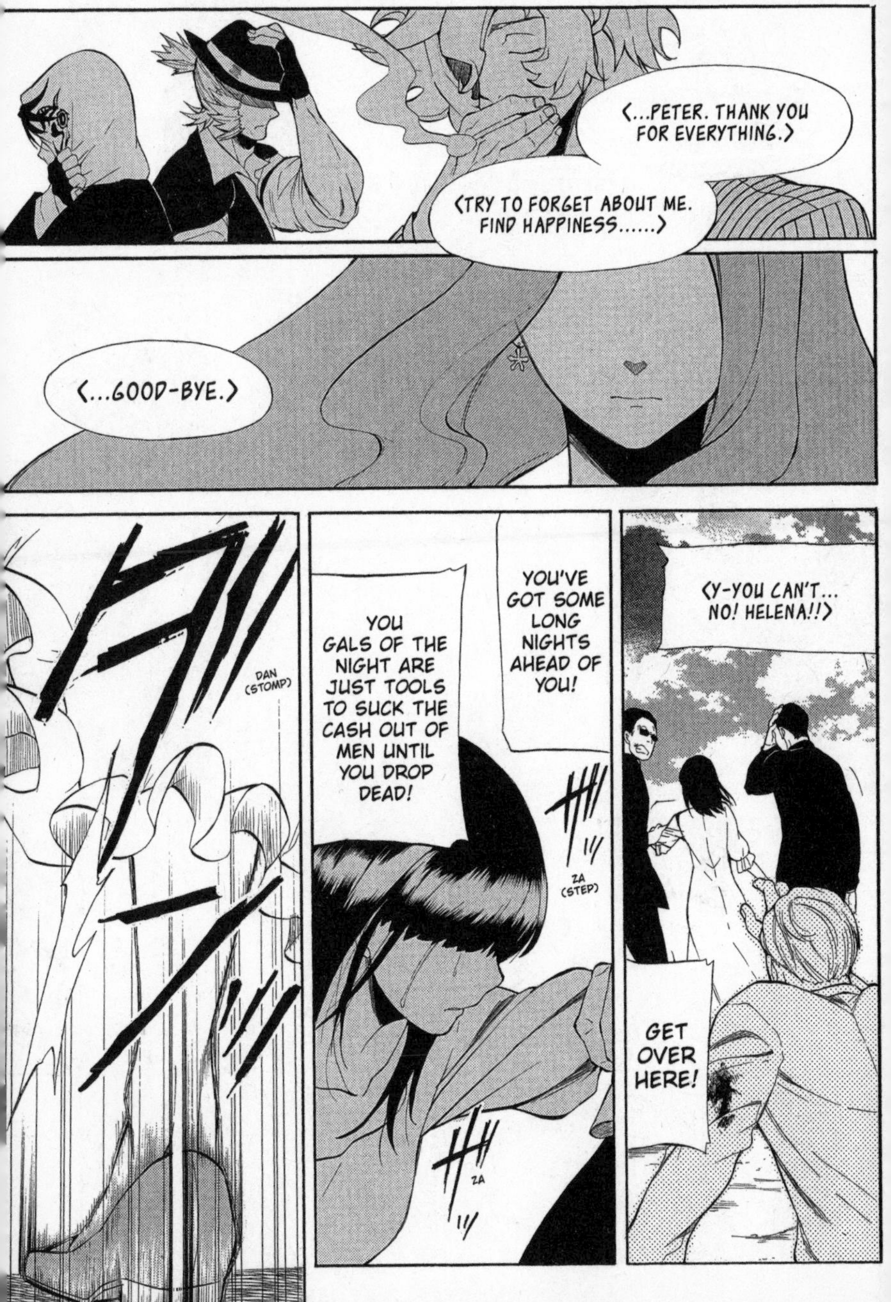
<...PETER. THANK YOU FOR EVERYTHING.>
<TRY TO FORGET ABOUT ME. FIND HAPPINESS......>
<...GOOD-BYE.>
<Y-YOU CAN'T... NO! HELENA!!>
GET OVER HERE!
YOU'VE GOT SOME LONG NIGHTS AHEAD OF YOU!
YOU GALS OF THE NIGHT ARE JUST TOOLS TO SUCK THE CASH OUT OF MEN UNTIL YOU DROP DEAD!
ZA (STEP)
ZA
DAN (STOMP)

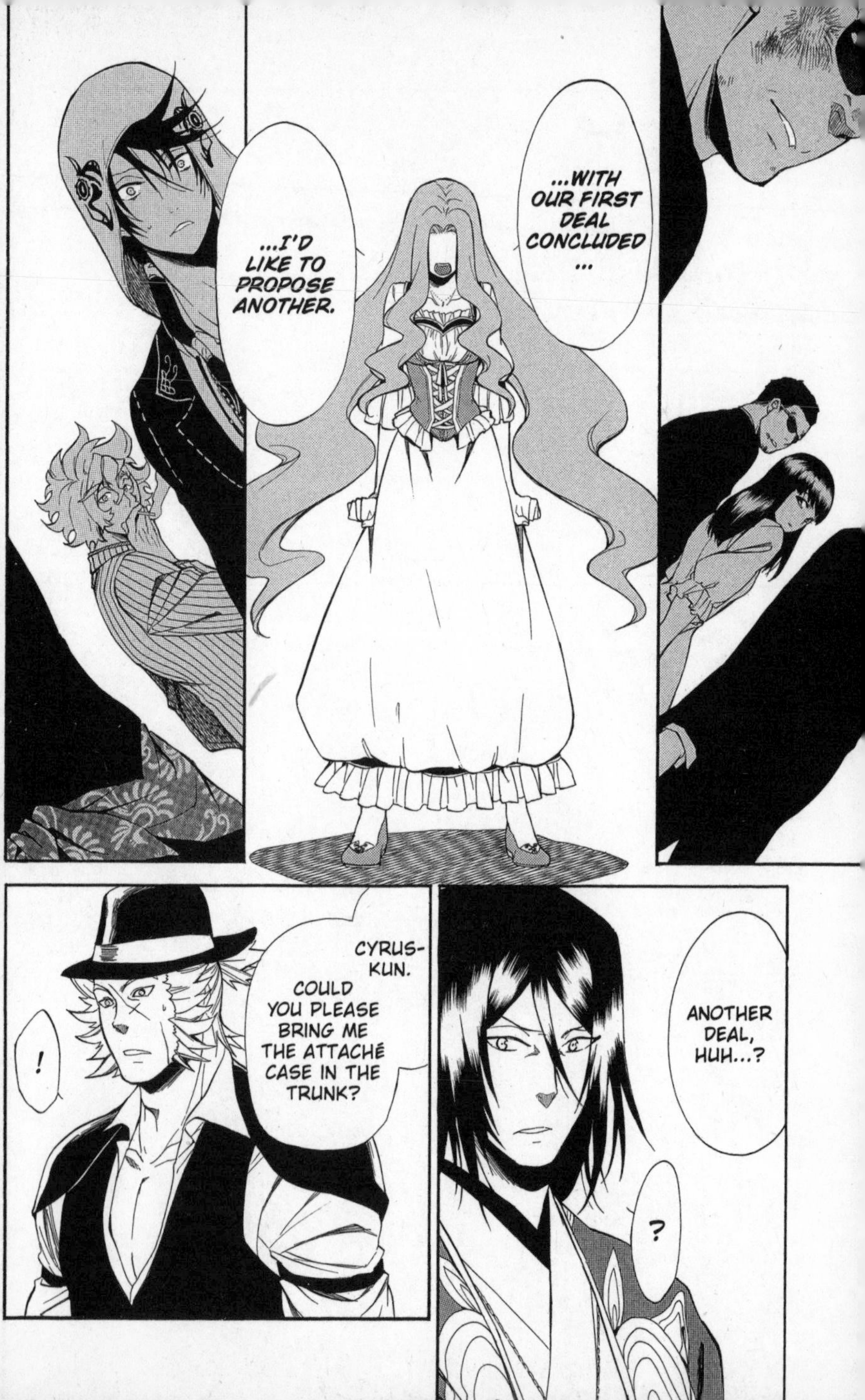
...WITH OUR FIRST DEAL CONCLUDED ...
...I'D LIKE TO PROPOSE ANOTHER.
ANOTHER DEAL, HUH...?
?
CYRUS-KUN.
COULD YOU PLEASE BRING ME THE ATTACHÉ CASE IN THE TRUNK?
!

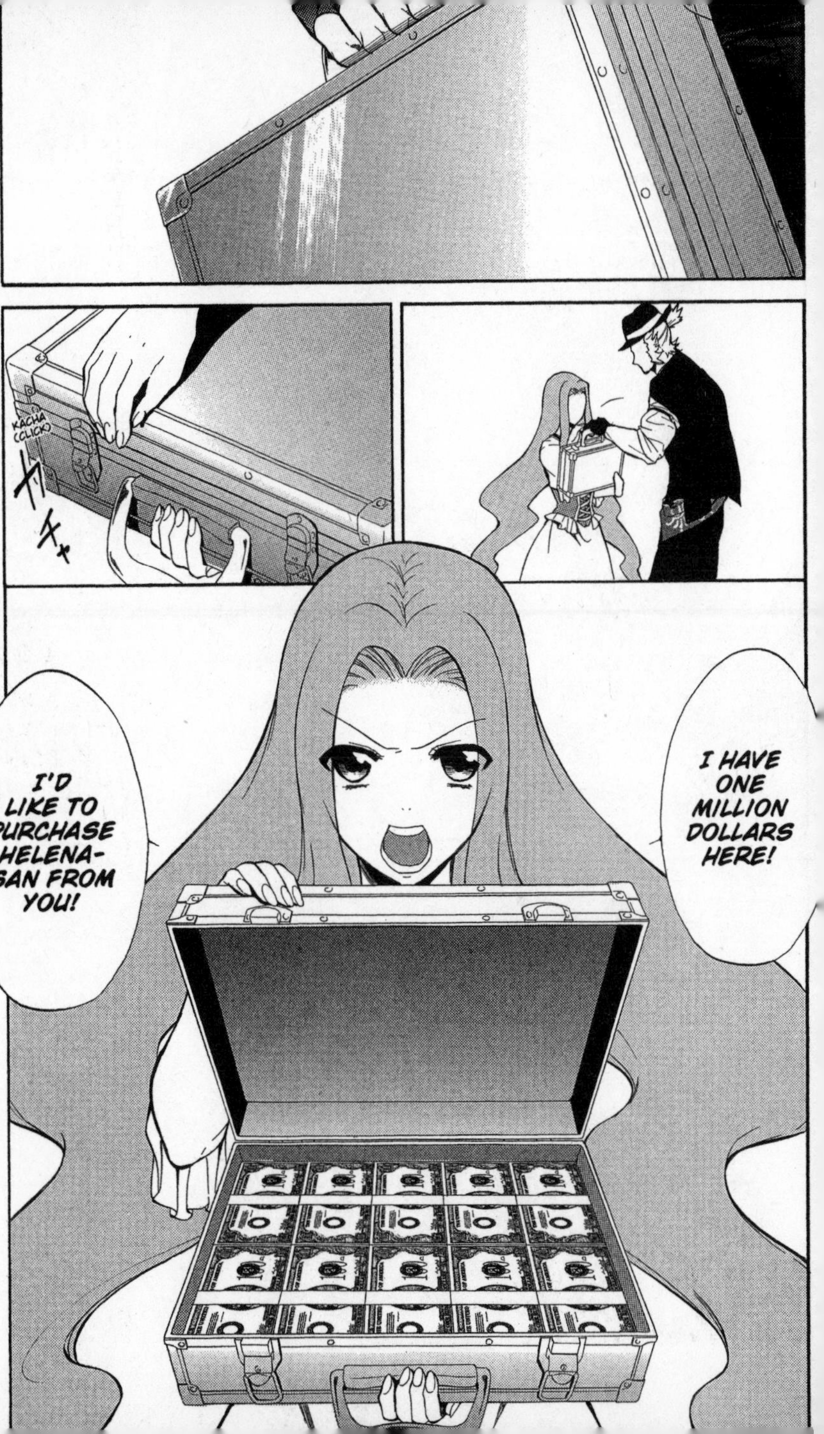
KACHA (CLICK)
I HAVE ONE MILLION DOLLARS HERE!
I'D LIKE TO PURCHASE HELENA-SAN FROM YOU!

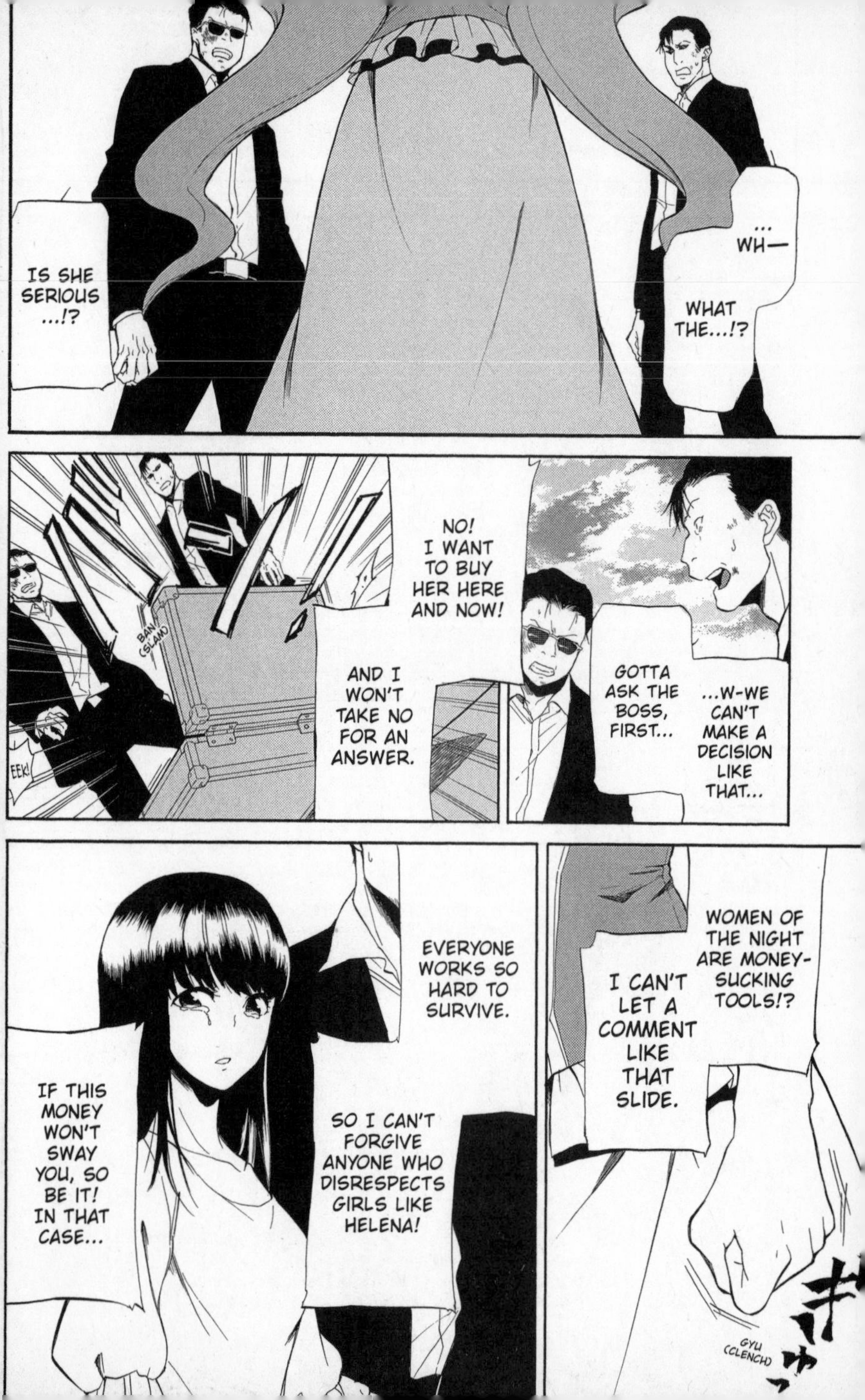

...WH— WHAT THE...!?
IS SHE SERIOUS ...!?
...W-WE CAN'T MAKE A DECISION LIKE THAT...
GOTTA ASK THE BOSS, FIRST...
NO! I WANT TO BUY HER HERE AND NOW!
AND I WON'T TAKE NO FOR AN ANSWER.
BAN (SLAM)
EEK!
WOMEN OF THE NIGHT ARE MONEY-SUCKING TOOLS!?
I CAN'T LET A COMMENT LIKE THAT SLIDE.
GYU (CLENCH)
EVERYONE WORKS SO HARD TO SURVIVE.
SO I CAN'T FORGIVE ANYONE WHO DISRESPECTS GIRLS LIKE HELENA!
IF THIS MONEY WON'T SWAY YOU, SO BE IT! IN THAT CASE...

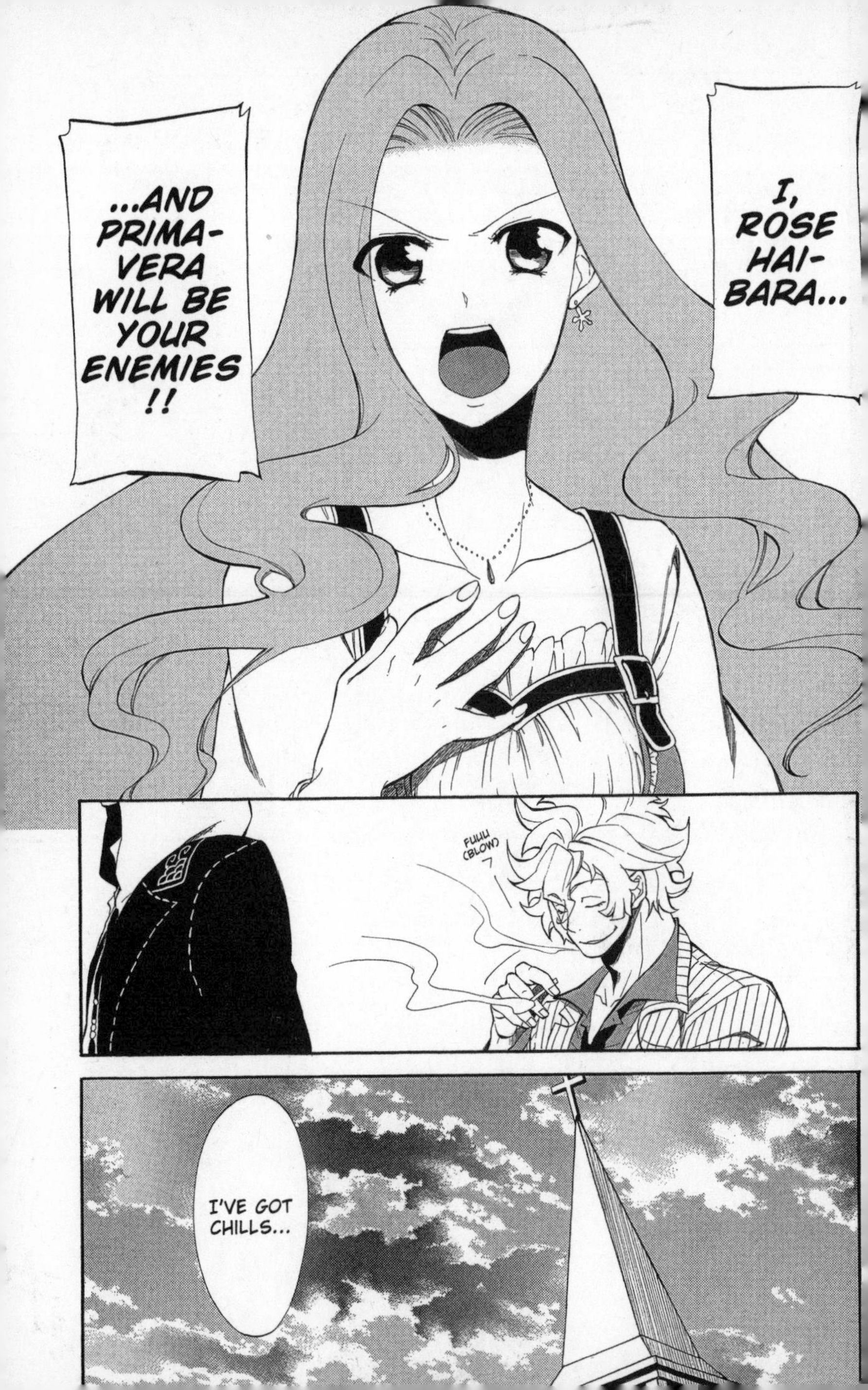
I, ROSE HAI-BARA...
...AND PRIMA-VERA WILL BE YOUR ENEMIES !!
FUUU (BLOW)
I'VE GOT CHILLS...

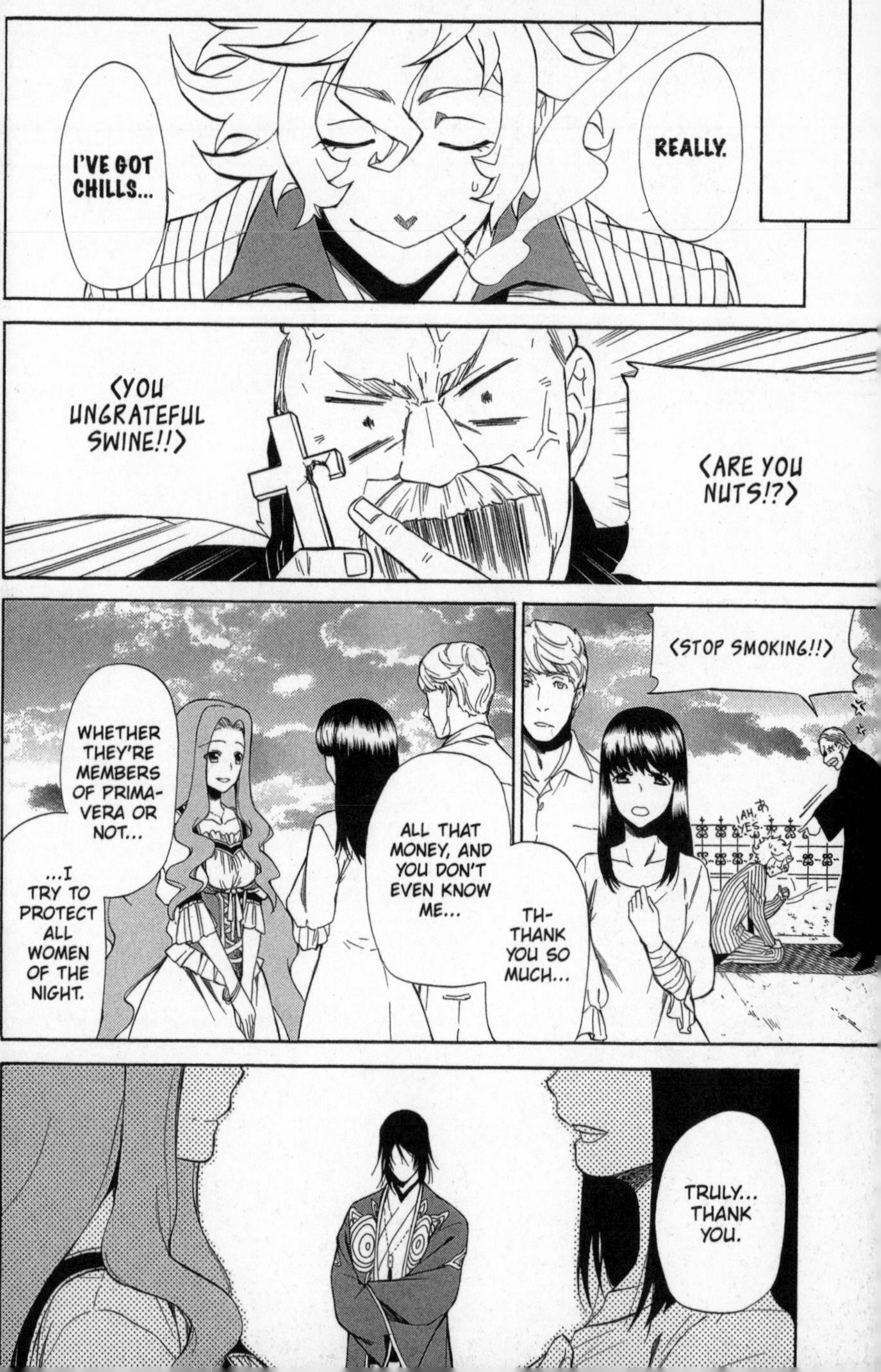
REALLY.
I'VE GOT CHILLS...
<ARE YOU NUTS!?>
<YOU UNGRATEFUL SWINE!!>
<STOP SMOKING!!>
AH, YES.
TH- THANK YOU SO MUCH...
ALL THAT MONEY, AND YOU DON'T EVEN KNOW ME...
WHETHER THEY'RE MEMBERS OF PRIMA-VERA OR NOT...
...I TRY TO PROTECT ALL WOMEN OF THE NIGHT.
TRULY... THANK YOU.

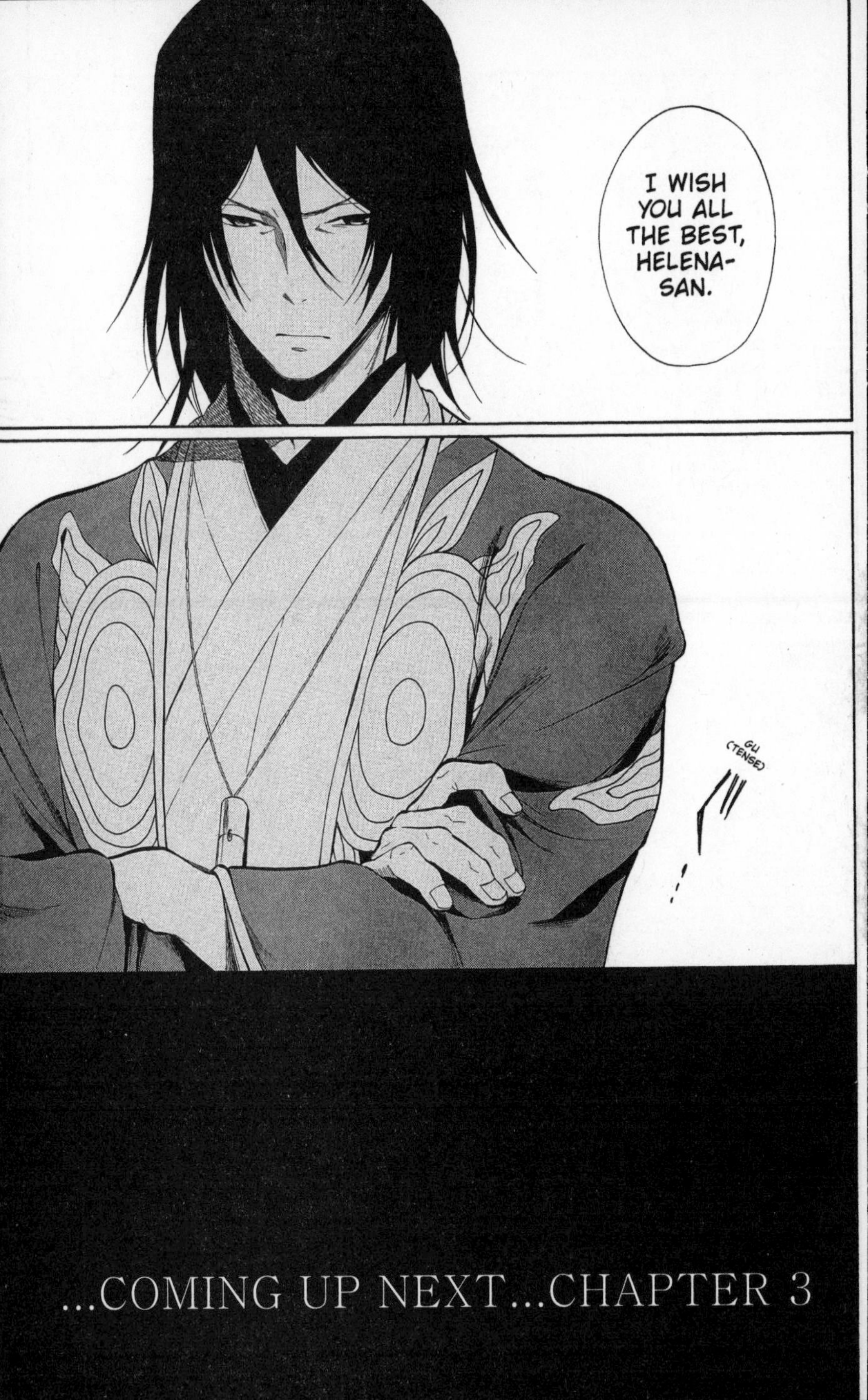
I WISH YOU ALL THE BEST, HELENA-SAN.
GU (TENSE)

...COMING UP NEXT...CHAPTER 3

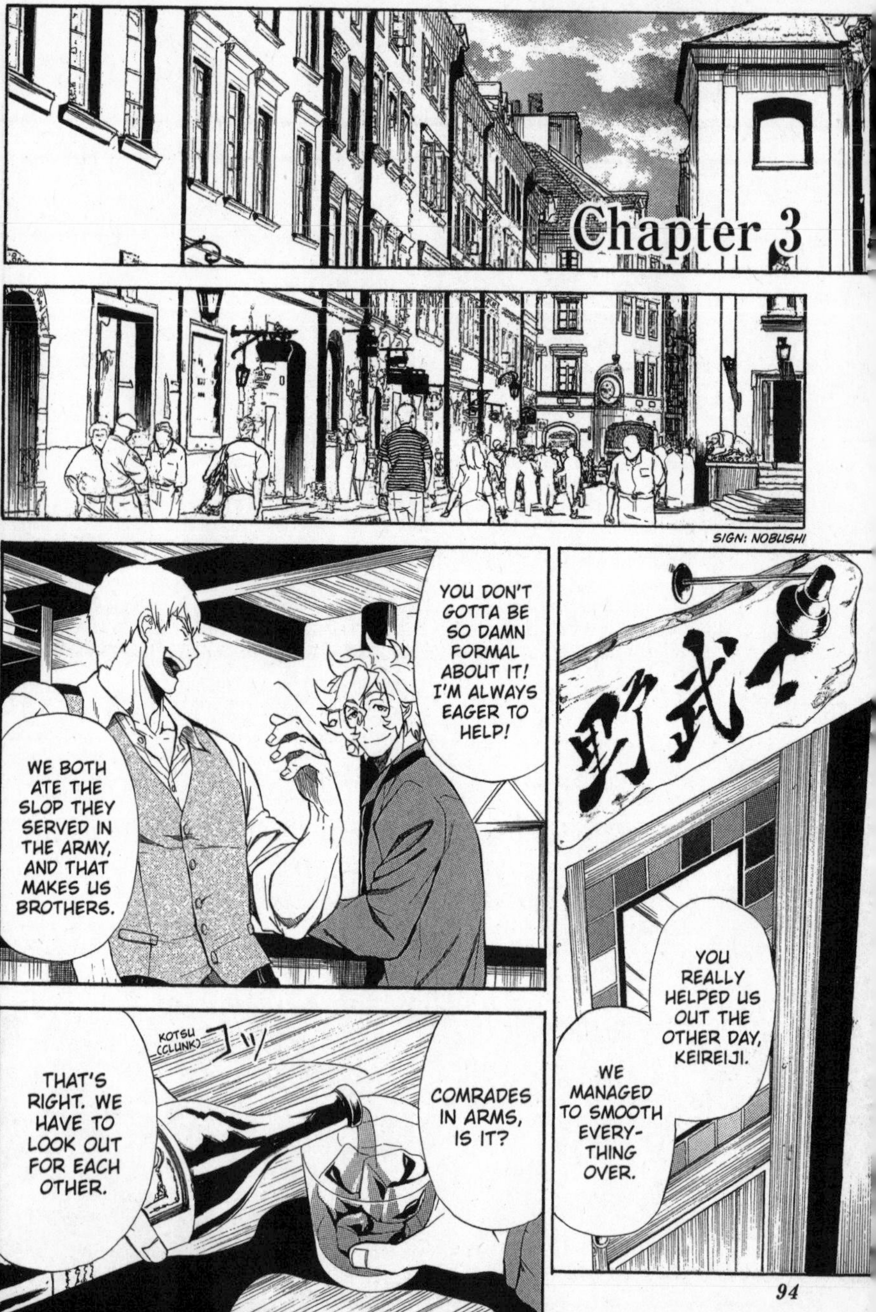
Chapter 3
SIGN: NOBUSHI
野武士
YOU REALLY HELPED US OUT THE OTHER DAY, KEIREIJI.
WE MANAGED TO SMOOTH EVERY-THING OVER.
YOU DON'T GOTTA BE SO DAMN FORMAL ABOUT IT! I'M ALWAYS EAGER TO HELP!
WE BOTH ATE THE SLOP THEY SERVED IN THE ARMY, AND THAT MAKES US BROTHERS.
KOTSU (CLUNK)
COMRADES IN ARMS, IS IT?
THAT'S RIGHT. WE HAVE TO LOOK OUT FOR EACH OTHER.

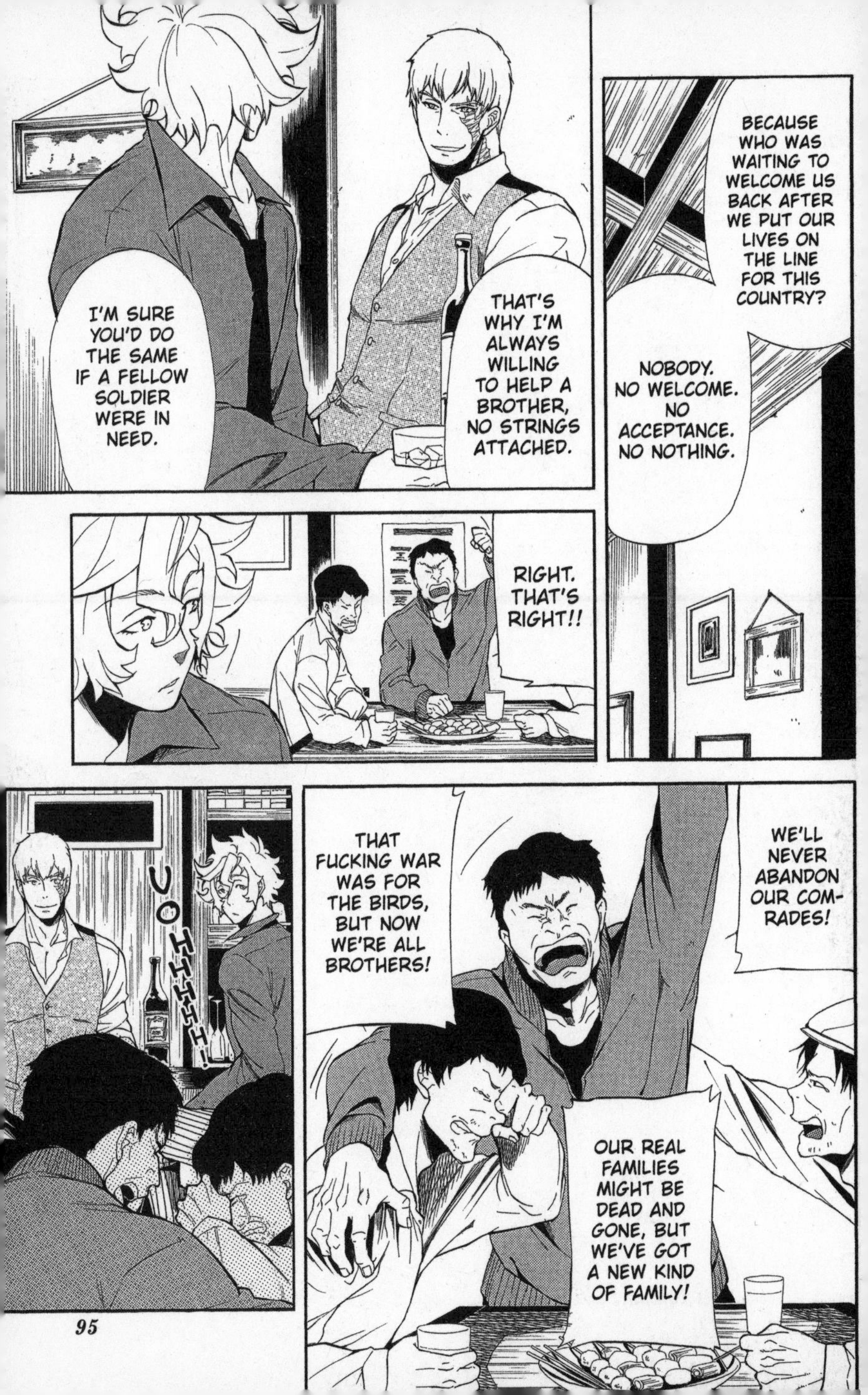
BECAUSE WHO WAS WAITING TO WELCOME US BACK AFTER WE PUT OUR LIVES ON THE LINE FOR THIS COUNTRY?
NOBODY. NO WELCOME. NO ACCEPTANCE. NO NOTHING.
THAT'S WHY I'M ALWAYS WILLING TO HELP A BROTHER, NO STRINGS ATTACHED.
I'M SURE YOU'D DO THE SAME IF A FELLOW SOLDIER WERE IN NEED.
RIGHT. THAT'S RIGHT!!
WE'LL NEVER ABANDON OUR COM-RADES!
THAT FUCKING WAR WAS FOR THE BIRDS, BUT NOW WE'RE ALL BROTHERS!
OUR REAL FAMILIES MIGHT BE DEAD AND GONE, BUT WE'VE GOT A NEW KIND OF FAMILY!
UOHHHHHH!

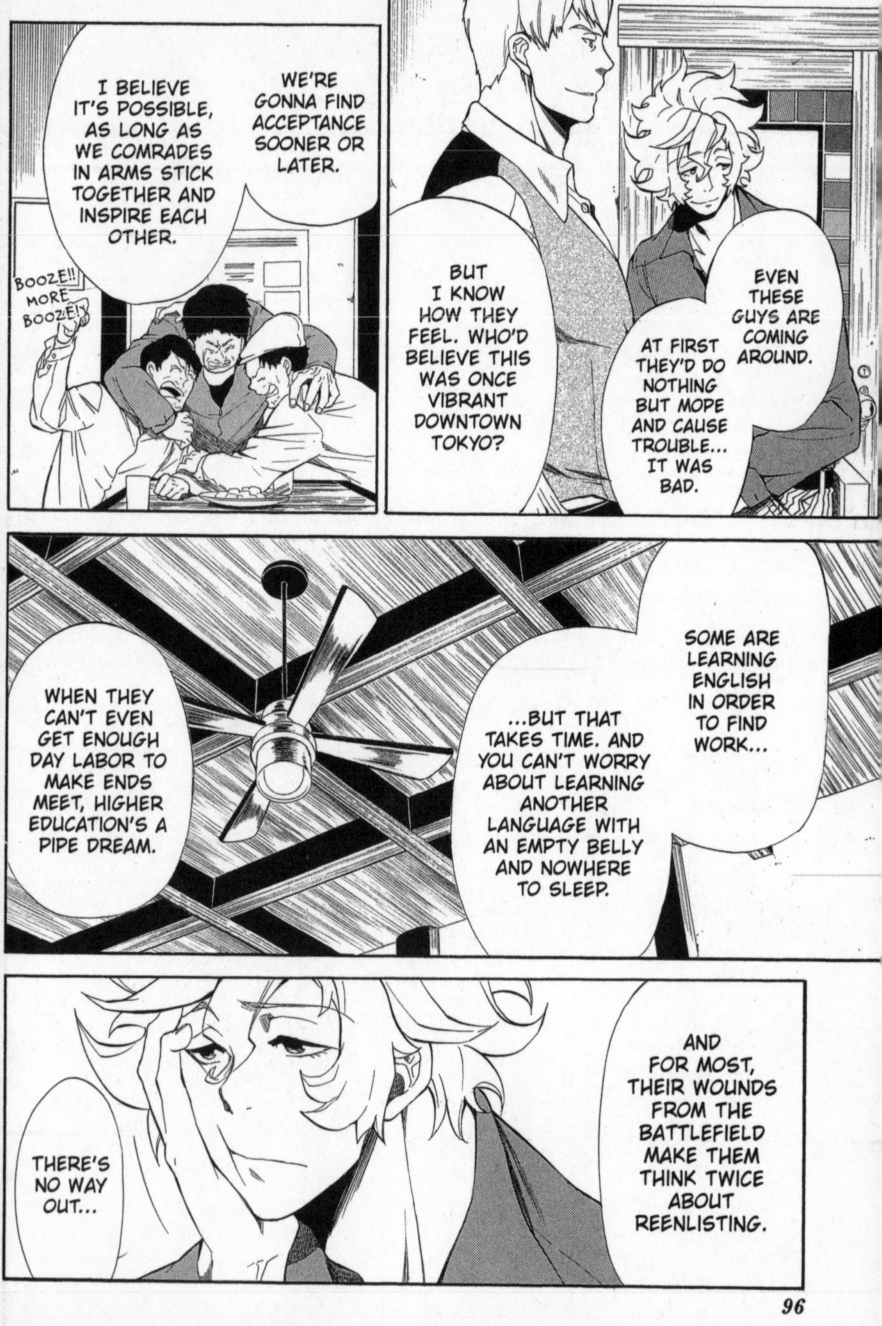
EVEN THESE GUYS ARE COMING AROUND.
AT FIRST THEY'D DO NOTHING BUT MOPE AND CAUSE TROUBLE... IT WAS BAD.
BUT I KNOW HOW THEY FEEL. WHO'D BELIEVE THIS WAS ONCE VIBRANT DOWNTOWN TOKYO?
WE'RE GONNA FIND ACCEPTANCE SOONER OR LATER.
I BELIEVE IT'S POSSIBLE, AS LONG AS WE COMRADES IN ARMS STICK TOGETHER AND INSPIRE EACH OTHER.
BOOZE!! MORE BOOZE!!
SOME ARE LEARNING ENGLISH IN ORDER TO FIND WORK...
...BUT THAT TAKES TIME. AND YOU CAN'T WORRY ABOUT LEARNING ANOTHER LANGUAGE WITH AN EMPTY BELLY AND NOWHERE TO SLEEP.
WHEN THEY CAN'T EVEN GET ENOUGH DAY LABOR TO MAKE ENDS MEET, HIGHER EDUCATION'S A PIPE DREAM.
AND FOR MOST, THEIR WOUNDS FROM THE BATTLEFIELD MAKE THEM THINK TWICE ABOUT REENLISTING.
THERE'S NO WAY OUT...

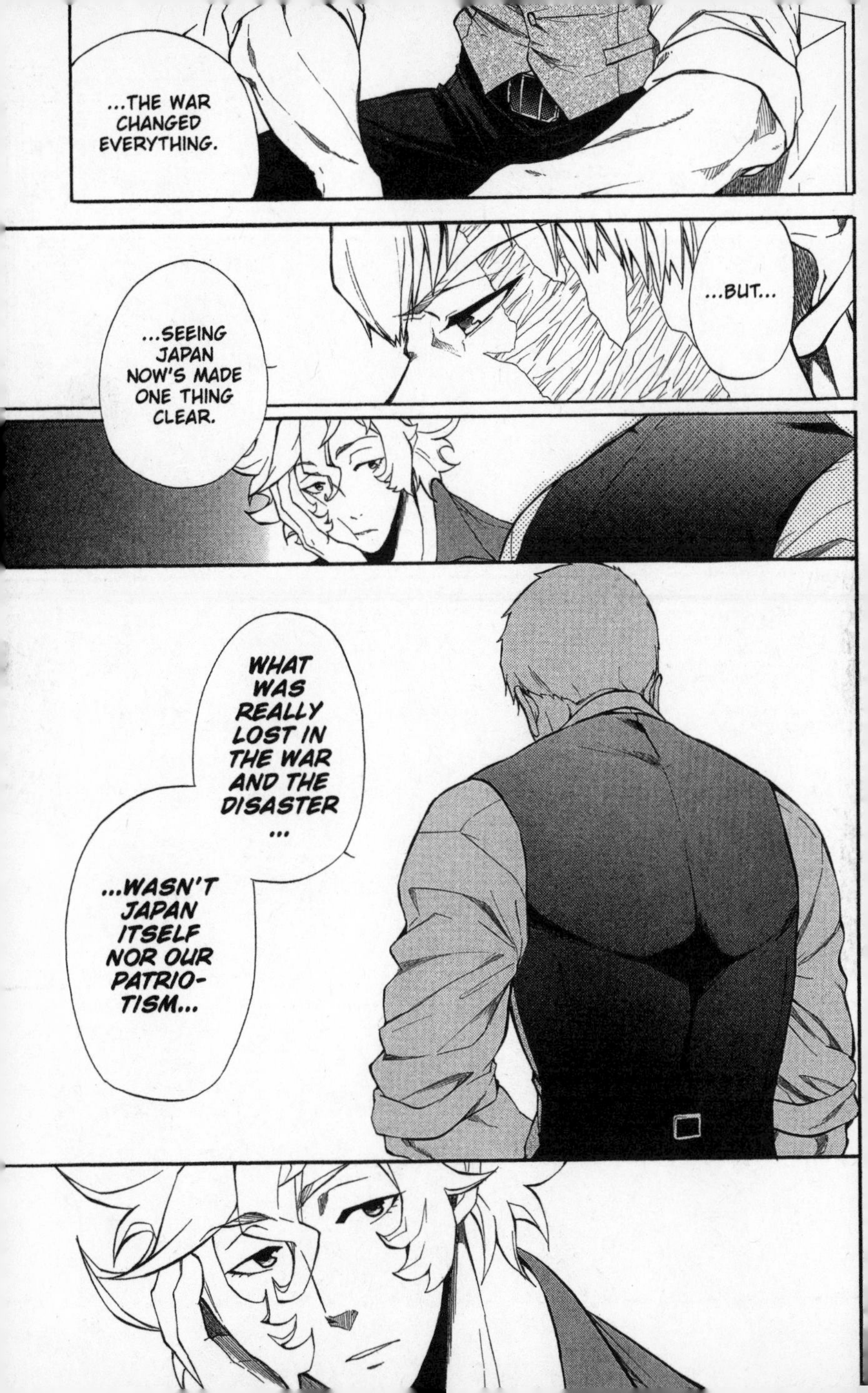
...THE WAR CHANGED EVERYTHING.
...BUT...
...SEEING JAPAN NOW'S MADE ONE THING CLEAR.
WHAT WAS REALLY LOST IN THE WAR AND THE DISASTER...
...WASN'T JAPAN ITSELF NOR OUR PATRIO-TISM...

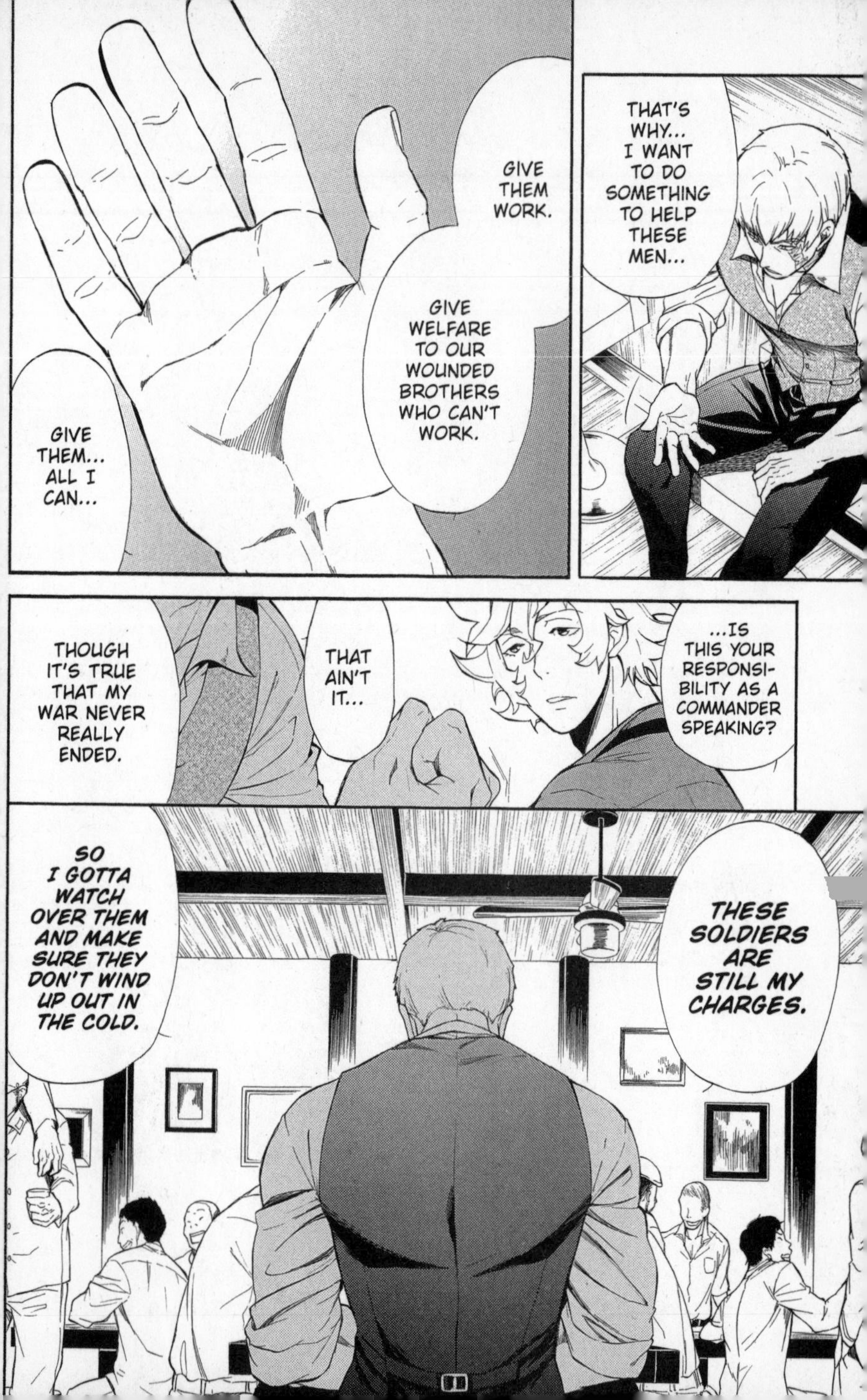
THAT'S WHY... I WANT TO DO SOMETHING TO HELP THESE MEN...
GIVE THEM WORK.
GIVE WELFARE TO OUR WOUNDED BROTHERS WHO CAN'T WORK.
GIVE THEM... ALL I CAN...
...IS THIS YOUR RESPONSIBILITY AS A COMMANDER SPEAKING?
THAT AIN'T IT...
THOUGH IT'S TRUE THAT MY WAR NEVER REALLY ENDED.
THESE SOLDIERS ARE STILL MY CHARGES.
SO I GOTTA WATCH OVER THEM AND MAKE SURE THEY DON'T WIND UP OUT IN THE COLD.

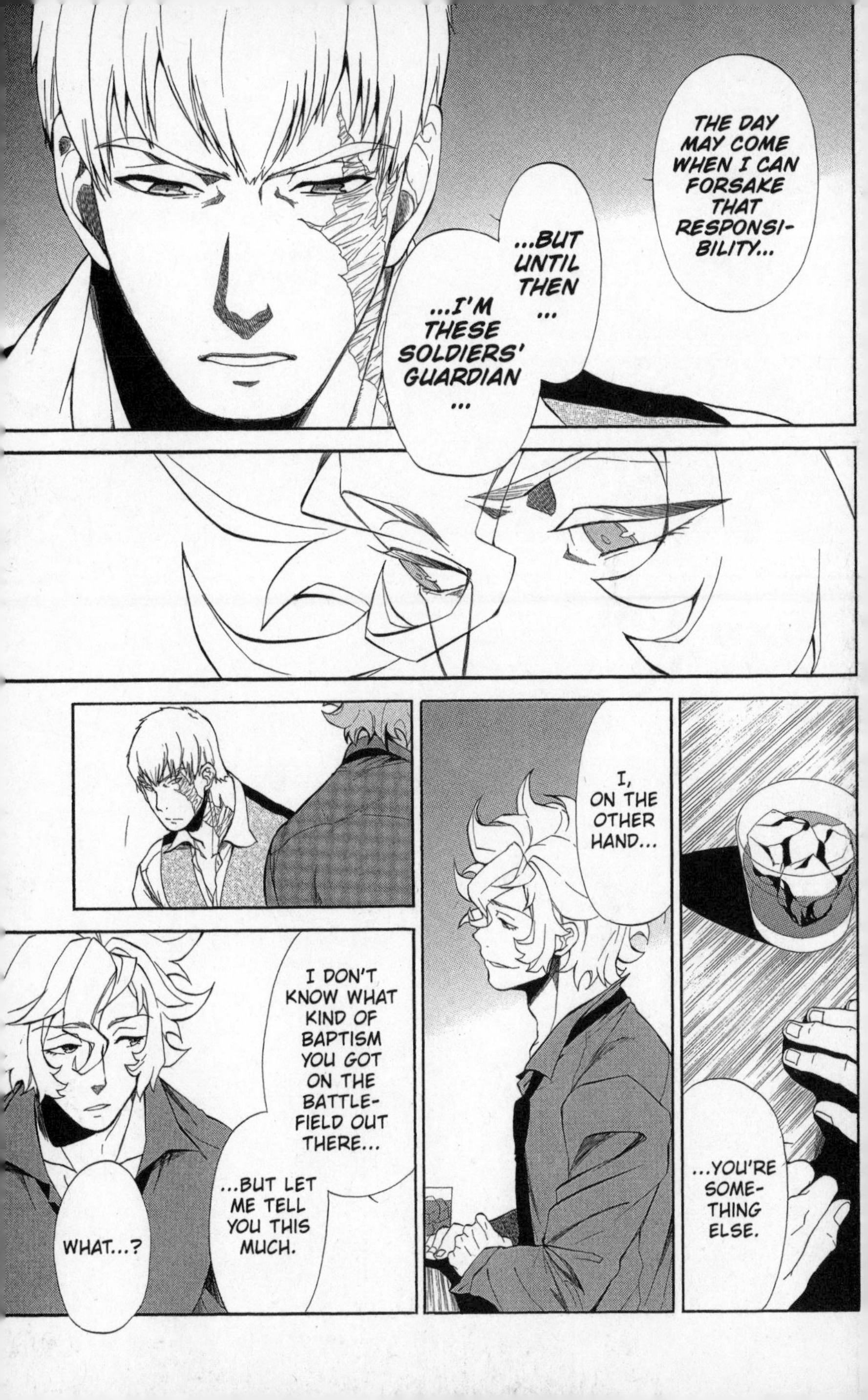
THE DAY MAY COME WHEN I CAN FORSAKE THAT RESPONSI-BILITY...
...BUT UNTIL THEN...
...I'M THESE SOLDIERS' GUARDIAN...
...YOU'RE SOME-THING ELSE.
I, ON THE OTHER HAND...
I DON'T KNOW WHAT KIND OF BAPTISM YOU GOT ON THE BATTLE-FIELD OUT THERE...
...BUT LET ME TELL YOU THIS MUCH.
WHAT...?

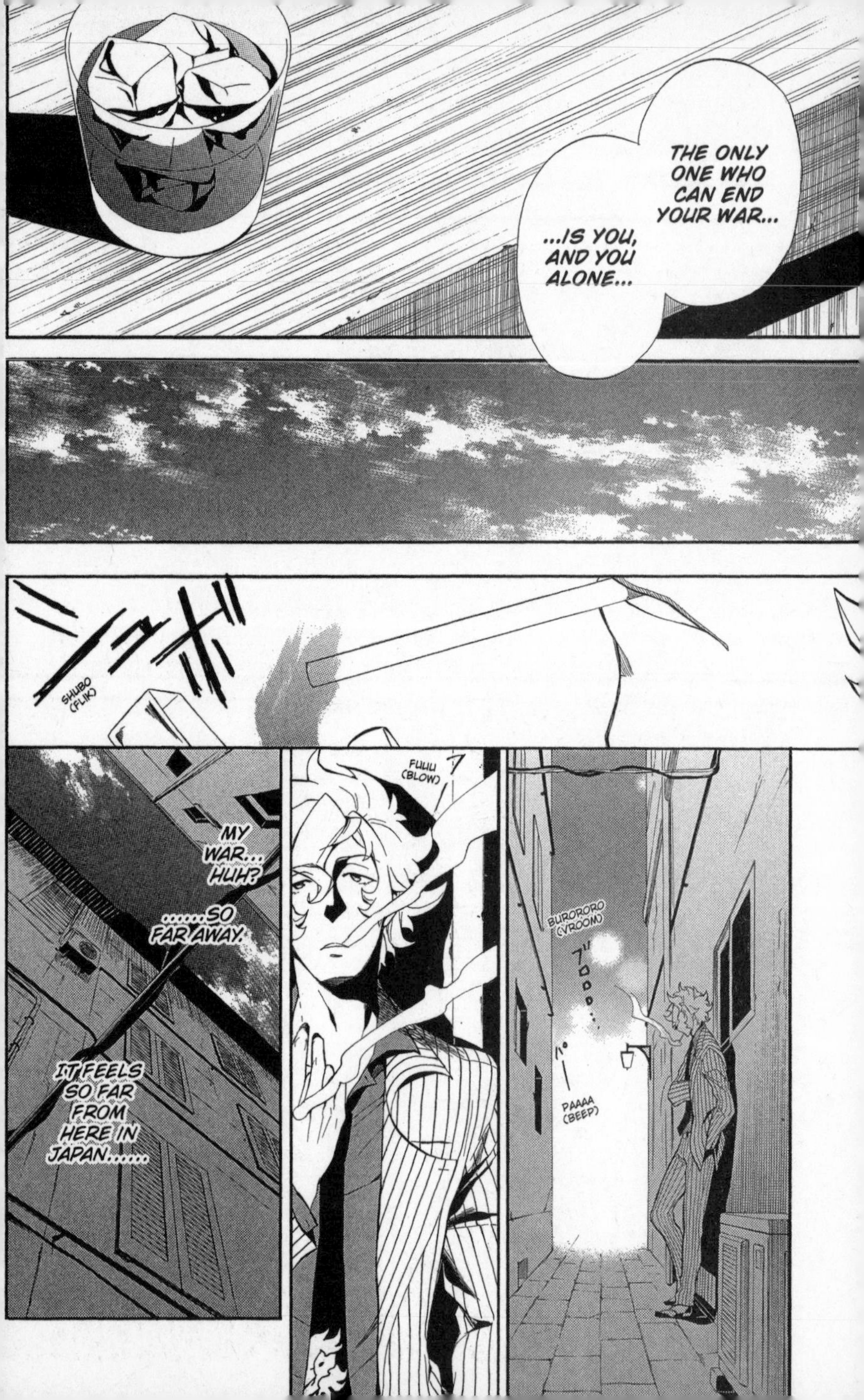
THE ONLY ONE WHO CAN END YOUR WAR...
...IS YOU, AND YOU ALONE...
シュボ
SHUBO (FLIK)
BURORORO (VROOM)
PAAAA (BEEP)
FUUU (BLOW)
MY WAR... HUH?
......SO FAR AWAY.
IT FEELS SO FAR FROM HERE IN JAPAN......

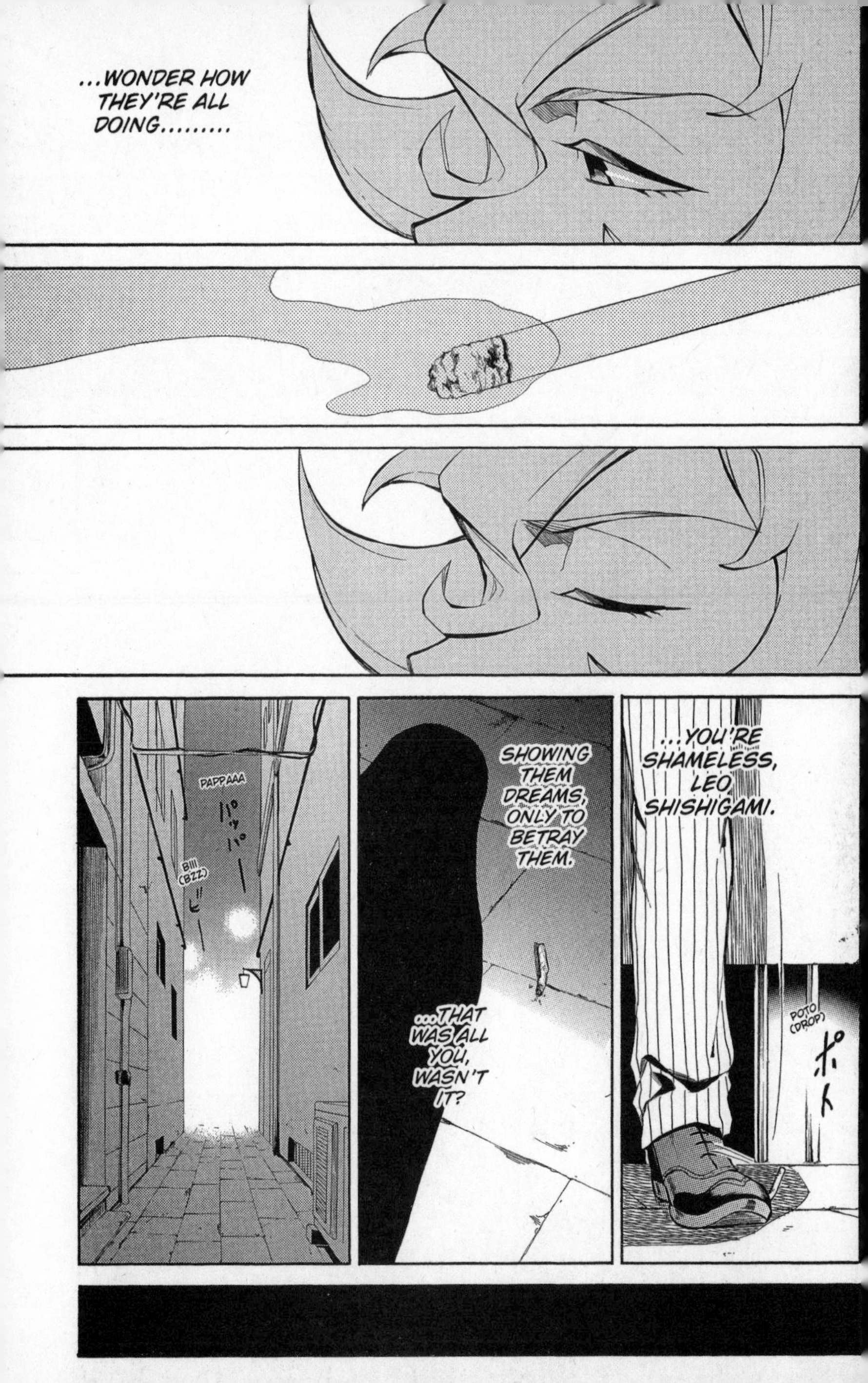
...WONDER HOW THEY'RE ALL DOING.........
...YOU'RE SHAMELESS, LEO, SHISHIGAMI.
POTO (DROP)
ポト
SHOWING THEM DREAMS, ONLY TO BETRAY THEM.
...THAT WAS ALL YOU, WASN'T IT?
PAPPAAA
パッパー
BIII (BZZ)
ビー

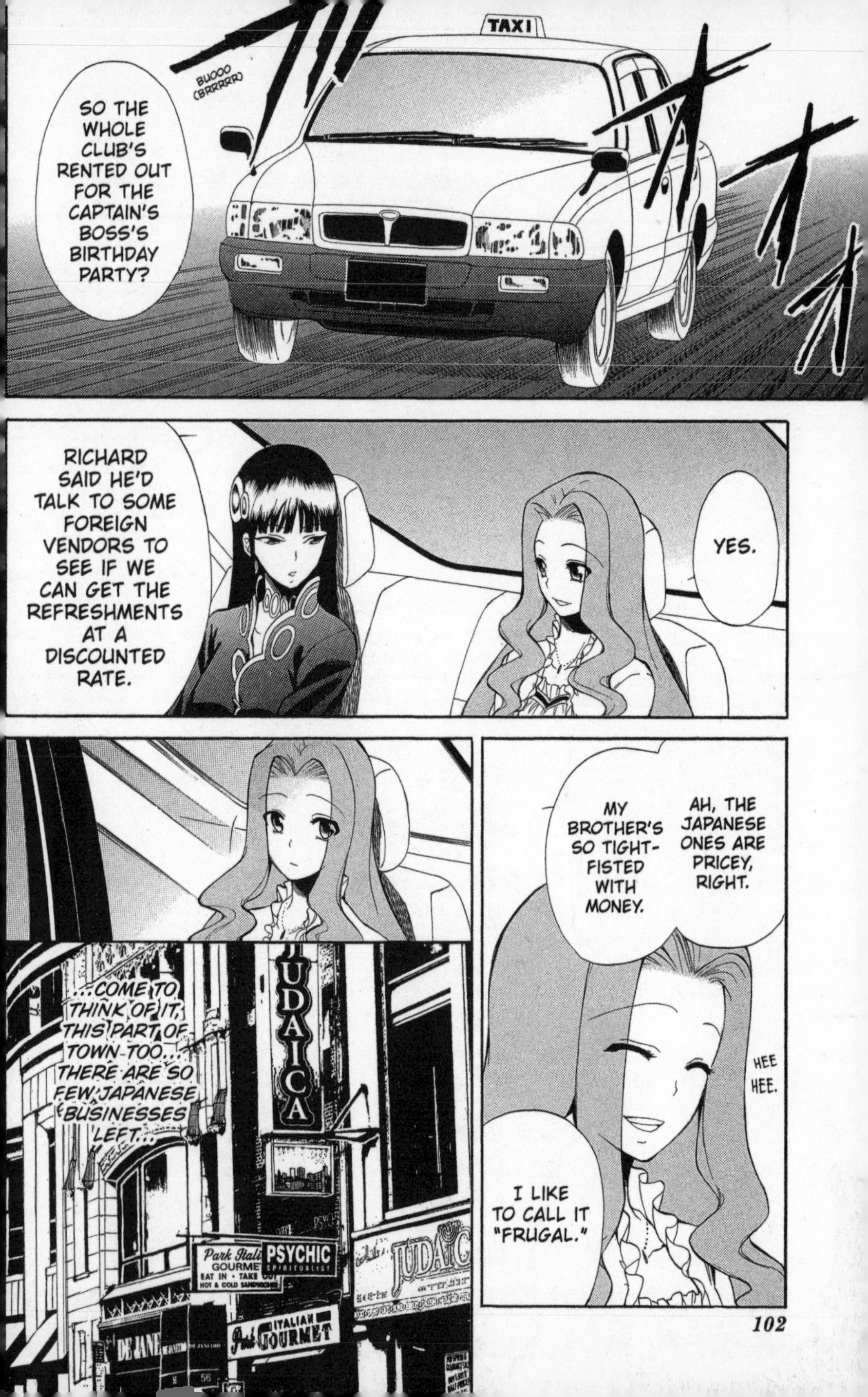
BUOOO (BRRRRR)
SO THE WHOLE CLUB'S RENTED OUT FOR THE CAPTAIN'S BOSS'S BIRTHDAY PARTY?
TAXI
RICHARD SAID HE'D TALK TO SOME FOREIGN VENDORS TO SEE IF WE CAN GET THE REFRESHMENTS AT A DISCOUNTED RATE.
YES.
AH, THE JAPANESE ONES ARE PRICEY, RIGHT.
MY BROTHER'S SO TIGHT-FISTED WITH MONEY.
HEE HEE.
I LIKE TO CALL IT "FRUGAL."
...COME TO THINK OF IT, THIS PART OF TOWN TOO... THERE ARE SO FEW JAPANESE BUSINESSES LEFT...
JUDAICA
PSYCHIC
SPIRITUALIST
ITALIAN GOURMET

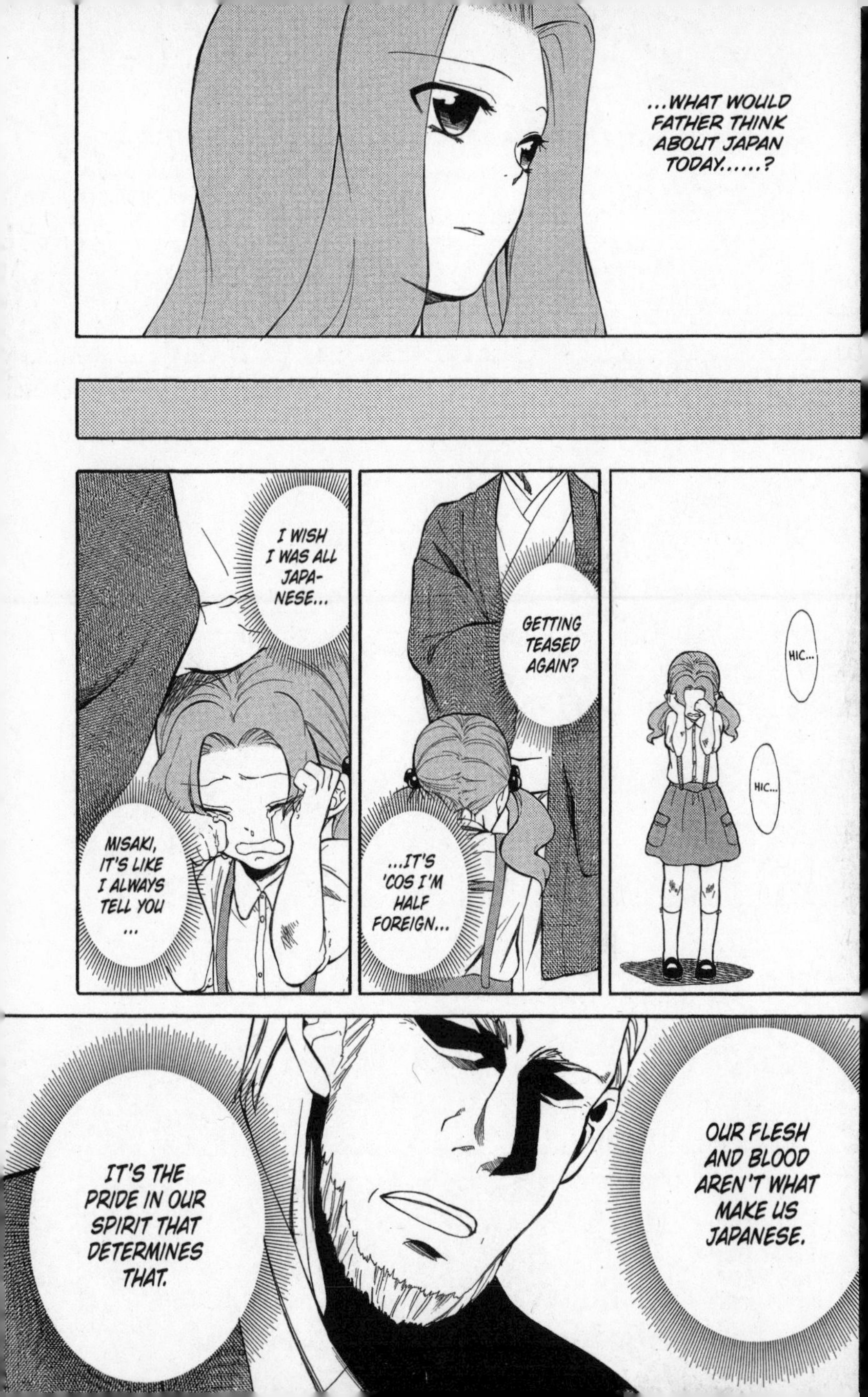
...WHAT WOULD FATHER THINK ABOUT JAPAN TODAY......?
HIC...
HIC...
GETTING TEASED AGAIN?
...IT'S 'COS I'M HALF FOREIGN...
I WISH I WAS ALL JAPA-NESE...
MISAKI, IT'S LIKE I ALWAYS TELL YOU ...
OUR FLESH AND BLOOD AREN'T WHAT MAKE US JAPANESE.
IT'S THE PRIDE IN OUR SPIRIT THAT DETERMINES THAT.

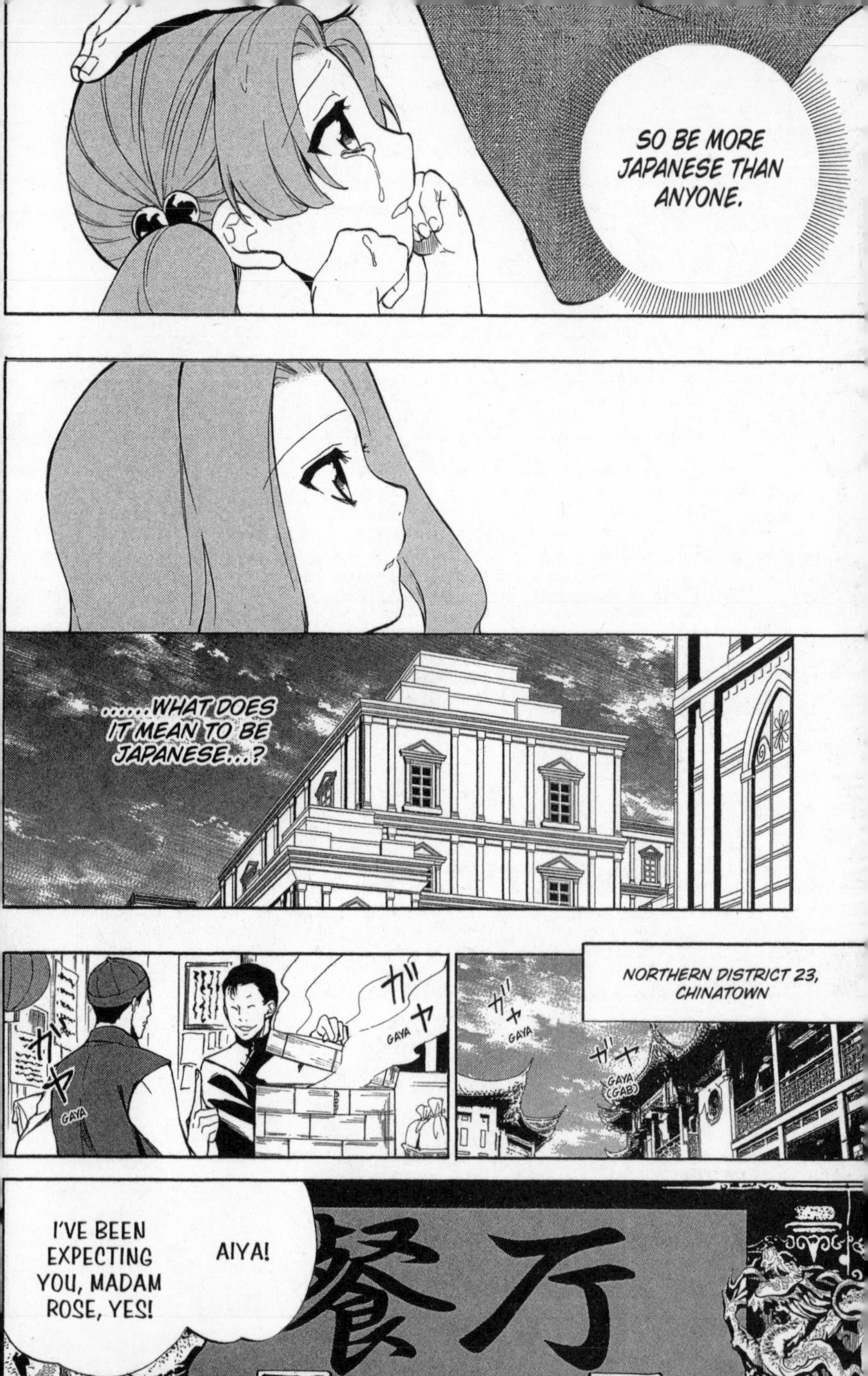
SO BE MORE JAPANESE THAN ANYONE.
......WHAT DOES IT MEAN TO BE JAPANESE...?
NORTHERN DISTRICT 23, CHINATOWN
ガヤ
GAYA
ガヤ
GAYA (GAB)
ガヤ
GAYA
ガヤ
GAYA
AIYA!
I'VE BEEN EXPECTING YOU, MADAM ROSE, YES!

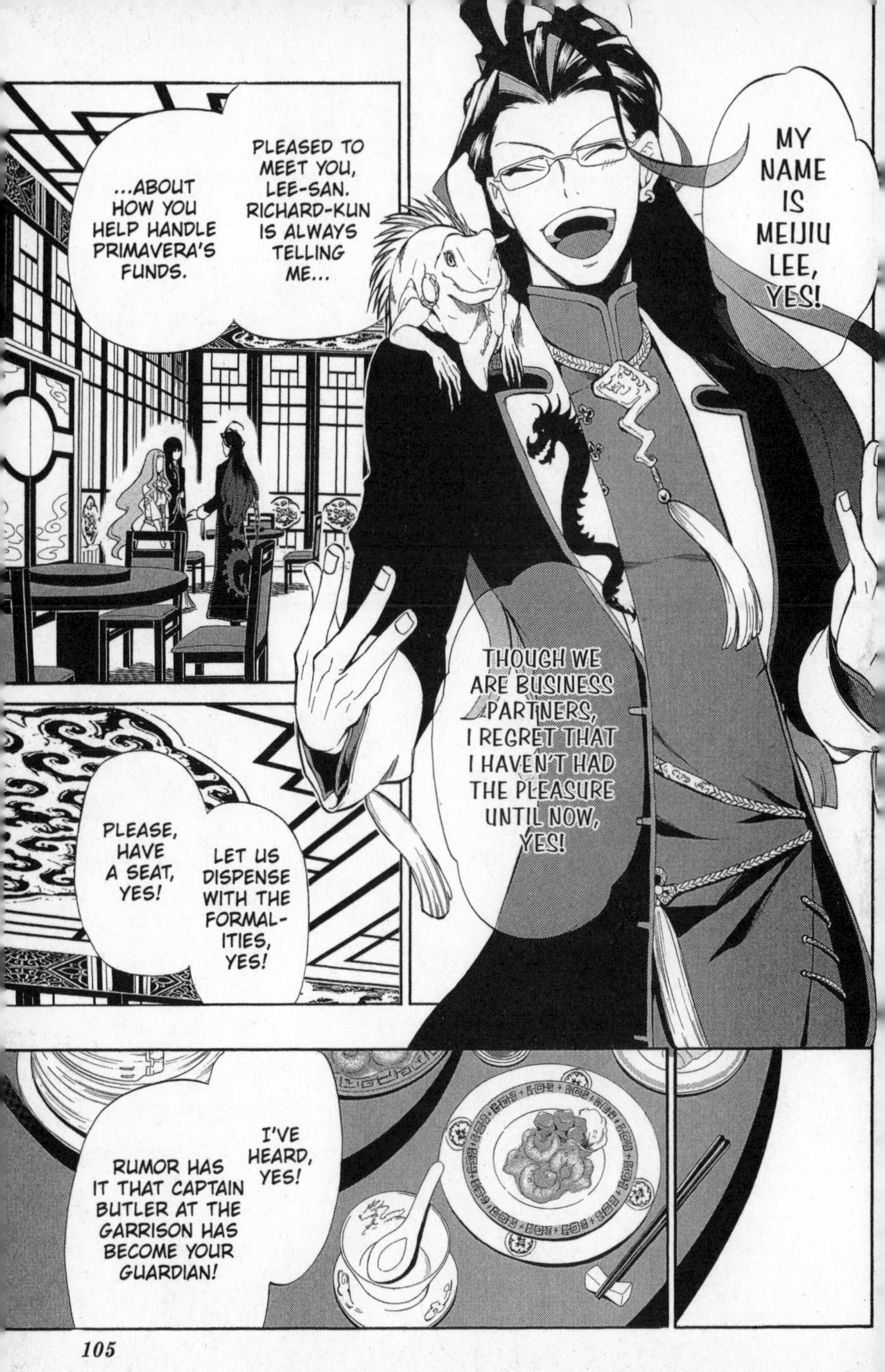
MY NAME IS MEIJIU LEE, YES!
THOUGH WE ARE BUSINESS PARTNERS, I REGRET THAT I HAVEN'T HAD THE PLEASURE UNTIL NOW, YES!
PLEASED TO MEET YOU, LEE-SAN. RICHARD-KUN IS ALWAYS TELLING ME...
...ABOUT HOW YOU HELP HANDLE PRIMAVERA'S FUNDS.
LET US DISPENSE WITH THE FORMAL-ITIES, YES!
PLEASE, HAVE A SEAT, YES!
I'VE HEARD, YES!
RUMOR HAS IT THAT CAPTAIN BUTLER AT THE GARRISON HAS BECOME YOUR GUARDIAN!

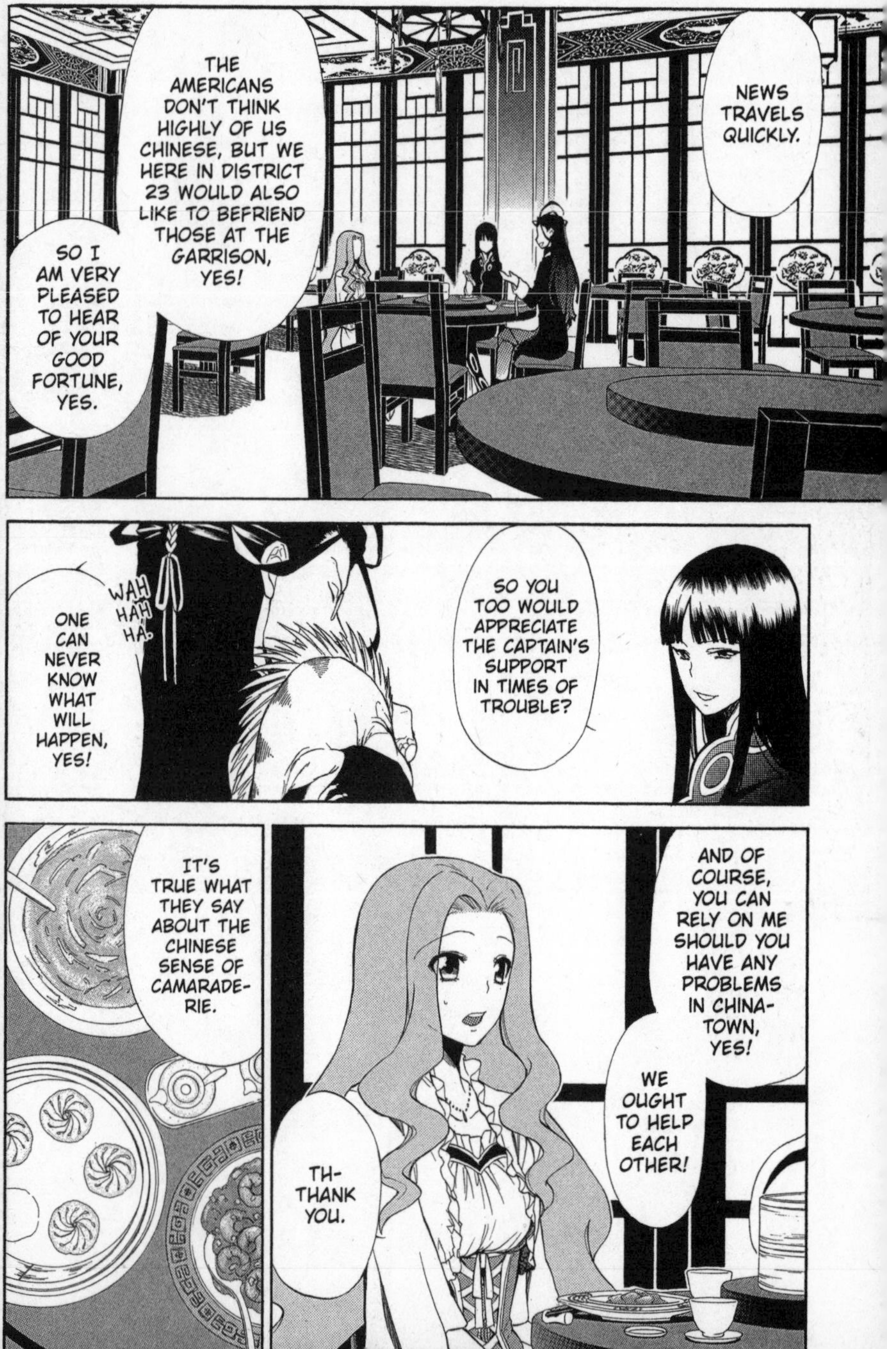
NEWS TRAVELS QUICKLY.
THE AMERICANS DON'T THINK HIGHLY OF US CHINESE, BUT WE HERE IN DISTRICT 23 WOULD ALSO LIKE TO BEFRIEND THOSE AT THE GARRISON, YES!
SO I AM VERY PLEASED TO HEAR OF YOUR GOOD FORTUNE, YES.
SO YOU TOO WOULD APPRECIATE THE CAPTAIN'S SUPPORT IN TIMES OF TROUBLE?
WAH HAH HA.
ONE CAN NEVER KNOW WHAT WILL HAPPEN, YES!
AND OF COURSE, YOU CAN RELY ON ME SHOULD YOU HAVE ANY PROBLEMS IN CHINA-TOWN, YES!
WE OUGHT TO HELP EACH OTHER!
TH-THANK YOU.
IT'S TRUE WHAT THEY SAY ABOUT THE CHINESE SENSE OF CAMARADE-RIE.

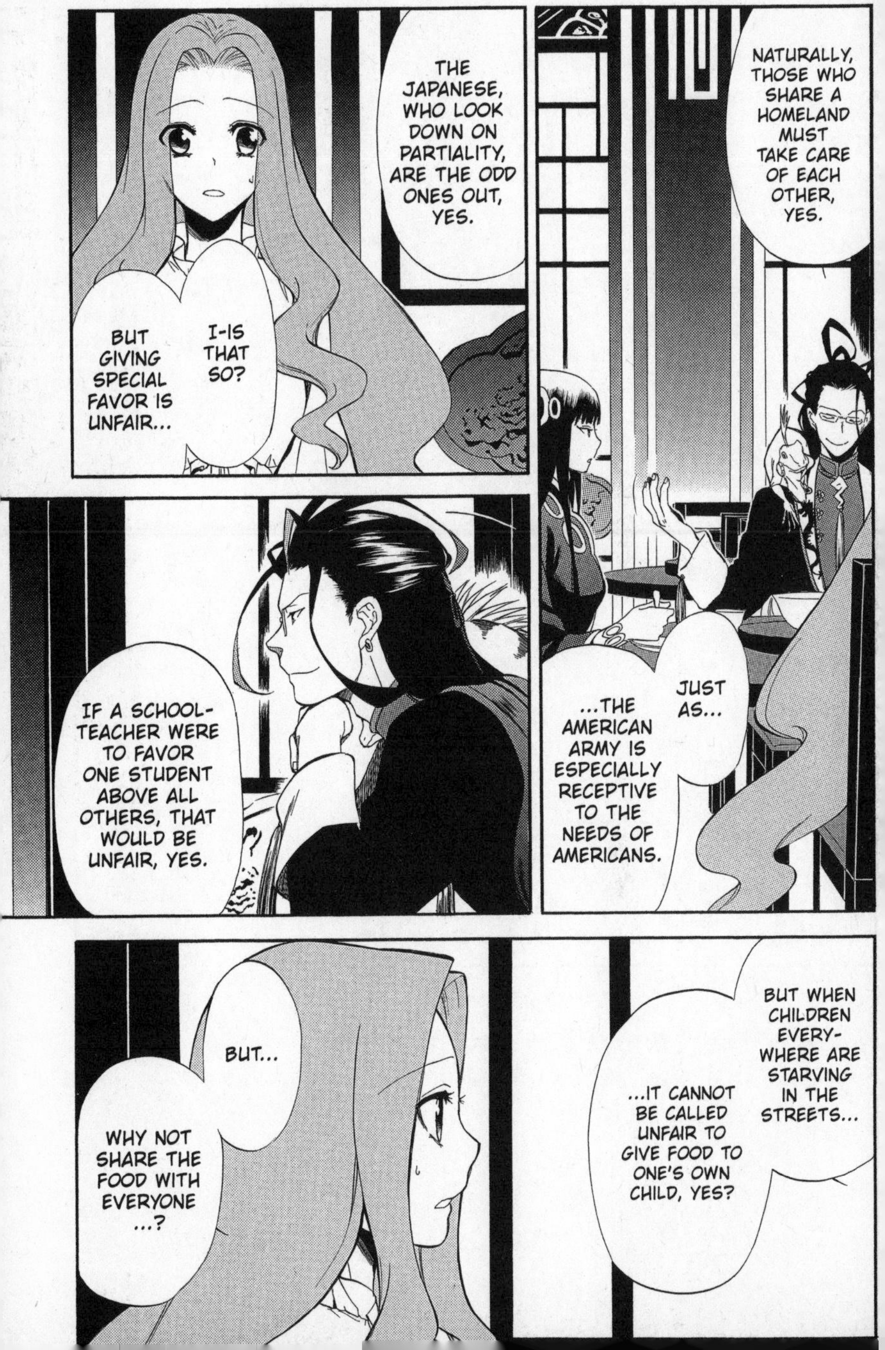
NATURALLY, THOSE WHO SHARE A HOMELAND MUST TAKE CARE OF EACH OTHER, YES.
JUST AS...
...THE AMERICAN ARMY IS ESPECIALLY RECEPTIVE TO THE NEEDS OF AMERICANS.
THE JAPANESE, WHO LOOK DOWN ON PARTIALITY, ARE THE ODD ONES OUT, YES.
I-IS THAT SO?
BUT GIVING SPECIAL FAVOR IS UNFAIR...
IF A SCHOOL-TEACHER WERE TO FAVOR ONE STUDENT ABOVE ALL OTHERS, THAT WOULD BE UNFAIR, YES.
BUT WHEN CHILDREN EVERY-WHERE ARE STARVING IN THE STREETS...
...IT CANNOT BE CALLED UNFAIR TO GIVE FOOD TO ONE'S OWN CHILD, YES?
BUT...
WHY NOT SHARE THE FOOD WITH EVERYONE ...?

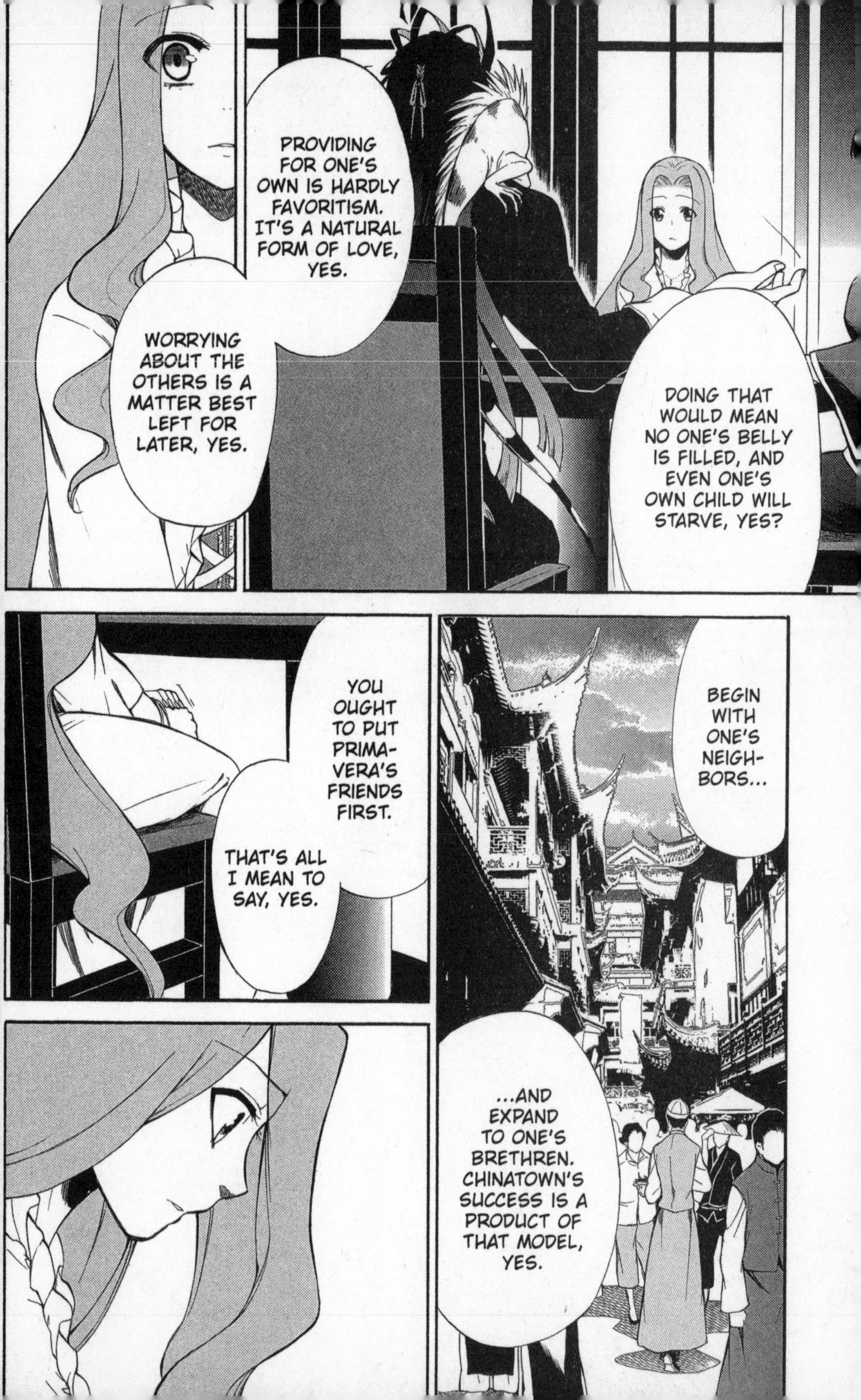
PROVIDING FOR ONE'S OWN IS HARDLY FAVORITISM. IT'S A NATURAL FORM OF LOVE, YES.
WORRYING ABOUT THE OTHERS IS A MATTER BEST LEFT FOR LATER, YES.
DOING THAT WOULD MEAN NO ONE'S BELLY IS FILLED, AND EVEN ONE'S OWN CHILD WILL STARVE, YES?
BEGIN WITH ONE'S NEIGH-BORS...
...AND EXPAND TO ONE'S BRETHREN. CHINATOWN'S SUCCESS IS A PRODUCT OF THAT MODEL, YES.
YOU OUGHT TO PUT PRIMA-VERA'S FRIENDS FIRST.
THAT'S ALL I MEAN TO SAY, YES.

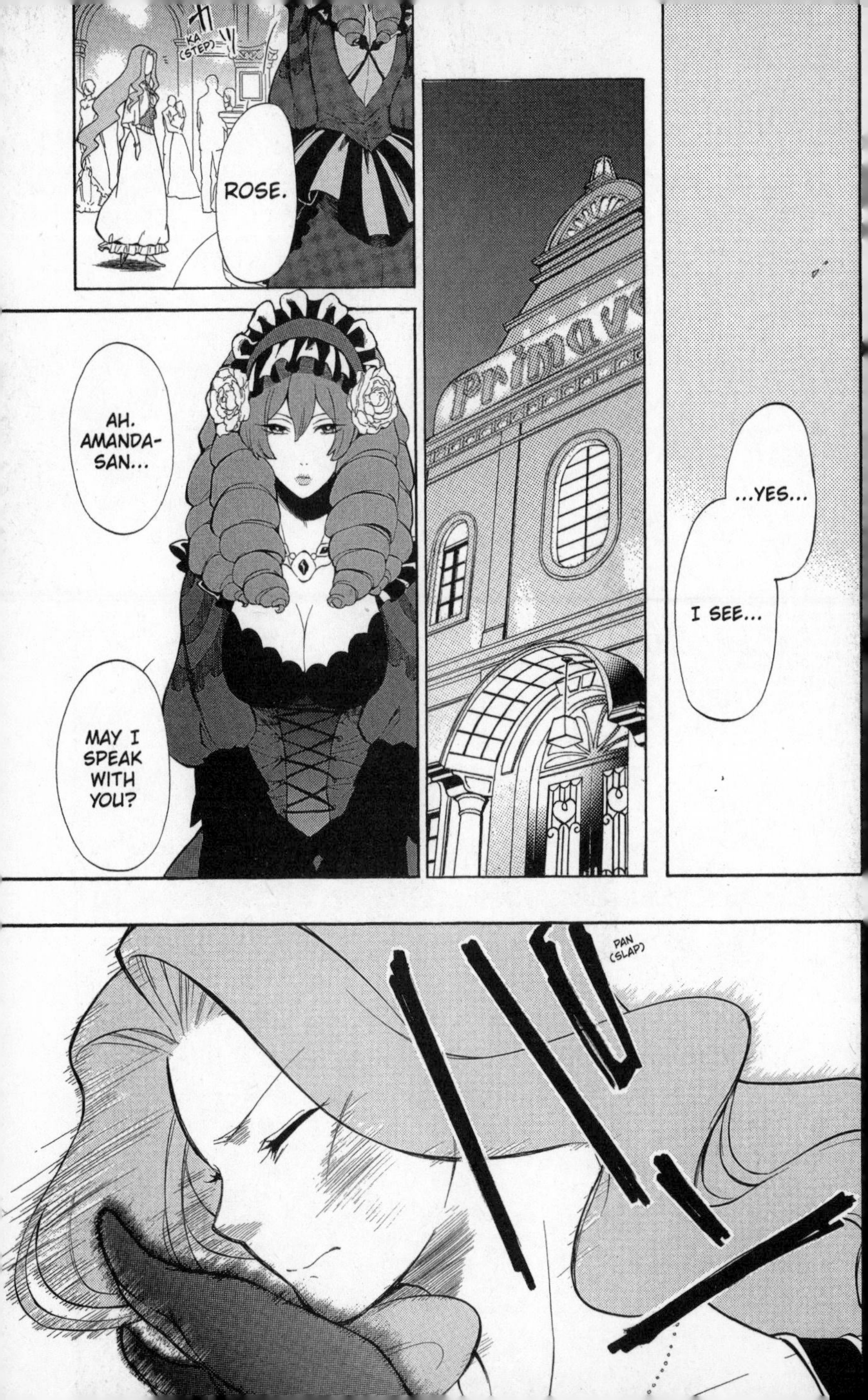
...YES...
I SEE...
KA (STEP)
ROSE.
AH. AMANDA-SAN...
MAY I SPEAK WITH YOU?
PAN (SLAP)

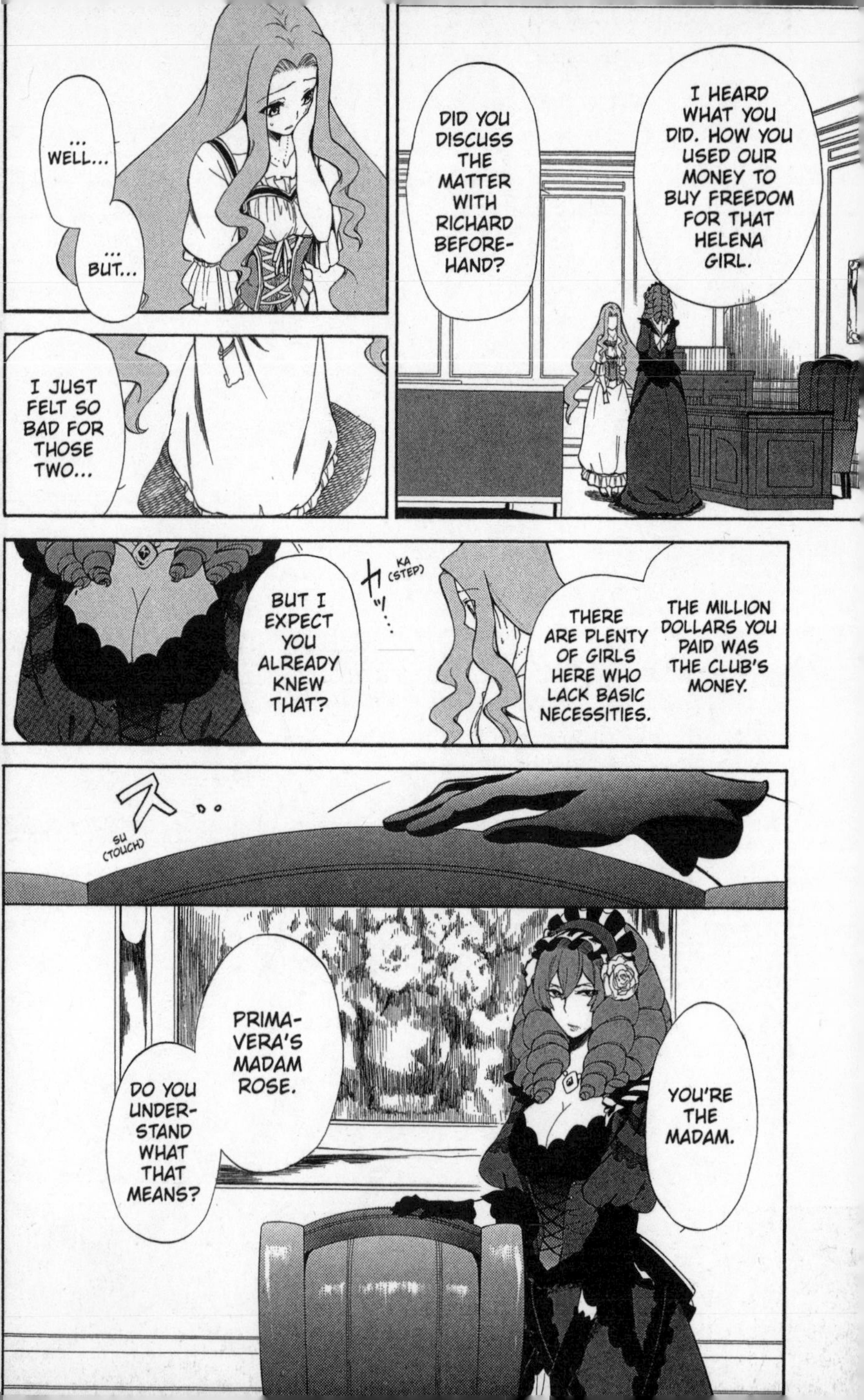
I HEARD WHAT YOU DID. HOW YOU USED OUR MONEY TO BUY FREEDOM FOR THAT HELENA GIRL.
DID YOU DISCUSS THE MATTER WITH RICHARD BEFORE-HAND?
... WELL...
... BUT...
I JUST FELT SO BAD FOR THOSE TWO...
THE MILLION DOLLARS YOU PAID WAS THE CLUB'S MONEY.
THERE ARE PLENTY OF GIRLS HERE WHO LACK BASIC NECESSITIES.
KA (STEP)
BUT I EXPECT YOU ALREADY KNEW THAT?
SU (TOUCH)
YOU'RE THE MADAM.
PRIMA-VERA'S MADAM ROSE.
DO YOU UNDER-STAND WHAT THAT MEANS?

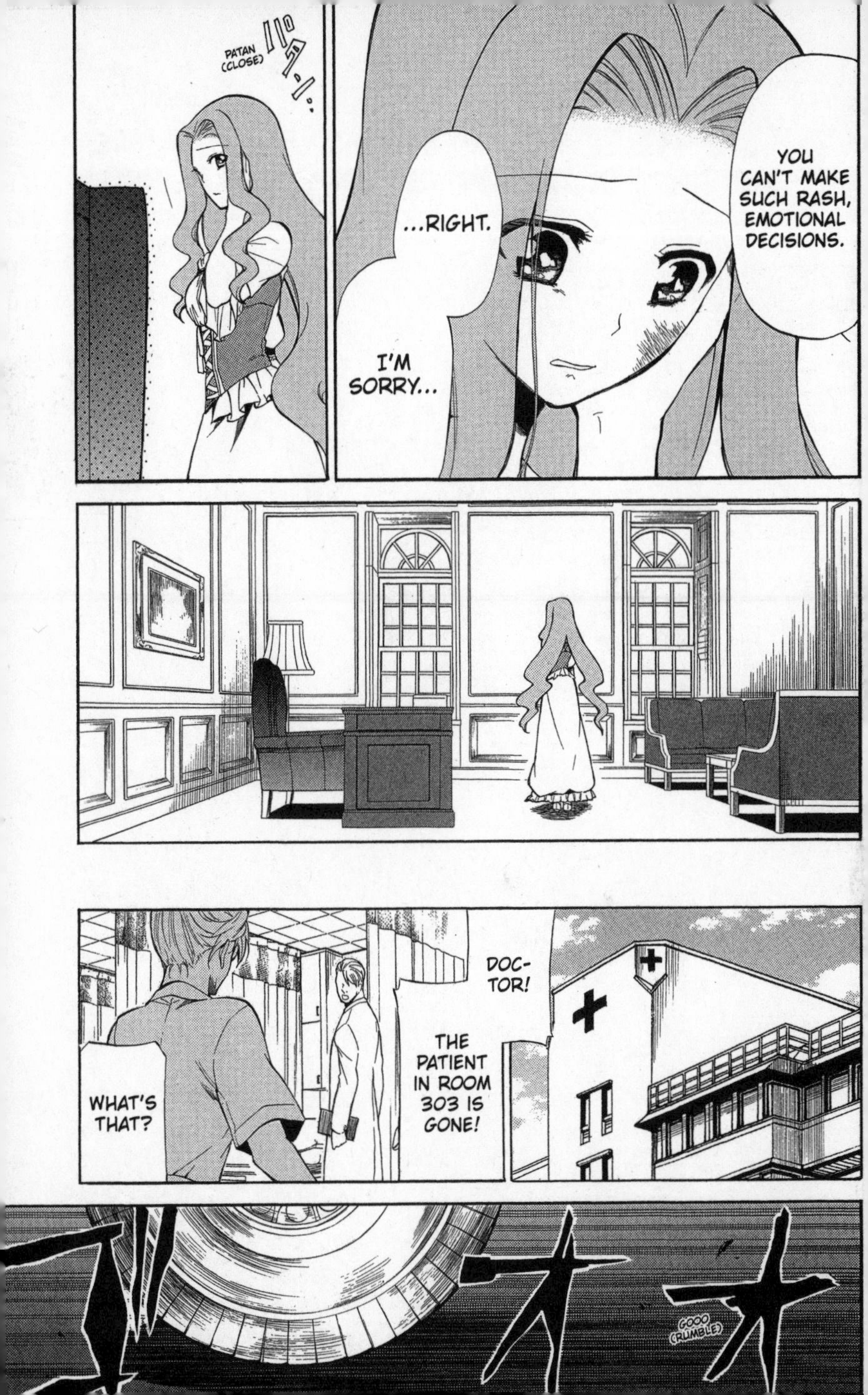
YOU CAN'T MAKE SUCH RASH, EMOTIONAL DECISIONS.
...RIGHT.
I'M SORRY...
PATAN (CLOSE)
DOC-TOR!
THE PATIENT IN ROOM 303 IS GONE!
WHAT'S THAT?
GOOO (RUMBLE)

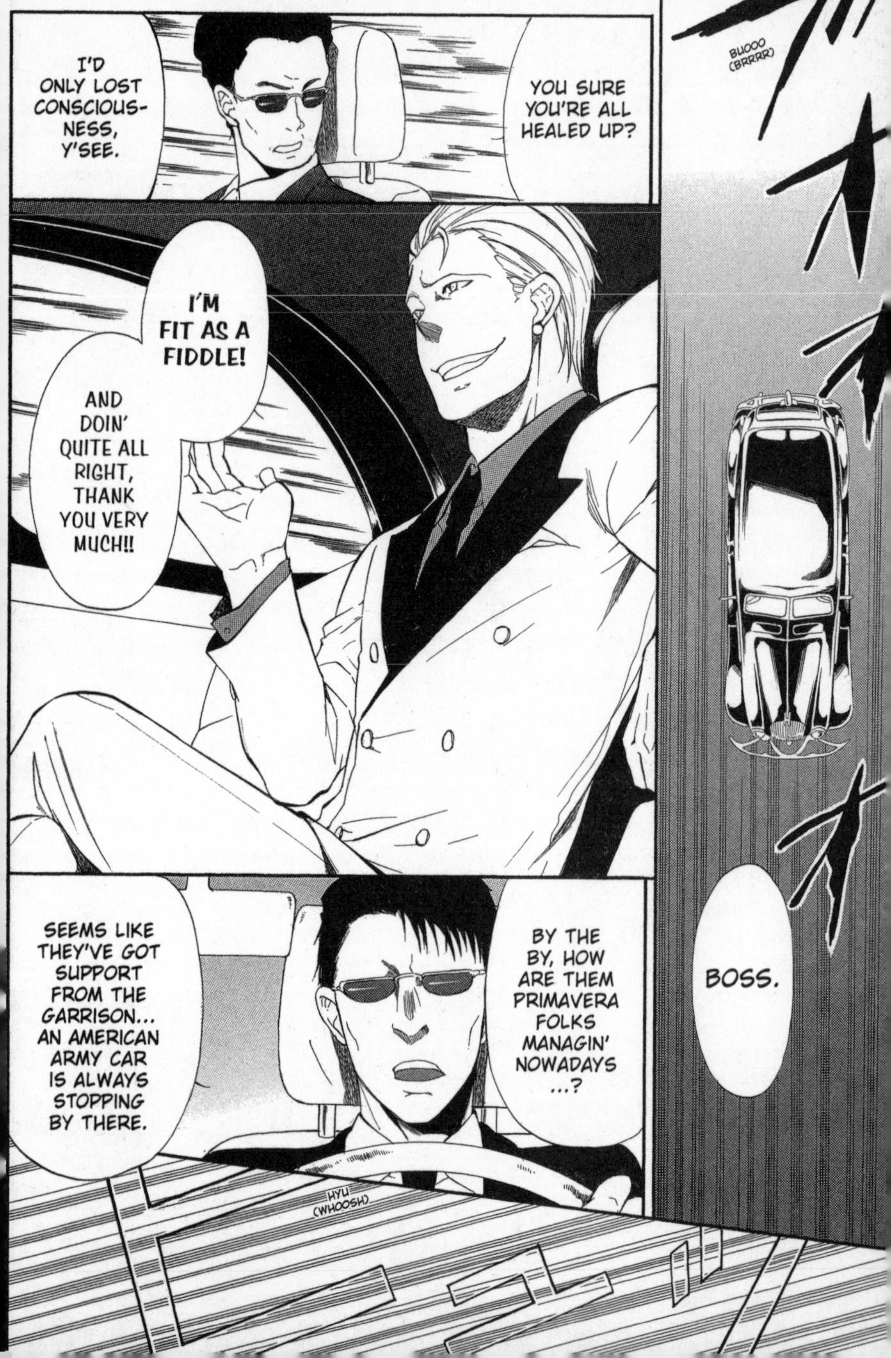
BUOOO (BRRRR)
BOSS.
YOU SURE YOU'RE ALL HEALED UP?
I'D ONLY LOST CONSCIOUS-NESS, Y'SEE.
I'M FIT AS A FIDDLE!
AND DOIN' QUITE ALL RIGHT, THANK YOU VERY MUCH!!
BY THE BY, HOW ARE THEM PRIMAVERA FOLKS MANAGIN' NOWADAYS...?
SEEMS LIKE THEY'VE GOT SUPPORT FROM THE GARRISON... AN AMERICAN ARMY CAR IS ALWAYS STOPPING BY THERE.
HYU (WHOOSH)

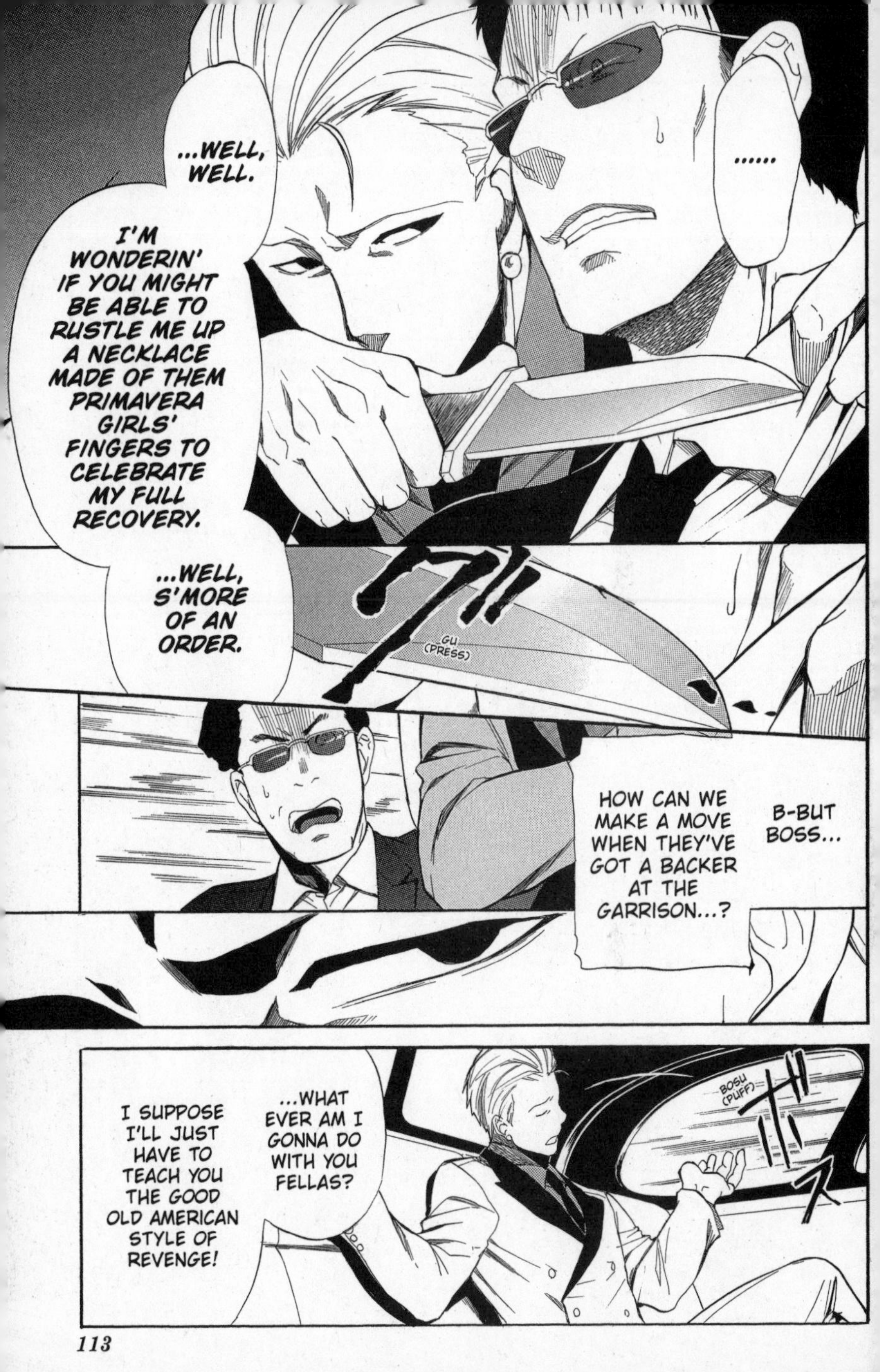
......
...WELL, WELL.
I'M WONDERIN' IF YOU MIGHT BE ABLE TO RUSTLE ME UP A NECKLACE MADE OF THEM PRIMAVERA GIRLS' FINGERS TO CELEBRATE MY FULL RECOVERY.
GU (PRESS)
...WELL, S'MORE OF AN ORDER.
B-BUT BOSS...
HOW CAN WE MAKE A MOVE WHEN THEY'VE GOT A BACKER AT THE GARRISON...?
BOSU (PUFF)
...WHAT EVER AM I GONNA DO WITH YOU FELLAS?
I SUPPOSE I'LL JUST HAVE TO TEACH YOU THE GOOD OLD AMERICAN STYLE OF REVENGE!

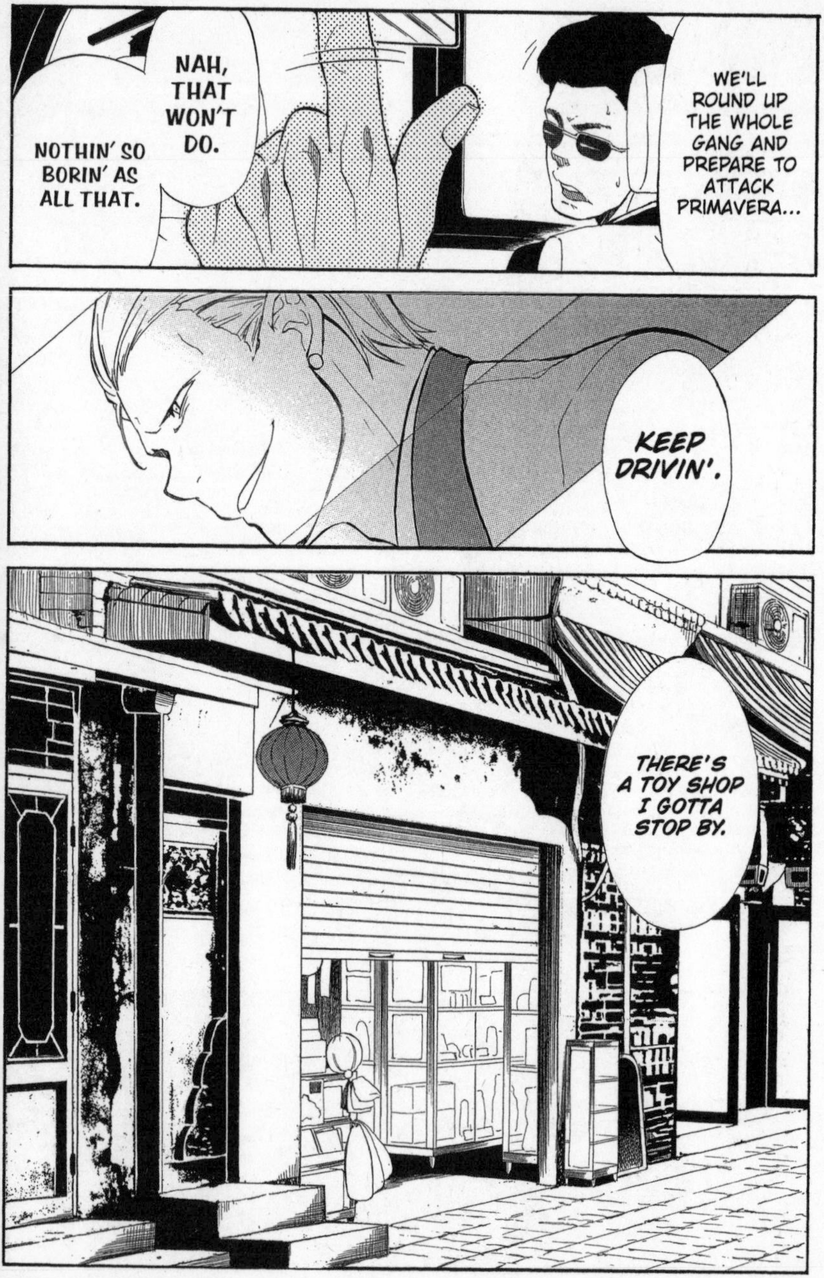
WE'LL ROUND UP THE WHOLE GANG AND PREPARE TO ATTACK PRIMAVERA...
NAH, THAT WON'T DO.
NOTHIN' SO BORIN' AS ALL THAT.
KEEP DRIVIN'.
THERE'S A TOY SHOP I GOTTA STOP BY.

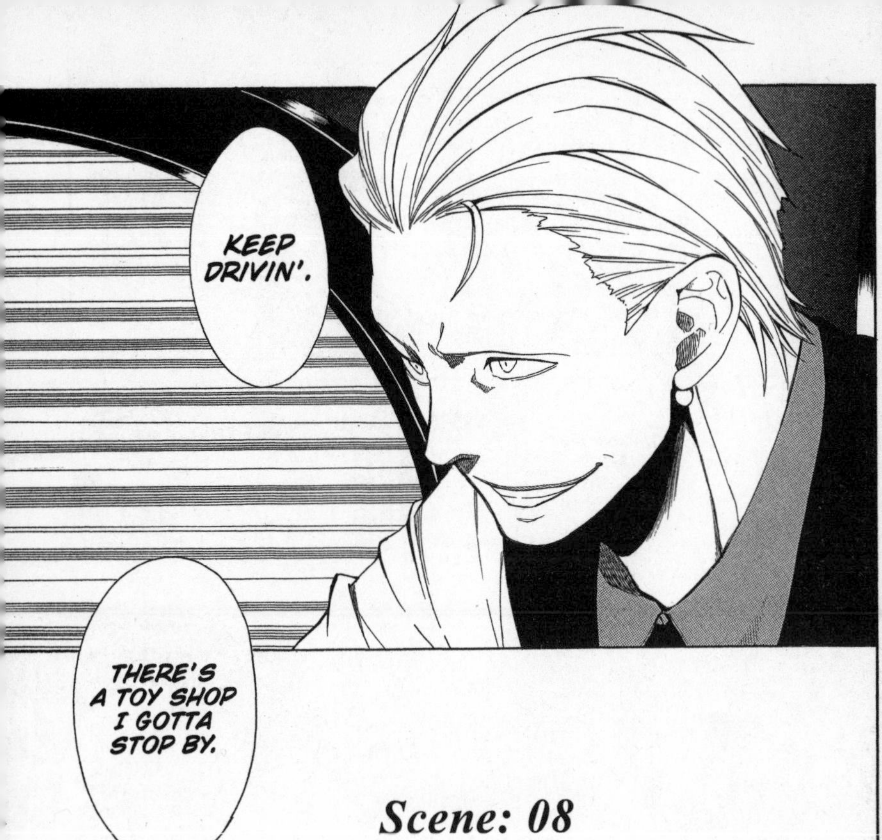
KEEP DRIVIN'.
THERE'S A TOY SHOP I GOTTA STOP BY.

Scene: 08

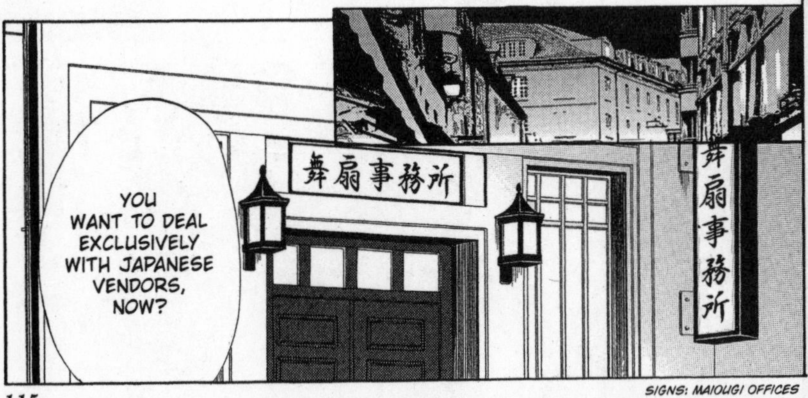
YOU WANT TO DEAL EXCLUSIVELY WITH JAPANESE VENDORS, NOW?
舞扇事務所
舞扇事務所

SIGNS: MAIOUGI OFFICES

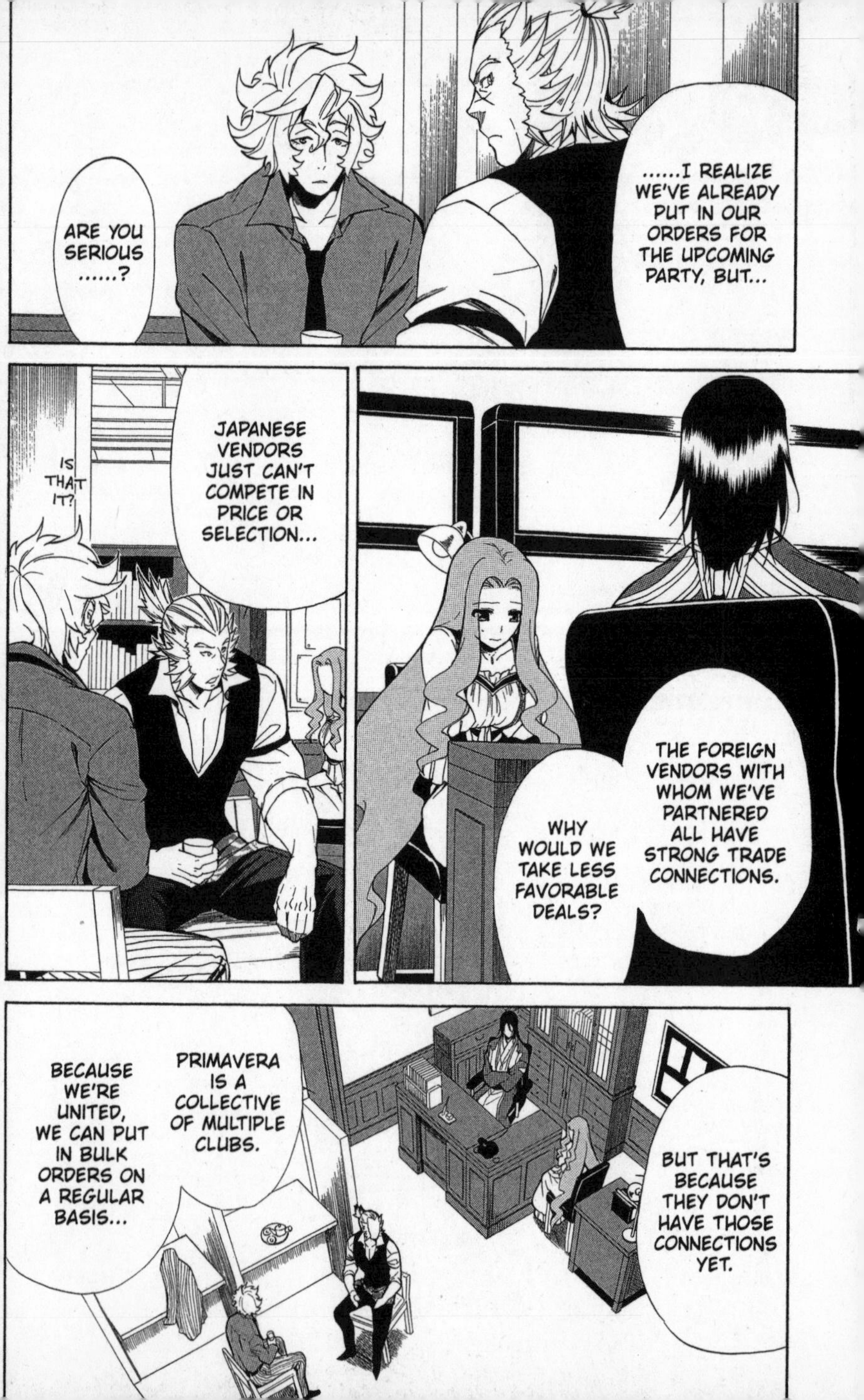
......I REALIZE WE'VE ALREADY PUT IN OUR ORDERS FOR THE UPCOMING PARTY, BUT...
ARE YOU SERIOUS ......?
THE FOREIGN VENDORS WITH WHOM WE'VE PARTNERED ALL HAVE STRONG TRADE CONNECTIONS.
WHY WOULD WE TAKE LESS FAVORABLE DEALS?
JAPANESE VENDORS JUST CAN'T COMPETE IN PRICE OR SELECTION...
IS THAT IT?
BUT THAT'S BECAUSE THEY DON'T HAVE THOSE CONNECTIONS YET.
PRIMAVERA IS A COLLECTIVE OF MULTIPLE CLUBS.
BECAUSE WE'RE UNITED, WE CAN PUT IN BULK ORDERS ON A REGULAR BASIS...

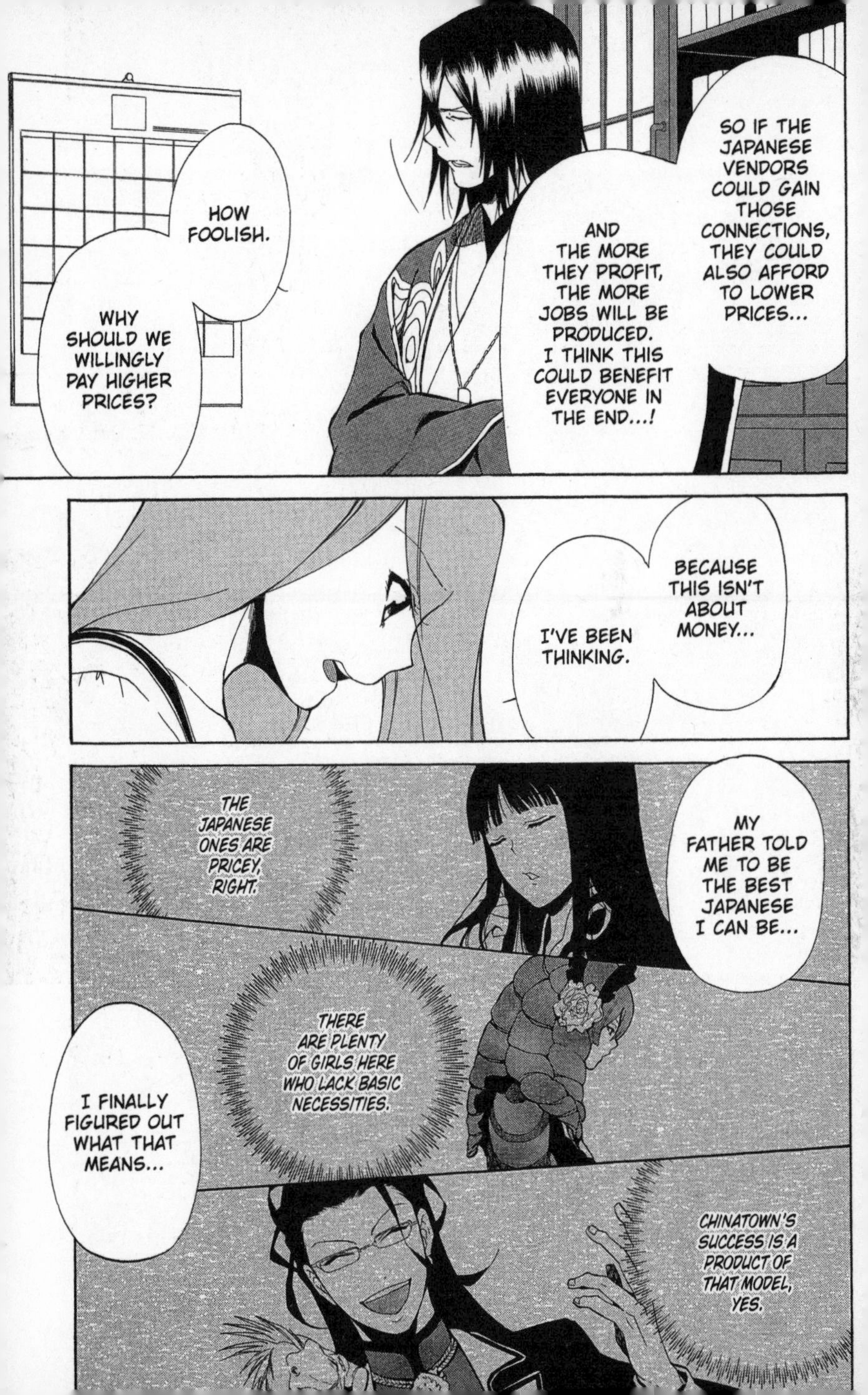
SO IF THE JAPANESE VENDORS COULD GAIN THOSE CONNECTIONS, THEY COULD ALSO AFFORD TO LOWER PRICES...
AND THE MORE THEY PROFIT, THE MORE JOBS WILL BE PRODUCED. I THINK THIS COULD BENEFIT EVERYONE IN THE END...!
HOW FOOLISH.
WHY SHOULD WE WILLINGLY PAY HIGHER PRICES?
BECAUSE THIS ISN'T ABOUT MONEY...
I'VE BEEN THINKING.
MY FATHER TOLD ME TO BE THE BEST JAPANESE I CAN BE...
THE JAPANESE ONES ARE PRICEY, RIGHT.
THERE ARE PLENTY OF GIRLS HERE WHO LACK BASIC NECESSITIES.
CHINATOWN'S SUCCESS IS A PRODUCT OF THAT MODEL, YES.
I FINALLY FIGURED OUT WHAT THAT MEANS...

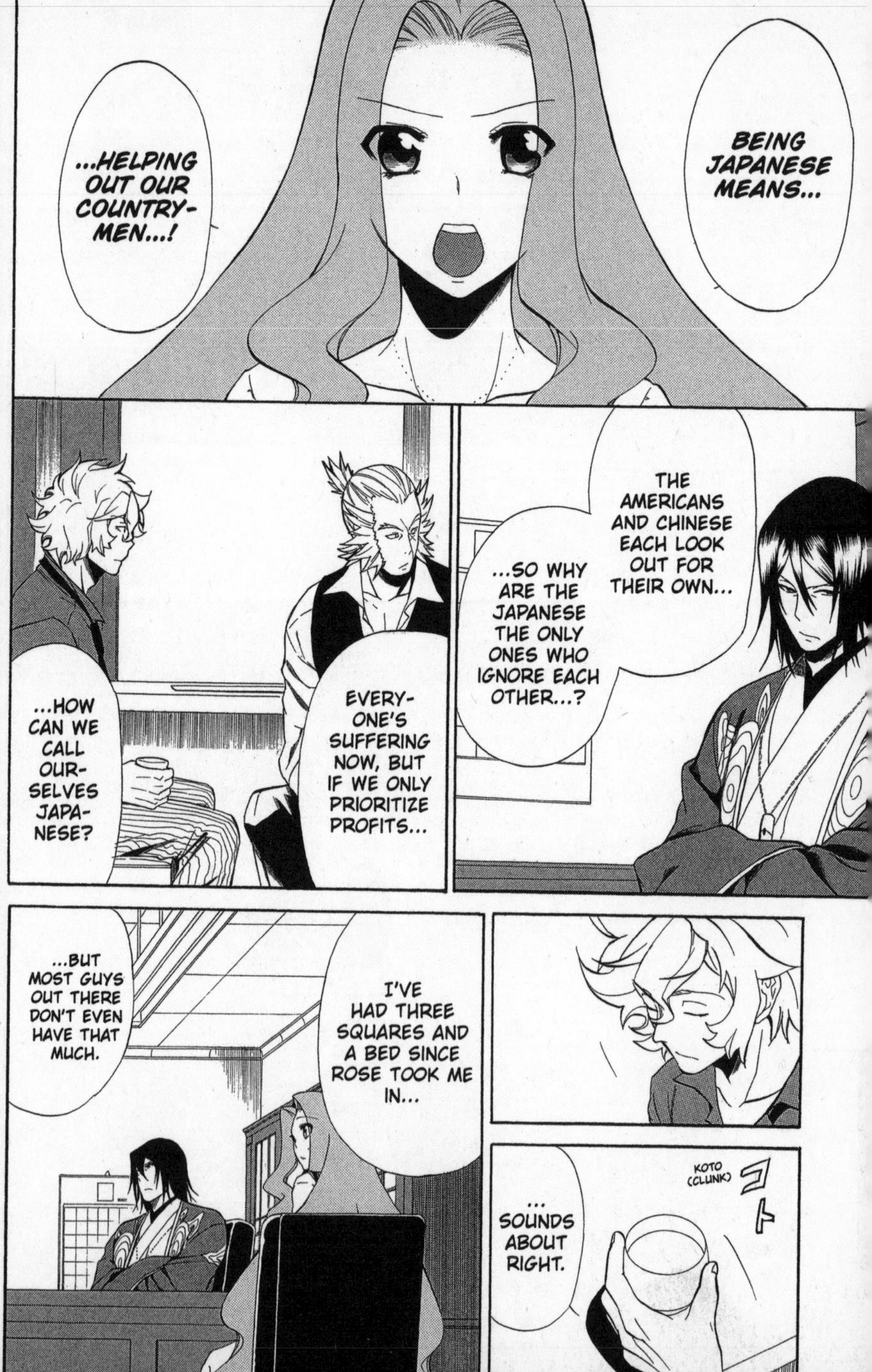
BEING JAPANESE MEANS...
...HELPING OUT OUR COUNTRY-MEN...!
THE AMERICANS AND CHINESE EACH LOOK OUT FOR THEIR OWN...
...SO WHY ARE THE JAPANESE THE ONLY ONES WHO IGNORE EACH OTHER...?
EVERY-ONE'S SUFFERING NOW, BUT IF WE ONLY PRIORITIZE PROFITS...
...HOW CAN WE CALL OUR-SELVES JAPA-NESE?
KOTO (CLUNK)
...SOUNDS ABOUT RIGHT.
I'VE HAD THREE SQUARES AND A BED SINCE ROSE TOOK ME IN...
...BUT MOST GUYS OUT THERE DON'T EVEN HAVE THAT MUCH.

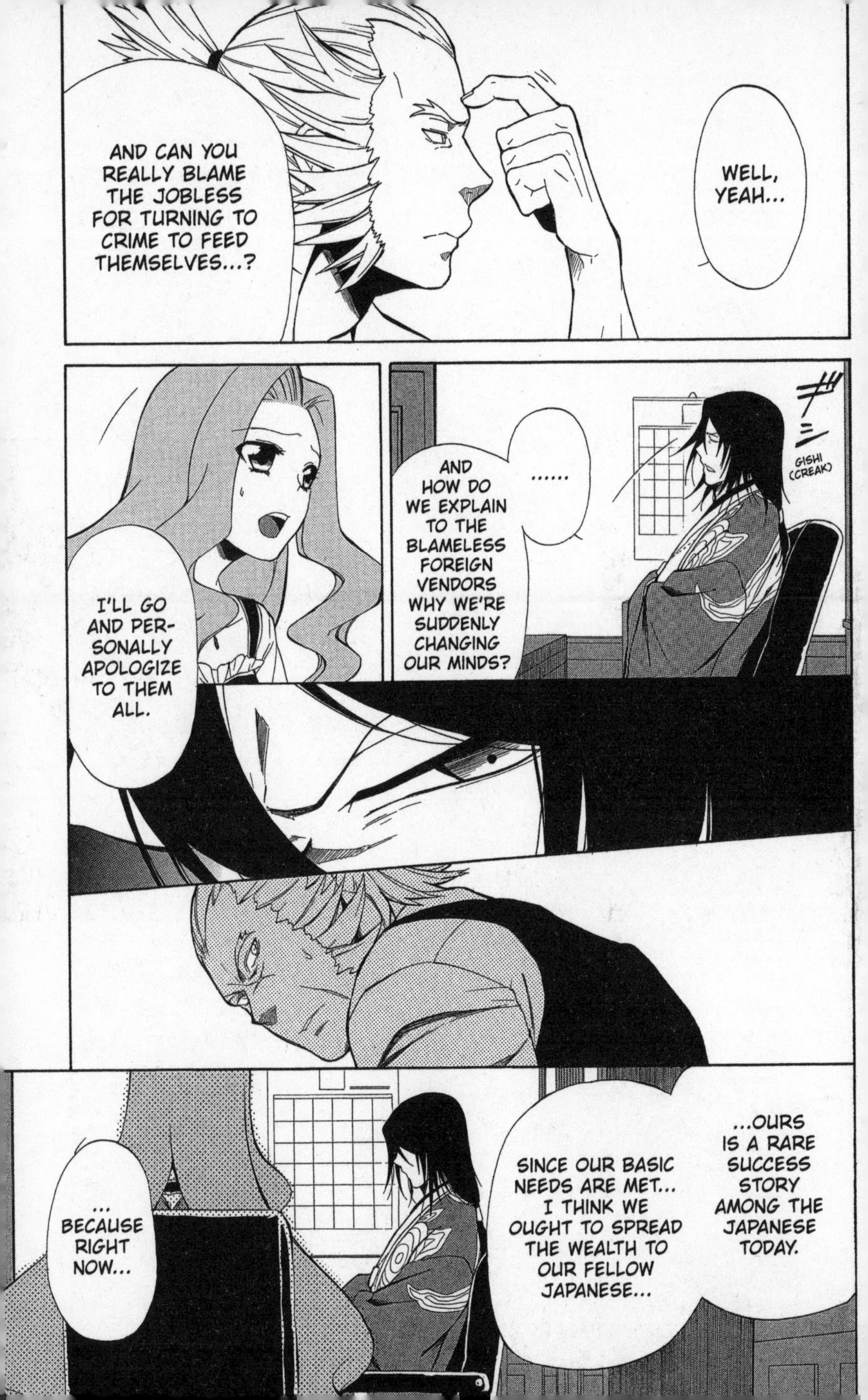
WELL, YEAH...
AND CAN YOU REALLY BLAME THE JOBLESS FOR TURNING TO CRIME TO FEED THEMSELVES...?
GISHI (CREAK)
......
AND HOW DO WE EXPLAIN TO THE BLAMELESS FOREIGN VENDORS WHY WE'RE SUDDENLY CHANGING OUR MINDS?
I'LL GO AND PER-SONALLY APOLOGIZE TO THEM ALL.
...OURS IS A RARE SUCCESS STORY AMONG THE JAPANESE TODAY.
SINCE OUR BASIC NEEDS ARE MET... I THINK WE OUGHT TO SPREAD THE WEALTH TO OUR FELLOW JAPANESE...
... BECAUSE RIGHT NOW...

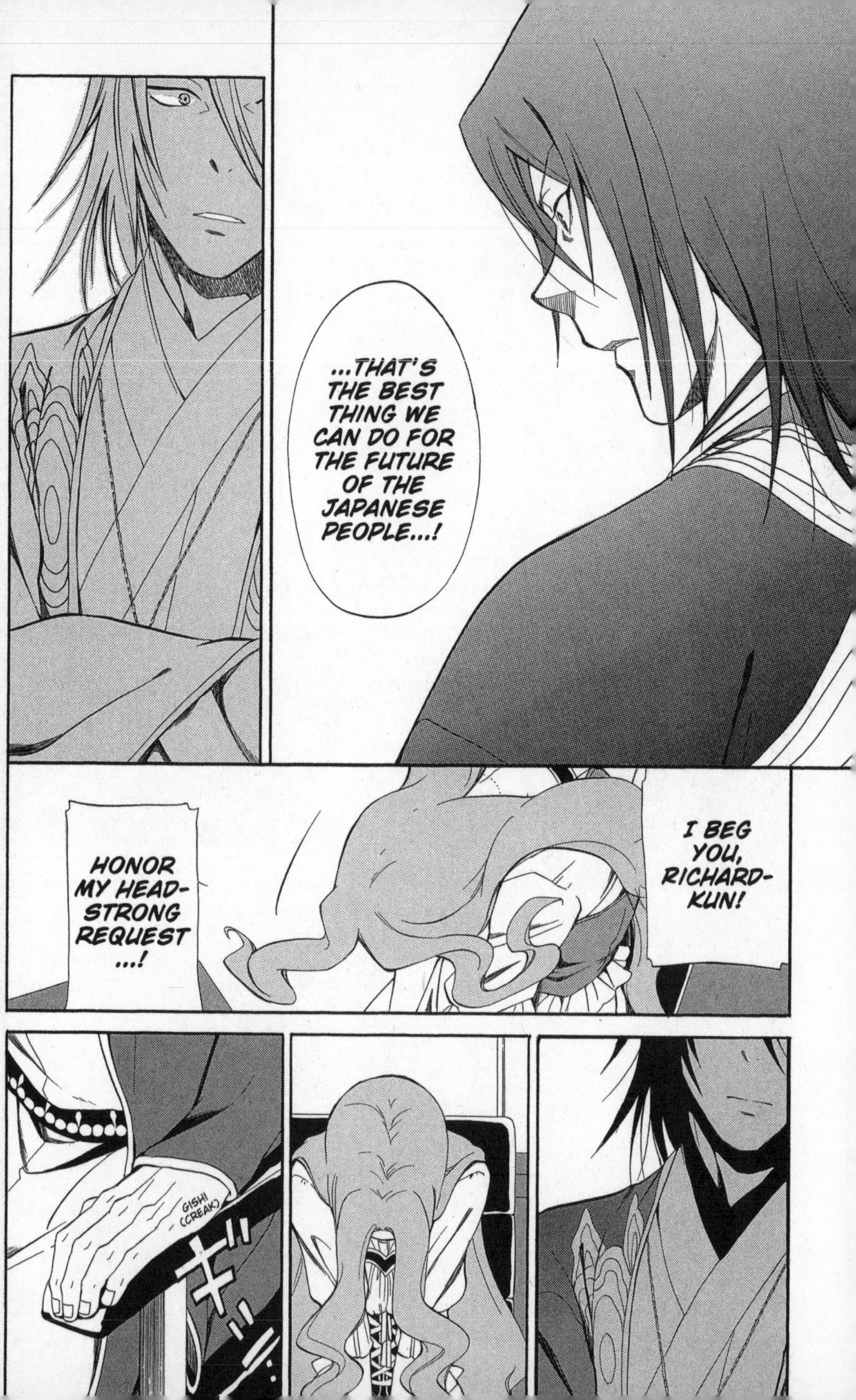
...THAT'S THE BEST THING WE CAN DO FOR THE FUTURE OF THE JAPANESE PEOPLE...!
I BEG YOU, RICHARD-KUN!
HONOR MY HEAD-STRONG REQUEST ...!
GISHI (CREAK)

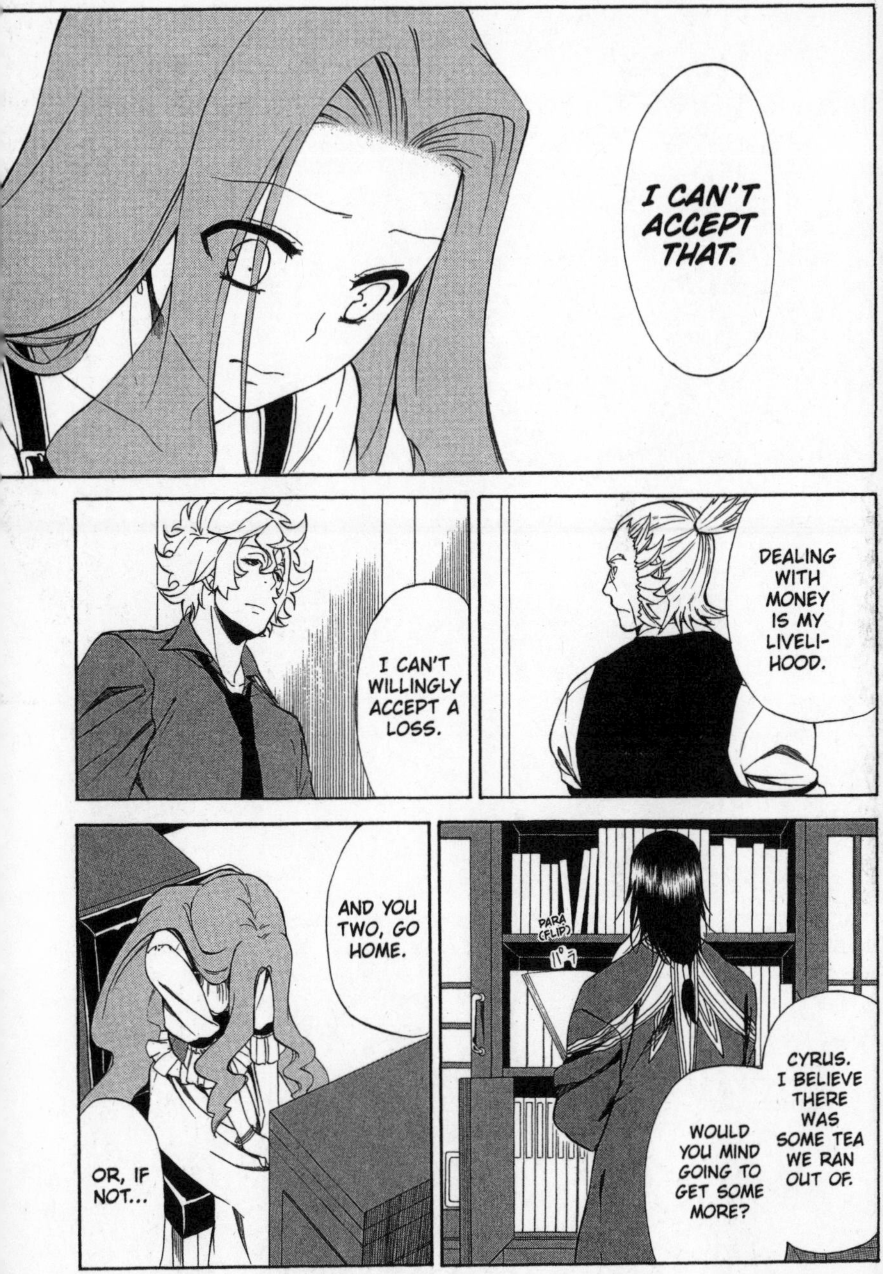
I CAN'T ACCEPT THAT.
DEALING WITH MONEY IS MY LIVELIHOOD.
I CAN'T WILLINGLY ACCEPT A LOSS.
PARA (FLIP)
パラ
CYRUS. I BELIEVE THERE WAS SOME TEA WE RAN OUT OF.
WOULD YOU MIND GOING TO GET SOME MORE?
AND YOU TWO, GO HOME.
OR, IF NOT...

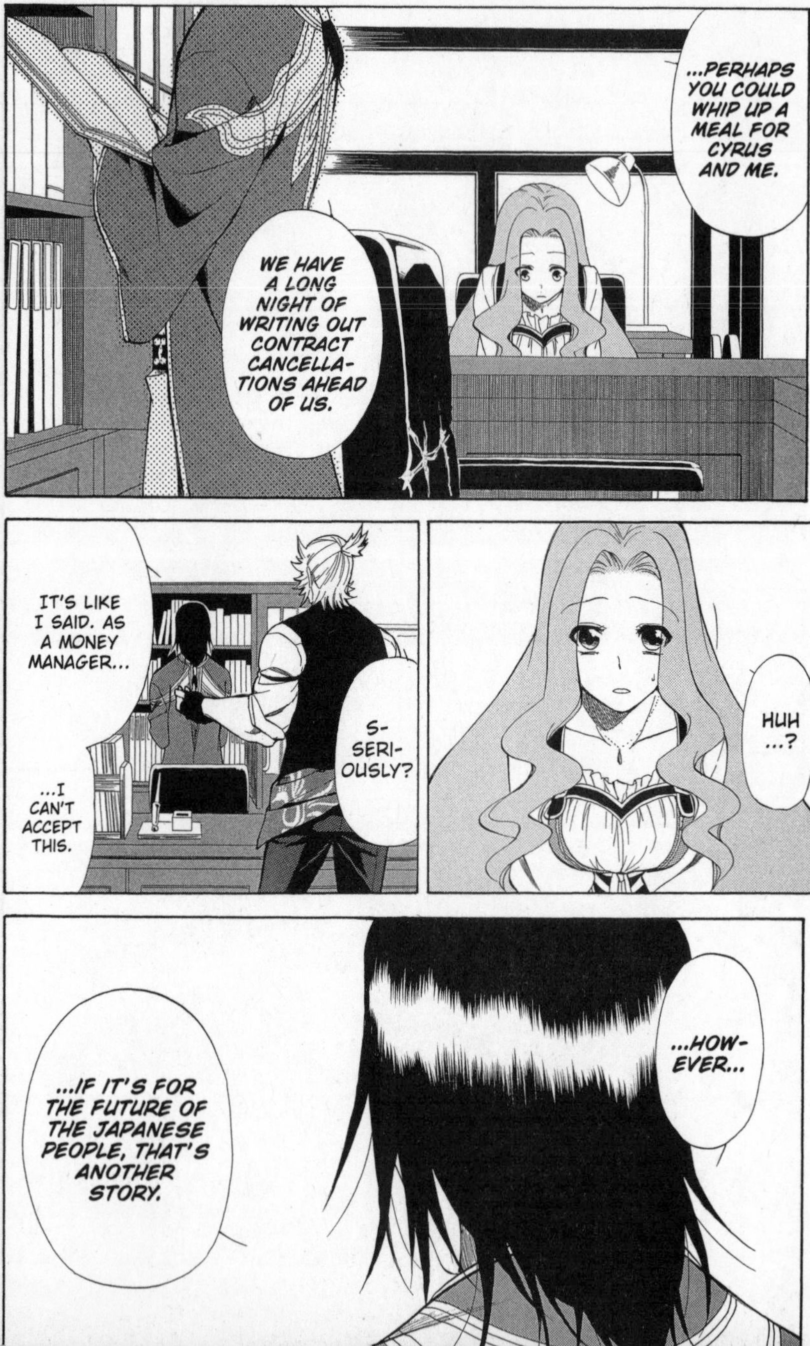
...PERHAPS YOU COULD WHIP UP A MEAL FOR CYRUS AND ME.
WE HAVE A LONG NIGHT OF WRITING OUT CONTRACT CANCELLA-TIONS AHEAD OF US.
HUH ...?
S-SERI-OUSLY?
IT'S LIKE I SAID. AS A MONEY MANAGER...
...I CAN'T ACCEPT THIS.
...HOW-EVER...
...IF IT'S FOR THE FUTURE OF THE JAPANESE PEOPLE, THAT'S ANOTHER STORY.

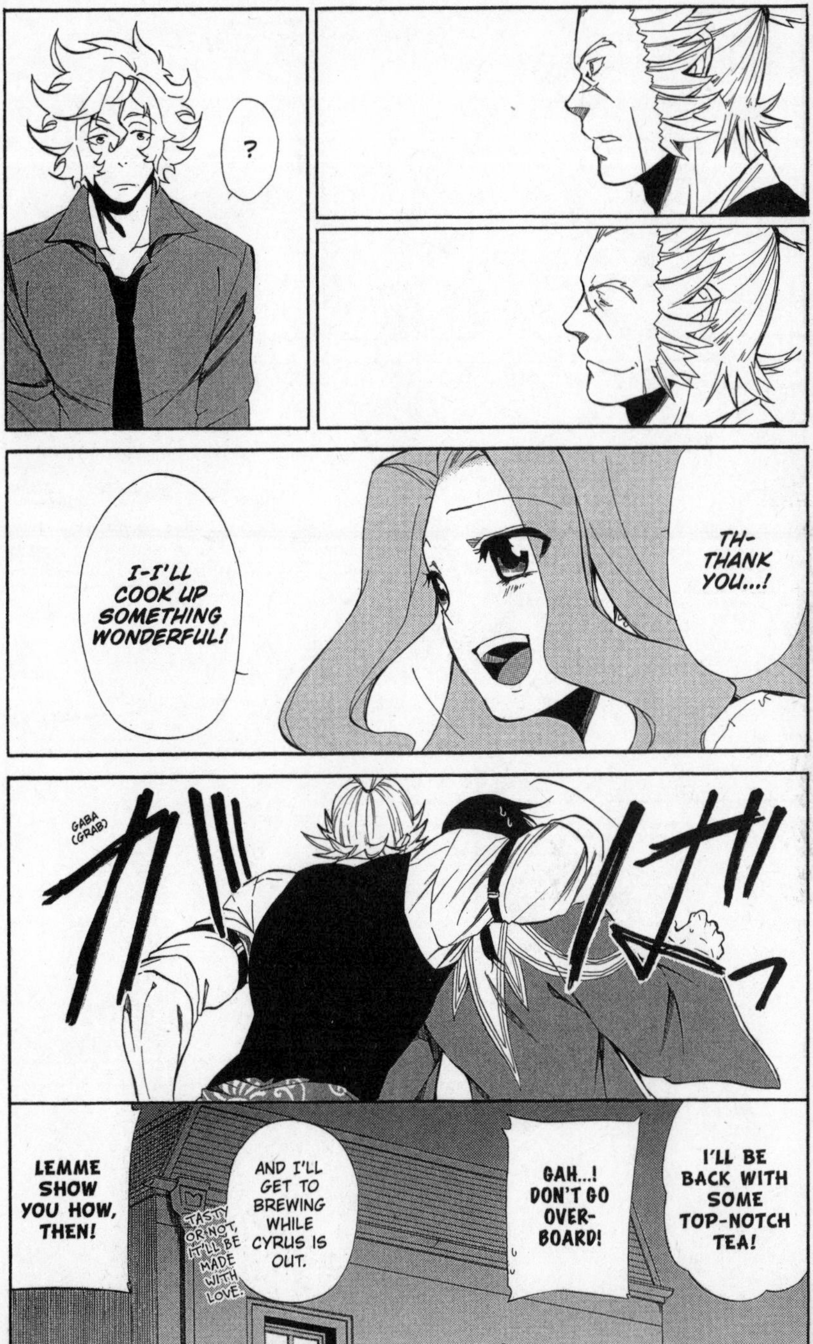
?
TH-THANK YOU...!
I-I'LL COOK UP SOMETHING WONDERFUL!
GABA (GRAB)
I'LL BE BACK WITH SOME TOP-NOTCH TEA!
GAH...! DON'T GO OVER-BOARD!
AND I'LL GET TO BREWING WHILE CYRUS IS OUT.
TASTY OR NOT, IT'LL BE MADE WITH LOVE.
LEMME SHOW YOU HOW, THEN!

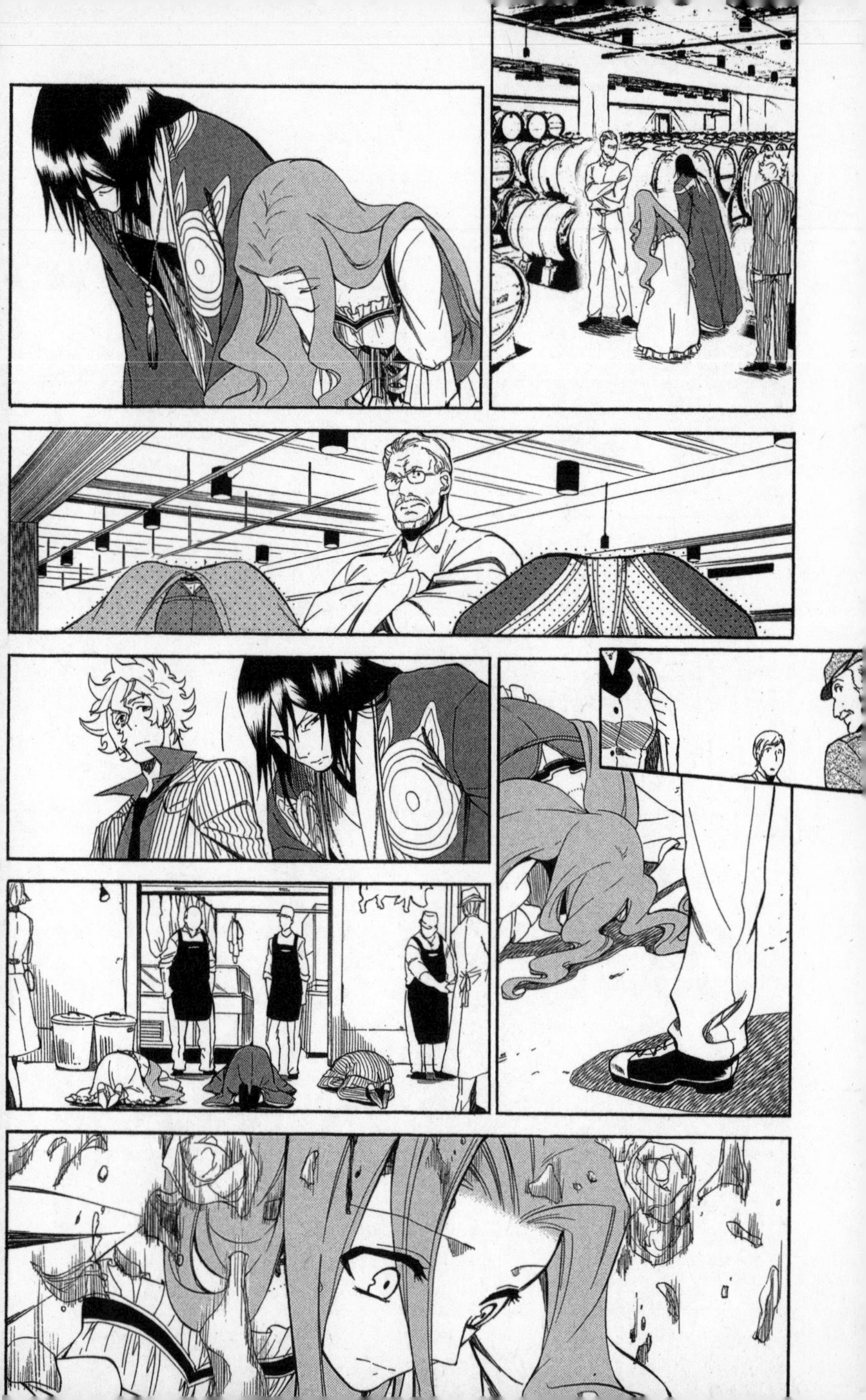

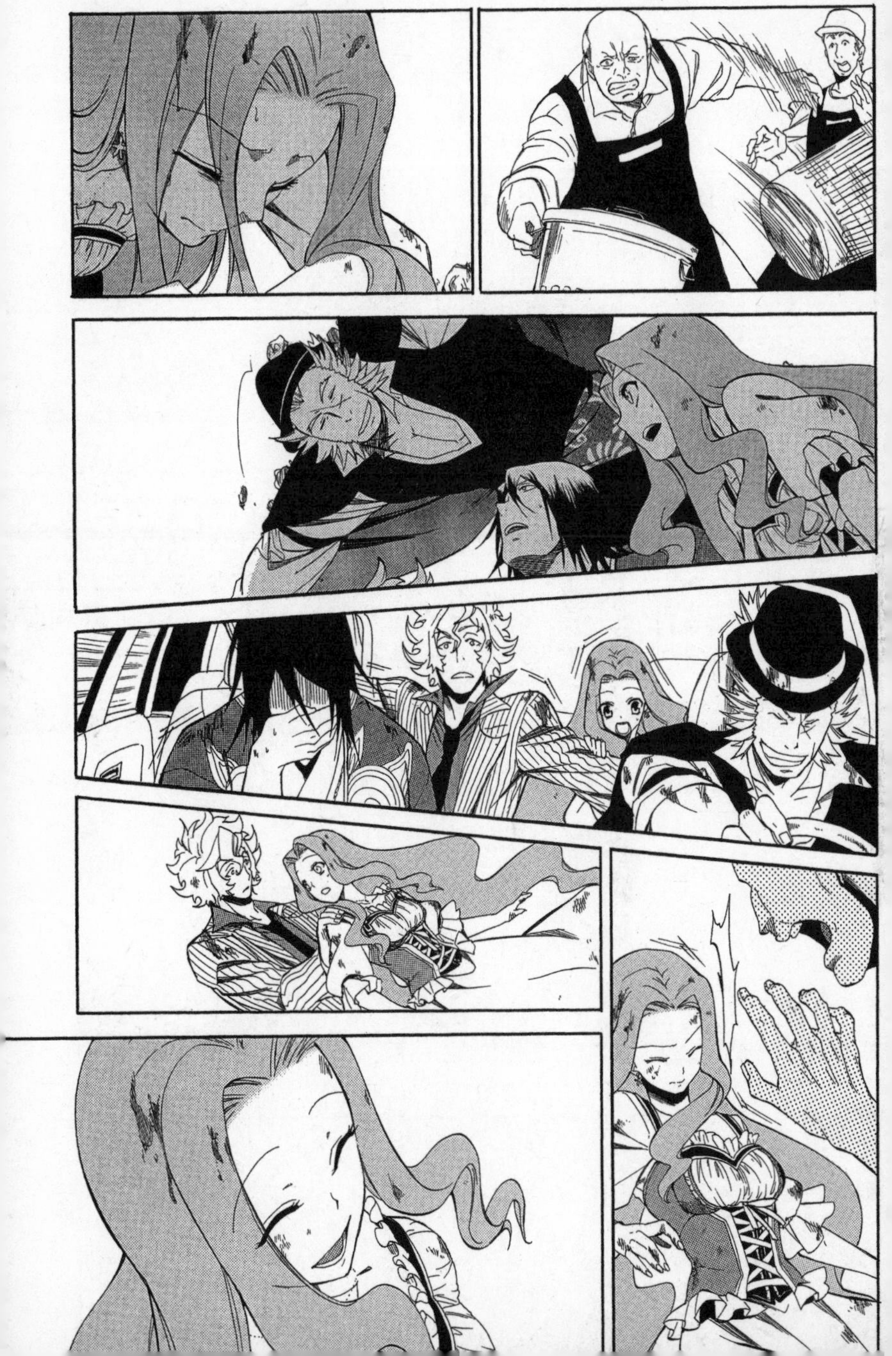

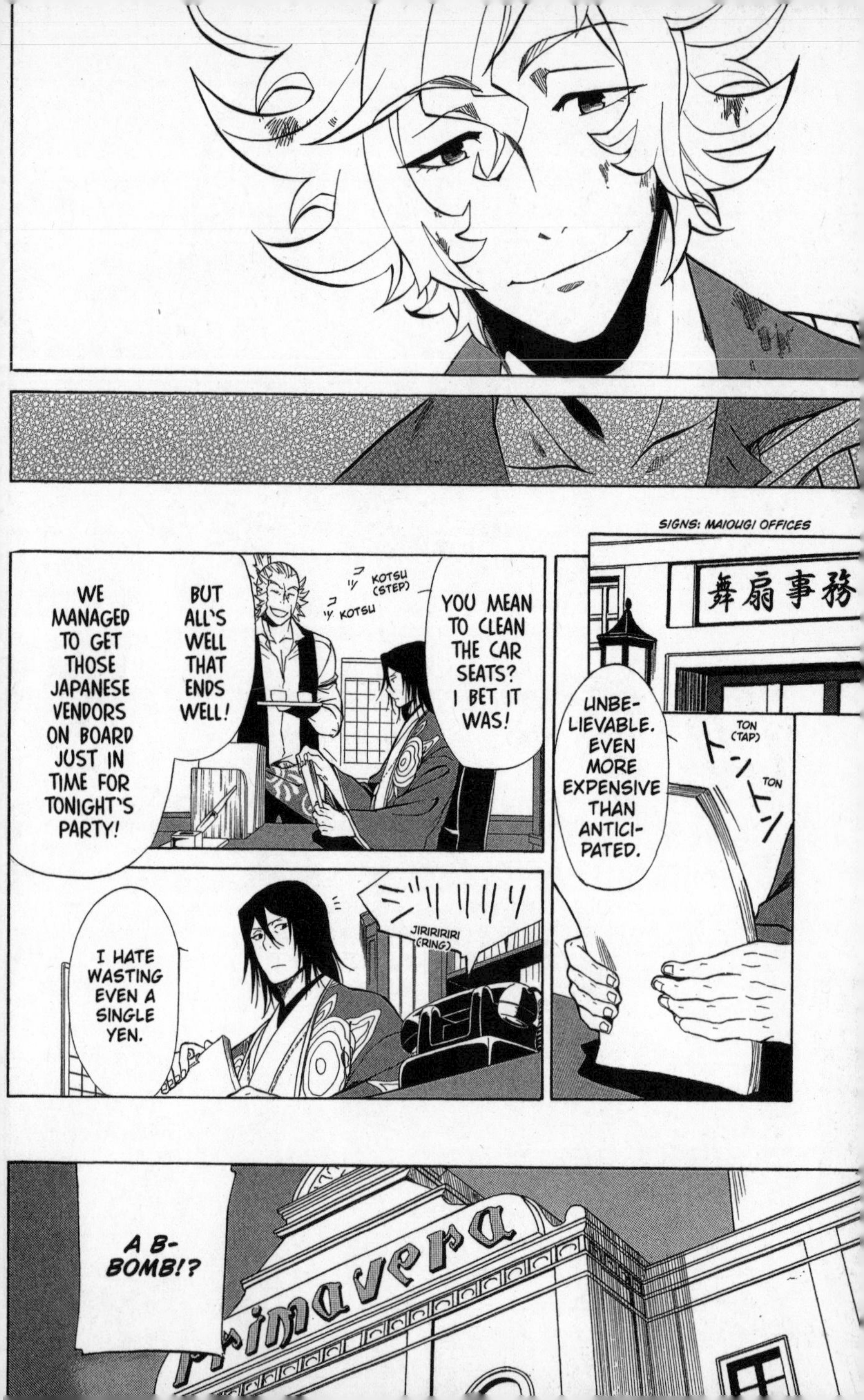
SIGNS: MAIOUGI OFFICES
舞扇事務
TON (TAP)
TON
UNBE-LIEVABLE. EVEN MORE EXPENSIVE THAN ANTICI-PATED.
YOU MEAN TO CLEAN THE CAR SEATS? I BET IT WAS!
KOTSU (STEP)
KOTSU
BUT ALL'S WELL THAT ENDS WELL!
WE MANAGED TO GET THOSE JAPANESE VENDORS ON BOARD JUST IN TIME FOR TONIGHT'S PARTY!
JIRIRIRIRI (RING)
I HATE WASTING EVEN A SINGLE YEN.
A B-BOMB!?
Primavera

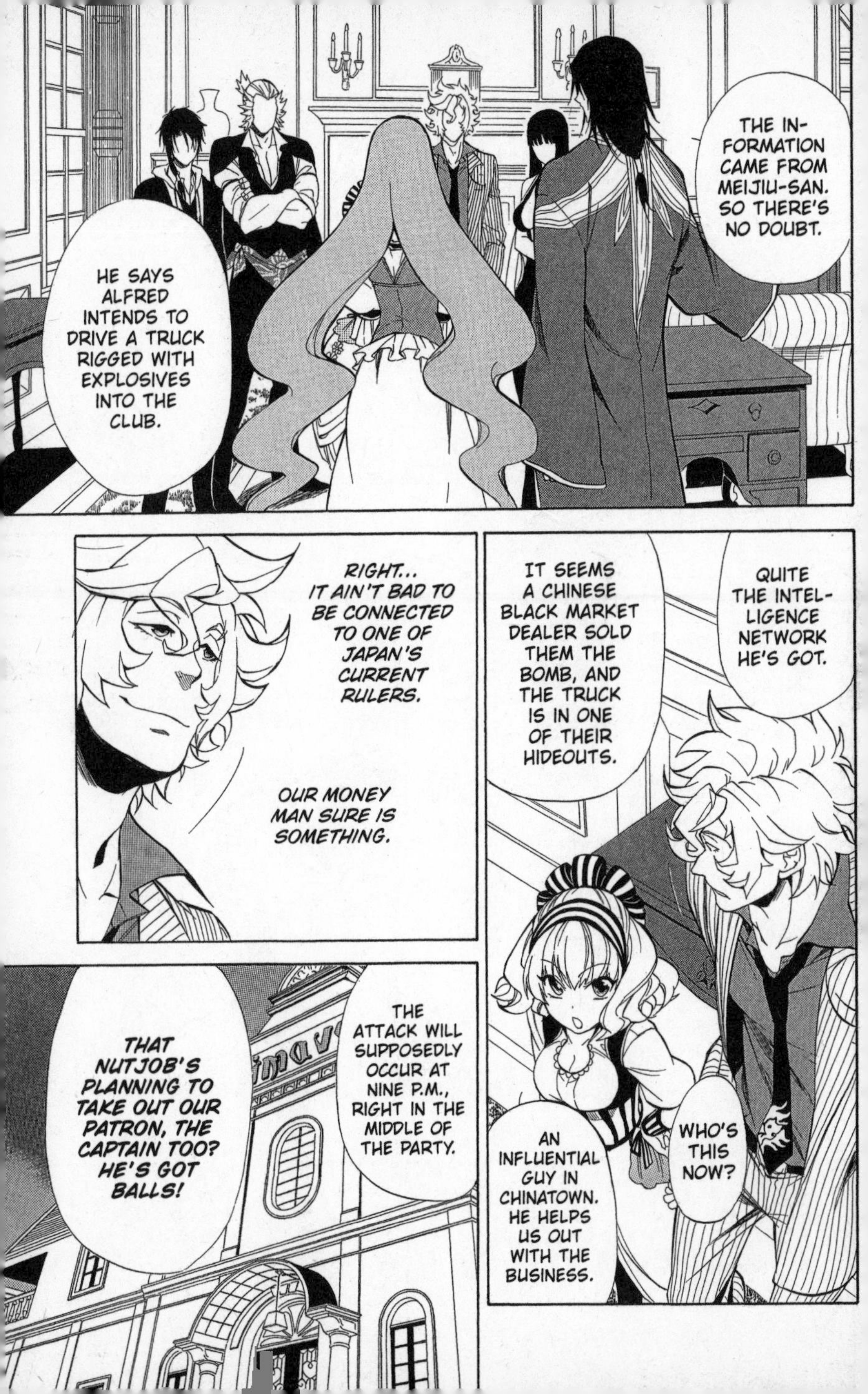
THE IN-FORMATION CAME FROM MEIJIU-SAN. SO THERE'S NO DOUBT.
HE SAYS ALFRED INTENDS TO DRIVE A TRUCK RIGGED WITH EXPLOSIVES INTO THE CLUB.
QUITE THE INTEL-LIGENCE NETWORK HE'S GOT.
IT SEEMS A CHINESE BLACK MARKET DEALER SOLD THEM THE BOMB, AND THE TRUCK IS IN ONE OF THEIR HIDEOUTS.
WHO'S THIS NOW?
AN INFLUENTIAL GUY IN CHINATOWN. HE HELPS US OUT WITH THE BUSINESS.
RIGHT... IT AIN'T BAD TO BE CONNECTED TO ONE OF JAPAN'S CURRENT RULERS.
OUR MONEY MAN SURE IS SOMETHING.
THE ATTACK WILL SUPPOSEDLY OCCUR AT NINE P.M., RIGHT IN THE MIDDLE OF THE PARTY.
THAT NUTJOB'S PLANNING TO TAKE OUT OUR PATRON, THE CAPTAIN TOO? HE'S GOT BALLS!

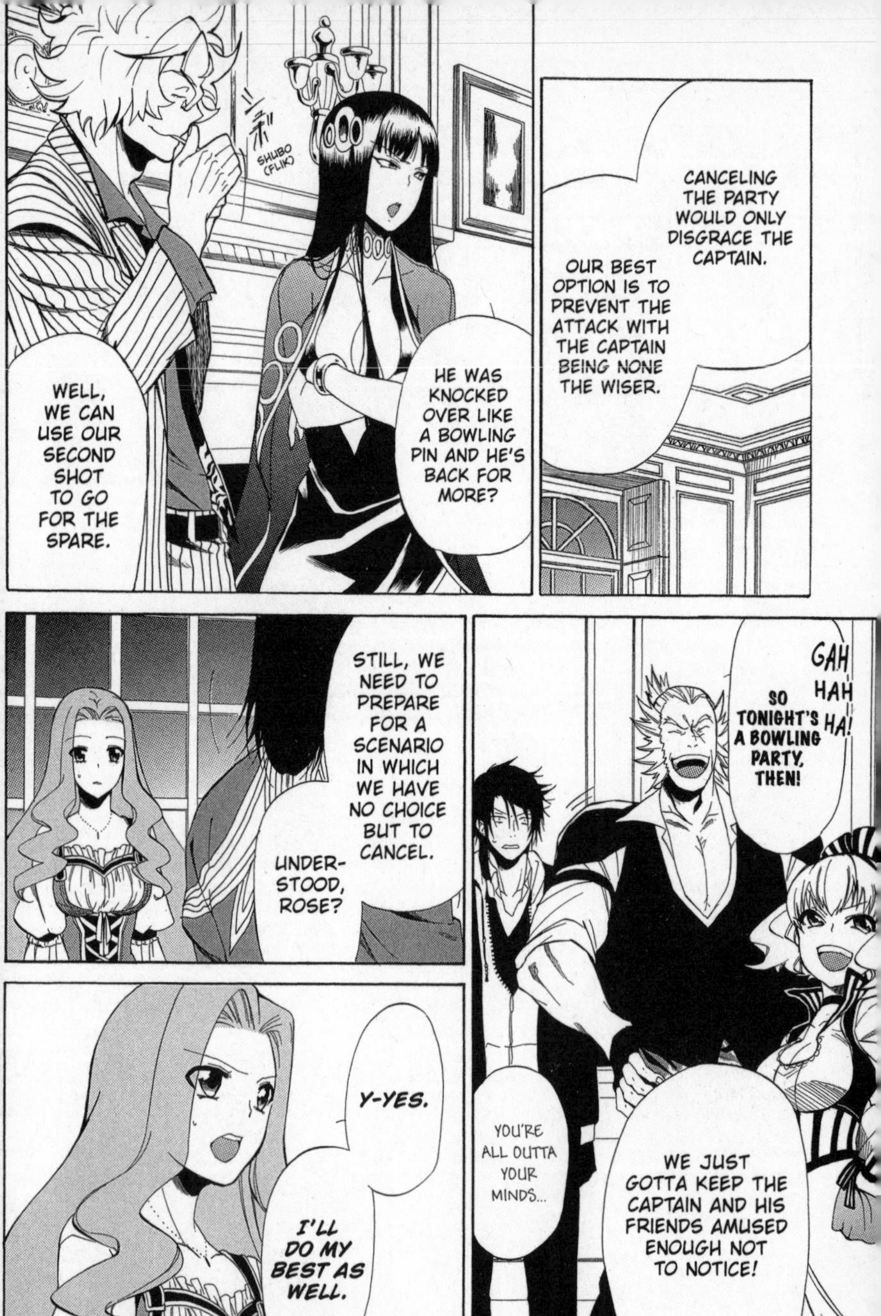
CANCELING THE PARTY WOULD ONLY DISGRACE THE CAPTAIN.
OUR BEST OPTION IS TO PREVENT THE ATTACK WITH THE CAPTAIN BEING NONE THE WISER.
SHUBO (FLIK)
HE WAS KNOCKED OVER LIKE A BOWLING PIN AND HE'S BACK FOR MORE?
WELL, WE CAN USE OUR SECOND SHOT TO GO FOR THE SPARE.
GAH HAH HA!
SO TONIGHT'S A BOWLING PARTY, THEN!
WE JUST GOTTA KEEP THE CAPTAIN AND HIS FRIENDS AMUSED ENOUGH NOT TO NOTICE!
YOU'RE ALL OUTTA YOUR MINDS...
STILL, WE NEED TO PREPARE FOR A SCENARIO IN WHICH WE HAVE NO CHOICE BUT TO CANCEL.
UNDER-STOOD, ROSE?
Y-YES.
I'LL DO MY BEST AS WELL.

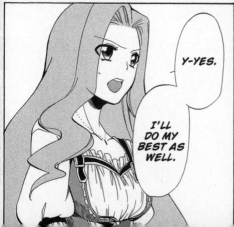

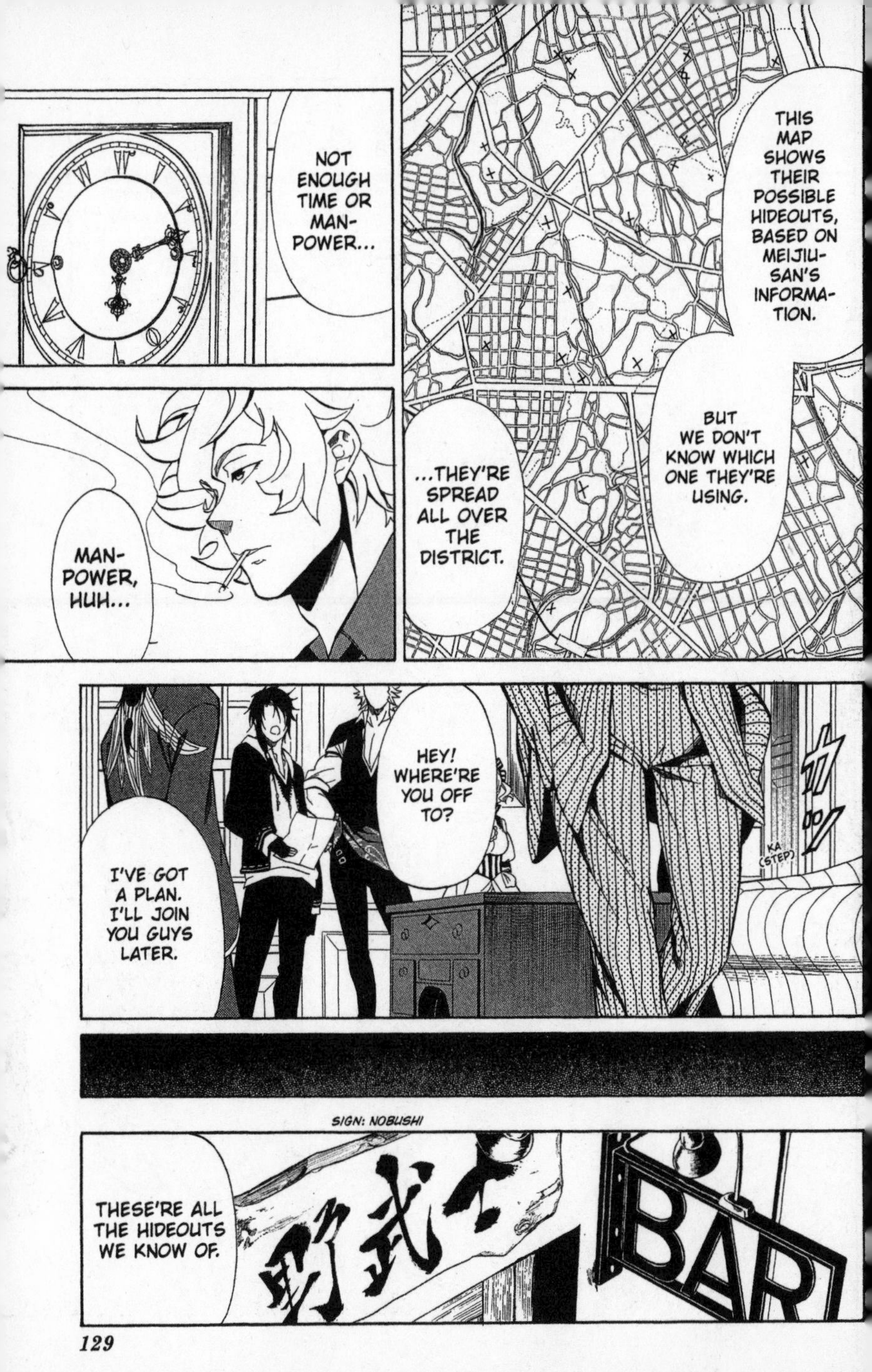
THIS MAP SHOWS THEIR POSSIBLE HIDEOUTS, BASED ON MEIJIU-SAN'S INFORMATION.
BUT WE DON'T KNOW WHICH ONE THEY'RE USING.
...THEY'RE SPREAD ALL OVER THE DISTRICT.
NOT ENOUGH TIME OR MAN-POWER...
MAN-POWER, HUH...
KA (STEP)
HEY! WHERE'RE YOU OFF TO?
I'VE GOT A PLAN. I'LL JOIN YOU GUYS LATER.
SIGN: NOBUSHI
野武士
BAR
THESE'RE ALL THE HIDEOUTS WE KNOW OF.

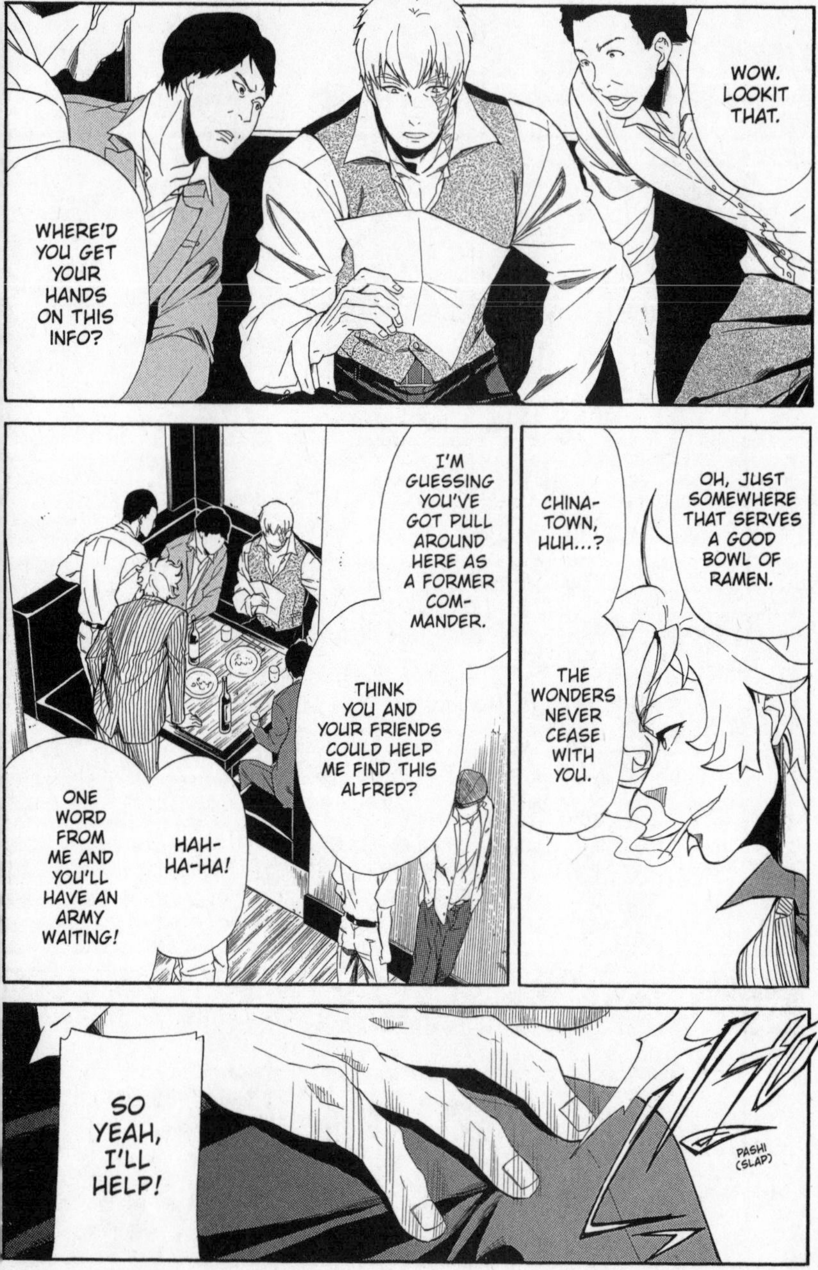
WOW. LOOKIT THAT.
WHERE'D YOU GET YOUR HANDS ON THIS INFO?
OH, JUST SOMEWHERE THAT SERVES A GOOD BOWL OF RAMEN.
CHINA-TOWN, HUH...?
THE WONDERS NEVER CEASE WITH YOU.
I'M GUESSING YOU'VE GOT PULL AROUND HERE AS A FORMER COM-MANDER.
THINK YOU AND YOUR FRIENDS COULD HELP ME FIND THIS ALFRED?
HAH-HA-HA!
ONE WORD FROM ME AND YOU'LL HAVE AN ARMY WAITING!
PASHI (SLAP)
SO YEAH, I'LL HELP!

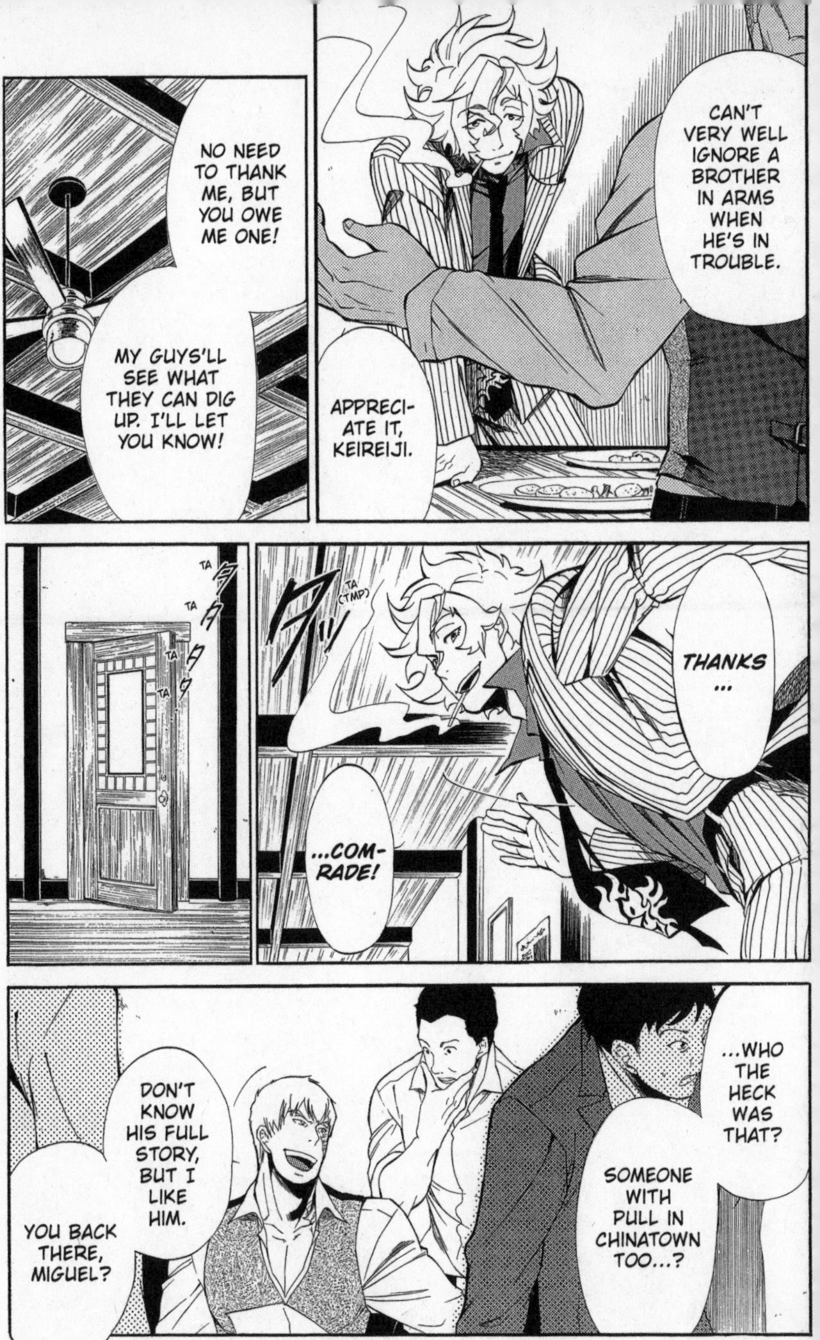
CAN'T VERY WELL IGNORE A BROTHER IN ARMS WHEN HE'S IN TROUBLE.
APPRECIATE IT, KEIREIJI.
NO NEED TO THANK ME, BUT YOU OWE ME ONE!
MY GUYS'LL SEE WHAT THEY CAN DIG UP. I'LL LET YOU KNOW!
THANKS ...
TA (TMP)
...COM-RADE!
TA
TA
TA
TA
...WHO THE HECK WAS THAT?
SOMEONE WITH PULL IN CHINATOWN TOO...?
DON'T KNOW HIS FULL STORY, BUT I LIKE HIM.
YOU BACK THERE, MIGUEL?

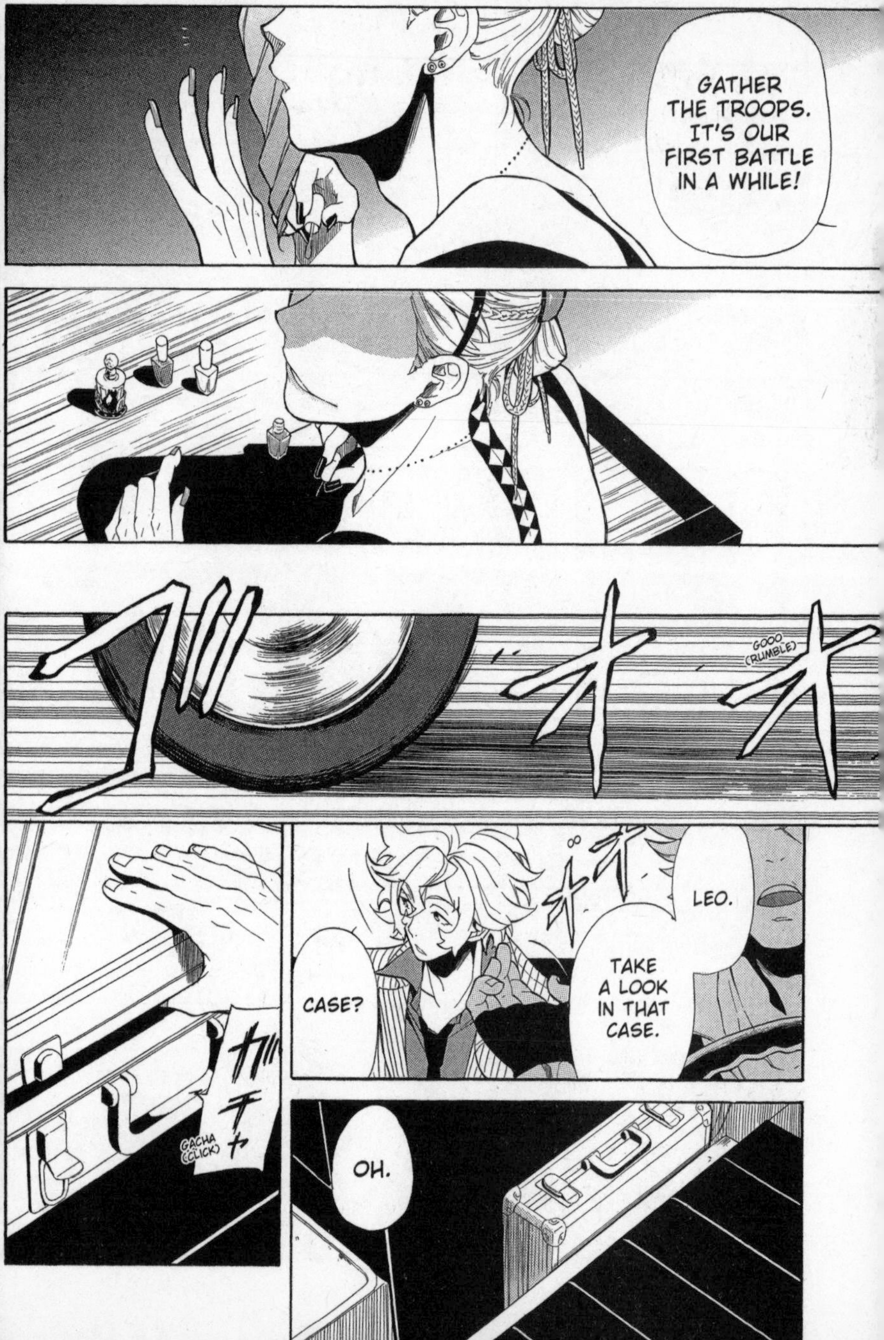
GATHER THE TROOPS. IT'S OUR FIRST BATTLE IN A WHILE!
GOOO (RUMBLE)
LEO.
TAKE A LOOK IN THAT CASE.
CASE?
OH.
GACHA (CLICK)

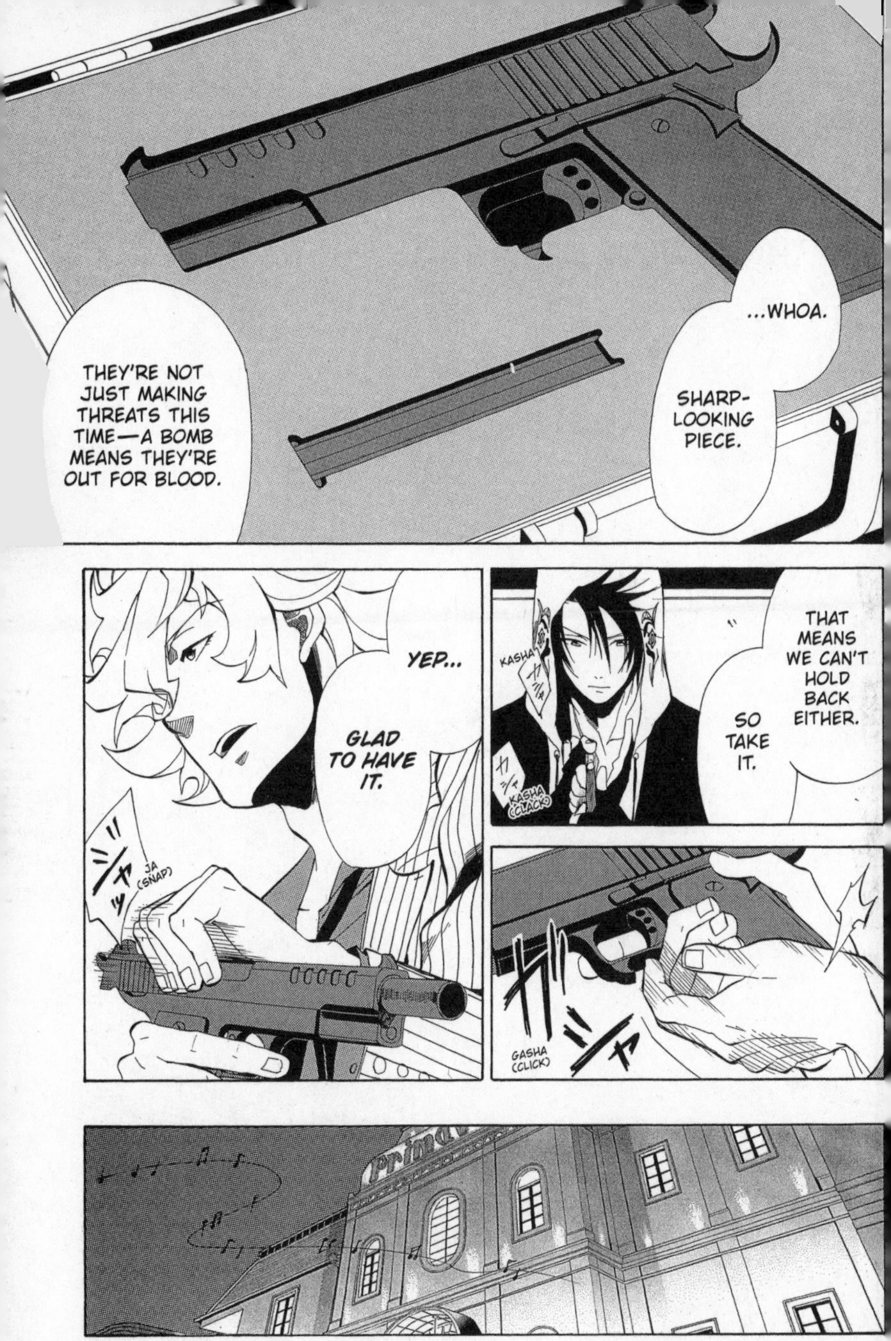
...WHOA.
SHARP-LOOKING PIECE.
THEY'RE NOT JUST MAKING THREATS THIS TIME—A BOMB MEANS THEY'RE OUT FOR BLOOD.
THAT MEANS WE CAN'T HOLD BACK EITHER.
SO TAKE IT.
KASHA
KASHA (CLICK)
GASHA (CLICK)
YEP...
GLAD TO HAVE IT.
JA (SNAP)

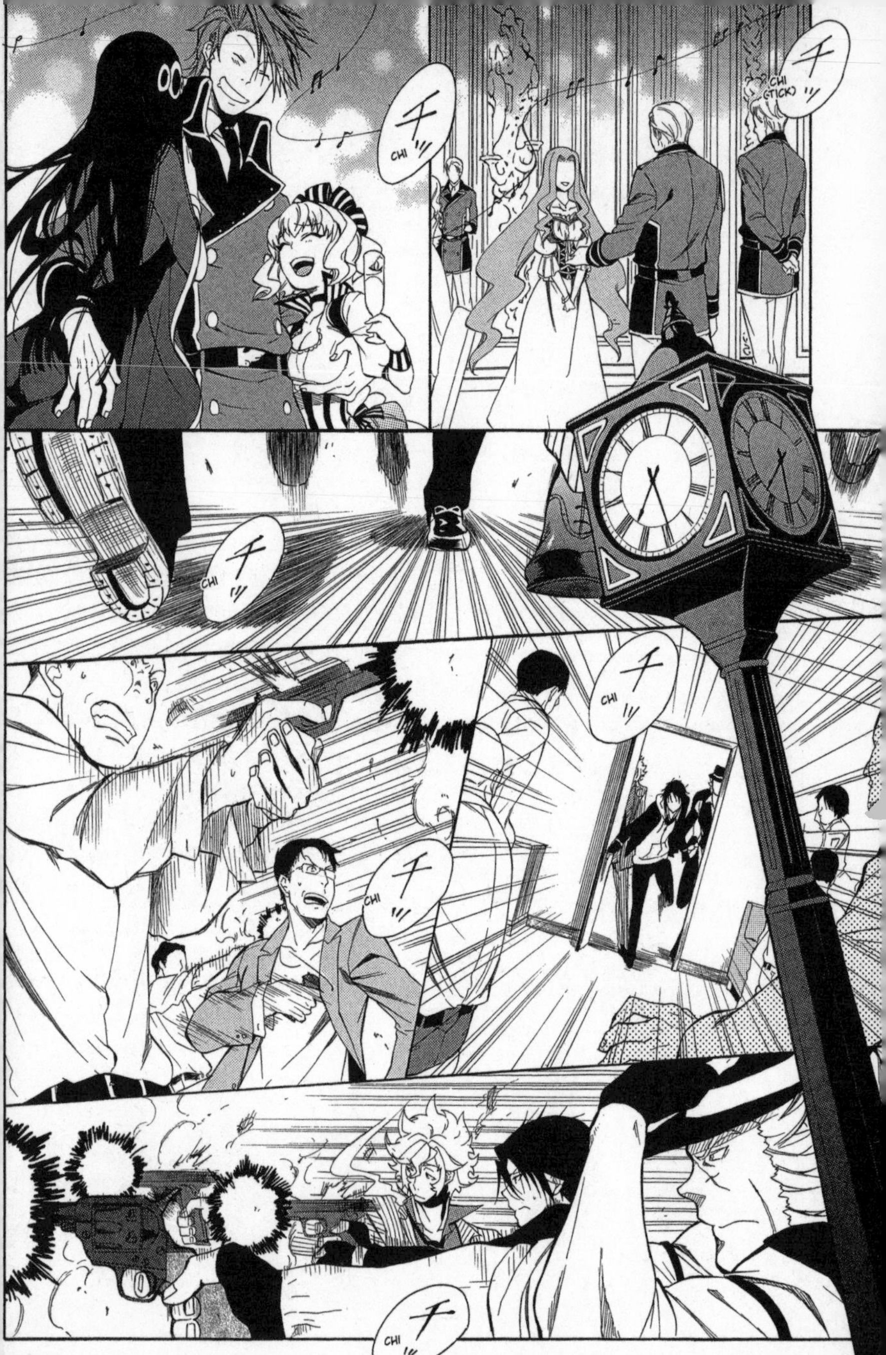
チ
CHI (TICK)
チ
CHI
チ
CHI
チ
CHI
チ
CHI
チ
CHI

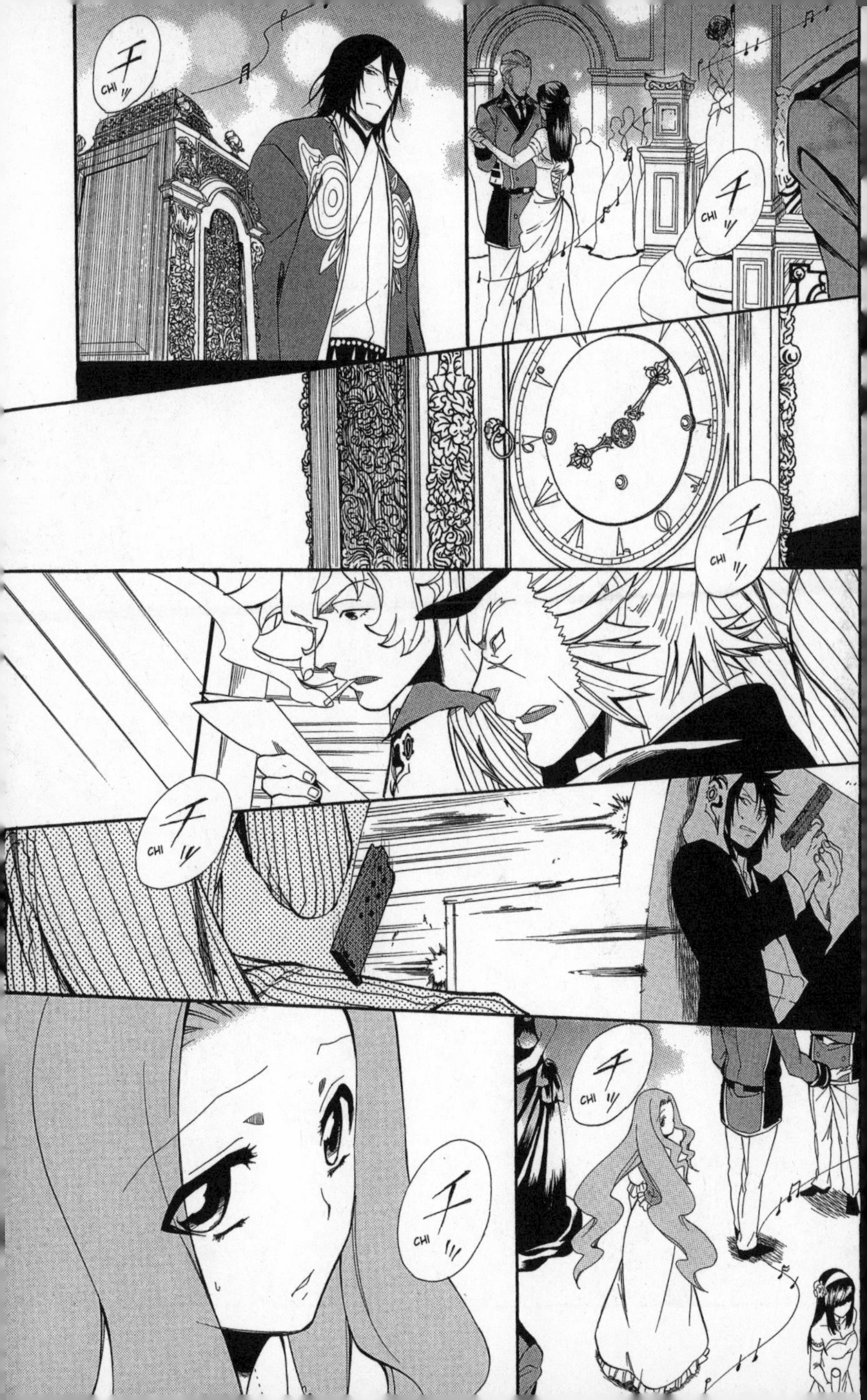
チ CHI
チ CHI
チ CHI
チ CHI
チ CHI
チ CHI
チ CHI

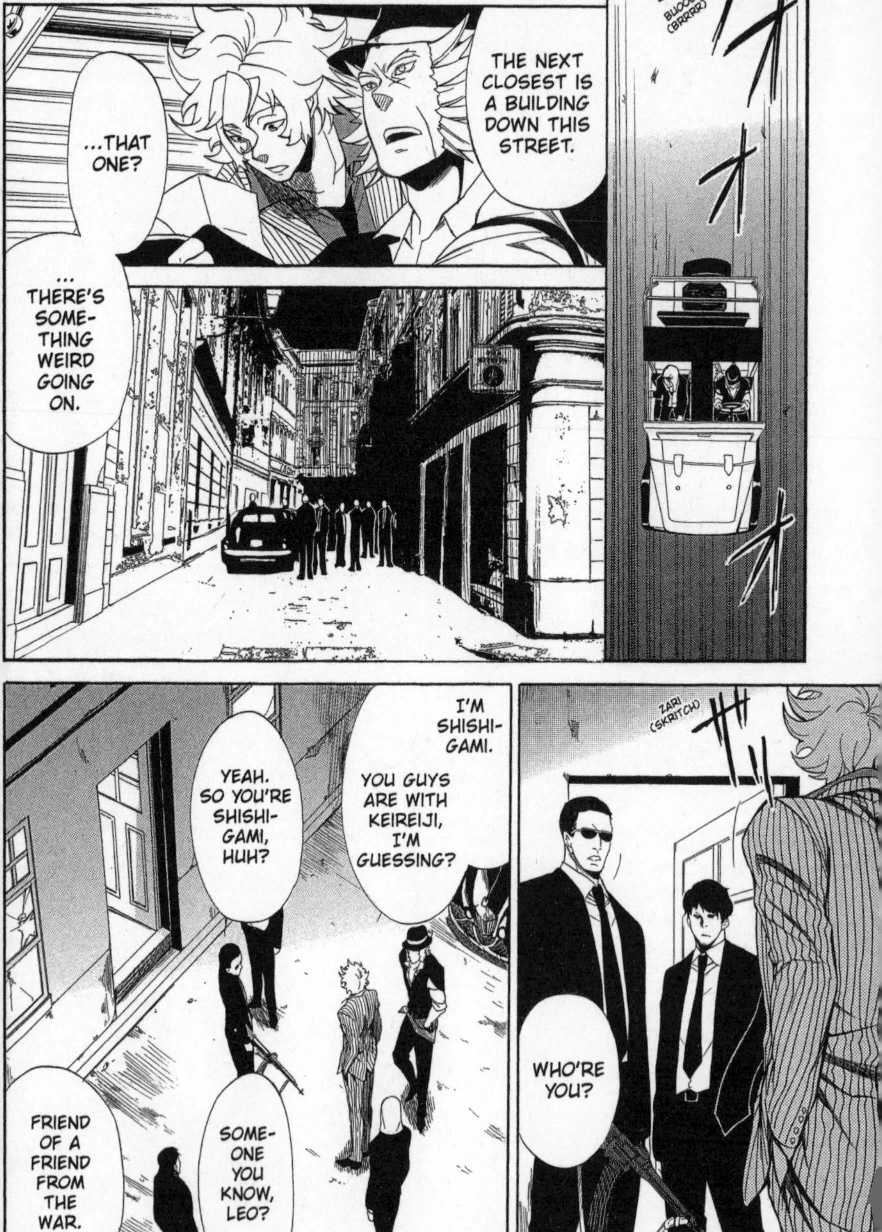
BUOOO (BRRRR)
THE NEXT CLOSEST IS A BUILDING DOWN THIS STREET.
...THAT ONE?
...THERE'S SOMETHING WEIRD GOING ON.
ZARI (SKRITCH)
WHO'RE YOU?
I'M SHISHIGAMI.
YOU GUYS ARE WITH KEIREIJI, I'M GUESSING?
YEAH. SO YOU'RE SHISHIGAMI, HUH?
SOMEONE YOU KNOW, LEO?
FRIEND OF A FRIEND FROM THE WAR.

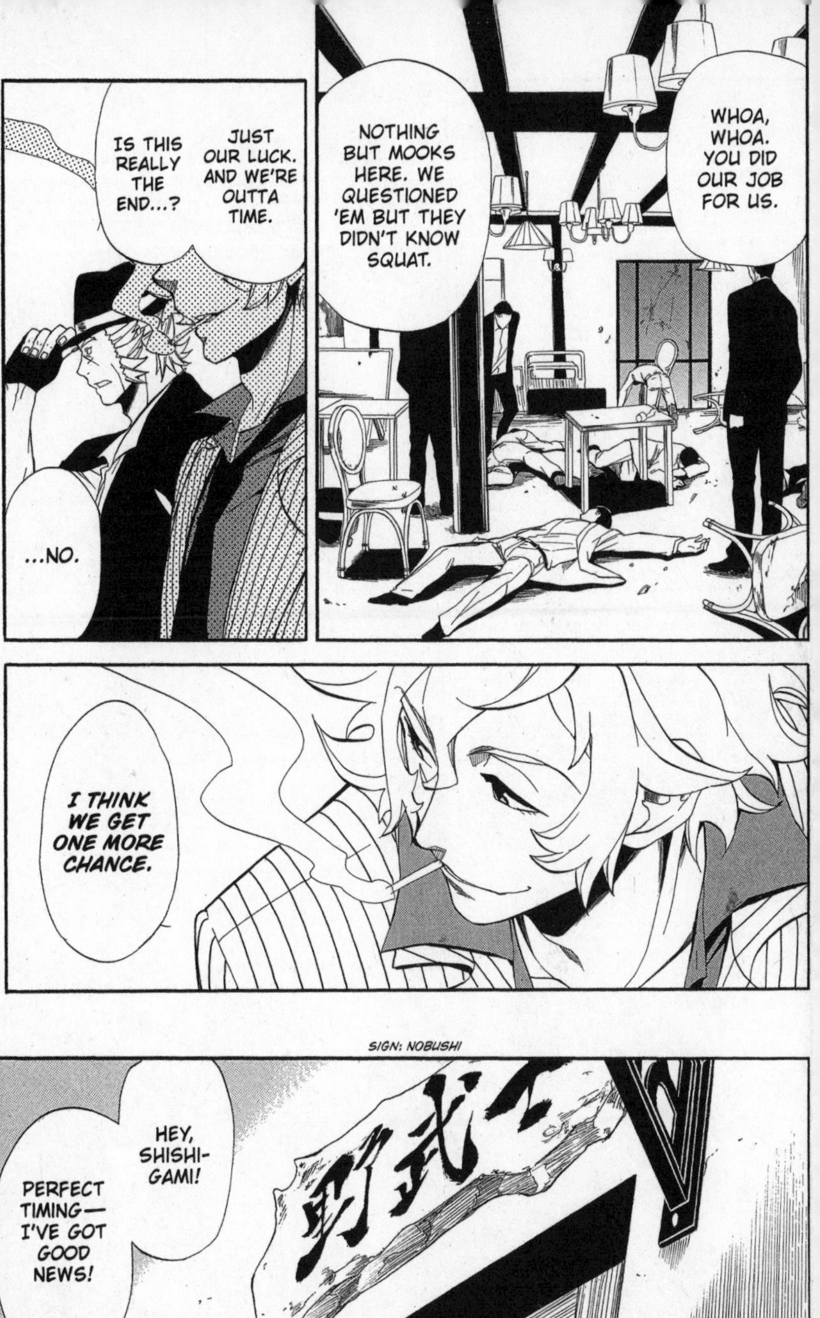
WHOA, WHOA. YOU DID OUR JOB FOR US.
NOTHING BUT MOOKS HERE. WE QUESTIONED 'EM BUT THEY DIDN'T KNOW SQUAT.
JUST OUR LUCK. AND WE'RE OUTTA TIME.
IS THIS REALLY THE END...?
...NO.
I THINK WE GET ONE MORE CHANCE.
SIGN: NOBUSHI
野武士
HEY, SHISHI-GAMI!
PERFECT TIMING—I'VE GOT GOOD NEWS!

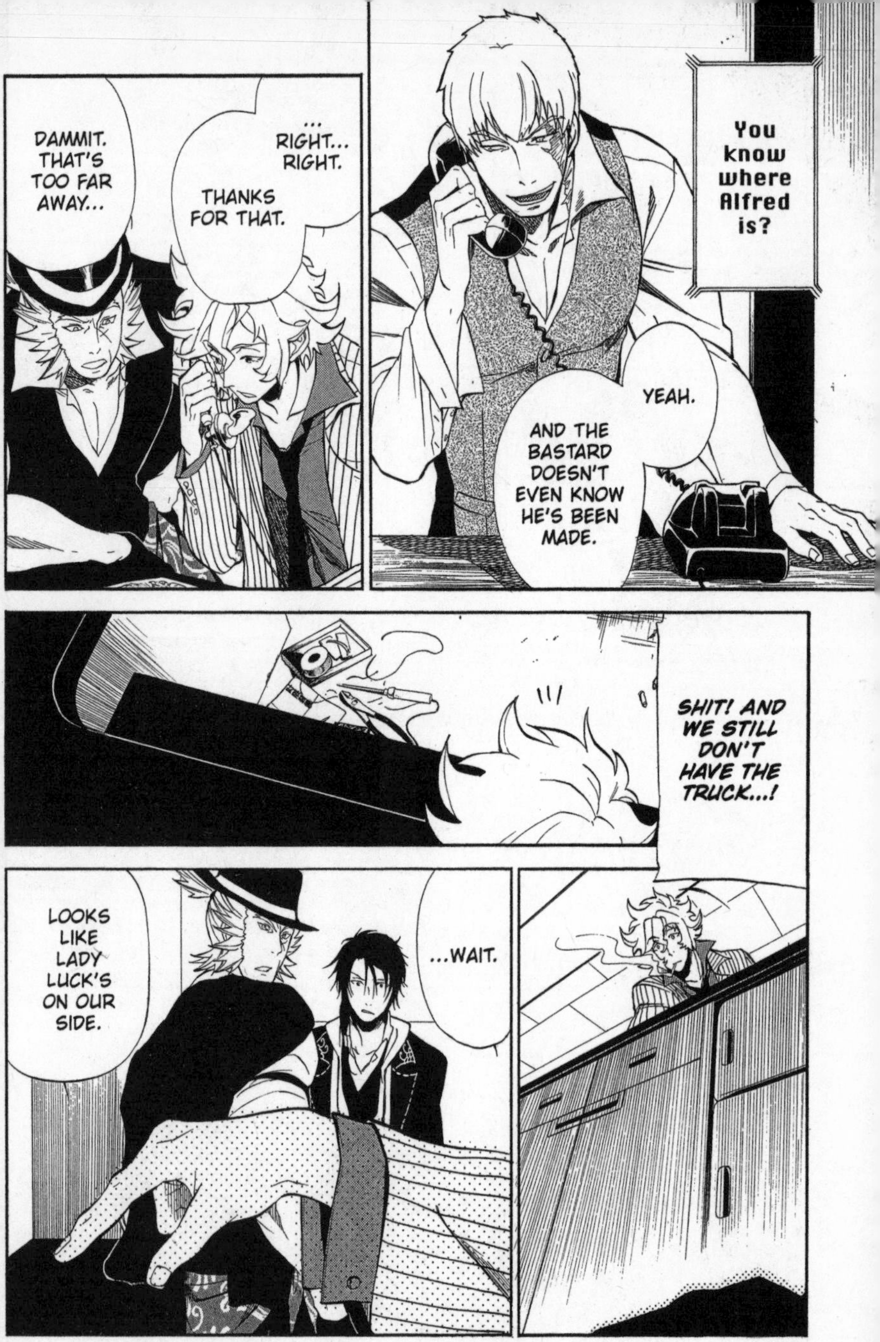
You know where Alfred is?
YEAH.
AND THE BASTARD DOESN'T EVEN KNOW HE'S BEEN MADE.
... RIGHT... RIGHT.
THANKS FOR THAT.
DAMMIT. THAT'S TOO FAR AWAY...
SHIT! AND WE STILL DON'T HAVE THE TRUCK...!
...WAIT.
LOOKS LIKE LADY LUCK'S ON OUR SIDE.

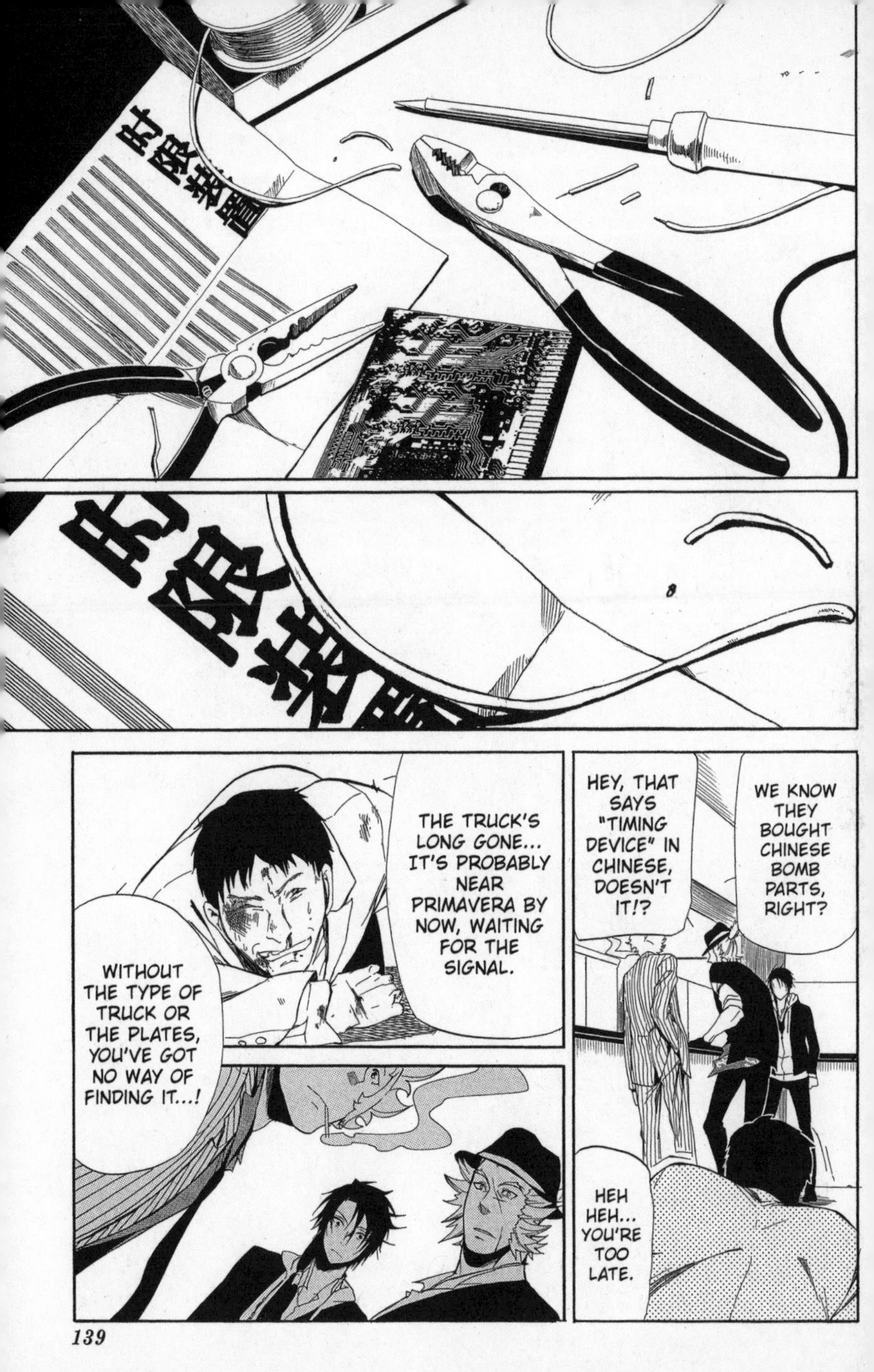
时限装置
WE KNOW THEY BOUGHT CHINESE BOMB PARTS, RIGHT?
HEY, THAT SAYS "TIMING DEVICE" IN CHINESE, DOESN'T IT!?
HEH HEH... YOU'RE TOO LATE.
THE TRUCK'S LONG GONE... IT'S PROBABLY NEAR PRIMAVERA BY NOW, WAITING FOR THE SIGNAL.
WITHOUT THE TYPE OF TRUCK OR THE PLATES, YOU'VE GOT NO WAY OF FINDING IT...!

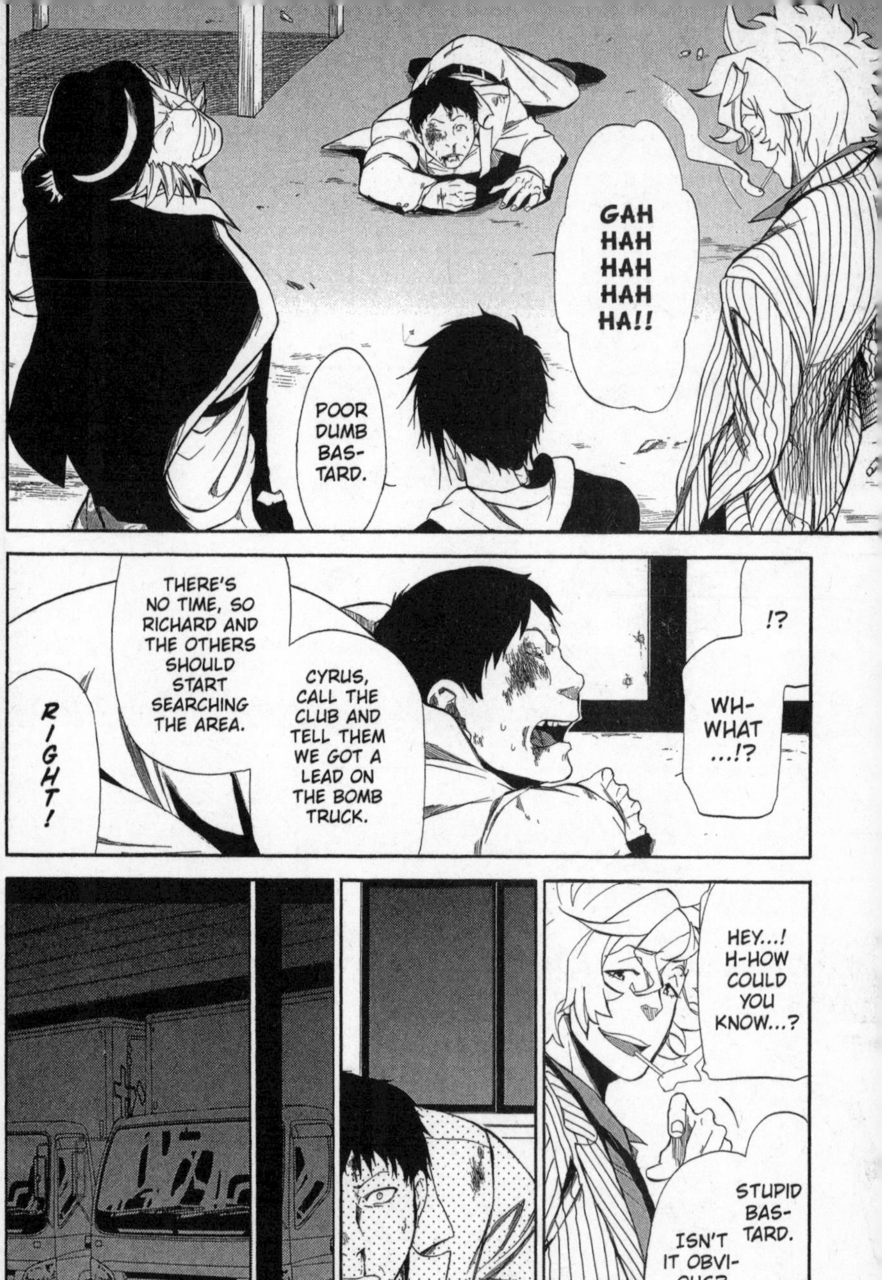
GAH HAH HAH HAH HA!!
POOR DUMB BASTARD.
!? WH-WHAT...!?
CYRUS, CALL THE CLUB AND TELL THEM WE GOT A LEAD ON THE BOMB TRUCK.
THERE'S NO TIME, SO RICHARD AND THE OTHERS SHOULD START SEARCHING THE AREA.
RIGHT!
HEY...! H-HOW COULD YOU KNOW...?
STUPID BASTARD.
ISN'T IT OBVIOUS?

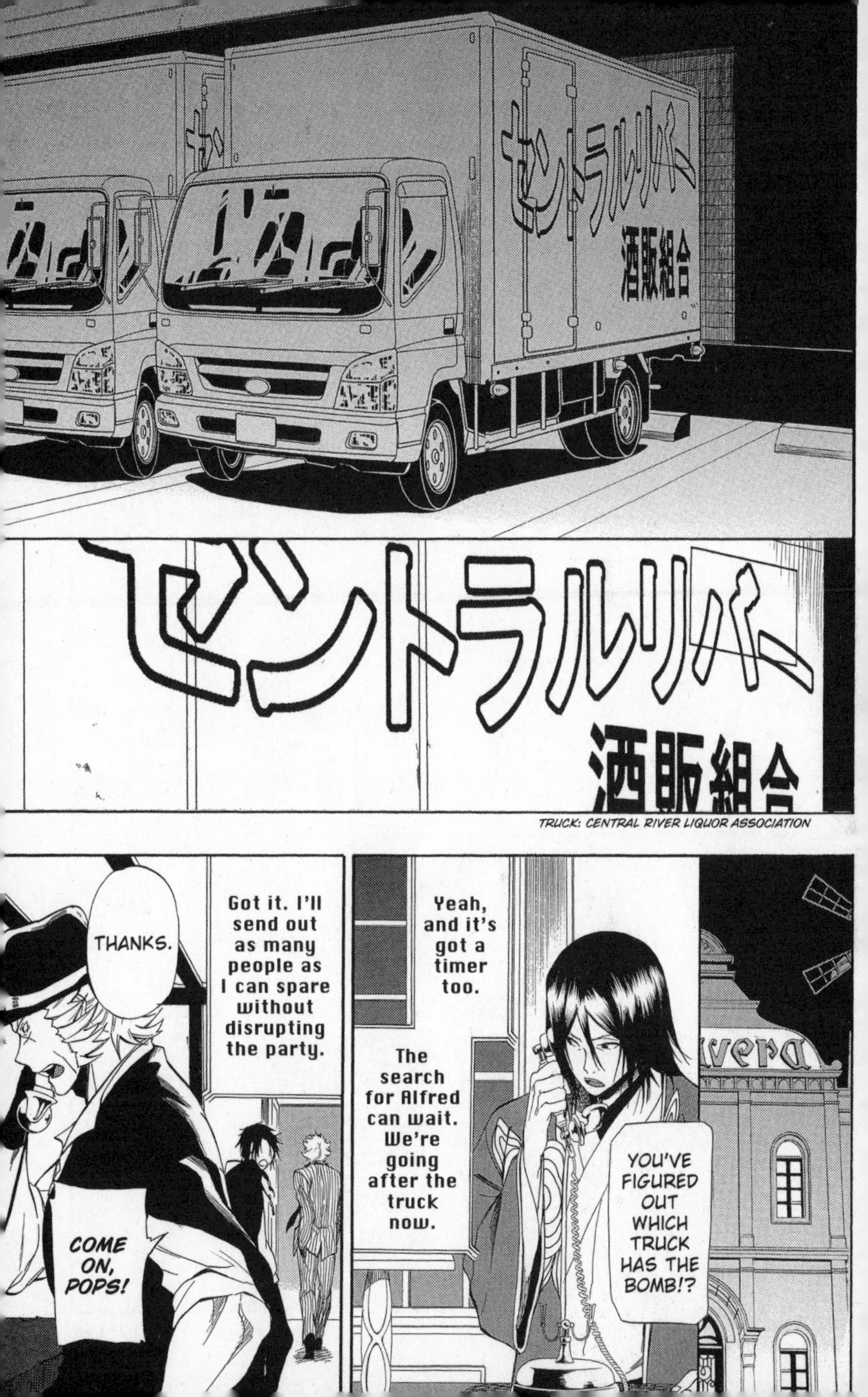

セントラルリバー
酒販組合
TRUCK: CENTRAL RIVER LIQUOR ASSOCIATION
YOU'VE FIGURED OUT WHICH TRUCK HAS THE BOMB!?
Yeah, and it's got a timer too.
The search for Alfred can wait. We're going after the truck now.
Got it. I'll send out as many people as I can spare without disrupting the party.
THANKS.
COME ON, POPS!

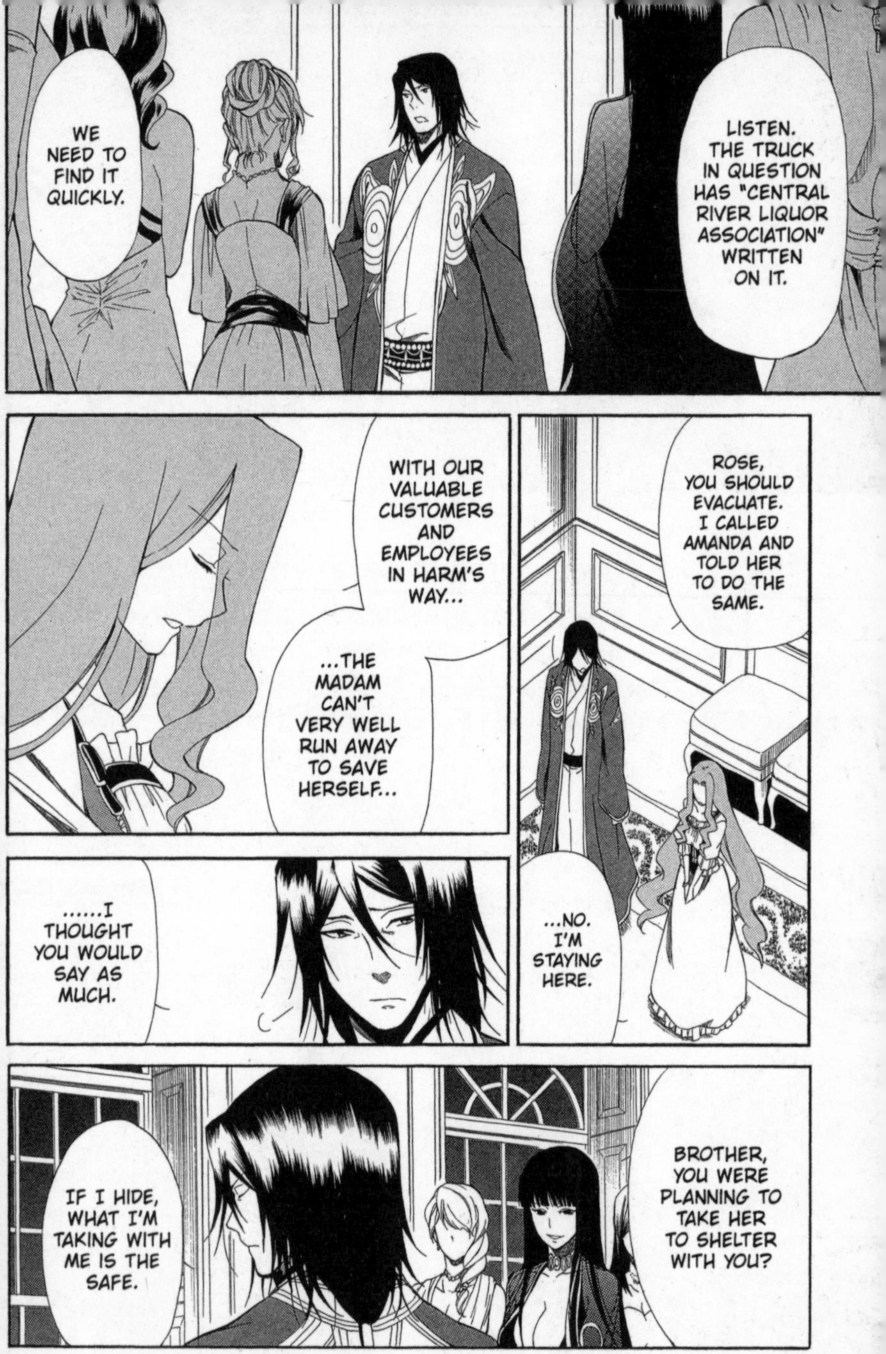
LISTEN. THE TRUCK IN QUESTION HAS "CENTRAL RIVER LIQUOR ASSOCIATION" WRITTEN ON IT.
WE NEED TO FIND IT QUICKLY.
ROSE, YOU SHOULD EVACUATE. I CALLED AMANDA AND TOLD HER TO DO THE SAME.
...NO. I'M STAYING HERE.
WITH OUR VALUABLE CUSTOMERS AND EMPLOYEES IN HARM'S WAY...
...THE MADAM CAN'T VERY WELL RUN AWAY TO SAVE HERSELF...
......I THOUGHT YOU WOULD SAY AS MUCH.
BROTHER, YOU WERE PLANNING TO TAKE HER TO SHELTER WITH YOU?
IF I HIDE, WHAT I'M TAKING WITH ME IS THE SAFE.

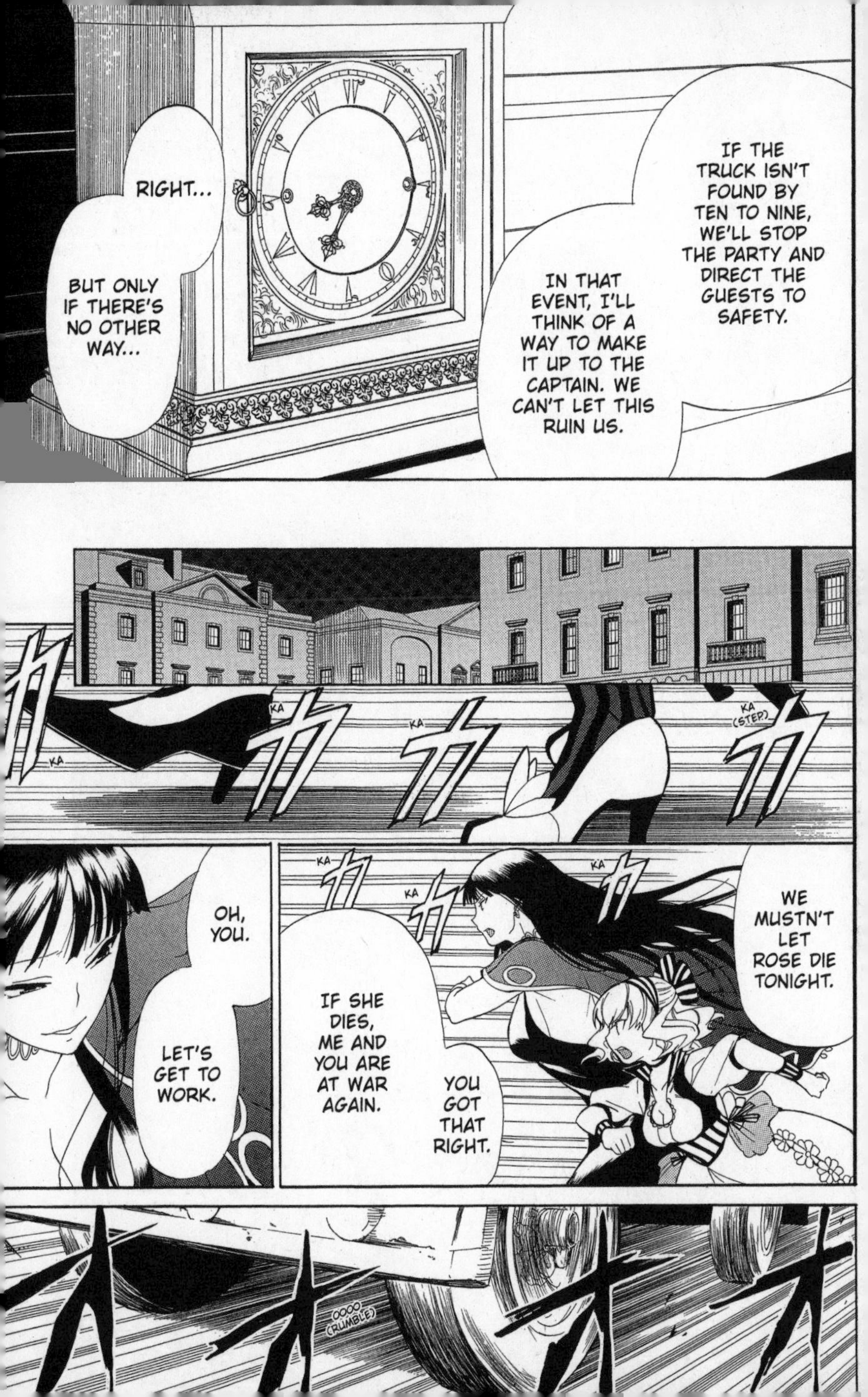
IF THE TRUCK ISN'T FOUND BY TEN TO NINE, WE'LL STOP THE PARTY AND DIRECT THE GUESTS TO SAFETY.
IN THAT EVENT, I'LL THINK OF A WAY TO MAKE IT UP TO THE CAPTAIN. WE CAN'T LET THIS RUIN US.
RIGHT...
BUT ONLY IF THERE'S NO OTHER WAY...
KA (STEP)
KA
KA
KA
WE MUSTN'T LET ROSE DIE TONIGHT.
KA
KA
KA
IF SHE DIES, ME AND YOU ARE AT WAR AGAIN.
YOU GOT THAT RIGHT.
OH, YOU.
LET'S GET TO WORK.
OOOO (RUMBLE)

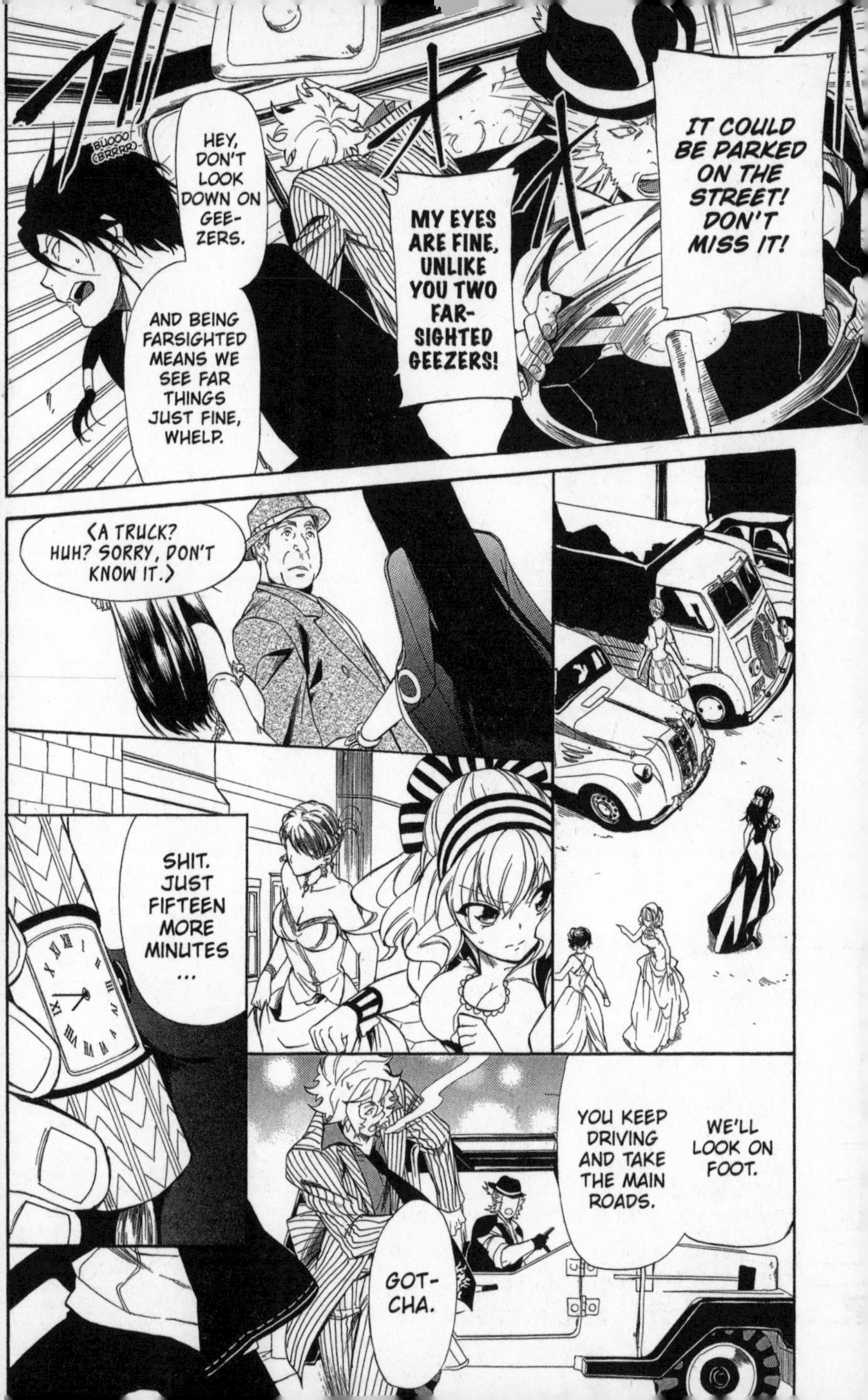
IT COULD BE PARKED ON THE STREET! DON'T MISS IT!
MY EYES ARE FINE, UNLIKE YOU TWO FAR-SIGHTED GEEZERS!
HEY, DON'T LOOK DOWN ON GEE-ZERS.
AND BEING FARSIGHTED MEANS WE SEE FAR THINGS JUST FINE, WHELP.
BUOOO (BRRRR)
<A TRUCK? HUH? SORRY, DON'T KNOW IT.>
SHIT. JUST FIFTEEN MORE MINUTES ...
WE'LL LOOK ON FOOT.
YOU KEEP DRIVING AND TAKE THE MAIN ROADS.
GOT-CHA.

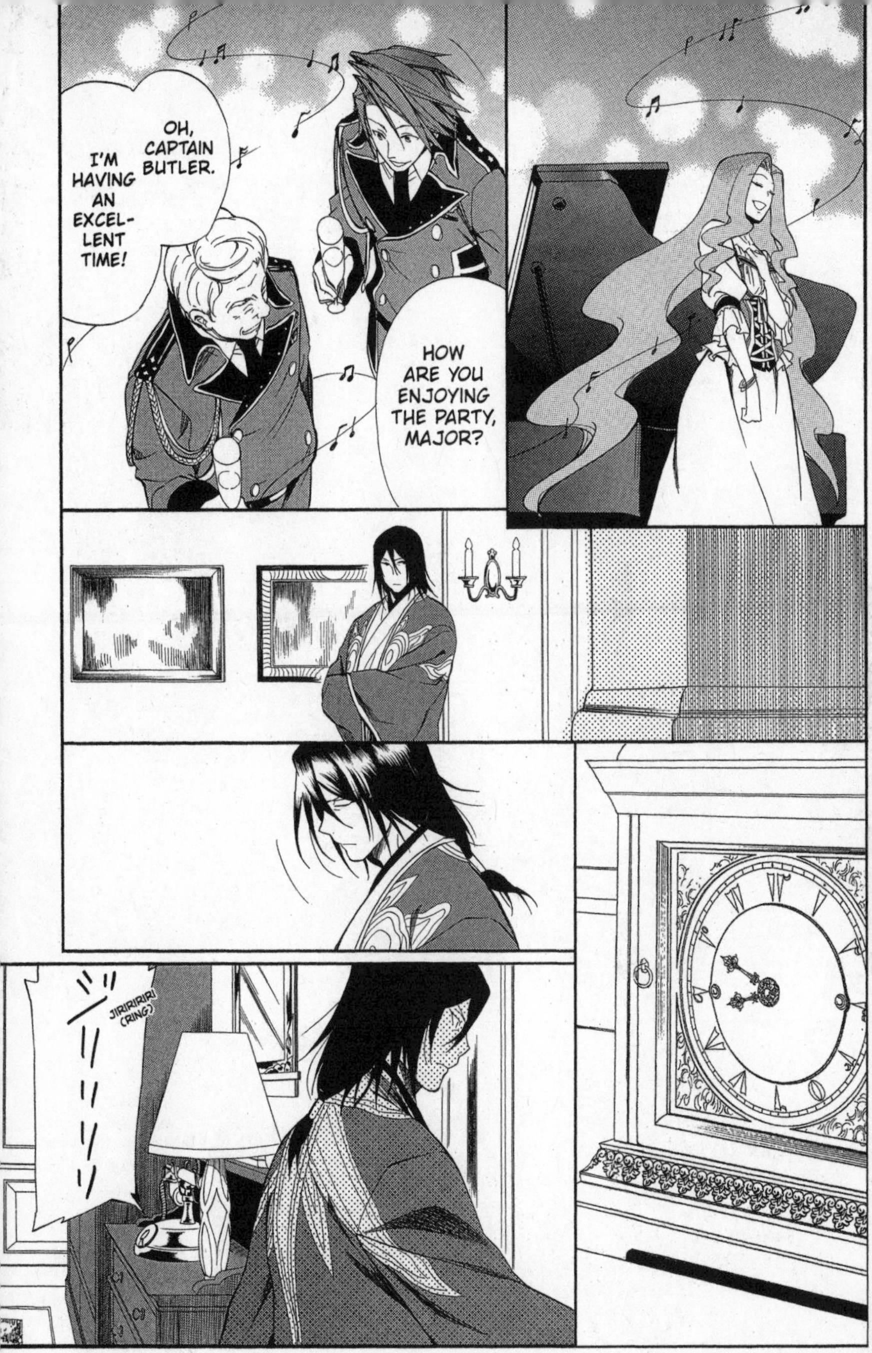
HOW ARE YOU ENJOYING THE PARTY, MAJOR?
OH, CAPTAIN BUTLER. I'M HAVING AN EXCEL-LENT TIME!
JIRIRIRIRI (RING)

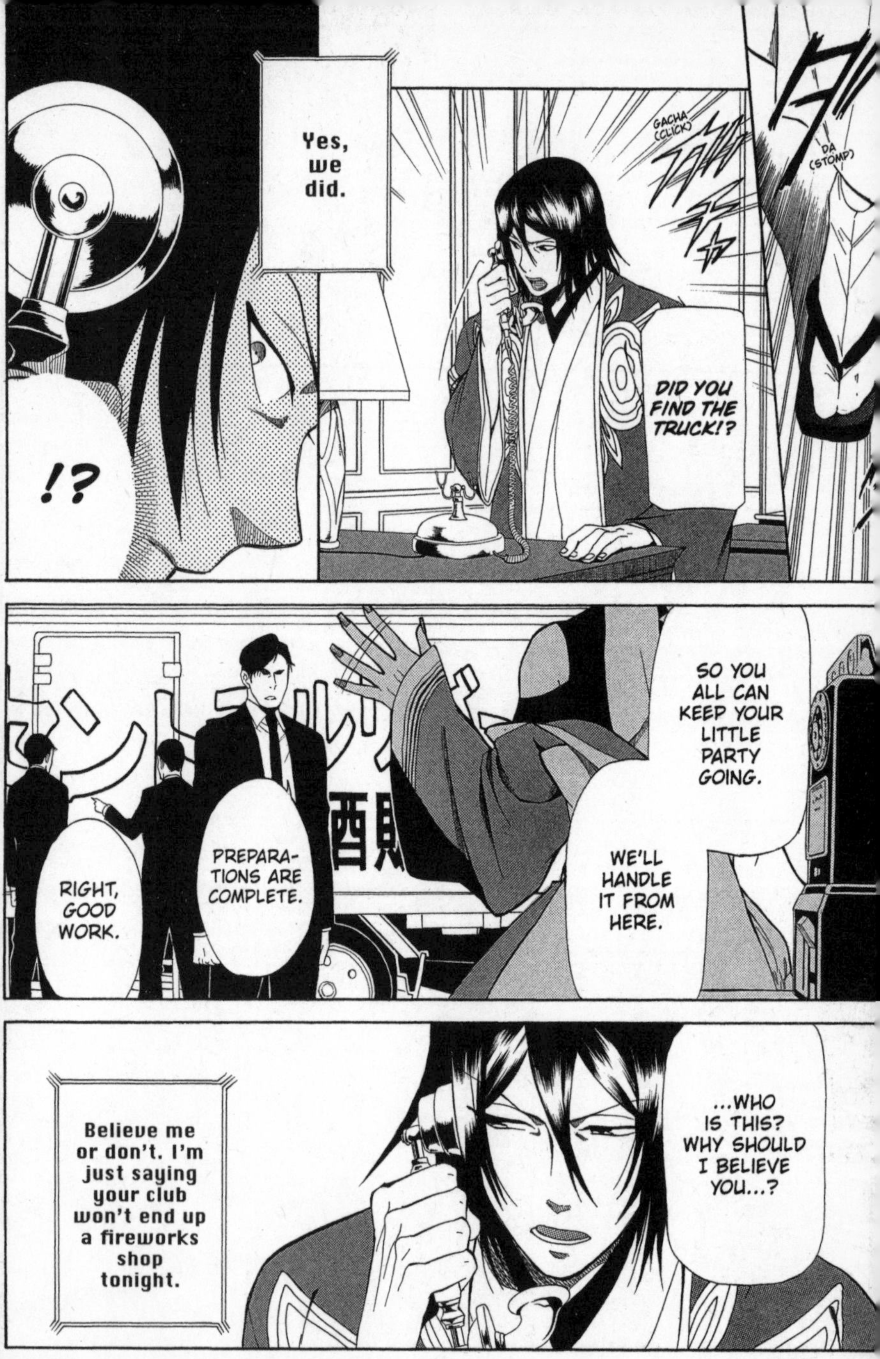
DA (STOMP)
GACHA (CLICK)
DID YOU FIND THE TRUCK!?
Yes, we did.
!?
SO YOU ALL CAN KEEP YOUR LITTLE PARTY GOING.
WE'LL HANDLE IT FROM HERE.
PREPARATIONS ARE COMPLETE.
RIGHT, GOOD WORK.
...WHO IS THIS? WHY SHOULD I BELIEVE YOU...?
Believe me or don't. I'm just saying your club won't end up a fireworks shop tonight.

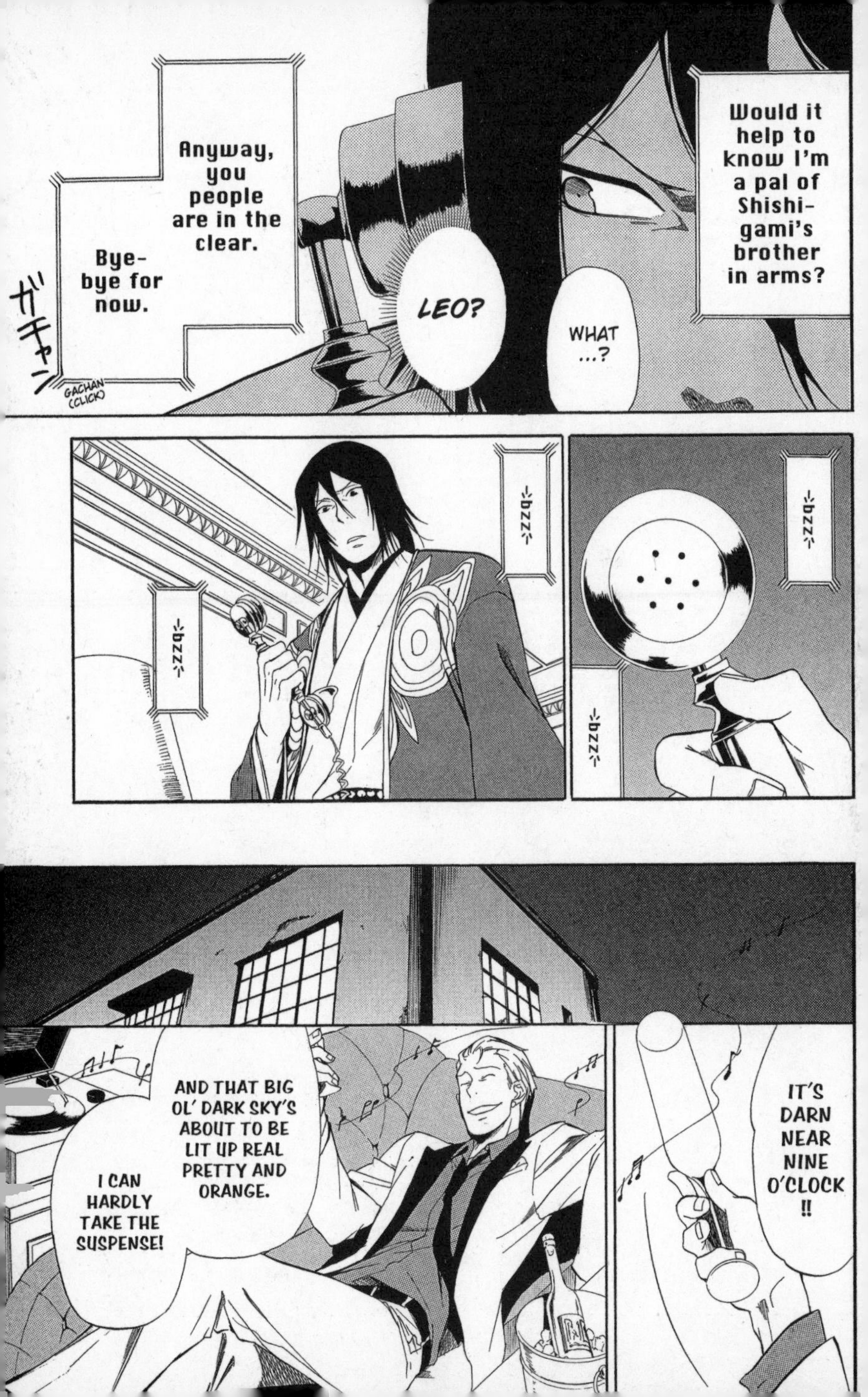
Would it help to know I'm a pal of Shishi-gami's brother in arms?
WHAT ...?
LEO?
Anyway, you people are in the clear.
Bye-bye for now.
ガチャン
GACHAN (CLICK)
bzz
bzz
bzz
bzz
IT'S DARN NEAR NINE O'CLOCK !!
AND THAT BIG OL' DARK SKY'S ABOUT TO BE LIT UP REAL PRETTY AND ORANGE.
I CAN HARDLY TAKE THE SUSPENSE!

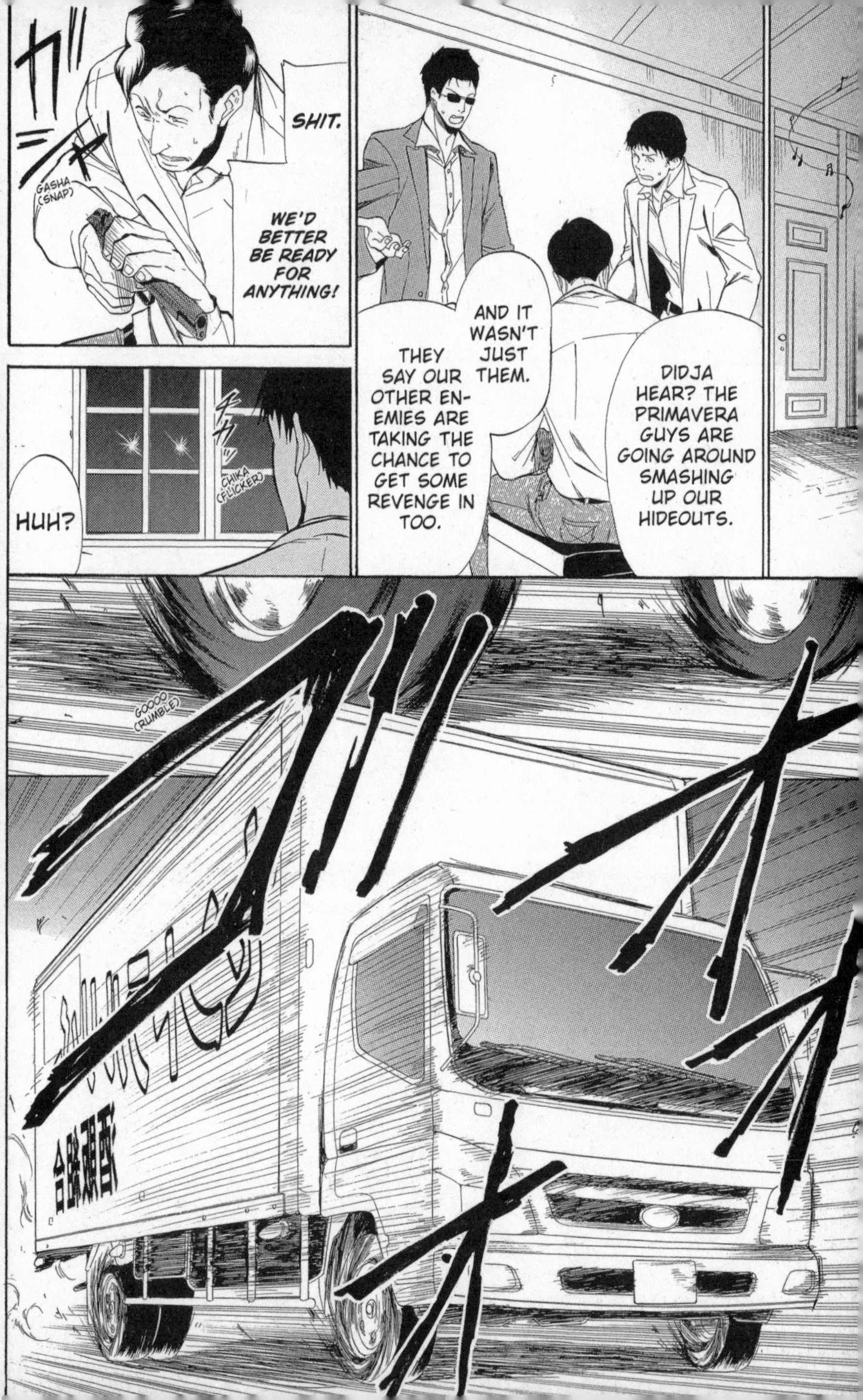
DIDJA HEAR? THE PRIMAVERA GUYS ARE GOING AROUND SMASHING UP OUR HIDEOUTS.
AND IT WASN'T JUST THEM.
THEY SAY OUR OTHER ENEMIES ARE TAKING THE CHANCE TO GET SOME REVENGE IN TOO.
SHIT.
GASHA (SNAP)
WE'D BETTER BE READY FOR ANYTHING!
CHIKA (FLICKER)
HUH?
GOOOO (RUMBLE)

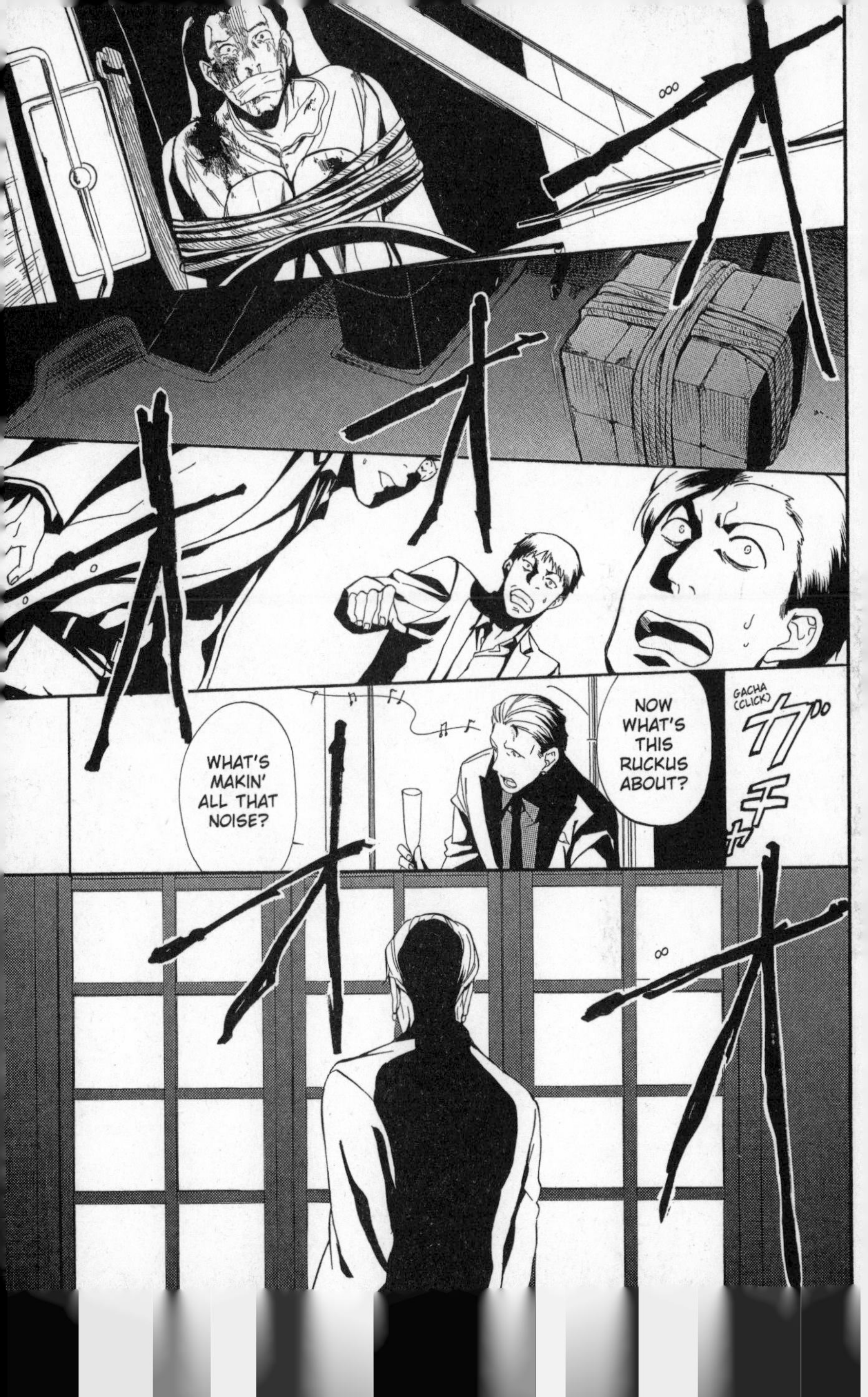
GACHA (CLICK)
NOW WHAT'S THIS RUCKUS ABOUT?
WHAT'S MAKIN' ALL THAT NOISE?

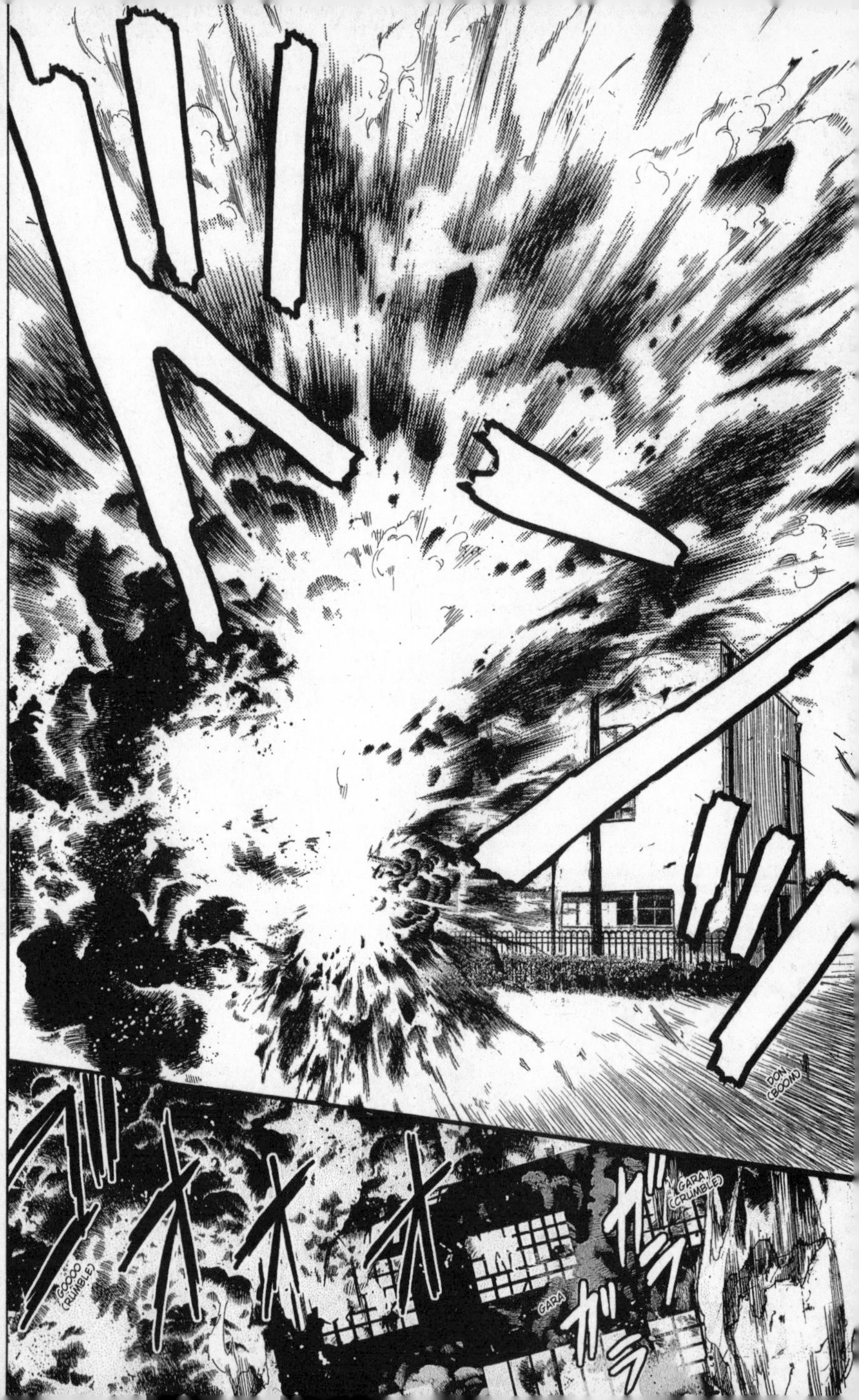
DON (BOOM)
GARA (CRUMBLE)
GARA
GOOOO (RUMBLE)

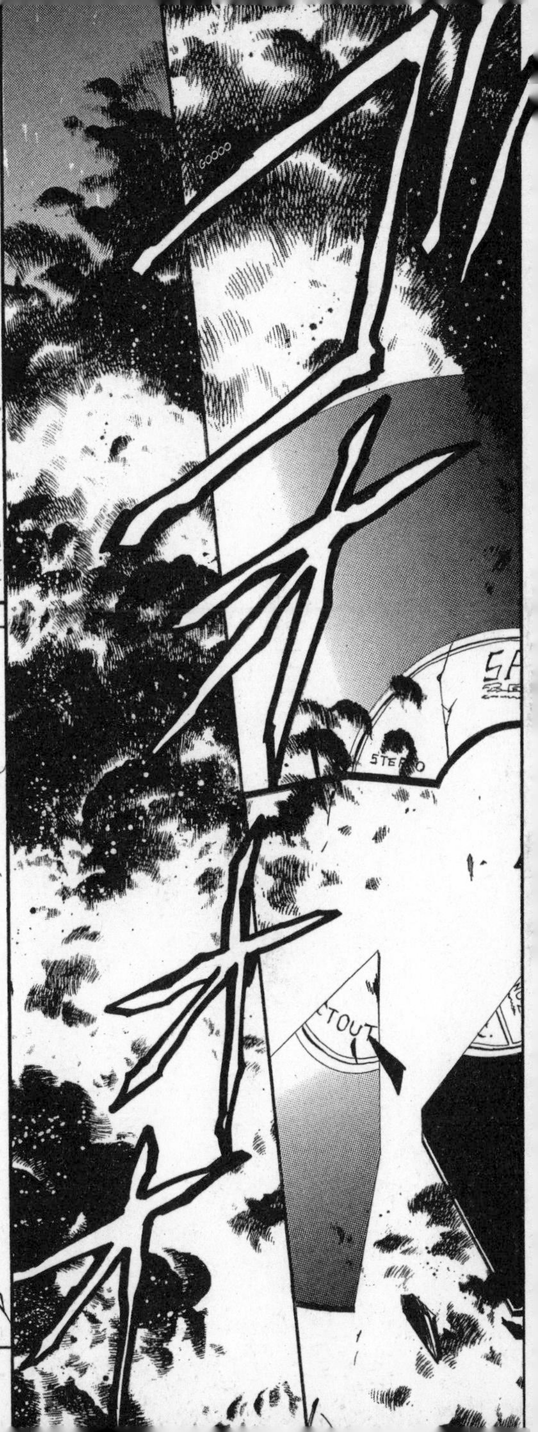
GOOOO
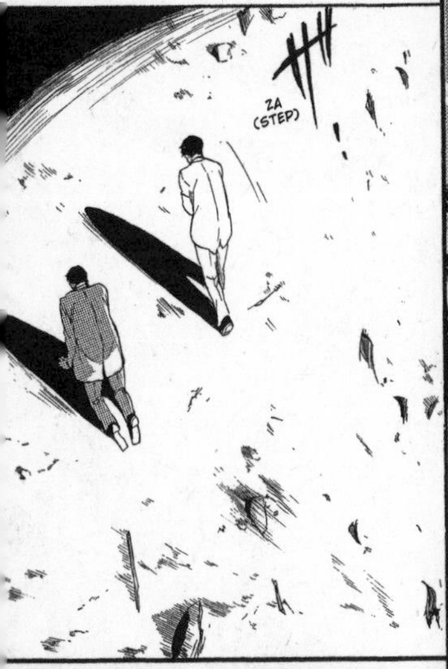
ZA (STEP)
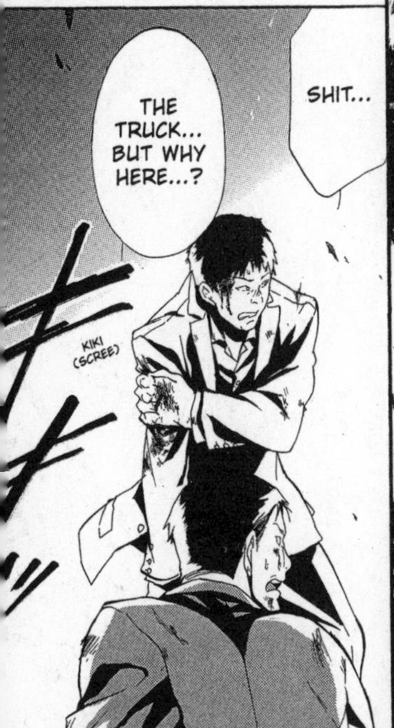
SHIT...
THE TRUCK... BUT WHY HERE...?
KIKI (SCREE)

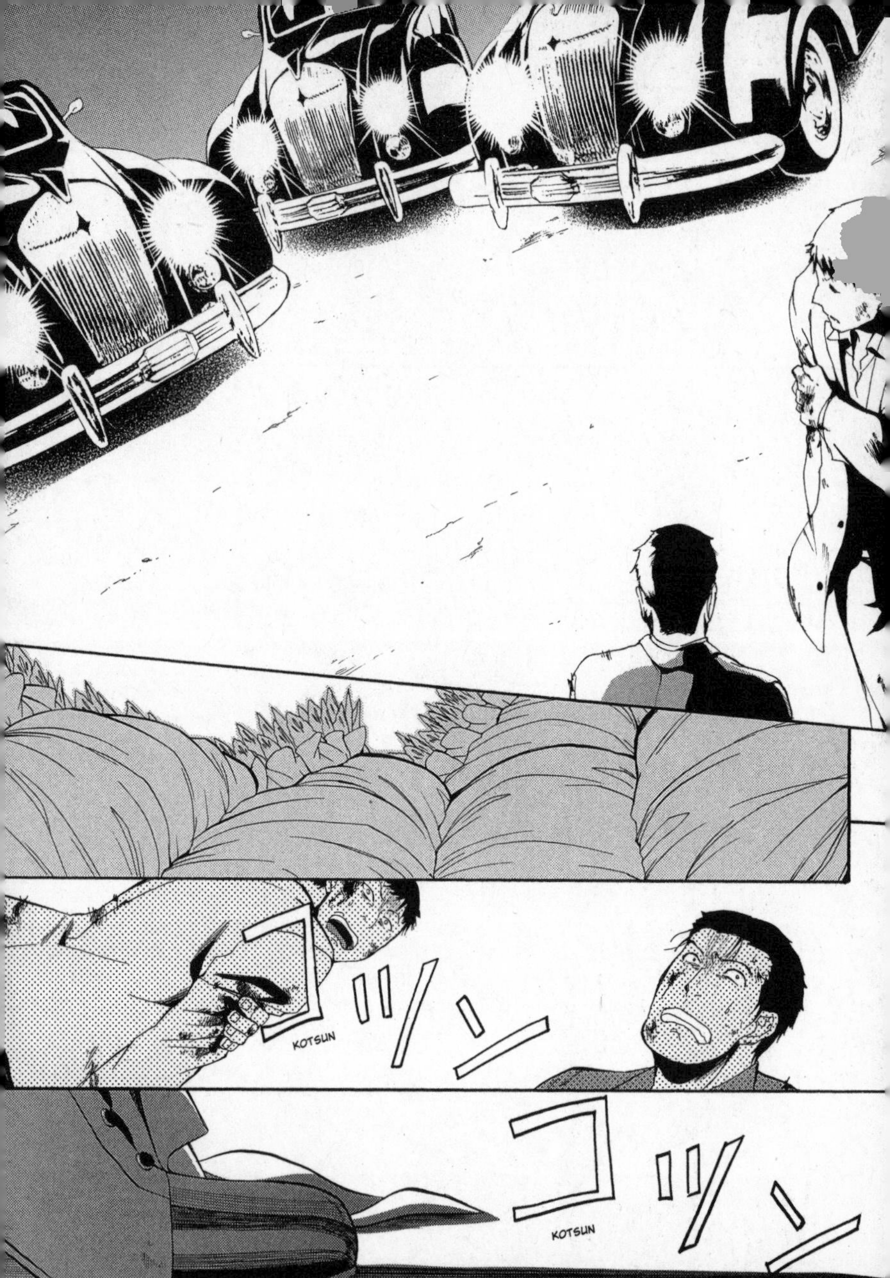
コッソン
KOTSUN
コッソン
KOTSUN

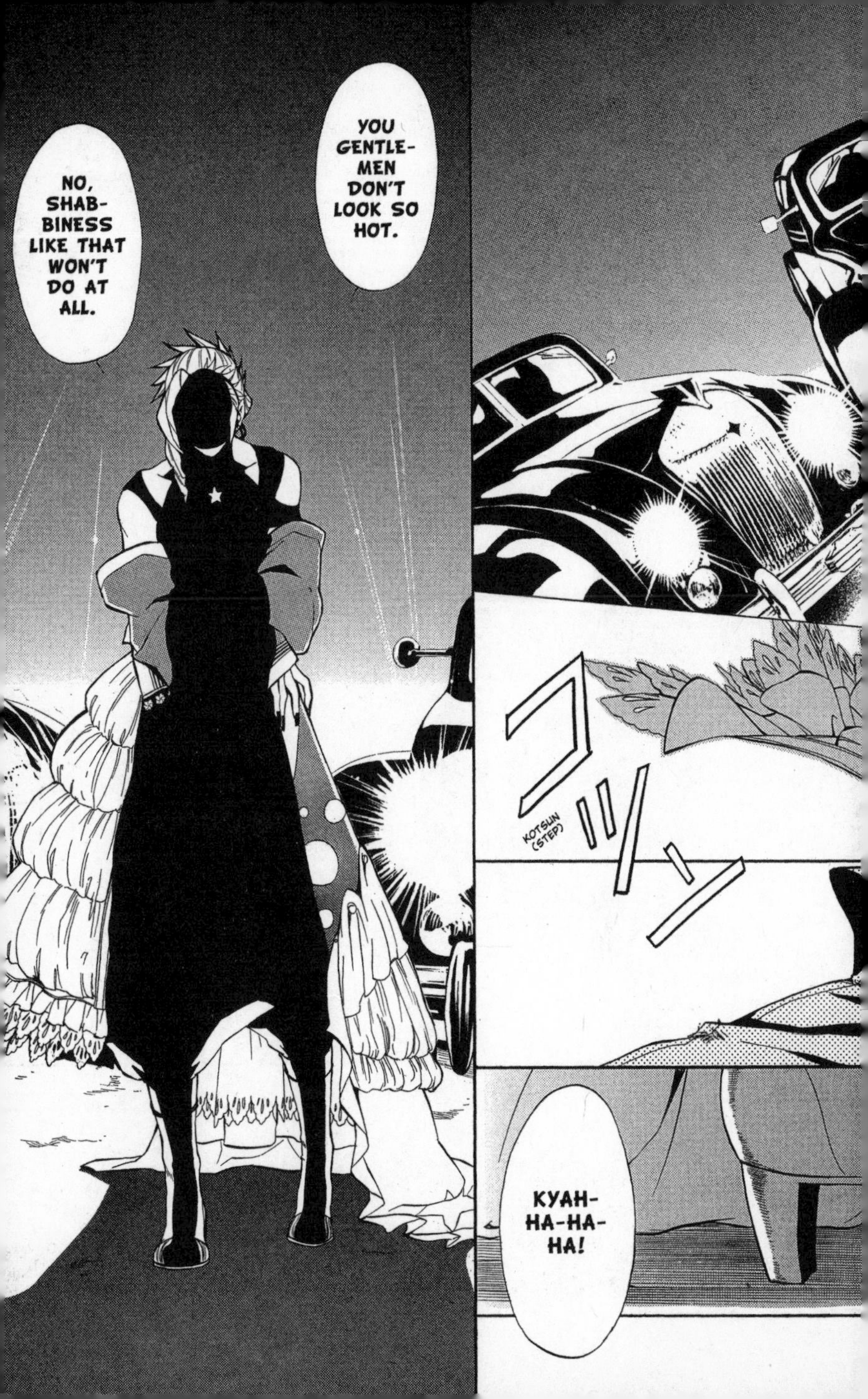
KOTSUN (STEP)
KYAH-HA-HA-HA!
YOU GENTLEMEN DON'T LOOK SO HOT.
NO, SHABBINESS LIKE THAT WON'T DO AT ALL.

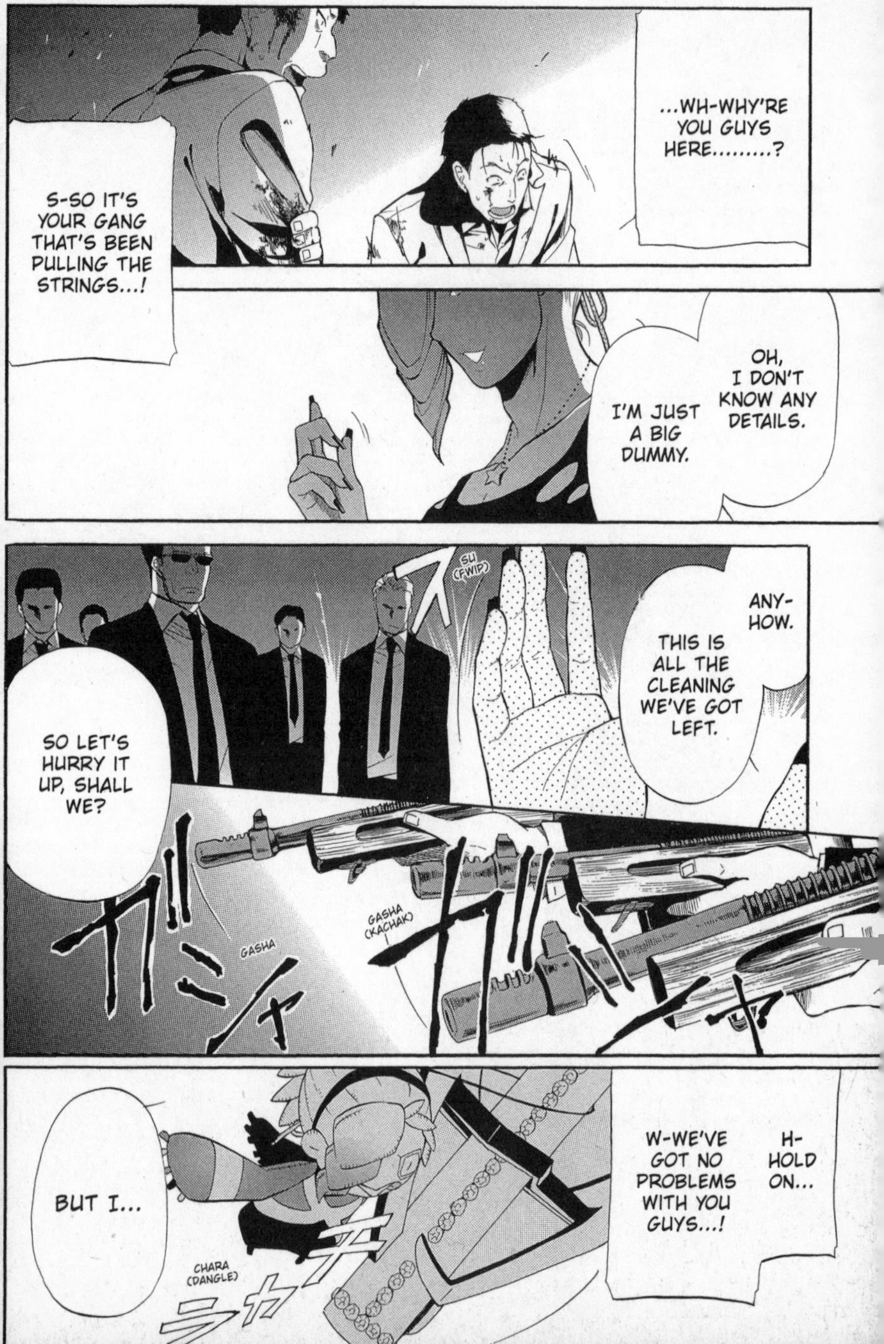
...WH-WHY'RE YOU GUYS HERE.........?
S-SO IT'S YOUR GANG THAT'S BEEN PULLING THE STRINGS...!
OH, I DON'T KNOW ANY DETAILS.
I'M JUST A BIG DUMMY.
ANY-HOW.
THIS IS ALL THE CLEANING WE'VE GOT LEFT.
SU (FWIP)
SO LET'S HURRY IT UP, SHALL WE?
GASHA (KACHAK)
GASHA
H-HOLD ON...
W-WE'VE GOT NO PROBLEMS WITH YOU GUYS...!
BUT I...
CHARA (DANGLE)

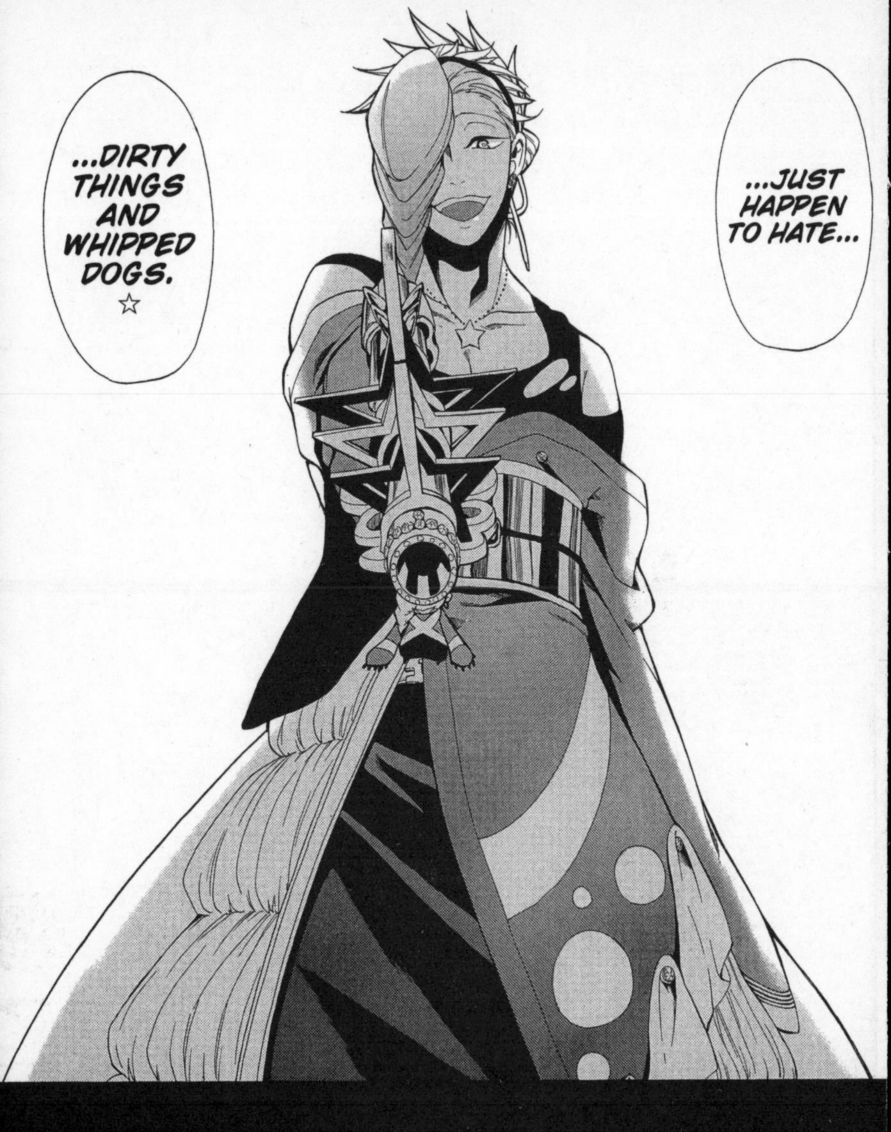
...JUST HAPPEN TO HATE...
...DIRTY THINGS AND WHIPPED DOGS. ☆

...COMING UP NEXT...CHAPTER 4

TRANSLATION NOTES

COMMON HONORIFICS

no honorific: Indicates familiarity or closeness; if used without permission or reason, addressing someone in this manner would constitute an insult.

-san: The Japanese equivalent of Mr./Mrs./Miss. If a situation calls for politeness, this is the fail-safe honorific.

-sama: Conveys great respect; may also indicate that the social status of the speaker is lower than that of the addressee.

-kun: Used most often when referring to boys, this indicates affection or familiarity. Occasionally used by older men among their peers, but it may also be used by anyone referring to a person of lower standing.

-chan: An affectionate honorific indicating familiarity used mostly in reference to girls; also used in reference to cute persons or animals of either gender.

-senpai: A suffix used to address upperclassmen or more experienced coworkers.

PAGE 19

Leo's demonstration of his limited English skills is an infamous one. The line, which comes from accidentally combining grade school-level textbook sentences, "This is a pen," and "I am a student," is well-known "bad" Japanese English.

PAGE 51

The bar Keireiji frequents is called "*Nobushi*," which means "The Wandering Samurai." It's a perfect metaphor for the state of the veterans in this version of Tokyo, who wander the streets without jobs, skills, or prospects.

PAGE 166

Leaving the cigarette (instead of an incense stick) and clapping his hands in prayer is Leo's traditional Japanese way of respecting the dead veteran.

Chapter 4

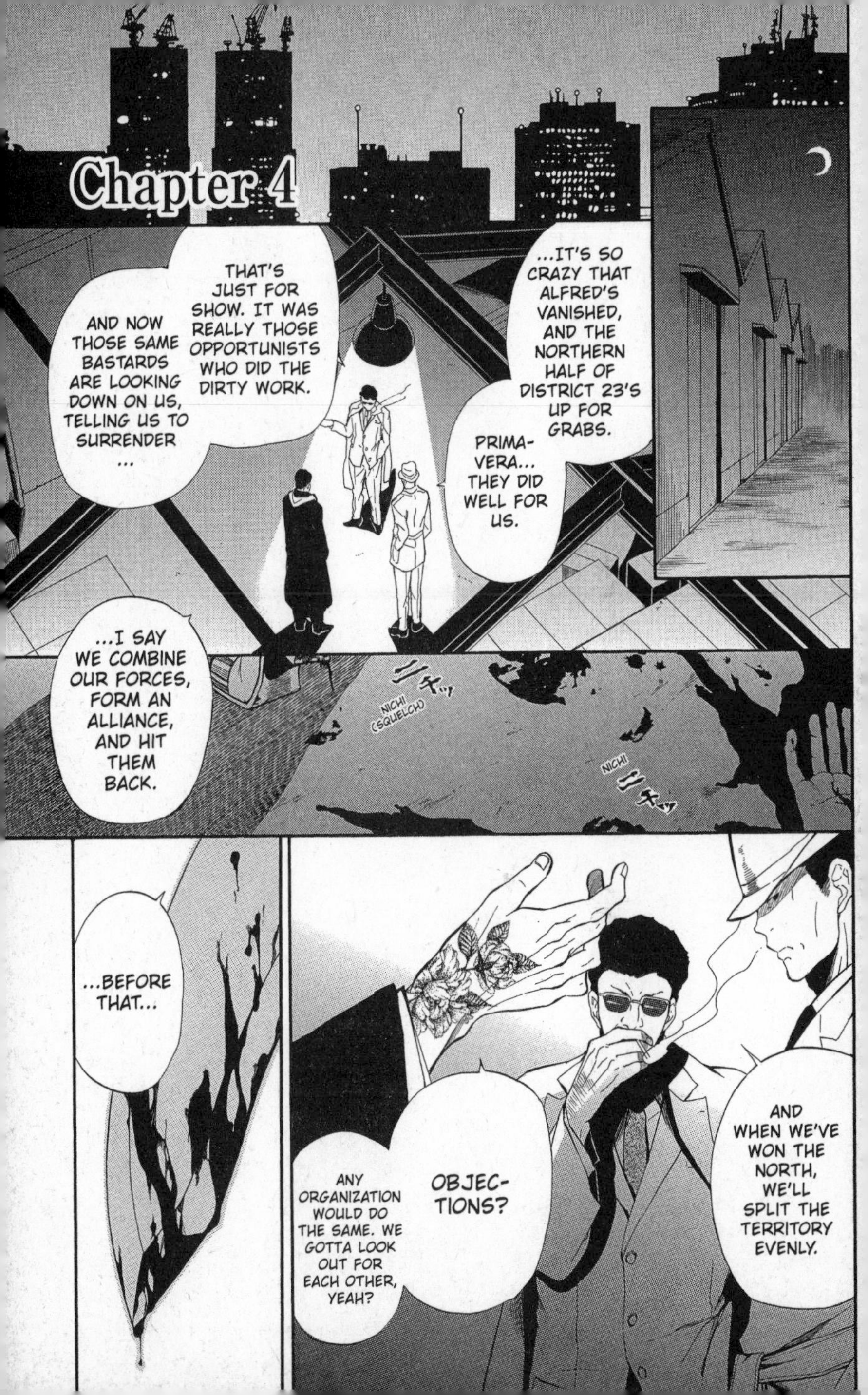
...IT'S SO CRAZY THAT ALFRED'S VANISHED, AND THE NORTHERN HALF OF DISTRICT 23'S UP FOR GRABS.
PRIMA-VERA... THEY DID WELL FOR US.
THAT'S JUST FOR SHOW. IT WAS REALLY THOSE OPPORTUNISTS WHO DID THE DIRTY WORK.
AND NOW THOSE SAME BASTARDS ARE LOOKING DOWN ON US, TELLING US TO SURRENDER ...
NICHI (SQUELCH)
NICHI
...I SAY WE COMBINE OUR FORCES, FORM AN ALLIANCE, AND HIT THEM BACK.
AND WHEN WE'VE WON THE NORTH, WE'LL SPLIT THE TERRITORY EVENLY.
OBJEC-TIONS?
ANY ORGANIZATION WOULD DO THE SAME. WE GOTTA LOOK OUT FOR EACH OTHER, YEAH?
...BEFORE THAT...

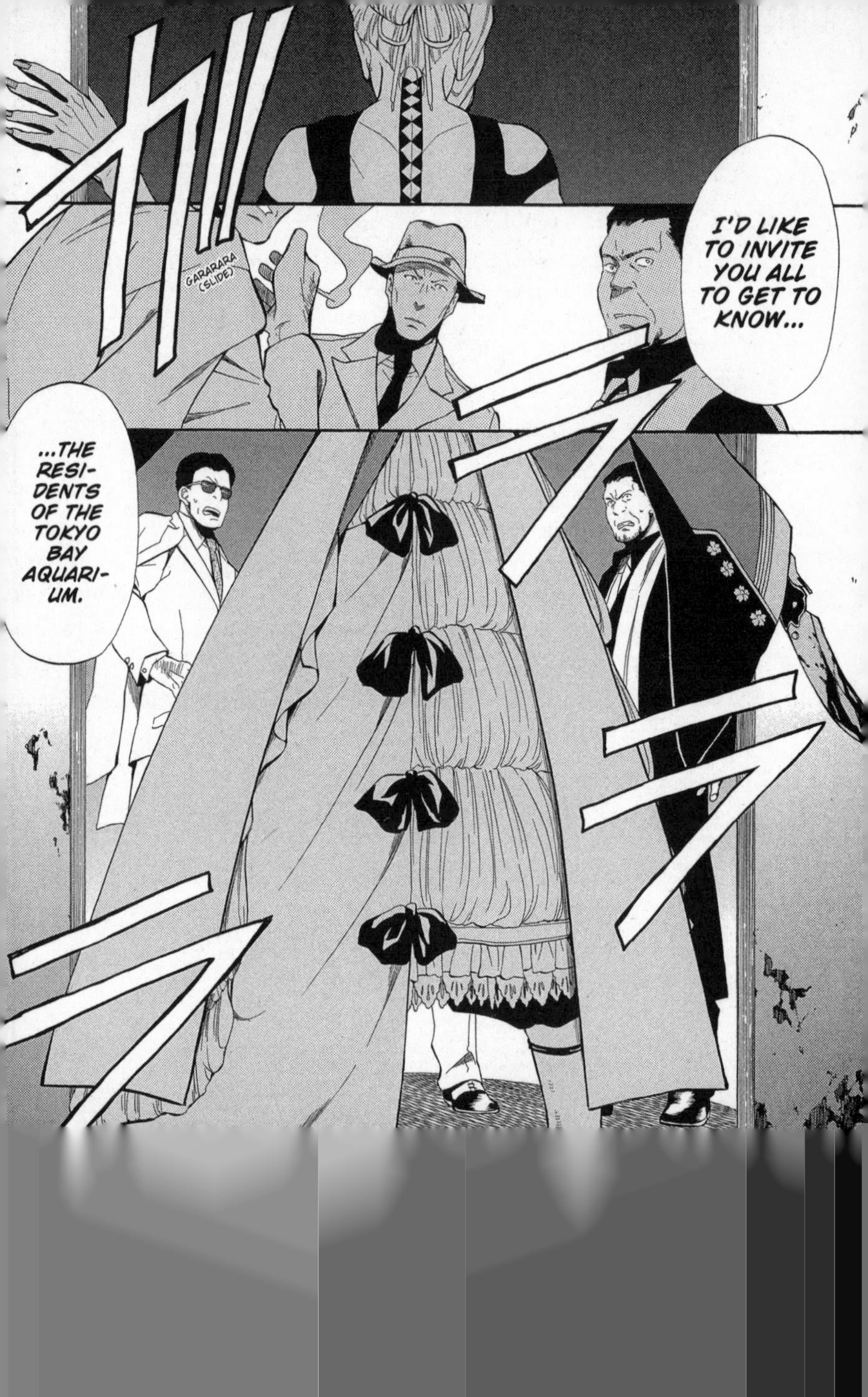
I'D LIKE TO INVITE YOU ALL TO GET TO KNOW...
GARARARA (SLIDE)
...THE RESI-DENTS OF THE TOKYO BAY AQUARI-UM.

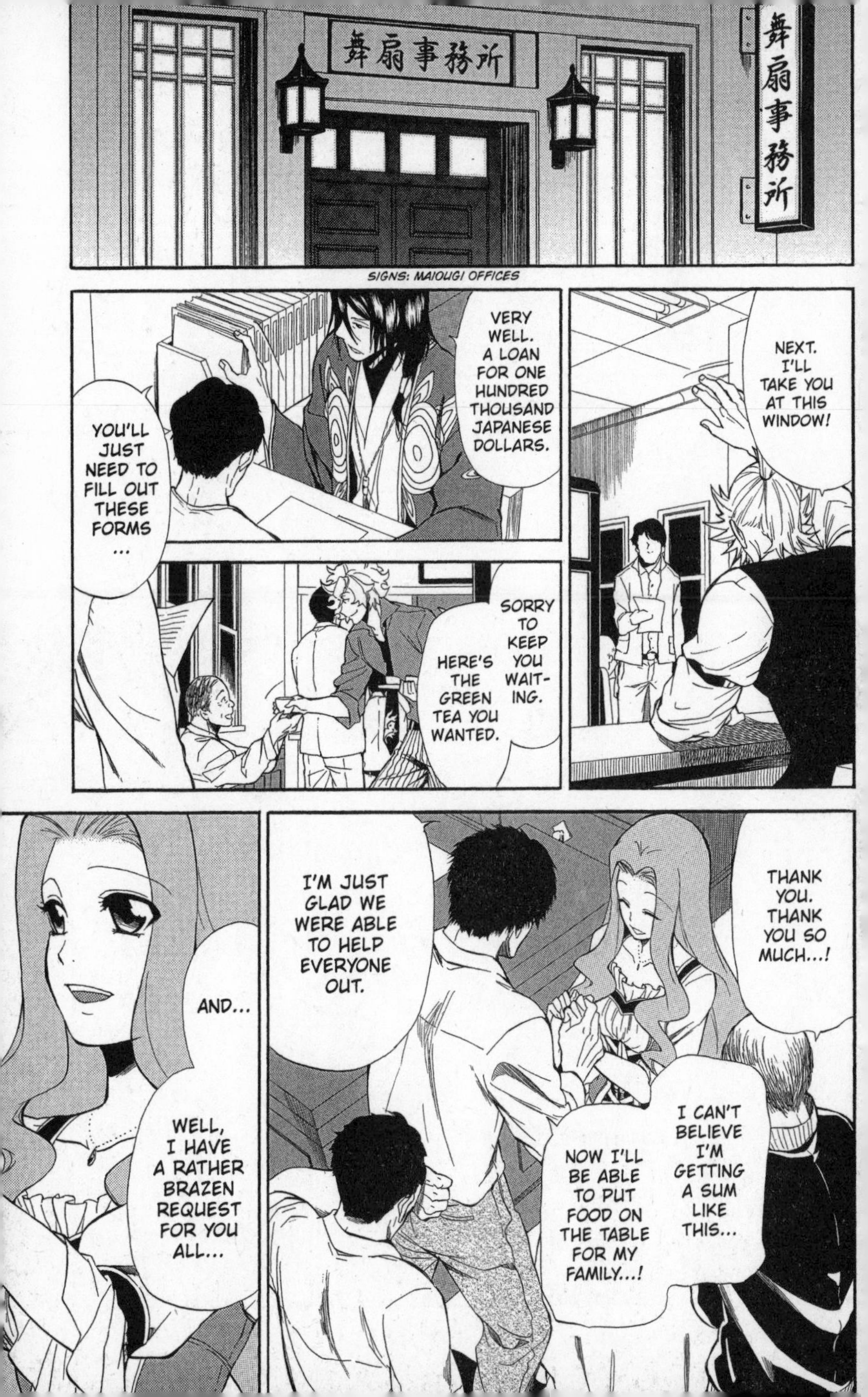
舞扇事務所
舞扇事務所
SIGNS: MAIOUGI OFFICES
NEXT. I'LL TAKE YOU AT THIS WINDOW!
VERY WELL. A LOAN FOR ONE HUNDRED THOUSAND JAPANESE DOLLARS.
YOU'LL JUST NEED TO FILL OUT THESE FORMS ...
SORRY TO KEEP YOU WAITING.
HERE'S THE GREEN TEA YOU WANTED.
THANK YOU. THANK YOU SO MUCH...!
I'M JUST GLAD WE WERE ABLE TO HELP EVERYONE OUT.
I CAN'T BELIEVE I'M GETTING A SUM LIKE THIS...
NOW I'LL BE ABLE TO PUT FOOD ON THE TABLE FOR MY FAMILY...!
AND...
WELL, I HAVE A RATHER BRAZEN REQUEST FOR YOU ALL...

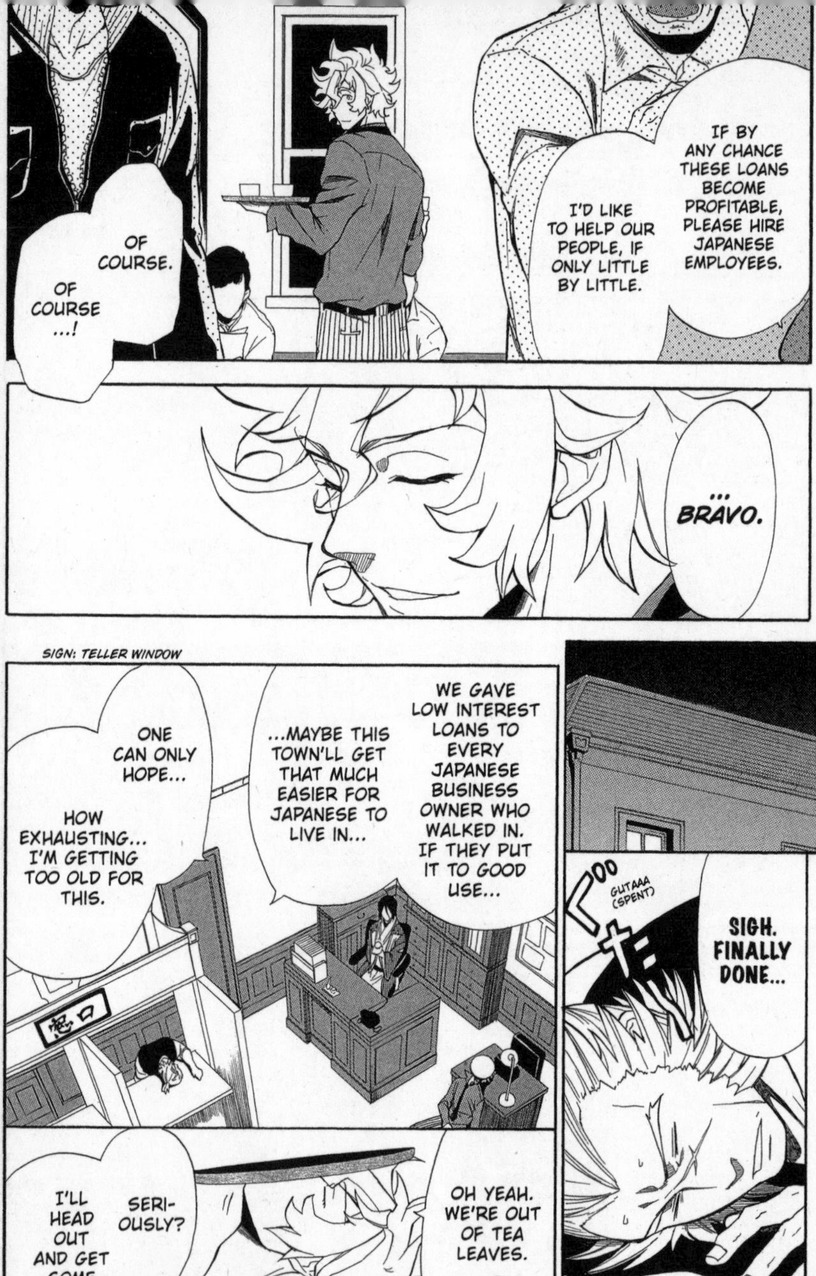
IF BY ANY CHANCE THESE LOANS BECOME PROFITABLE, PLEASE HIRE JAPANESE EMPLOYEES.
I'D LIKE TO HELP OUR PEOPLE, IF ONLY LITTLE BY LITTLE.
OF COURSE.
OF COURSE ...!
... BRAVO.
GUTAAA (SPENT)
SIGH. FINALLY DONE...
SIGN: TELLER WINDOW
WE GAVE LOW INTEREST LOANS TO EVERY JAPANESE BUSINESS OWNER WHO WALKED IN. IF THEY PUT IT TO GOOD USE...
...MAYBE THIS TOWN'LL GET THAT MUCH EASIER FOR JAPANESE TO LIVE IN...
ONE CAN ONLY HOPE...
HOW EXHAUSTING... I'M GETTING TOO OLD FOR THIS.
OH YEAH. WE'RE OUT OF TEA LEAVES.
EVEN THOUGH WE JUST BOUGHT SOME.
SERI-OUSLY?
I'LL HEAD OUT AND GET SOME MORE.

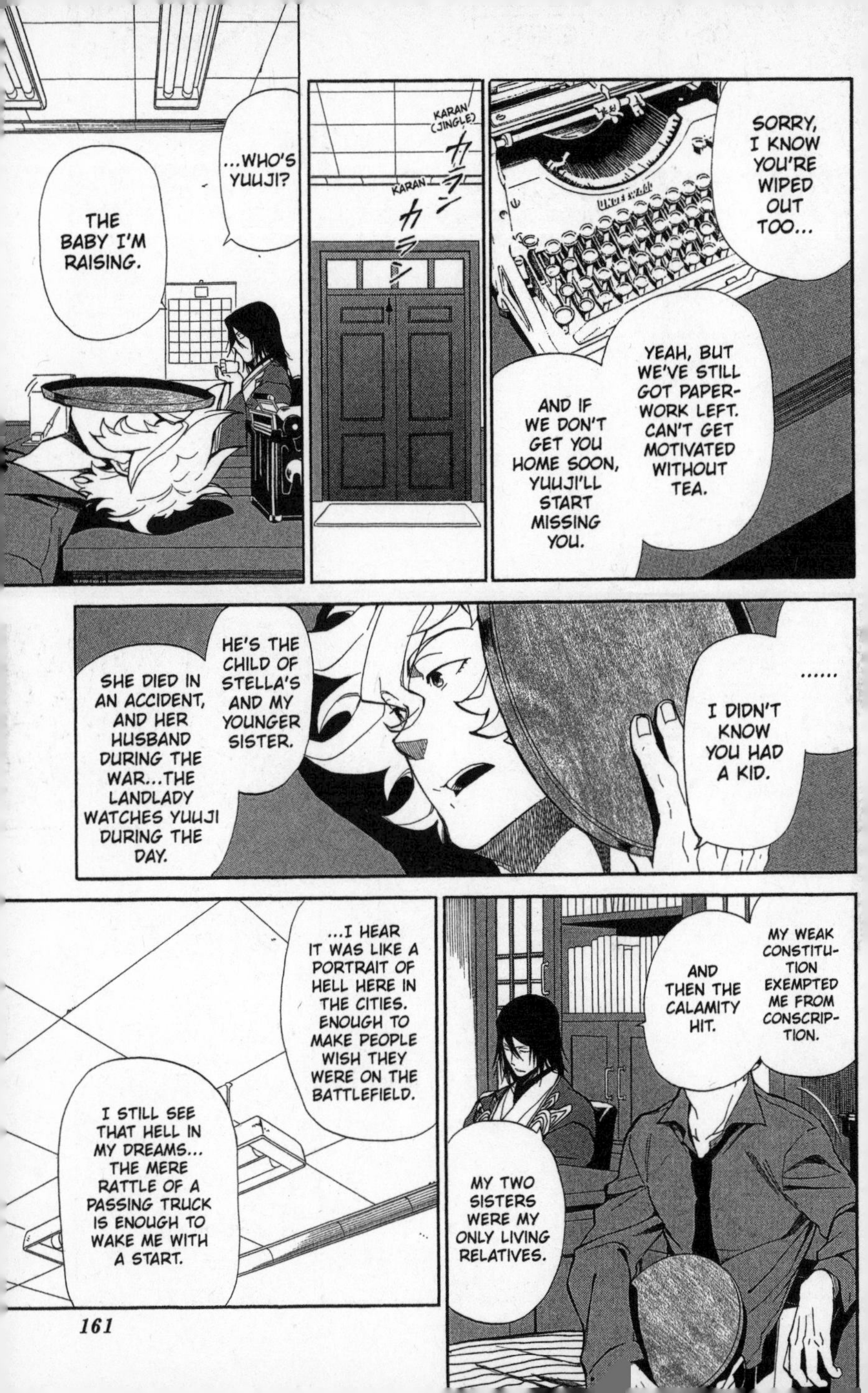
SORRY, I KNOW YOU'RE WIPED OUT TOO...
YEAH, BUT WE'VE STILL GOT PAPER-WORK LEFT. CAN'T GET MOTIVATED WITHOUT TEA.
AND IF WE DON'T GET YOU HOME SOON, YUUJI'LL START MISSING YOU.
KARAN (JINGLE)
カラン
KARAN
カラン
...WHO'S YUUJI?
THE BABY I'M RAISING.
......
I DIDN'T KNOW YOU HAD A KID.
HE'S THE CHILD OF STELLA'S AND MY YOUNGER SISTER.
SHE DIED IN AN ACCIDENT, AND HER HUSBAND DURING THE WAR...THE LANDLADY WATCHES YUUJI DURING THE DAY.
MY WEAK CONSTITU-TION EXEMPTED ME FROM CONSCRIP-TION.
AND THEN THE CALAMITY HIT.
MY TWO SISTERS WERE MY ONLY LIVING RELATIVES.
...I HEAR IT WAS LIKE A PORTRAIT OF HELL HERE IN THE CITIES. ENOUGH TO MAKE PEOPLE WISH THEY WERE ON THE BATTLEFIELD.
I STILL SEE THAT HELL IN MY DREAMS... THE MERE RATTLE OF A PASSING TRUCK IS ENOUGH TO WAKE ME WITH A START.

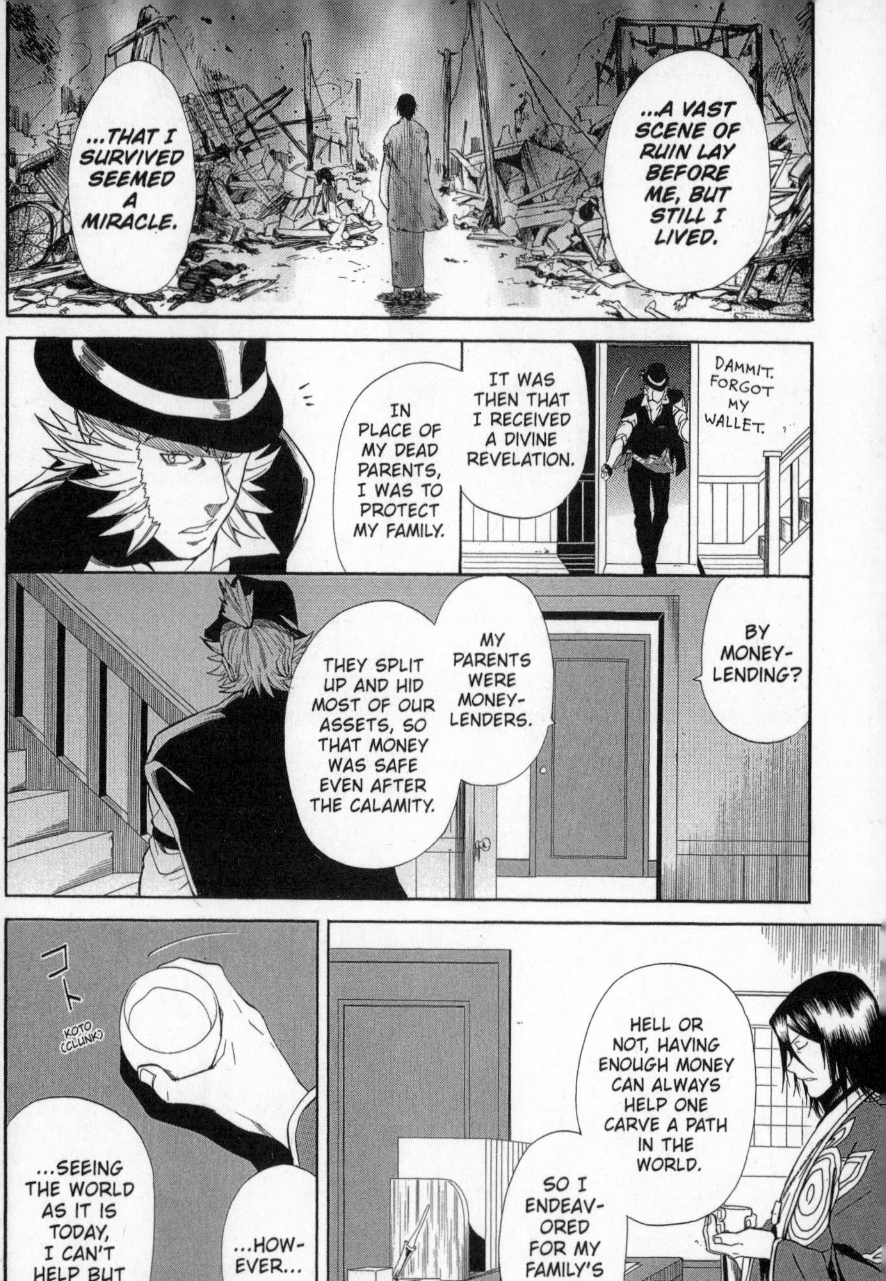
...A VAST SCENE OF RUIN LAY BEFORE ME, BUT STILL I LIVED.
...THAT I SURVIVED SEEMED A MIRACLE.
DAMMIT. FORGOT MY WALLET.
IT WAS THEN THAT I RECEIVED A DIVINE REVELATION.
IN PLACE OF MY DEAD PARENTS, I WAS TO PROTECT MY FAMILY.
BY MONEY-LENDING?
MY PARENTS WERE MONEY-LENDERS.
THEY SPLIT UP AND HID MOST OF OUR ASSETS, SO THAT MONEY WAS SAFE EVEN AFTER THE CALAMITY.
HELL OR NOT, HAVING ENOUGH MONEY CAN ALWAYS HELP ONE CARVE A PATH IN THE WORLD.
SO I ENDEAVORED FOR MY FAMILY'S SAKE.
コト
KOTO (CLUNK)
...HOWEVER...
...SEEING THE WORLD AS IT IS TODAY, I CAN'T HELP BUT WORRY...

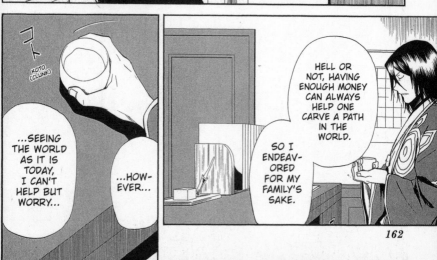

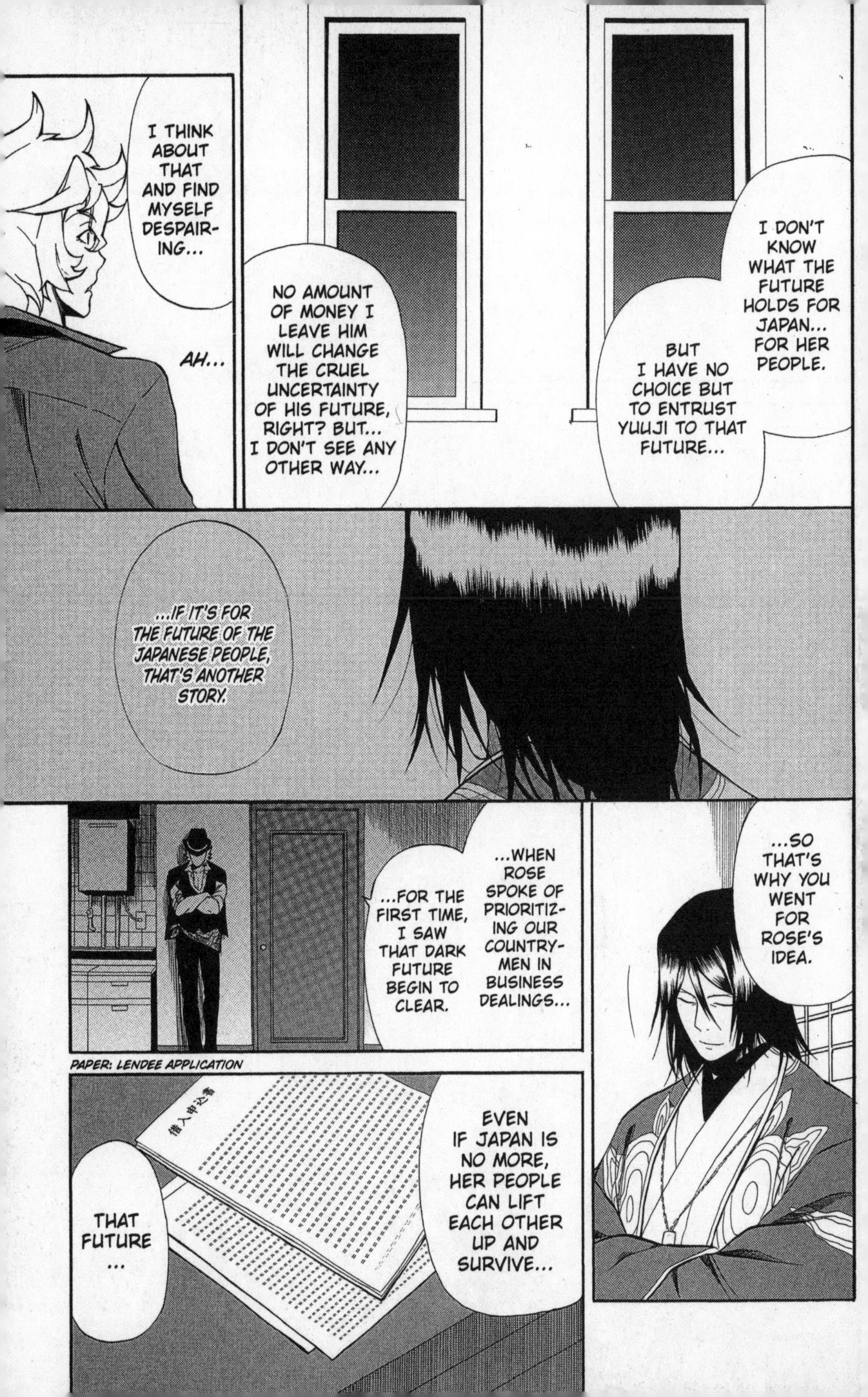
I DON'T KNOW WHAT THE FUTURE HOLDS FOR JAPAN... FOR HER PEOPLE.
BUT I HAVE NO CHOICE BUT TO ENTRUST YUUJI TO THAT FUTURE...
NO AMOUNT OF MONEY I LEAVE HIM WILL CHANGE THE CRUEL UNCERTAINTY OF HIS FUTURE, RIGHT? BUT... I DON'T SEE ANY OTHER WAY...
I THINK ABOUT THAT AND FIND MYSELF DESPAIR-ING...
AH...
...IF IT'S FOR THE FUTURE OF THE JAPANESE PEOPLE, THAT'S ANOTHER STORY.
...SO THAT'S WHY YOU WENT FOR ROSE'S IDEA.
...WHEN ROSE SPOKE OF PRIORITIZ-ING OUR COUNTRY-MEN IN BUSINESS DEALINGS...
...FOR THE FIRST TIME, I SAW THAT DARK FUTURE BEGIN TO CLEAR.
PAPER: LENDEE APPLICATION
借入申込書
EVEN IF JAPAN IS NO MORE, HER PEOPLE CAN LIFT EACH OTHER UP AND SURVIVE...
THAT FUTURE ...

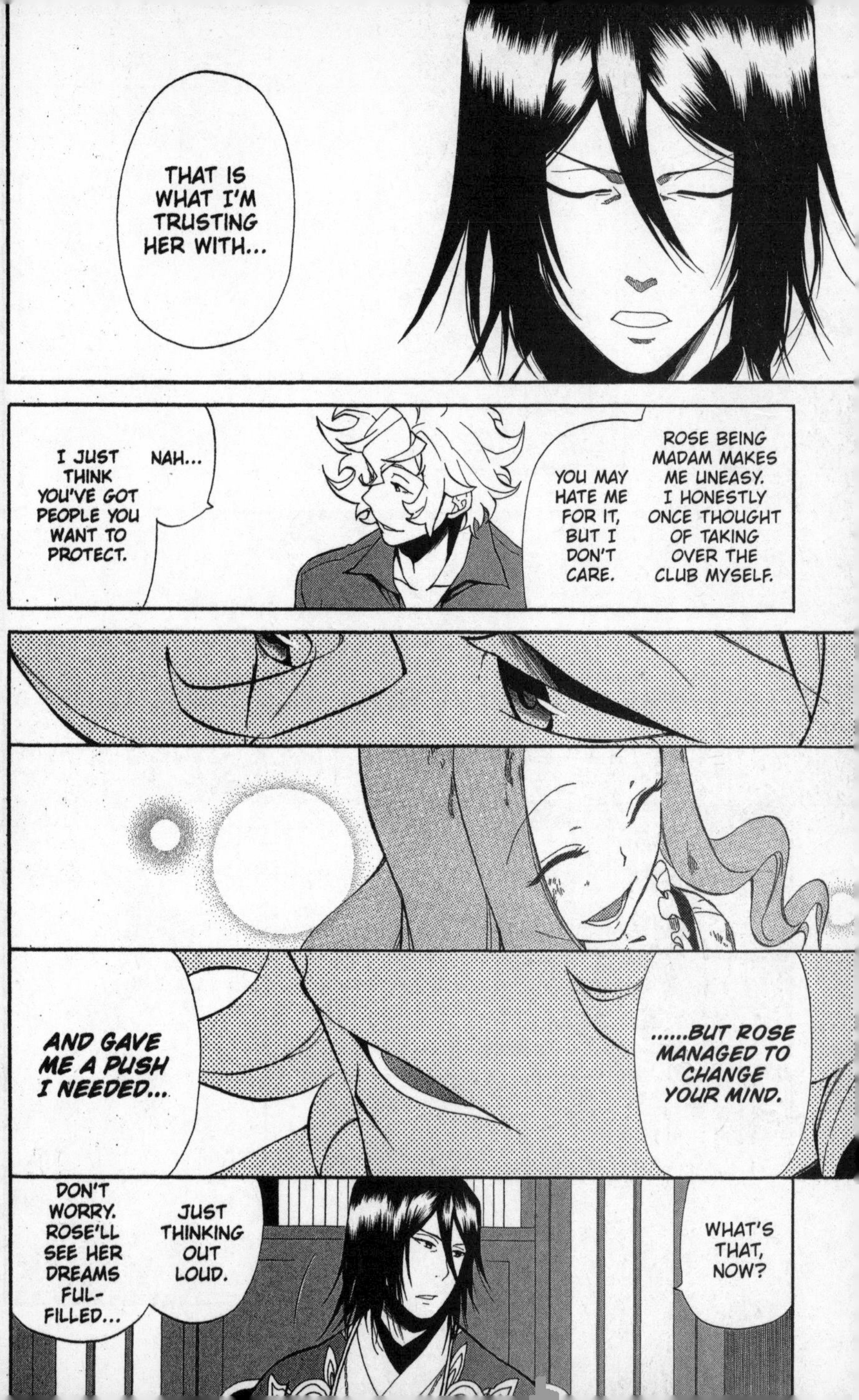
THAT IS WHAT I'M TRUSTING HER WITH...
ROSE BEING MADAM MAKES ME UNEASY. I HONESTLY ONCE THOUGHT OF TAKING OVER THE CLUB MYSELF.
YOU MAY HATE ME FOR IT, BUT I DON'T CARE.
NAH...
I JUST THINK YOU'VE GOT PEOPLE YOU WANT TO PROTECT.
......BUT ROSE MANAGED TO CHANGE YOUR MIND.
AND GAVE ME A PUSH I NEEDED...
WHAT'S THAT, NOW?
JUST THINKING OUT LOUD.
DON'T WORRY. ROSE'LL SEE HER DREAMS FUL-FILLED...

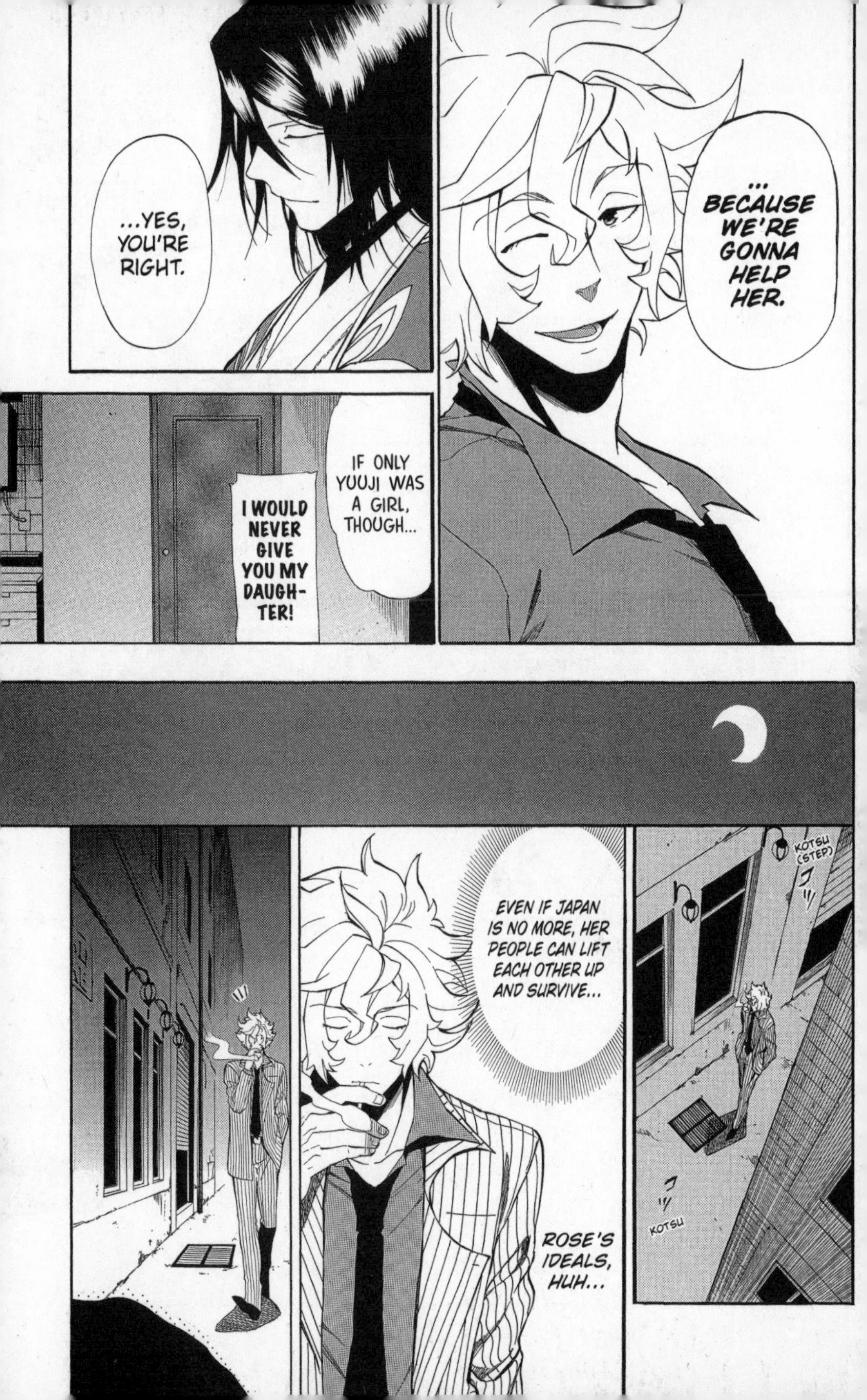
...BECAUSE WE'RE GONNA HELP HER.
...YES, YOU'RE RIGHT.
IF ONLY YUUJI WAS A GIRL, THOUGH...
I WOULD NEVER GIVE YOU MY DAUGH-TER!
KOTSU (STEP)
KOTSU
EVEN IF JAPAN IS NO MORE, HER PEOPLE CAN LIFT EACH OTHER UP AND SURVIVE...
ROSE'S IDEALS, HUH...

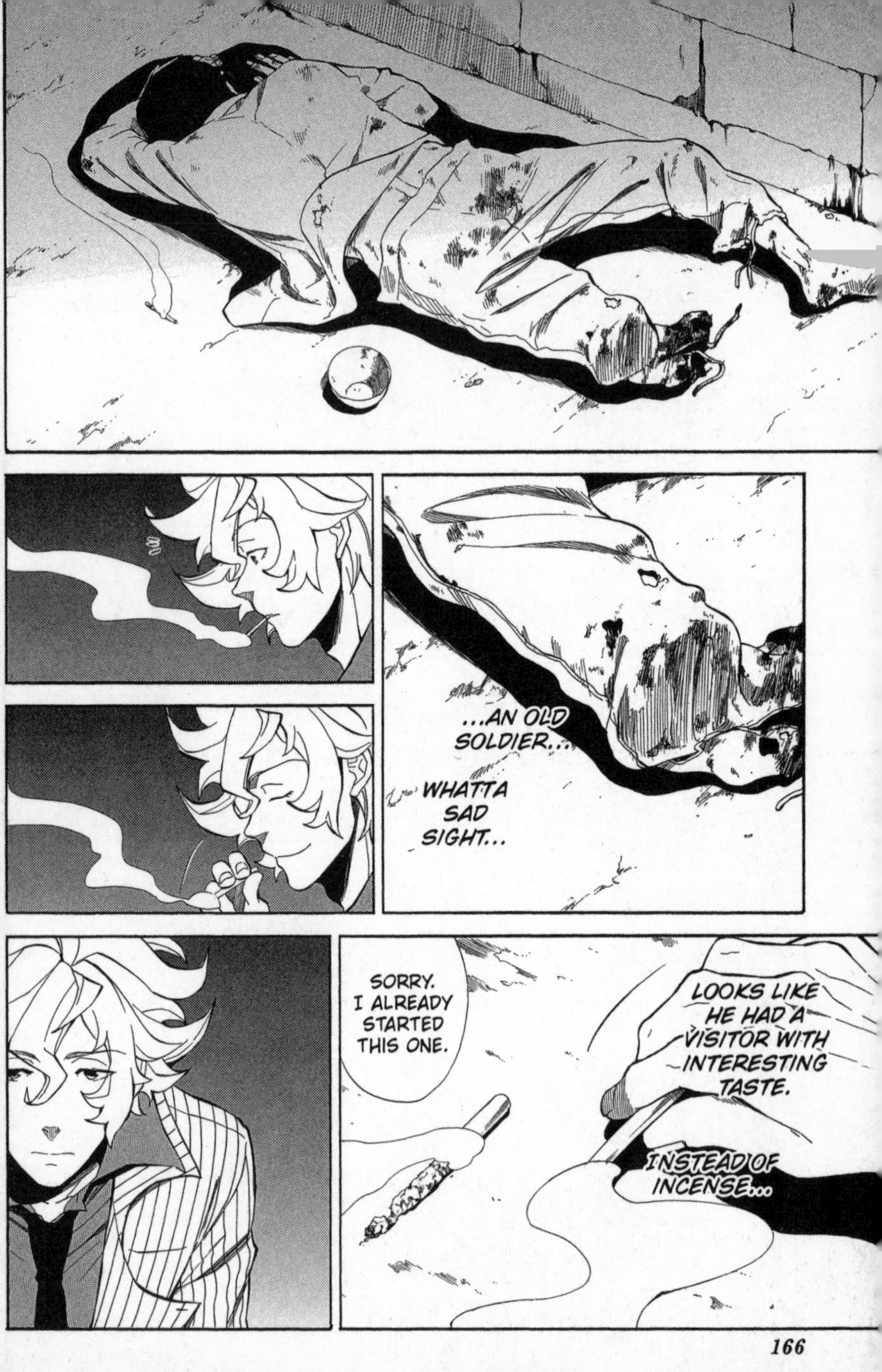
...AN OLD SOLDIER...
WHATTA SAD SIGHT...
LOOKS LIKE HE HAD A VISITOR WITH INTERESTING TASTE.
INSTEAD OF INCENSE...
SORRY. I ALREADY STARTED THIS ONE.

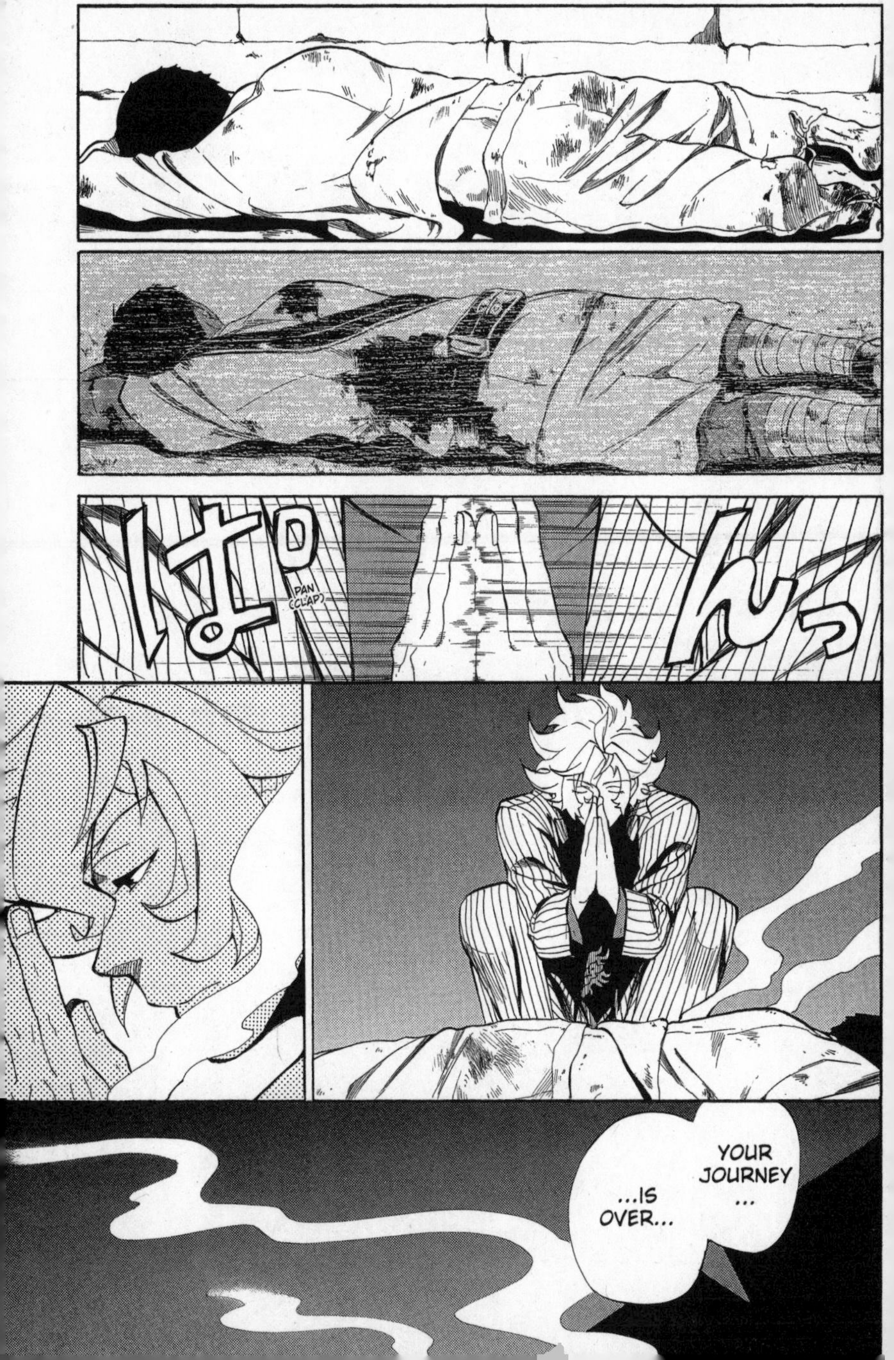
ぱ
PAN (CLAP)
んっ
YOUR JOURNEY ...
...IS OVER...

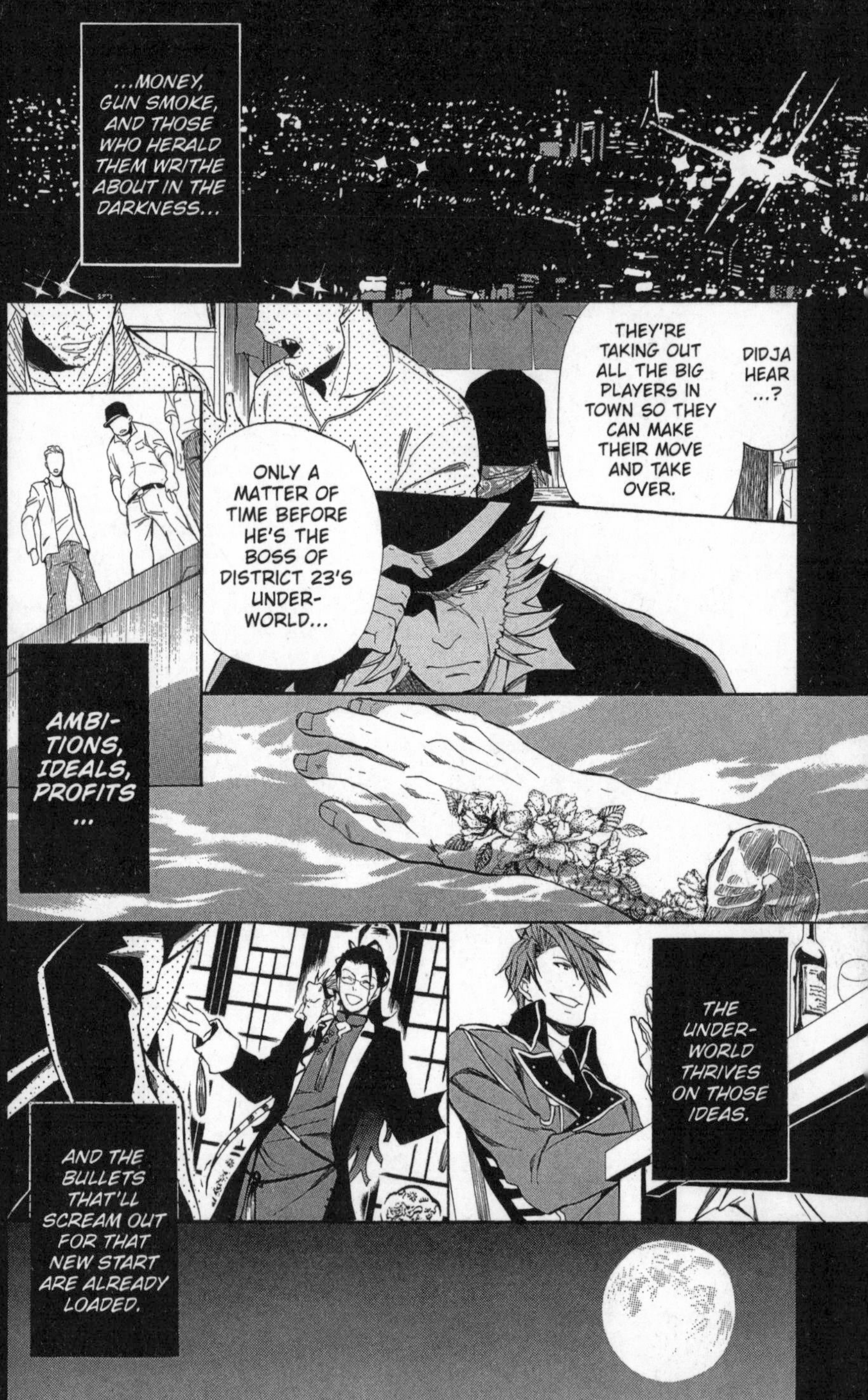
...MONEY, GUN SMOKE, AND THOSE WHO HERALD THEM WRITHE ABOUT IN THE DARKNESS...
DIDJA HEAR ...?
THEY'RE TAKING OUT ALL THE BIG PLAYERS IN TOWN SO THEY CAN MAKE THEIR MOVE AND TAKE OVER.
ONLY A MATTER OF TIME BEFORE HE'S THE BOSS OF DISTRICT 23'S UNDER-WORLD...
AMBI-TIONS, IDEALS, PROFITS ...
THE UNDER-WORLD THRIVES ON THOSE IDEAS.
AND THE BULLETS THAT'LL SCREAM OUT FOR THAT NEW START ARE ALREADY LOADED.

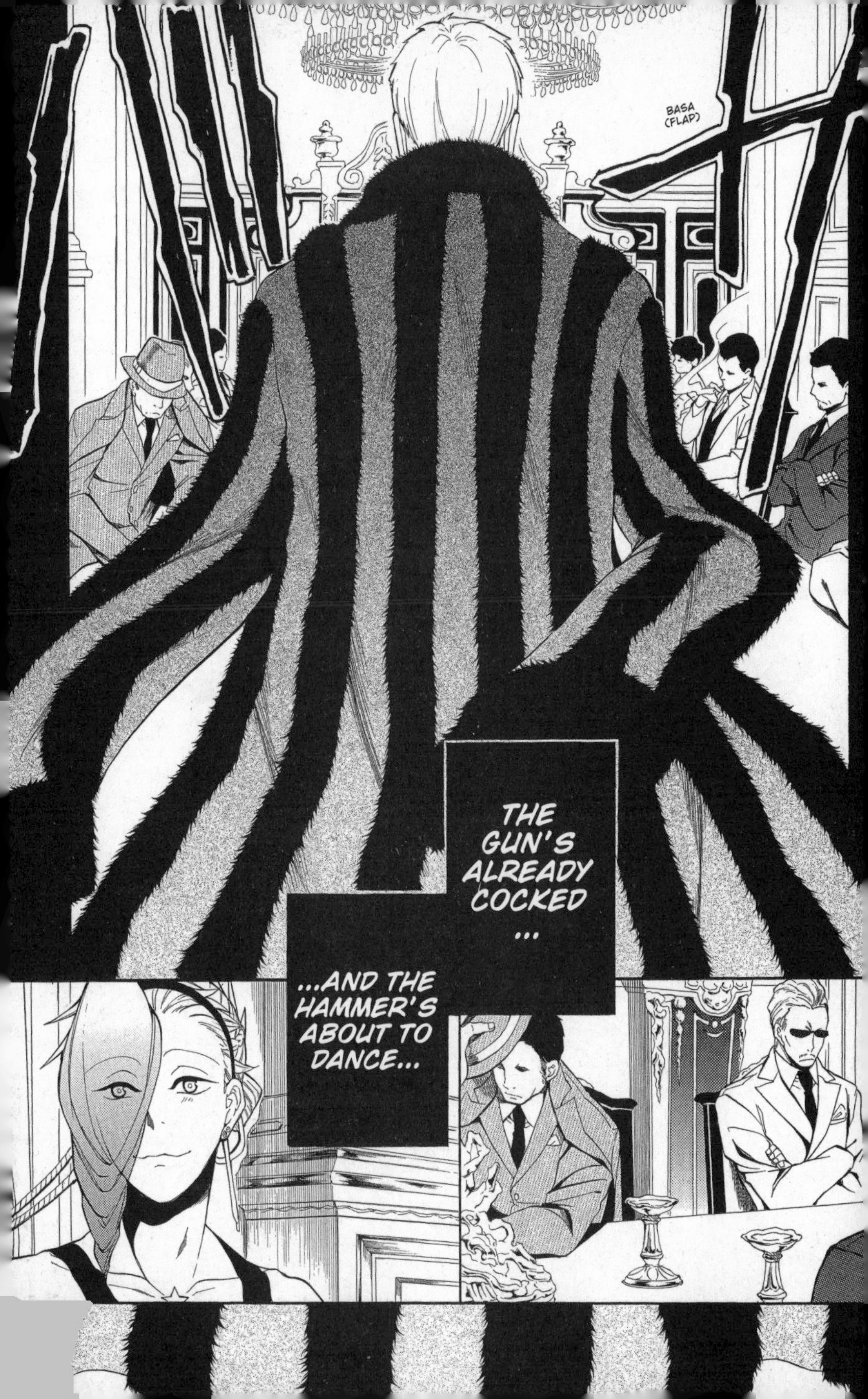
BASA (FLAP)
THE GUN'S ALREADY COCKED ...
...AND THE HAMMER'S ABOUT TO DANCE...

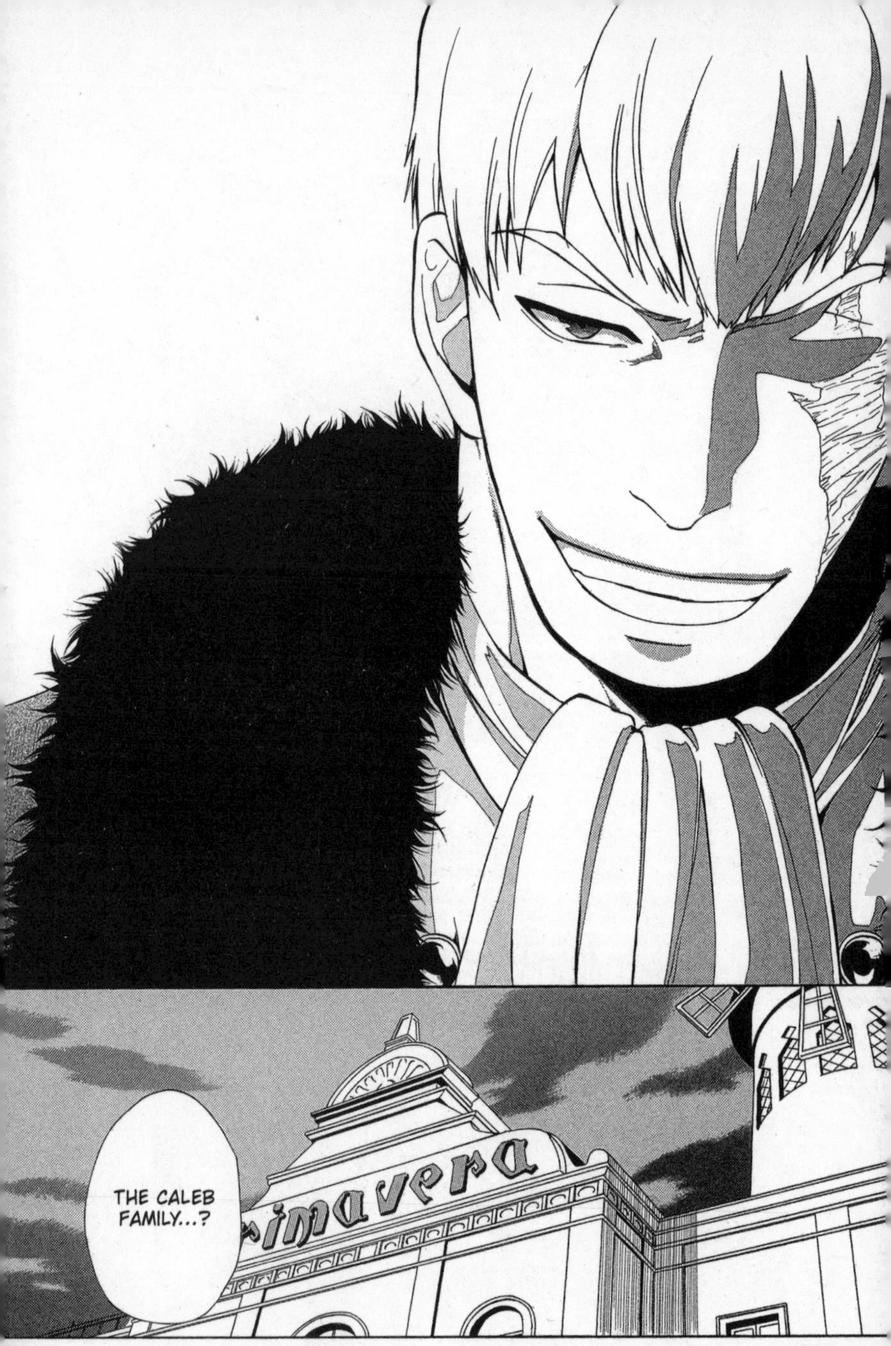
THE CALEB FAMILY...?

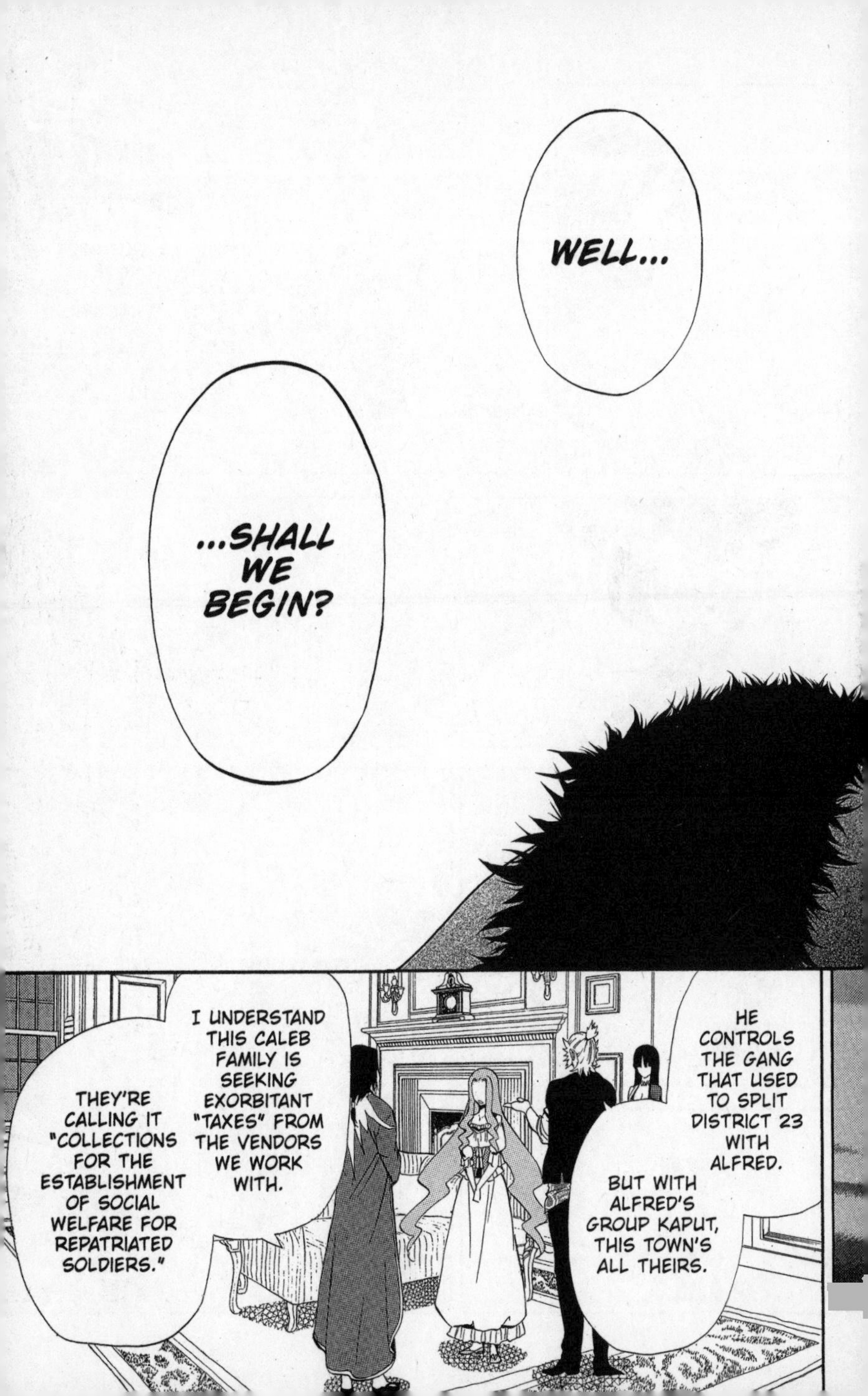
WELL...
...SHALL WE BEGIN?
HE CONTROLS THE GANG THAT USED TO SPLIT DISTRICT 23 WITH ALFRED.
BUT WITH ALFRED'S GROUP KAPUT, THIS TOWN'S ALL THEIRS.
I UNDERSTAND THIS CALEB FAMILY IS SEEKING EXORBITANT "TAXES" FROM THE VENDORS WE WORK WITH.
THEY'RE CALLING IT "COLLECTIONS FOR THE ESTABLISHMENT OF SOCIAL WELFARE FOR REPATRIATED SOLDIERS."

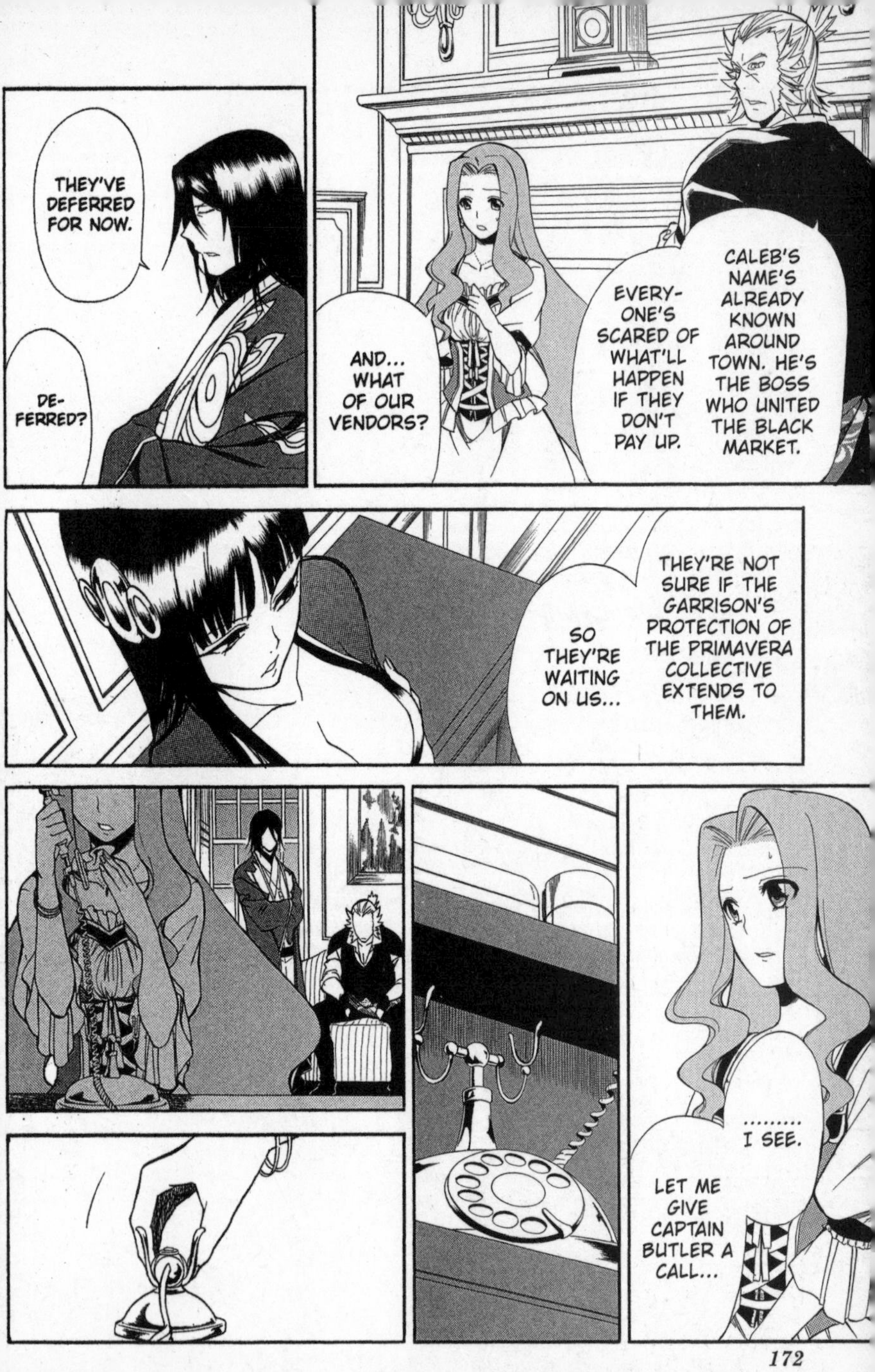
CALEB'S NAME'S ALREADY KNOWN AROUND TOWN. HE'S THE BOSS WHO UNITED THE BLACK MARKET.
EVERY-ONE'S SCARED OF WHAT'LL HAPPEN IF THEY DON'T PAY UP.
AND... WHAT OF OUR VENDORS?
THEY'VE DEFERRED FOR NOW.
DE-FERRED?
THEY'RE NOT SURE IF THE GARRISON'S PROTECTION OF THE PRIMAVERA COLLECTIVE EXTENDS TO THEM.
SO THEY'RE WAITING ON US...
.... I SEE.
LET ME GIVE CAPTAIN BUTLER A CALL...

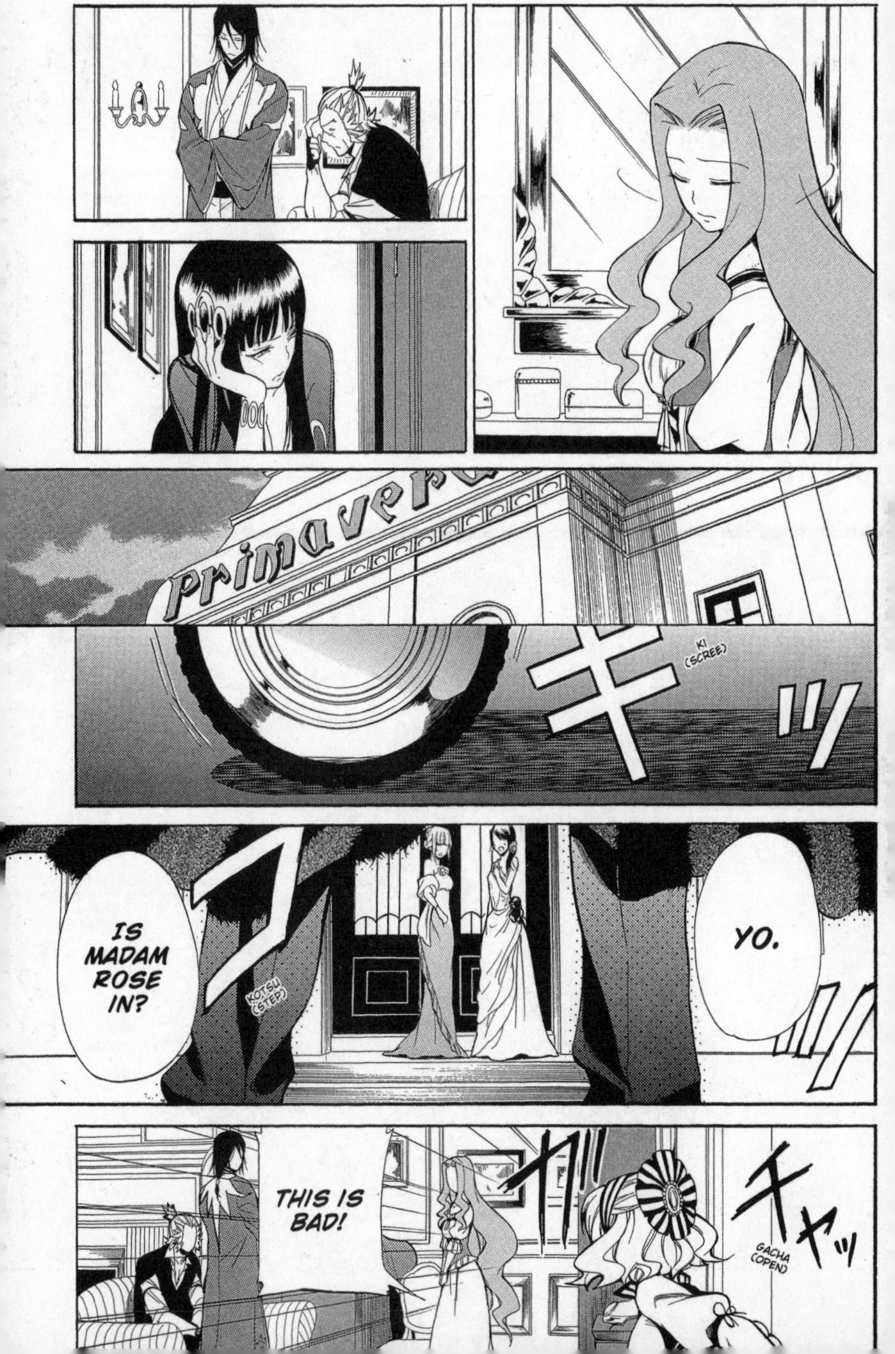
Primavera
KI (SCREE)
YO.
IS MADAM ROSE IN?
KOTSU (STEP)
GACHA (OPEN)
THIS IS BAD!

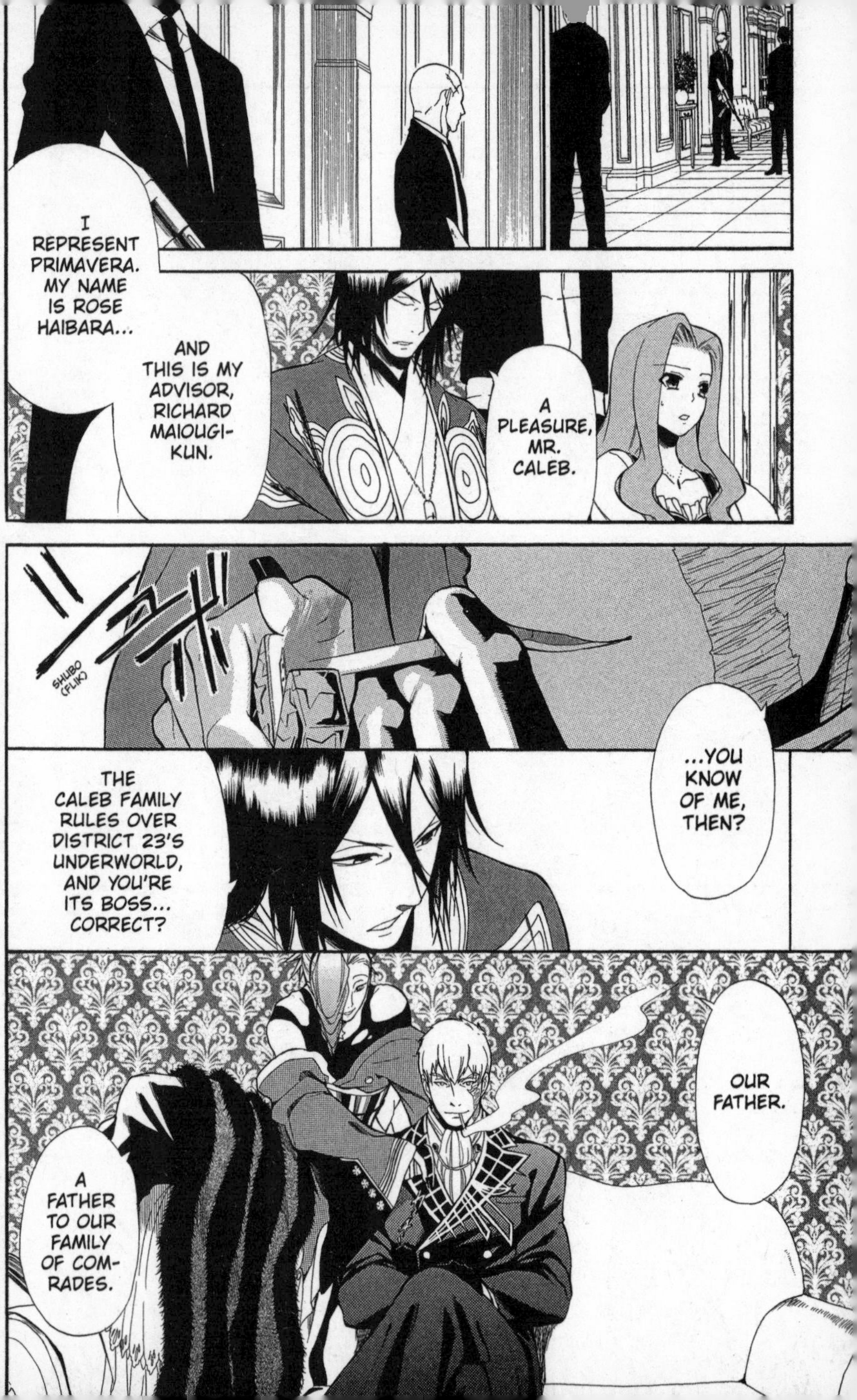

I REPRESENT PRIMAVERA. MY NAME IS ROSE HAIBARA...
AND THIS IS MY ADVISOR, RICHARD MAIOUGI-KUN.
A PLEASURE, MR. CALEB.
SHUBO (FLIK)
...YOU KNOW OF ME, THEN?
THE CALEB FAMILY RULES OVER DISTRICT 23'S UNDERWORLD, AND YOU'RE ITS BOSS... CORRECT?
OUR FATHER.
A FATHER TO OUR FAMILY OF COM-RADES.

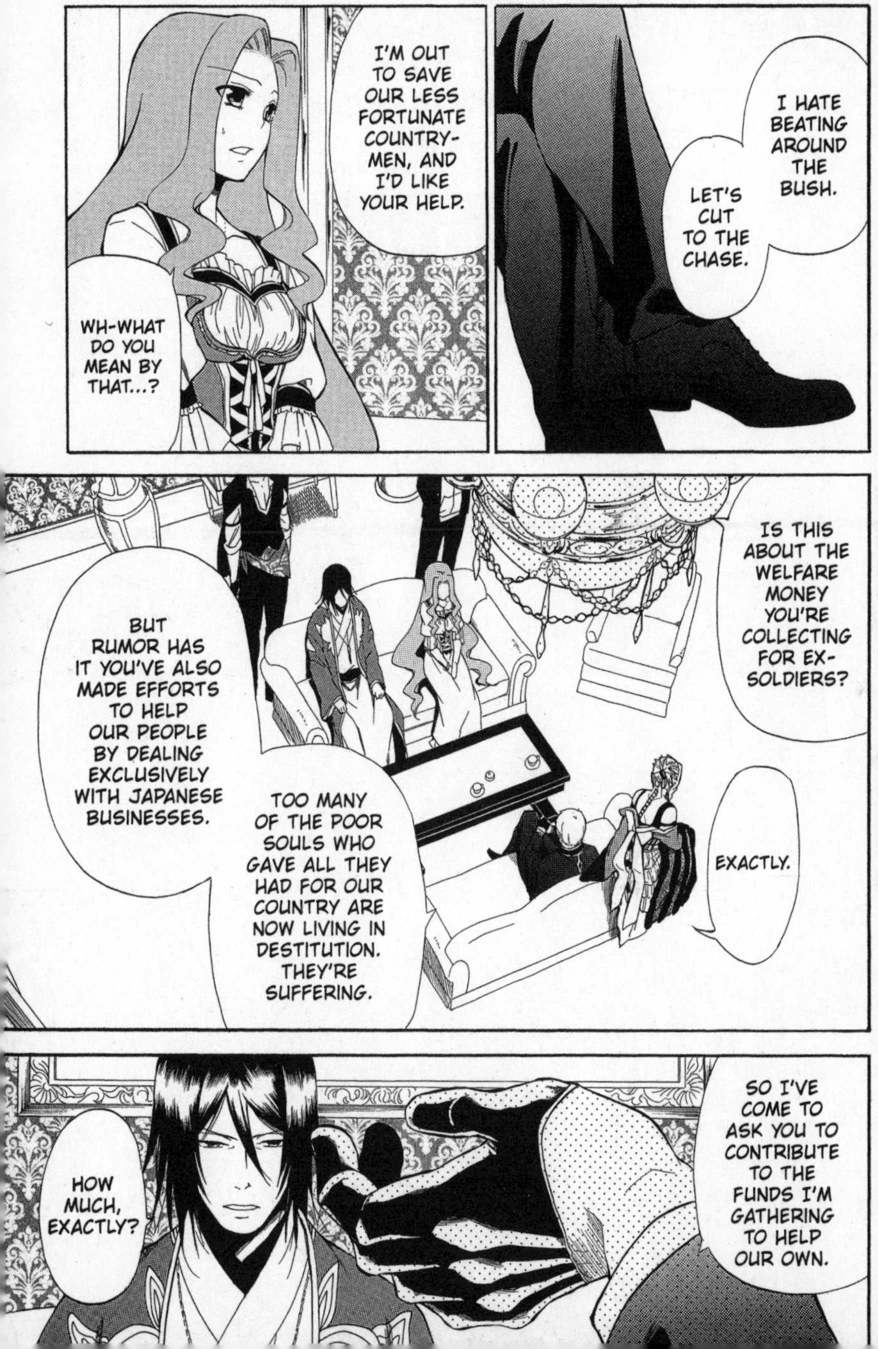
I HATE BEATING AROUND THE BUSH.
LET'S CUT TO THE CHASE.
I'M OUT TO SAVE OUR LESS FORTUNATE COUNTRYMEN, AND I'D LIKE YOUR HELP.
WH-WHAT DO YOU MEAN BY THAT...?
IS THIS ABOUT THE WELFARE MONEY YOU'RE COLLECTING FOR EX-SOLDIERS?
EXACTLY.
TOO MANY OF THE POOR SOULS WHO GAVE ALL THEY HAD FOR OUR COUNTRY ARE NOW LIVING IN DESTITUTION. THEY'RE SUFFERING.
BUT RUMOR HAS IT YOU'VE ALSO MADE EFFORTS TO HELP OUR PEOPLE BY DEALING EXCLUSIVELY WITH JAPANESE BUSINESSES.
SO I'VE COME TO ASK YOU TO CONTRIBUTE TO THE FUNDS I'M GATHERING TO HELP OUR OWN.
HOW MUCH, EXACTLY?

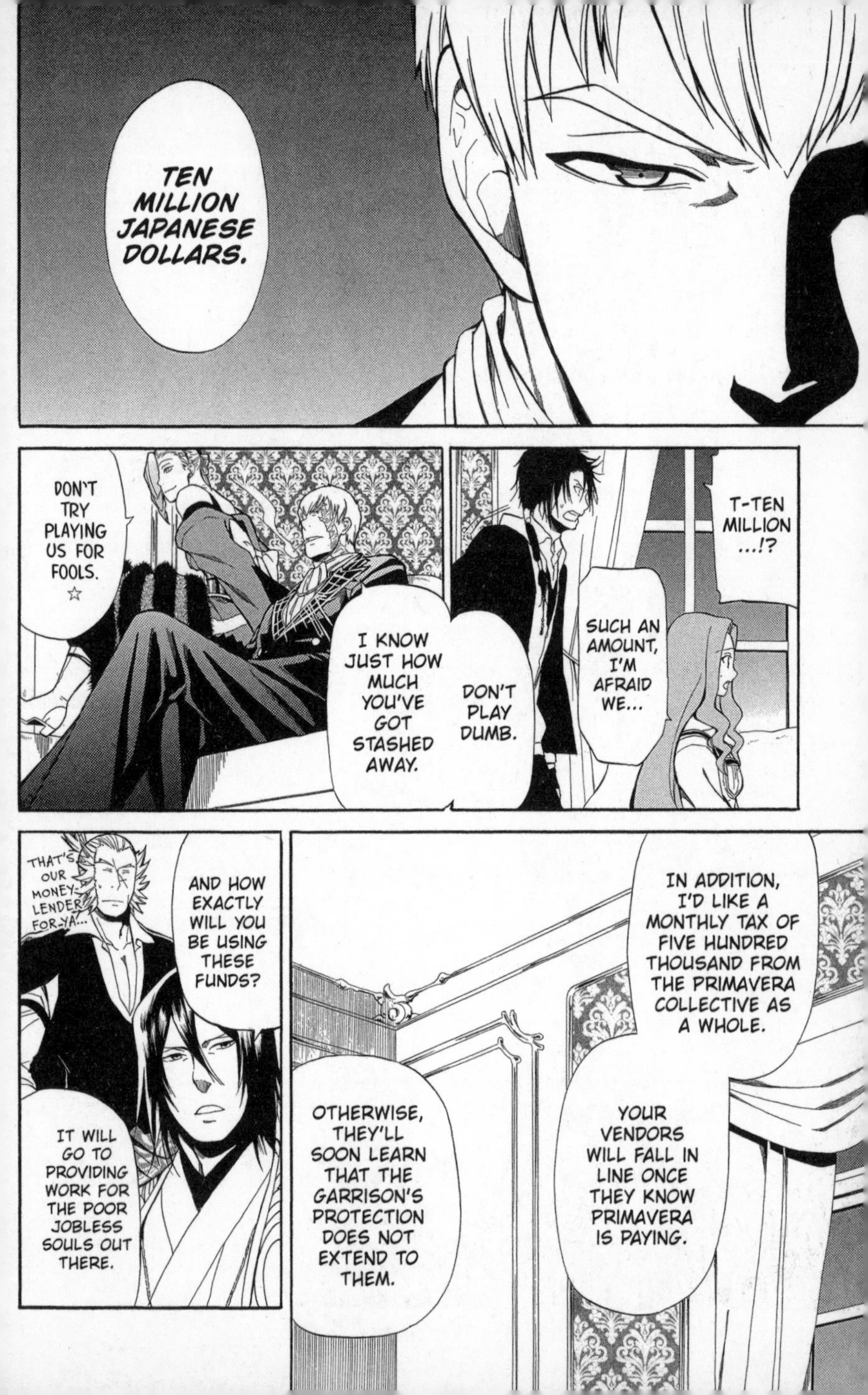
TEN MILLION JAPANESE DOLLARS.
T-TEN MILLION ...!?
SUCH AN AMOUNT, I'M AFRAID WE...
DON'T PLAY DUMB.
I KNOW JUST HOW MUCH YOU'VE GOT STASHED AWAY.
DON'T TRY PLAYING US FOR FOOLS. ☆
IN ADDITION, I'D LIKE A MONTHLY TAX OF FIVE HUNDRED THOUSAND FROM THE PRIMAVERA COLLECTIVE AS A WHOLE.
YOUR VENDORS WILL FALL IN LINE ONCE THEY KNOW PRIMAVERA IS PAYING.
OTHERWISE, THEY'LL SOON LEARN THAT THE GARRISON'S PROTECTION DOES NOT EXTEND TO THEM.
AND HOW EXACTLY WILL YOU BE USING THESE FUNDS?
THAT'S OUR MONEY-LENDER FOR YA...
IT WILL GO TO PROVIDING WORK FOR THE POOR JOBLESS SOULS OUT THERE.

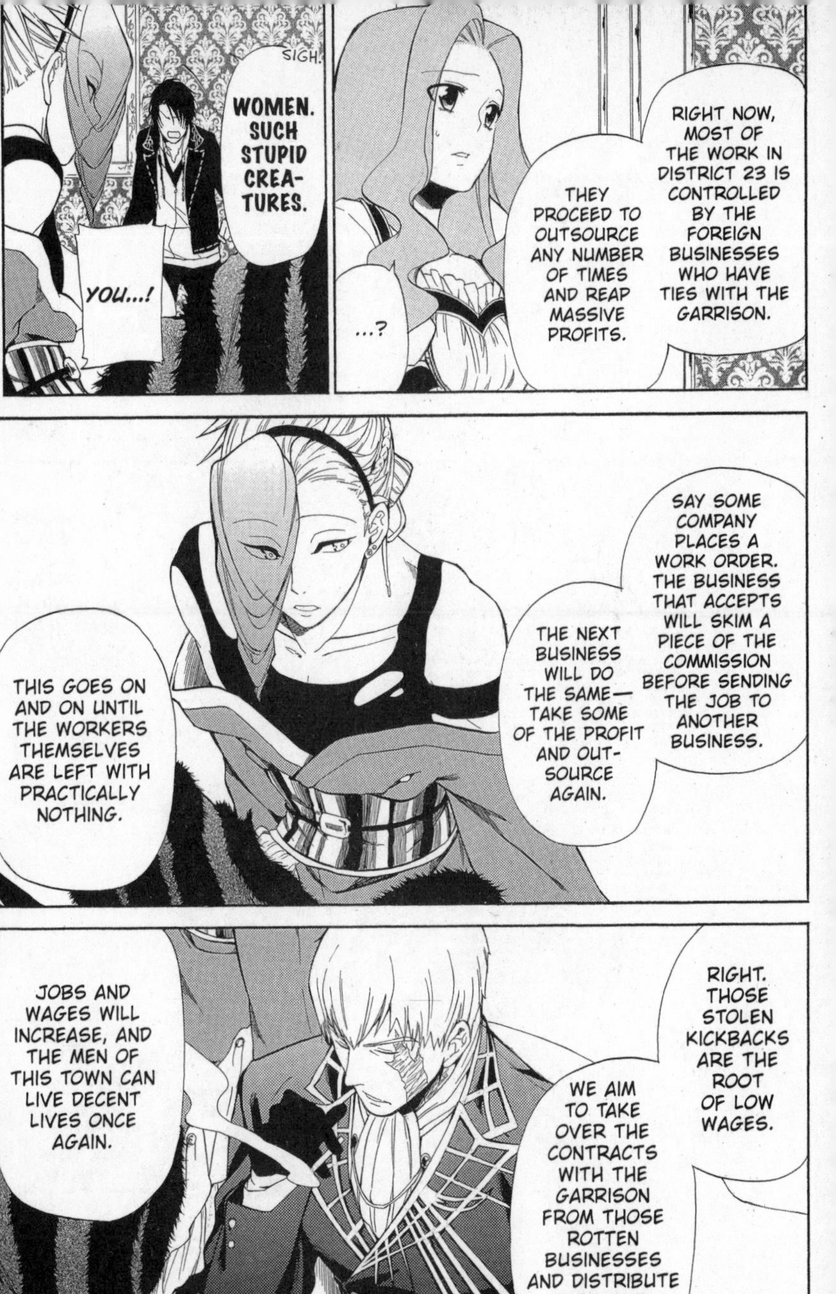
RIGHT NOW, MOST OF THE WORK IN DISTRICT 23 IS CONTROLLED BY THE FOREIGN BUSINESSES WHO HAVE TIES WITH THE GARRISON.
THEY PROCEED TO OUTSOURCE ANY NUMBER OF TIMES AND REAP MASSIVE PROFITS.
...?
SIGH.
WOMEN. SUCH STUPID CREA-TURES.
YOU...!
SAY SOME COMPANY PLACES A WORK ORDER. THE BUSINESS THAT ACCEPTS WILL SKIM A PIECE OF THE COMMISSION BEFORE SENDING THE JOB TO ANOTHER BUSINESS.
THE NEXT BUSINESS WILL DO THE SAME—TAKE SOME OF THE PROFIT AND OUT-SOURCE AGAIN.
THIS GOES ON AND ON UNTIL THE WORKERS THEMSELVES ARE LEFT WITH PRACTICALLY NOTHING.
RIGHT. THOSE STOLEN KICKBACKS ARE THE ROOT OF LOW WAGES.
WE AIM TO TAKE OVER THE CONTRACTS WITH THE GARRISON FROM THOSE ROTTEN BUSINESSES AND DISTRIBUTE THEM OUR-SELVES.
JOBS AND WAGES WILL INCREASE, AND THE MEN OF THIS TOWN CAN LIVE DECENT LIVES ONCE AGAIN.

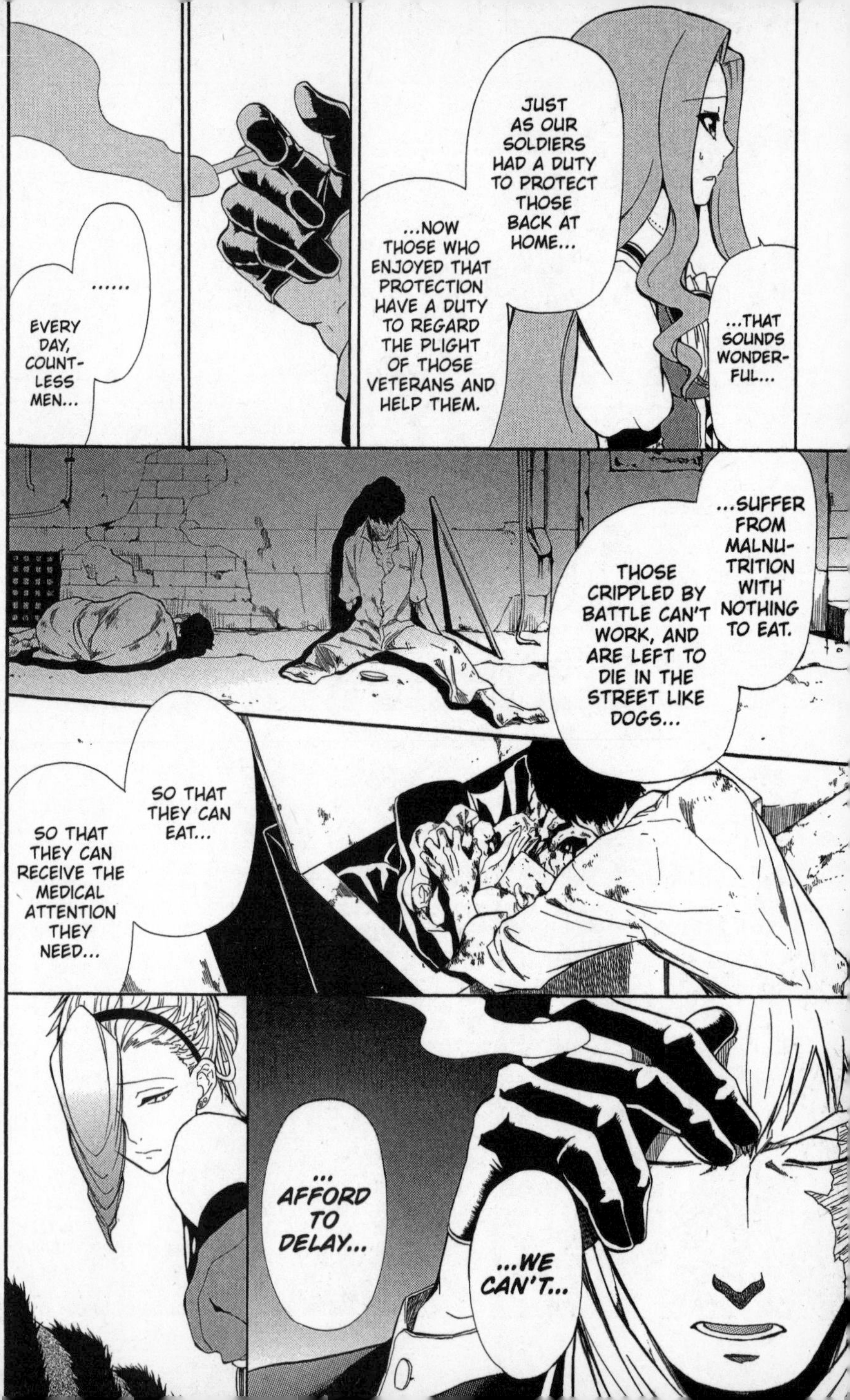
...THAT SOUNDS WONDERFUL...
JUST AS OUR SOLDIERS HAD A DUTY TO PROTECT THOSE BACK AT HOME...
...NOW THOSE WHO ENJOYED THAT PROTECTION HAVE A DUTY TO REGARD THE PLIGHT OF THOSE VETERANS AND HELP THEM.
......
EVERY DAY, COUNTLESS MEN...
...SUFFER FROM MALNUTRITION WITH NOTHING TO EAT.
THOSE CRIPPLED BY BATTLE CAN'T WORK, AND ARE LEFT TO DIE IN THE STREET LIKE DOGS...
SO THAT THEY CAN EAT...
SO THAT THEY CAN RECEIVE THE MEDICAL ATTENTION THEY NEED...
...WE CAN'T...
...AFFORD TO DELAY...

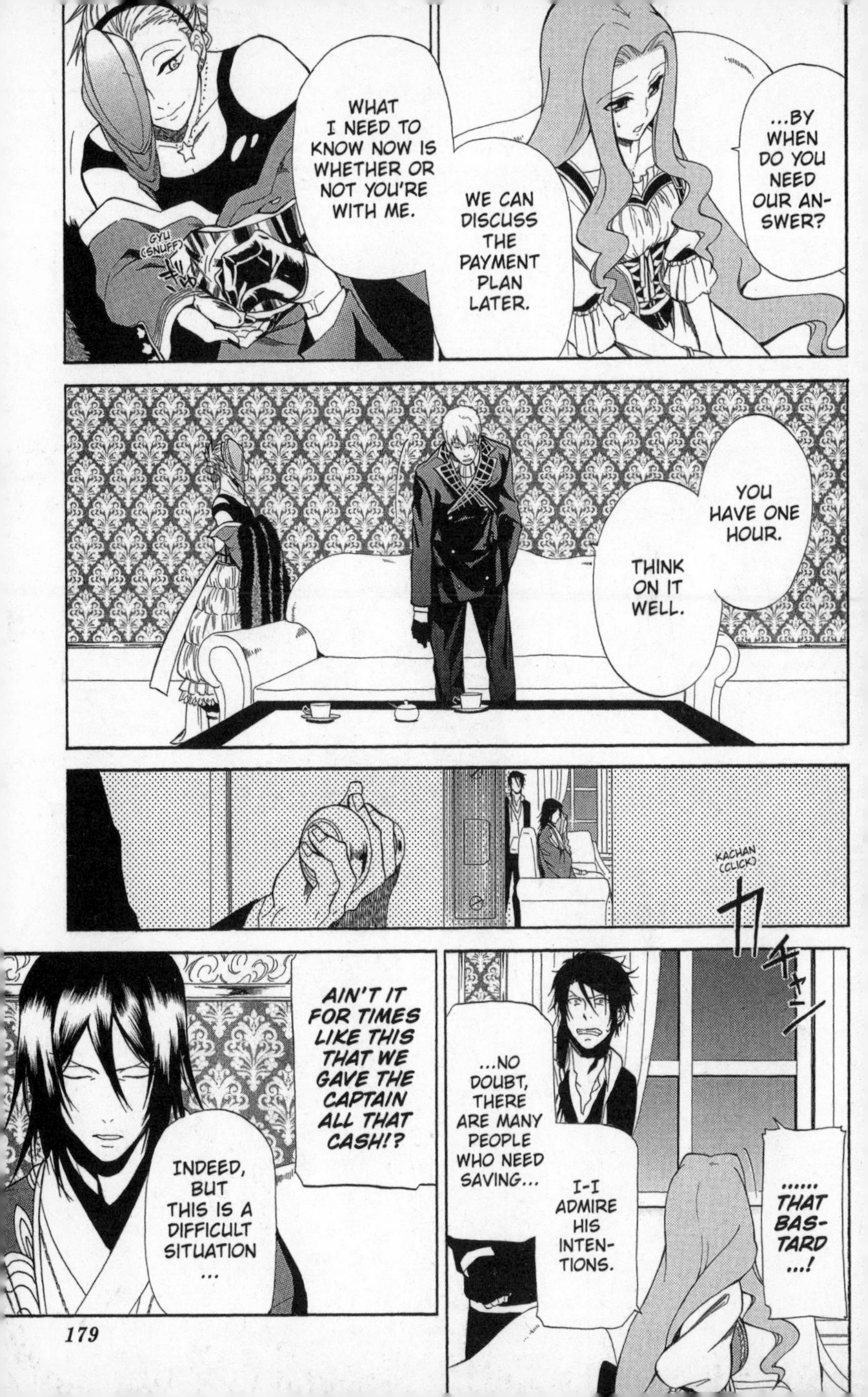
...BY WHEN DO YOU NEED OUR AN-SWER?
WE CAN DISCUSS THE PAYMENT PLAN LATER.
WHAT I NEED TO KNOW NOW IS WHETHER OR NOT YOU'RE WITH ME.
GYU (SNUFF)
YOU HAVE ONE HOUR.
THINK ON IT WELL.
KACHAN (CLICK)
......THAT BAS-TARD ...!
I-I ADMIRE HIS INTEN-TIONS.
...NO DOUBT, THERE ARE MANY PEOPLE WHO NEED SAVING...
AIN'T IT FOR TIMES LIKE THIS THAT WE GAVE THE CAPTAIN ALL THAT CASH!?
INDEED, BUT THIS IS A DIFFICULT SITUATION ...

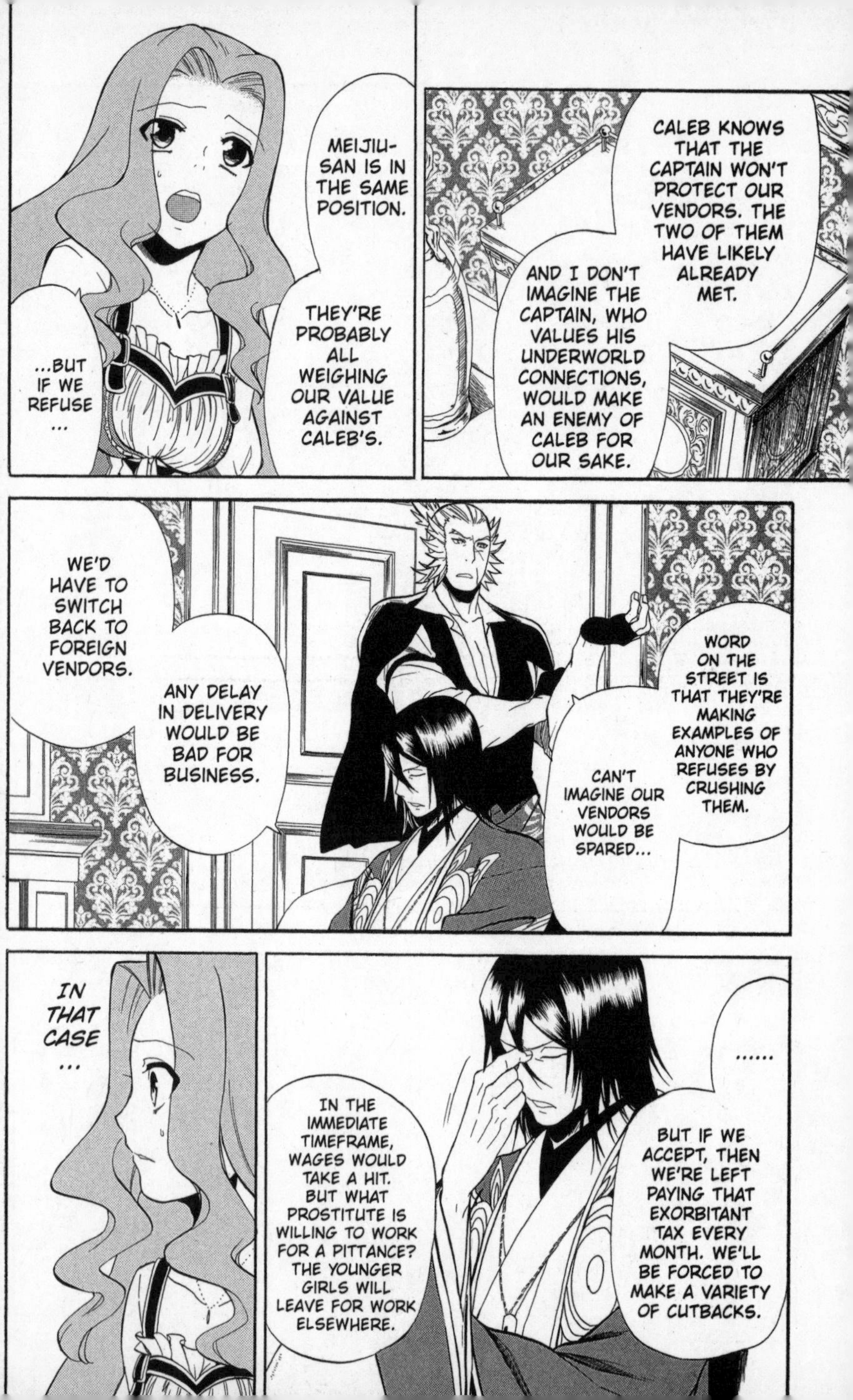
CALEB KNOWS THAT THE CAPTAIN WON'T PROTECT OUR VENDORS. THE TWO OF THEM HAVE LIKELY ALREADY MET.
AND I DON'T IMAGINE THE CAPTAIN, WHO VALUES HIS UNDERWORLD CONNECTIONS, WOULD MAKE AN ENEMY OF CALEB FOR OUR SAKE.
MEIJIU-SAN IS IN THE SAME POSITION.
THEY'RE PROBABLY ALL WEIGHING OUR VALUE AGAINST CALEB'S.
...BUT IF WE REFUSE...
WORD ON THE STREET IS THAT THEY'RE MAKING EXAMPLES OF ANYONE WHO REFUSES BY CRUSHING THEM.
CAN'T IMAGINE OUR VENDORS WOULD BE SPARED...
WE'D HAVE TO SWITCH BACK TO FOREIGN VENDORS.
ANY DELAY IN DELIVERY WOULD BE BAD FOR BUSINESS.
......
BUT IF WE ACCEPT, THEN WE'RE LEFT PAYING THAT EXORBITANT TAX EVERY MONTH. WE'LL BE FORCED TO MAKE A VARIETY OF CUTBACKS.
IN THE IMMEDIATE TIMEFRAME, WAGES WOULD TAKE A HIT. BUT WHAT PROSTITUTE IS WILLING TO WORK FOR A PITTANCE? THE YOUNGER GIRLS WILL LEAVE FOR WORK ELSEWHERE.
IN THAT CASE...

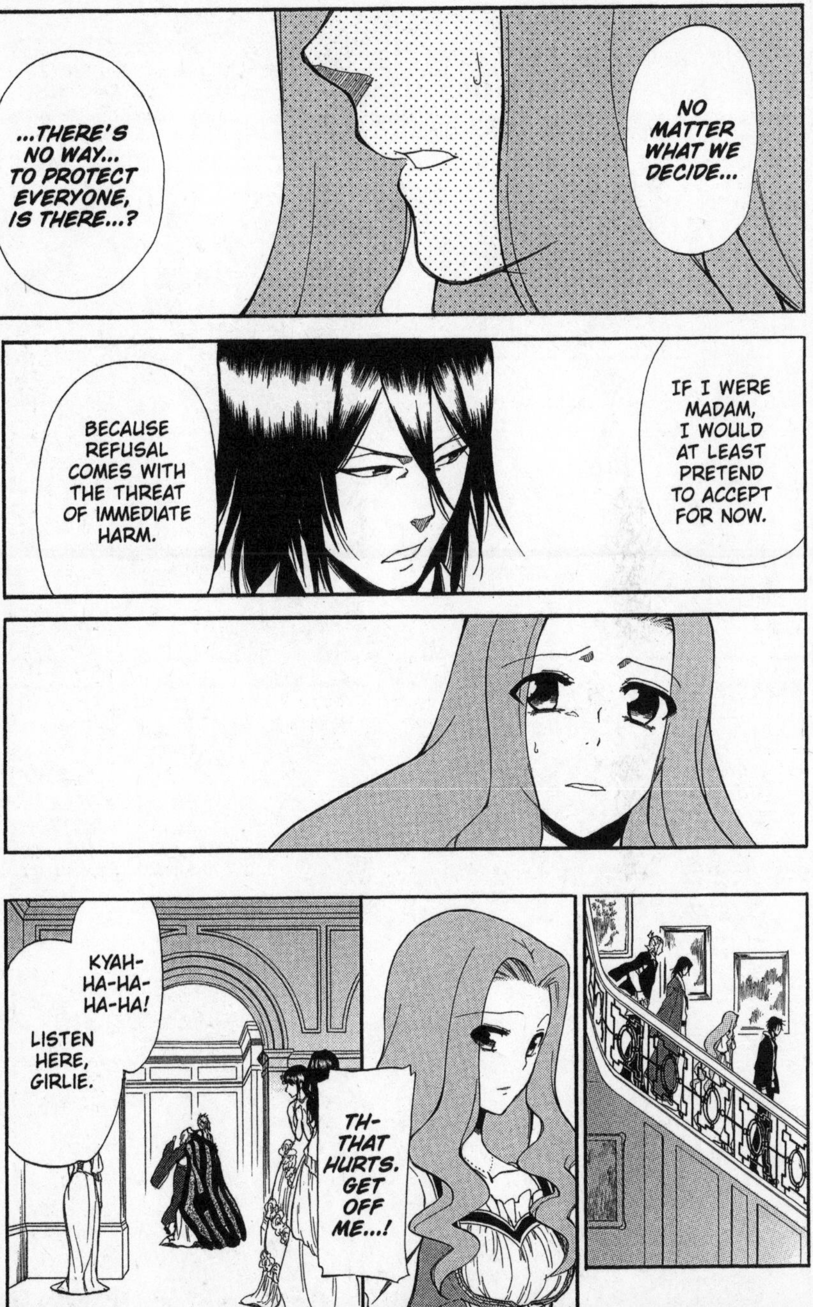
NO MATTER WHAT WE DECIDE...
...THERE'S NO WAY... TO PROTECT EVERYONE, IS THERE...?
IF I WERE MADAM, I WOULD AT LEAST PRETEND TO ACCEPT FOR NOW.
BECAUSE REFUSAL COMES WITH THE THREAT OF IMMEDIATE HARM.
TH- THAT HURTS. GET OFF ME...!
KYAH-HA-HA-HA-HA!
LISTEN HERE, GIRLIE.

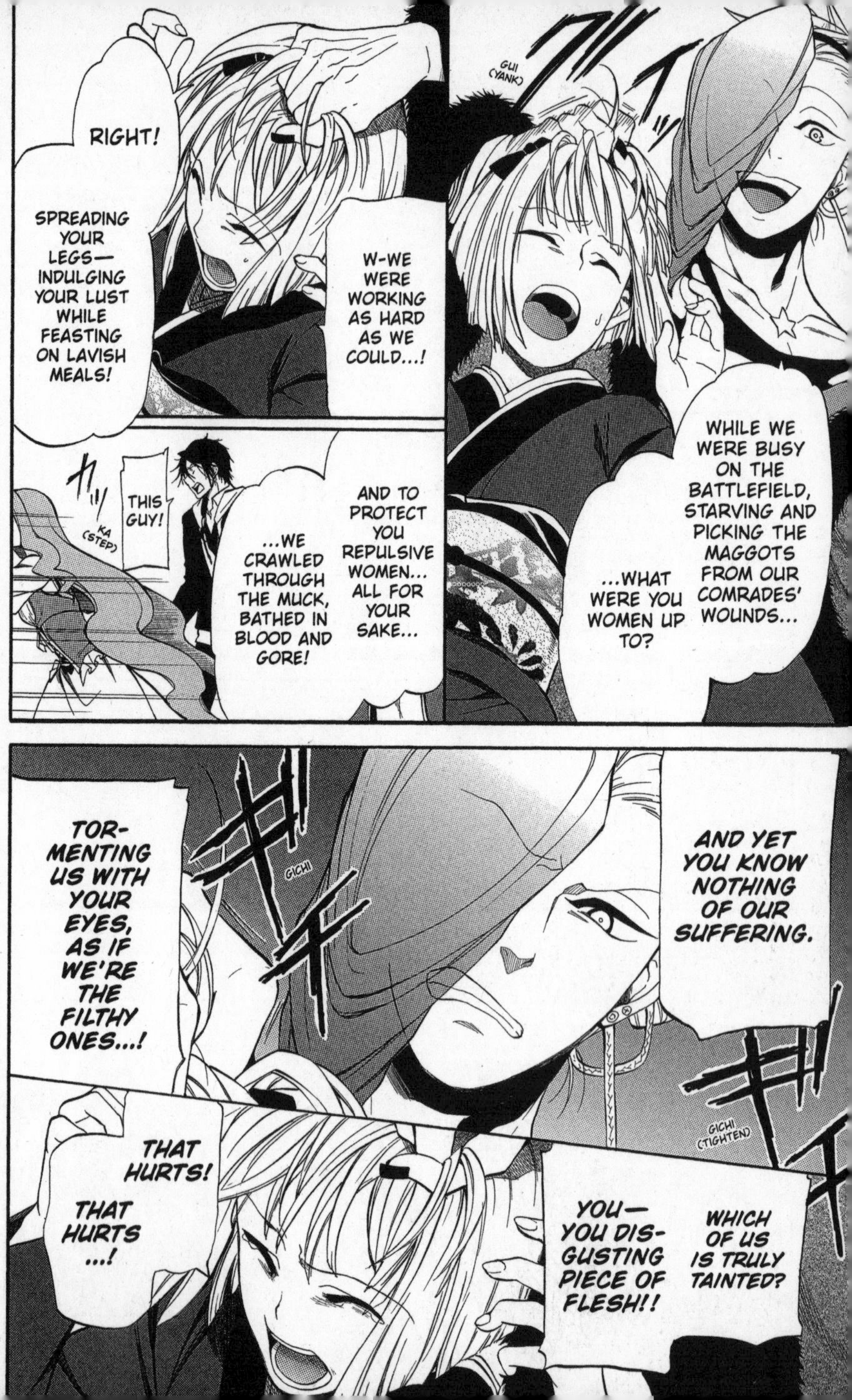
GUI (YANK)
WHILE WE WERE BUSY ON THE BATTLEFIELD, STARVING AND PICKING THE MAGGOTS FROM OUR COMRADES' WOUNDS...
...WHAT WERE YOU WOMEN UP TO?
W-WE WERE WORKING AS HARD AS WE COULD...!
RIGHT!
SPREADING YOUR LEGS—INDULGING YOUR LUST WHILE FEASTING ON LAVISH MEALS!
AND TO PROTECT YOU REPULSIVE WOMEN... ALL FOR YOUR SAKE...
...WE CRAWLED THROUGH THE MUCK, BATHED IN BLOOD AND GORE!
THIS GUY!
KA (STEP)
AND YET YOU KNOW NOTHING OF OUR SUFFERING.
GICHI
TOR-MENTING US WITH YOUR EYES, AS IF WE'RE THE FILTHY ONES...!
GICHI (TIGHTEN)
WHICH OF US IS TRULY TAINTED?
YOU—YOU DIS-GUSTING PIECE OF FLESH!!
THAT HURTS!
THAT HURTS...!

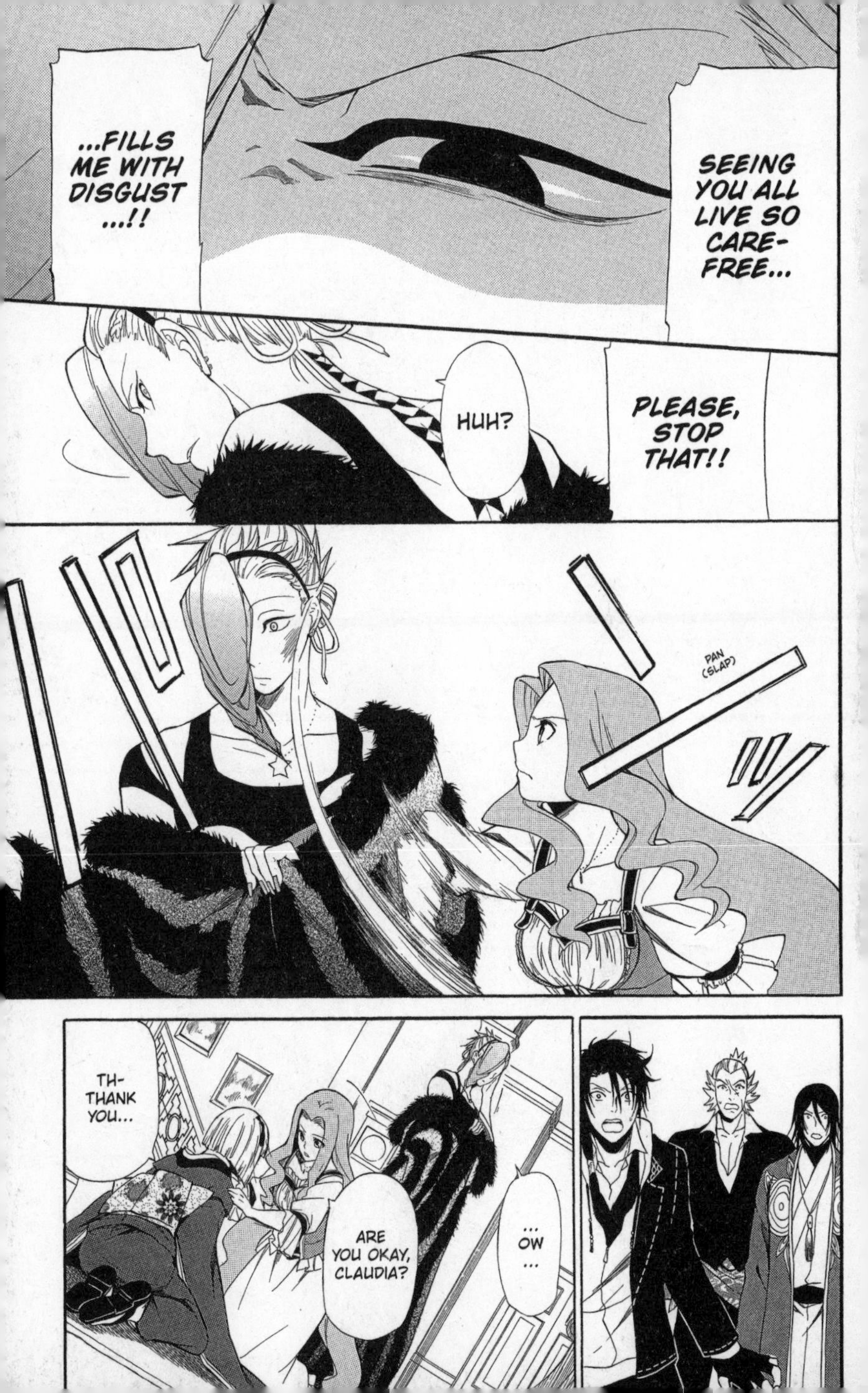
SEEING YOU ALL LIVE SO CARE-FREE...
...FILLS ME WITH DISGUST...!!
PLEASE, STOP THAT!!
HUH?
PAN (SLAP)
... OW ...
ARE YOU OKAY, CLAUDIA?
TH-THANK YOU...

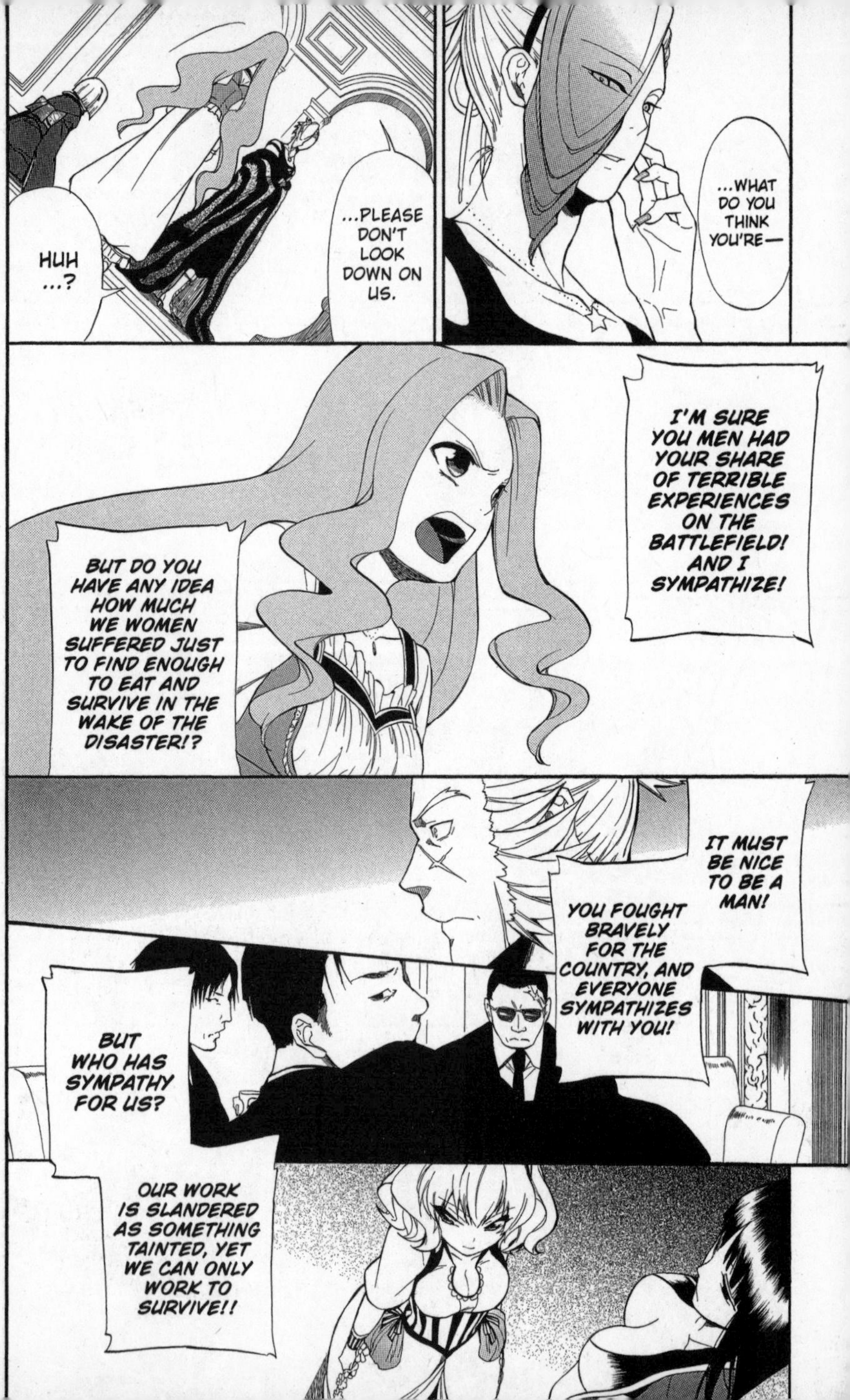
...WHAT DO YOU THINK YOU'RE—
...PLEASE DON'T LOOK DOWN ON US.
HUH ...?
I'M SURE YOU MEN HAD YOUR SHARE OF TERRIBLE EXPERIENCES ON THE BATTLEFIELD! AND I SYMPATHIZE!
BUT DO YOU HAVE ANY IDEA HOW MUCH WE WOMEN SUFFERED JUST TO FIND ENOUGH TO EAT AND SURVIVE IN THE WAKE OF THE DISASTER!?
IT MUST BE NICE TO BE A MAN!
YOU FOUGHT BRAVELY FOR THE COUNTRY, AND EVERYONE SYMPATHIZES WITH YOU!
BUT WHO HAS SYMPATHY FOR US?
OUR WORK IS SLANDERED AS SOMETHING TAINTED, YET WE CAN ONLY WORK TO SURVIVE!!

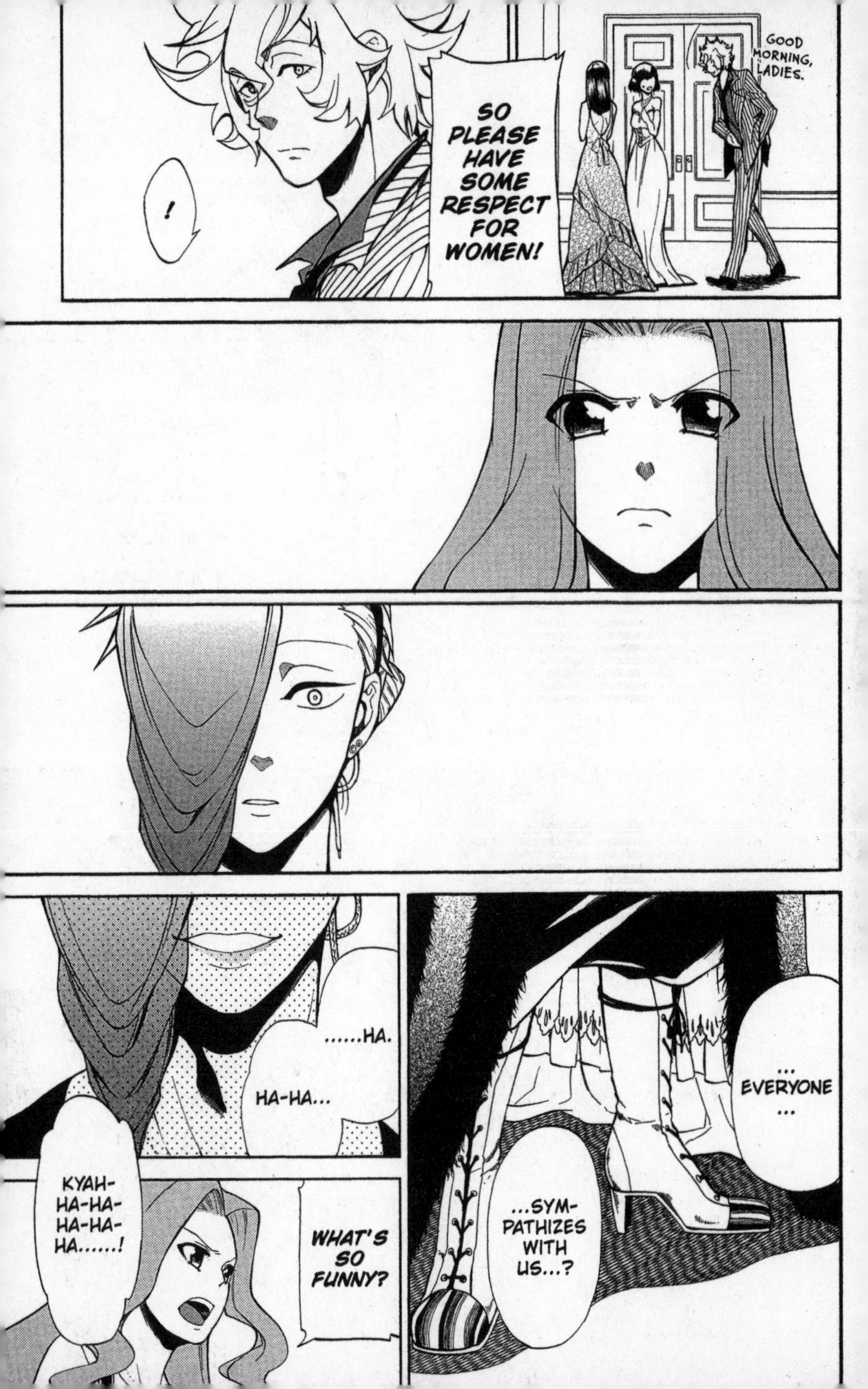
GOOD MORNING, LADIES.
SO PLEASE HAVE SOME RESPECT FOR WOMEN!
!
...EVERYONE...
...SYMPATHIZES WITH US...?
......HA.
HA-HA...
WHAT'S SO FUNNY?
KYAH-HA-HA-HA-HA-HA......!

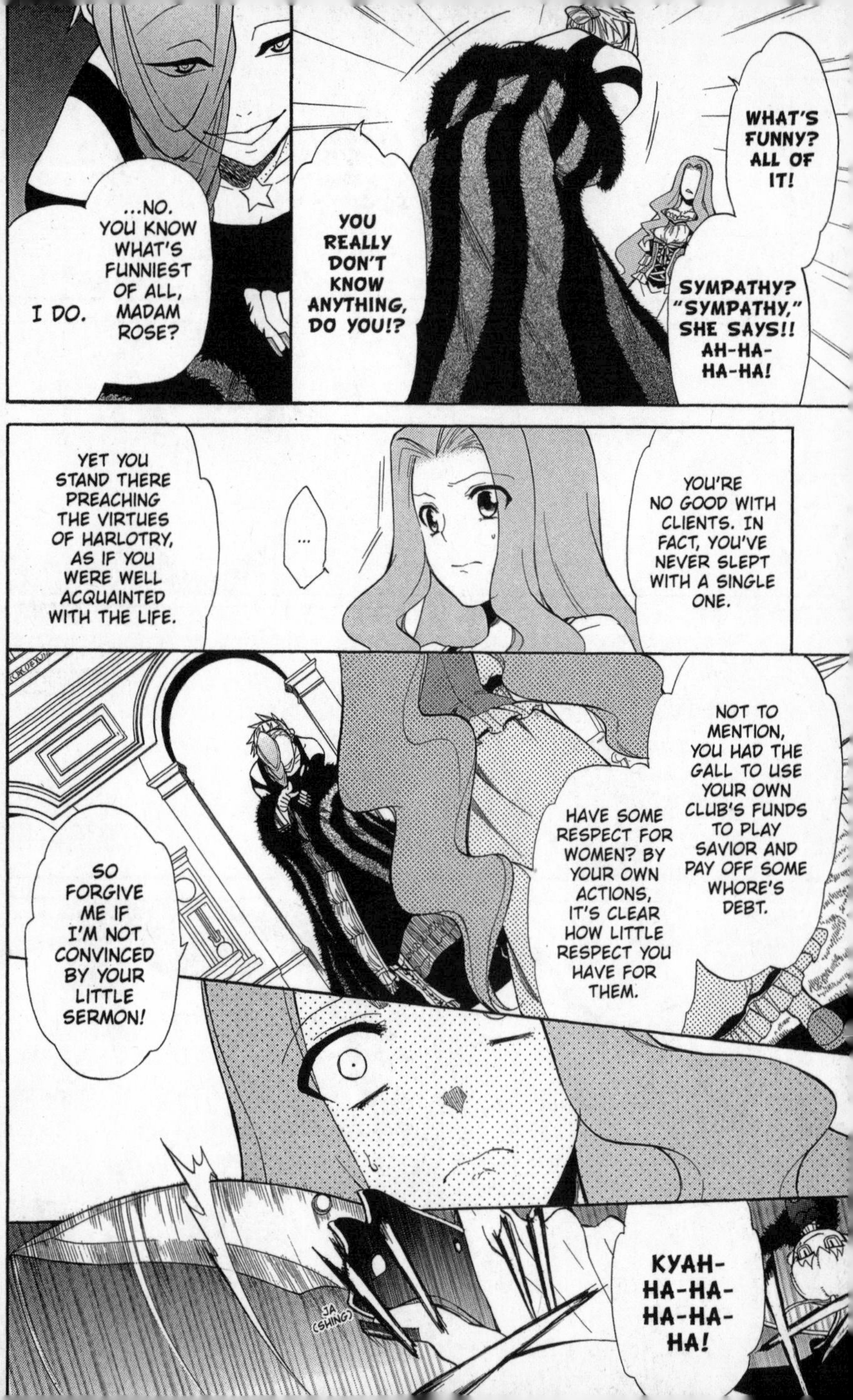
WHAT'S FUNNY? ALL OF IT!
SYMPATHY? "SYMPATHY," SHE SAYS!! AH-HA-HA-HA!
YOU REALLY DON'T KNOW ANYTHING, DO YOU!?
...NO. YOU KNOW WHAT'S FUNNIEST OF ALL, MADAM ROSE?
I DO.
YOU'RE NO GOOD WITH CLIENTS. IN FACT, YOU'VE NEVER SLEPT WITH A SINGLE ONE.
...
YET YOU STAND THERE PREACHING THE VIRTUES OF HARLOTRY, AS IF YOU WERE WELL ACQUAINTED WITH THE LIFE.
NOT TO MENTION, YOU HAD THE GALL TO USE YOUR OWN CLUB'S FUNDS TO PLAY SAVIOR AND PAY OFF SOME WHORE'S DEBT.
HAVE SOME RESPECT FOR WOMEN? BY YOUR OWN ACTIONS, IT'S CLEAR HOW LITTLE RESPECT YOU HAVE FOR THEM.
SO FORGIVE ME IF I'M NOT CONVINCED BY YOUR LITTLE SERMON!
KYAH-HA-HA-HA-HA-HA!
JA (SHING)

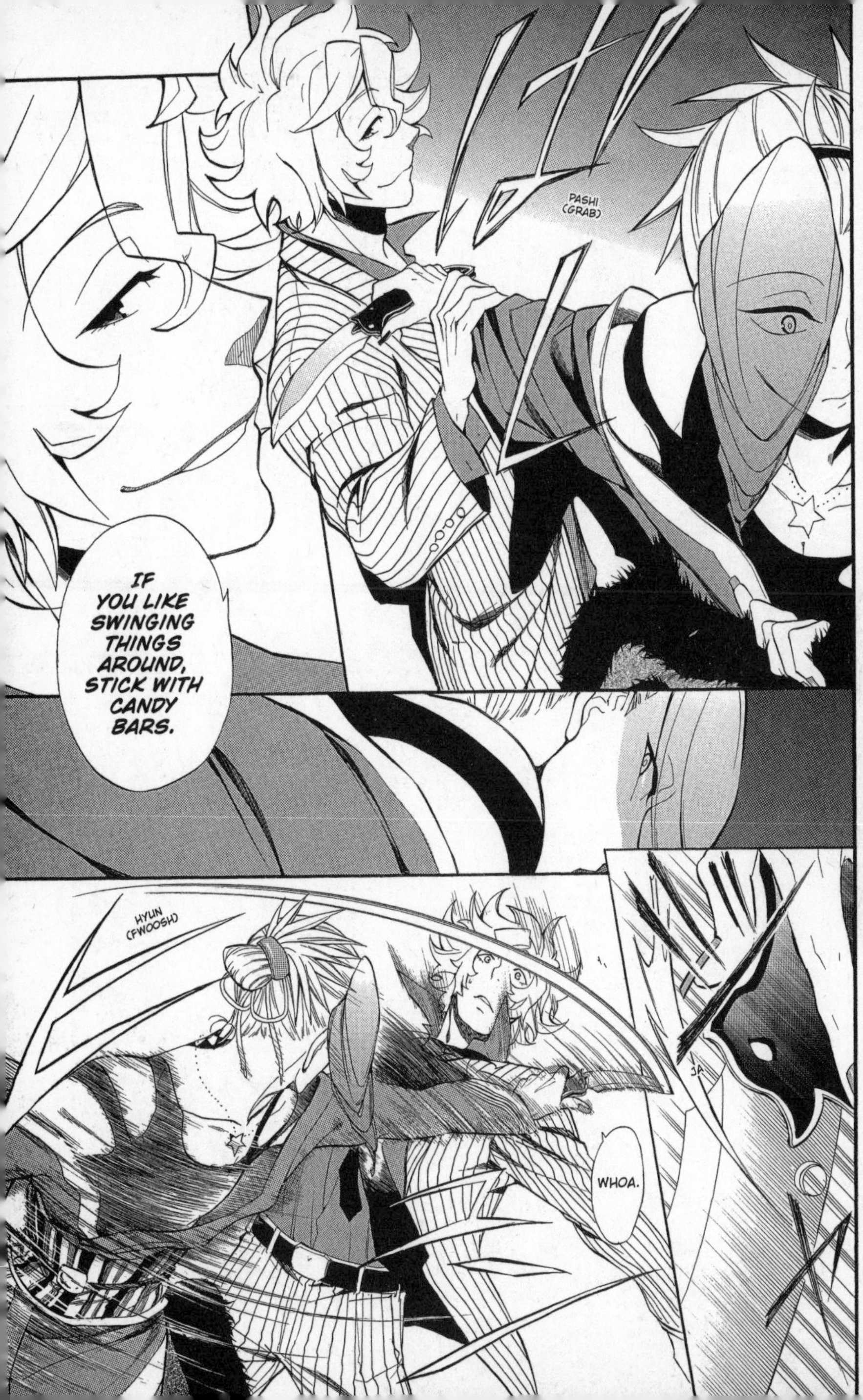
PASHI (GRAB)
IF YOU LIKE SWINGING THINGS AROUND, STICK WITH CANDY BARS.
JA
WHOA.
HYUN (FWOOSH)

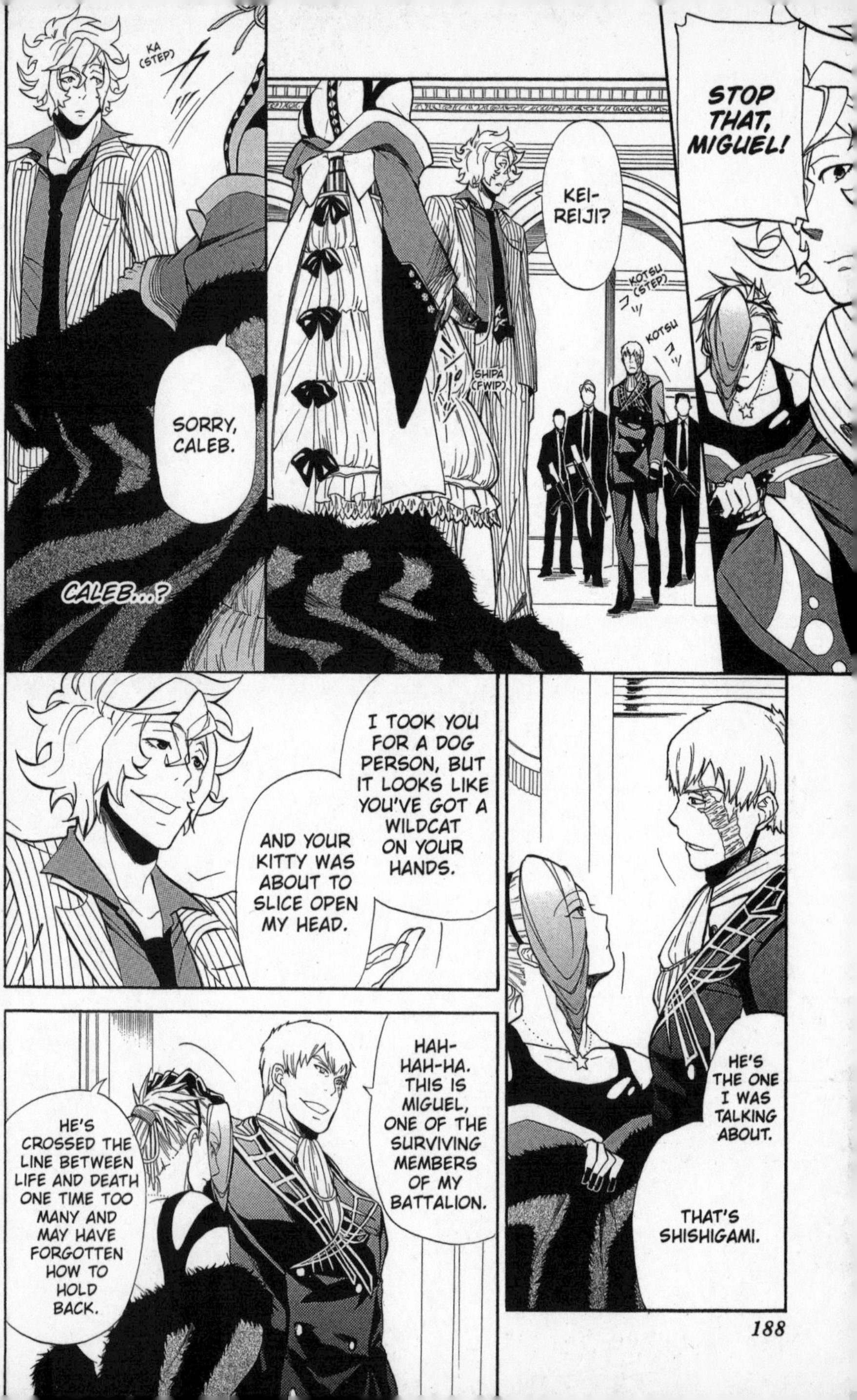

STOP THAT, MIGUEL!
KEI-REIJI?
KOTSU (STEP)
KOTSU
SHIPA (FWIP)
KA (STEP)
SORRY, CALEB.
CALEB...?
HE'S THE ONE I WAS TALKING ABOUT.
THAT'S SHISHIGAMI.
I TOOK YOU FOR A DOG PERSON, BUT IT LOOKS LIKE YOU'VE GOT A WILDCAT ON YOUR HANDS.
AND YOUR KITTY WAS ABOUT TO SLICE OPEN MY HEAD.
HAH-HAH-HA. THIS IS MIGUEL, ONE OF THE SURVIVING MEMBERS OF MY BATTALION.
HE'S CROSSED THE LINE BETWEEN LIFE AND DEATH ONE TIME TOO MANY AND MAY HAVE FORGOTTEN HOW TO HOLD BACK.

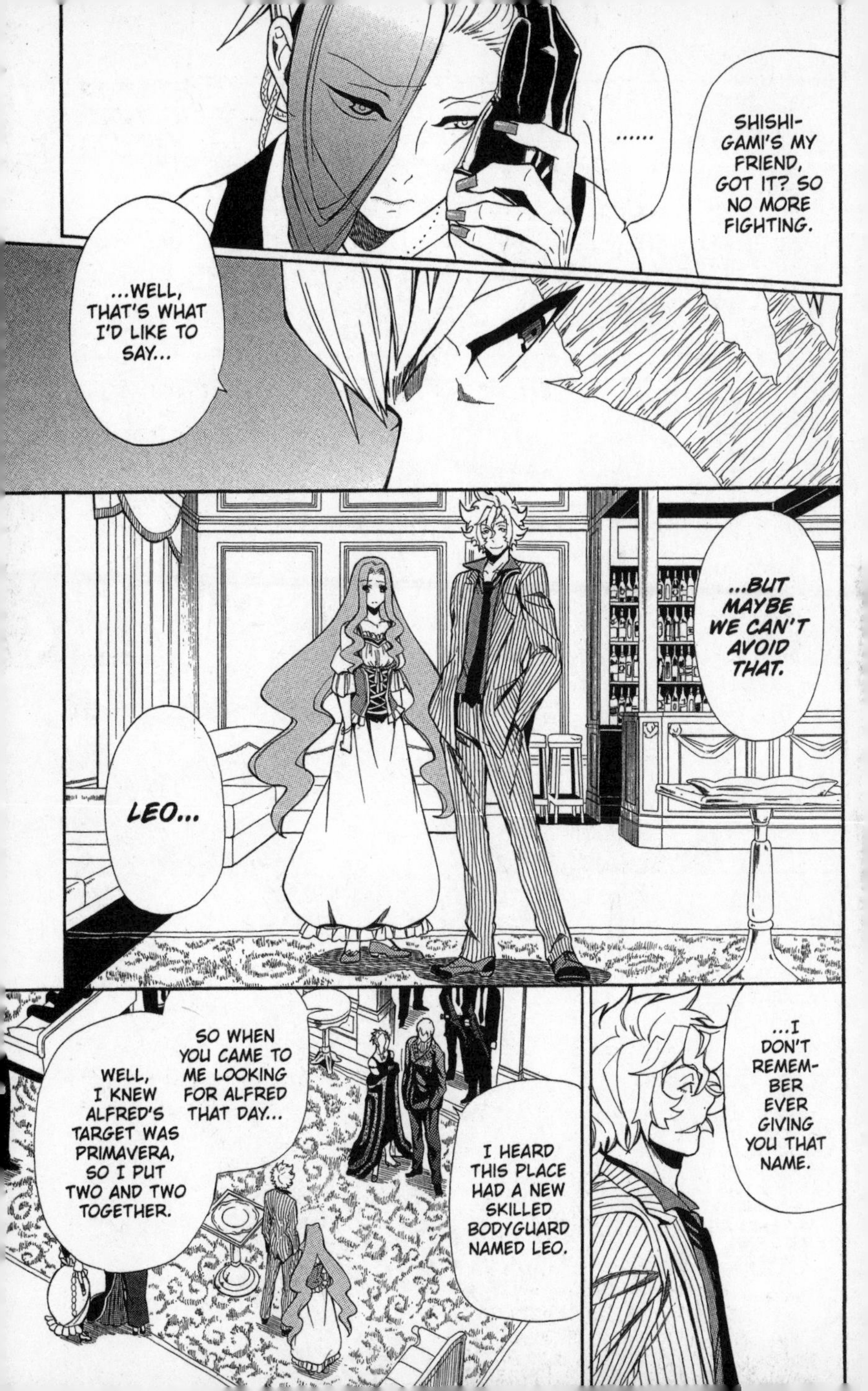
SHISHI-GAMI'S MY FRIEND, GOT IT? SO NO MORE FIGHTING.
......
...WELL, THAT'S WHAT I'D LIKE TO SAY...
...BUT MAYBE WE CAN'T AVOID THAT.
LEO...
...I DON'T REMEM-BER EVER GIVING YOU THAT NAME.
I HEARD THIS PLACE HAD A NEW SKILLED BODYGUARD NAMED LEO.
SO WHEN YOU CAME TO ME LOOKING FOR ALFRED THAT DAY...
WELL, I KNEW ALFRED'S TARGET WAS PRIMAVERA, SO I PUT TWO AND TWO TOGETHER.

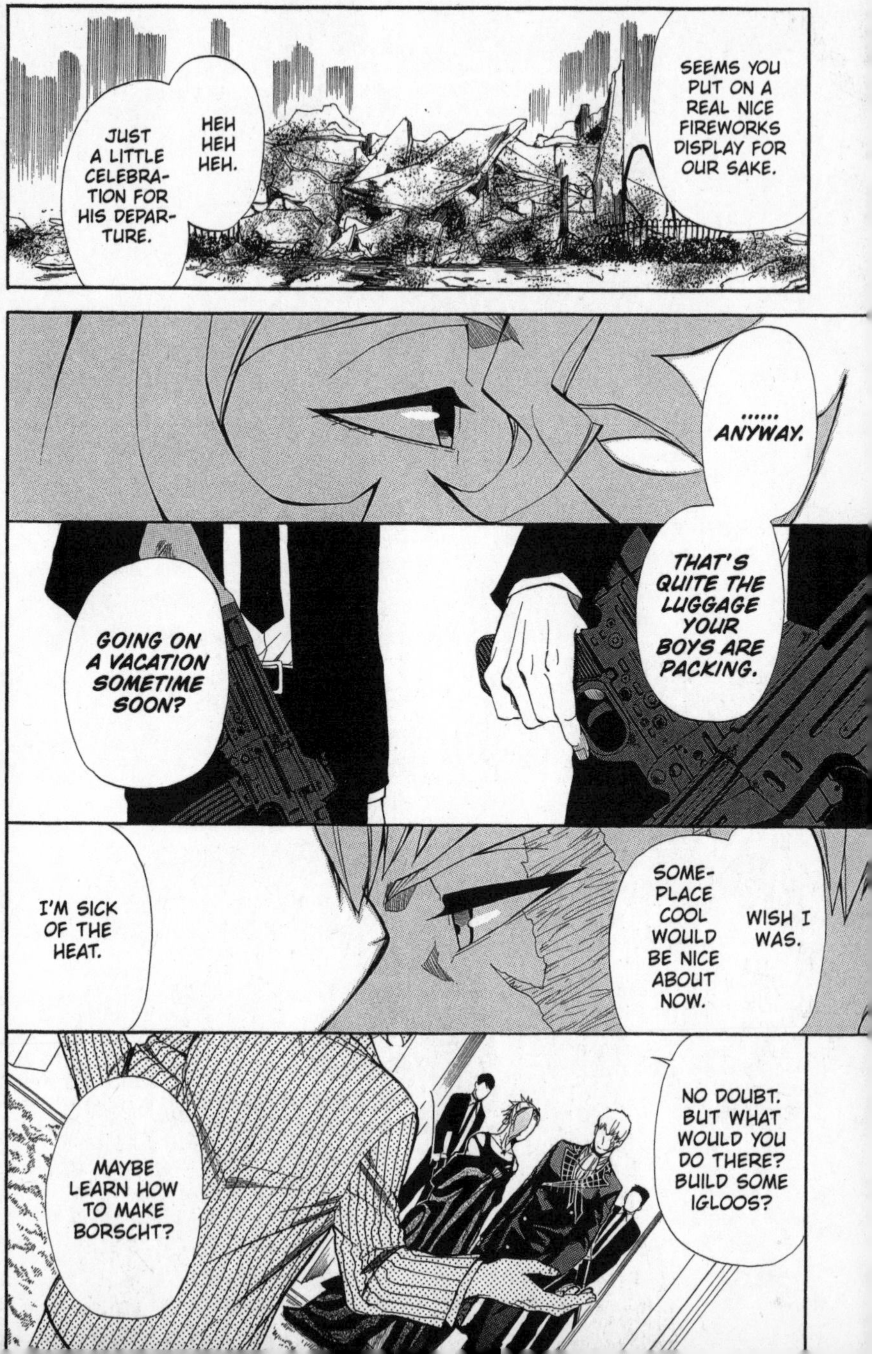
SEEMS YOU PUT ON A REAL NICE FIREWORKS DISPLAY FOR OUR SAKE.
HEH HEH HEH.
JUST A LITTLE CELEBRATION FOR HIS DEPARTURE.
...... ANYWAY.
THAT'S QUITE THE LUGGAGE YOUR BOYS ARE PACKING.
GOING ON A VACATION SOMETIME SOON?
WISH I WAS.
SOMEPLACE COOL WOULD BE NICE ABOUT NOW.
I'M SICK OF THE HEAT.
NO DOUBT. BUT WHAT WOULD YOU DO THERE? BUILD SOME IGLOOS?
MAYBE LEARN HOW TO MAKE BORSCHT?

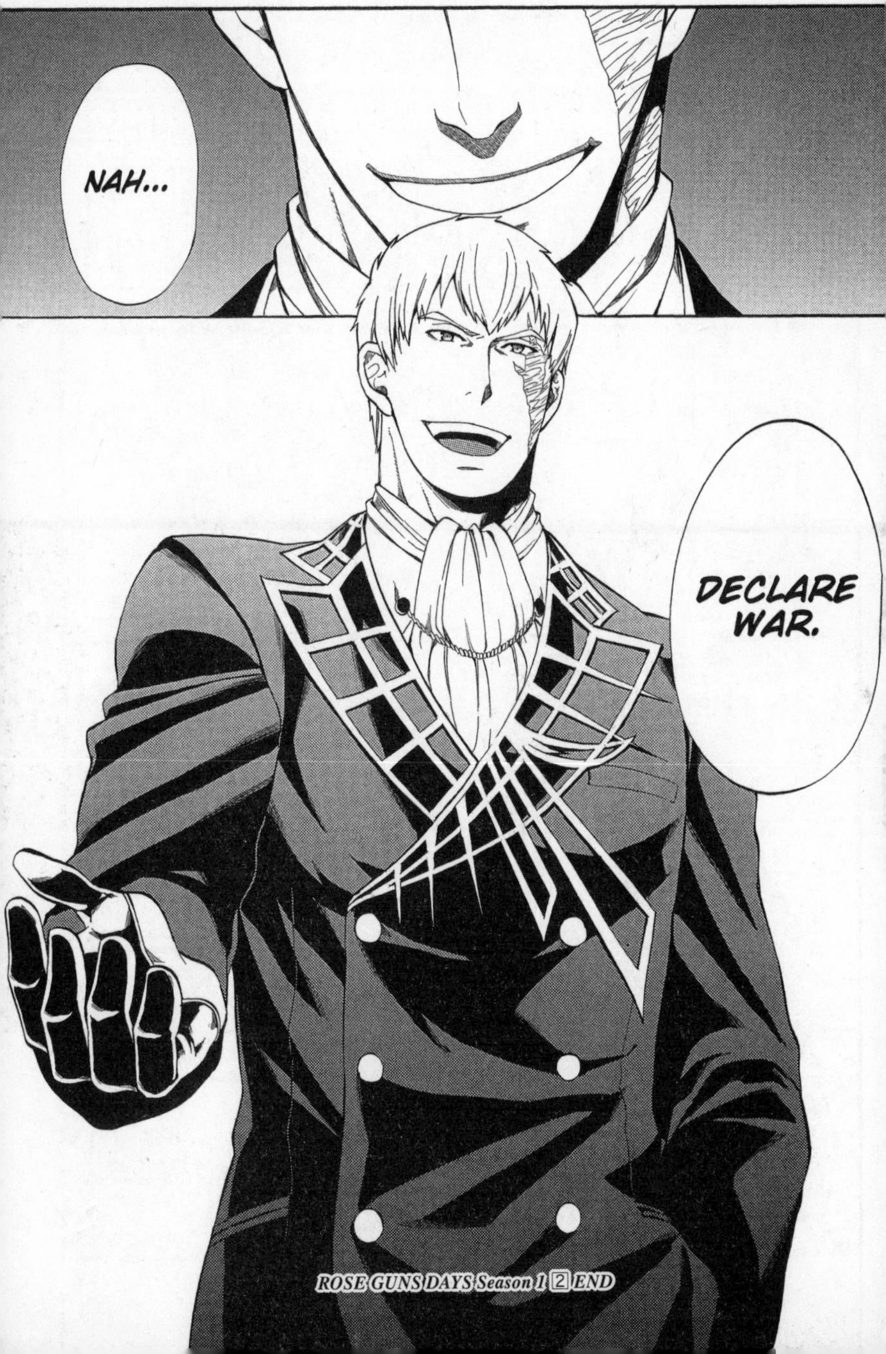
NAH...
DECLARE WAR.
ROSE GUNS DAYS Season 1 2 END

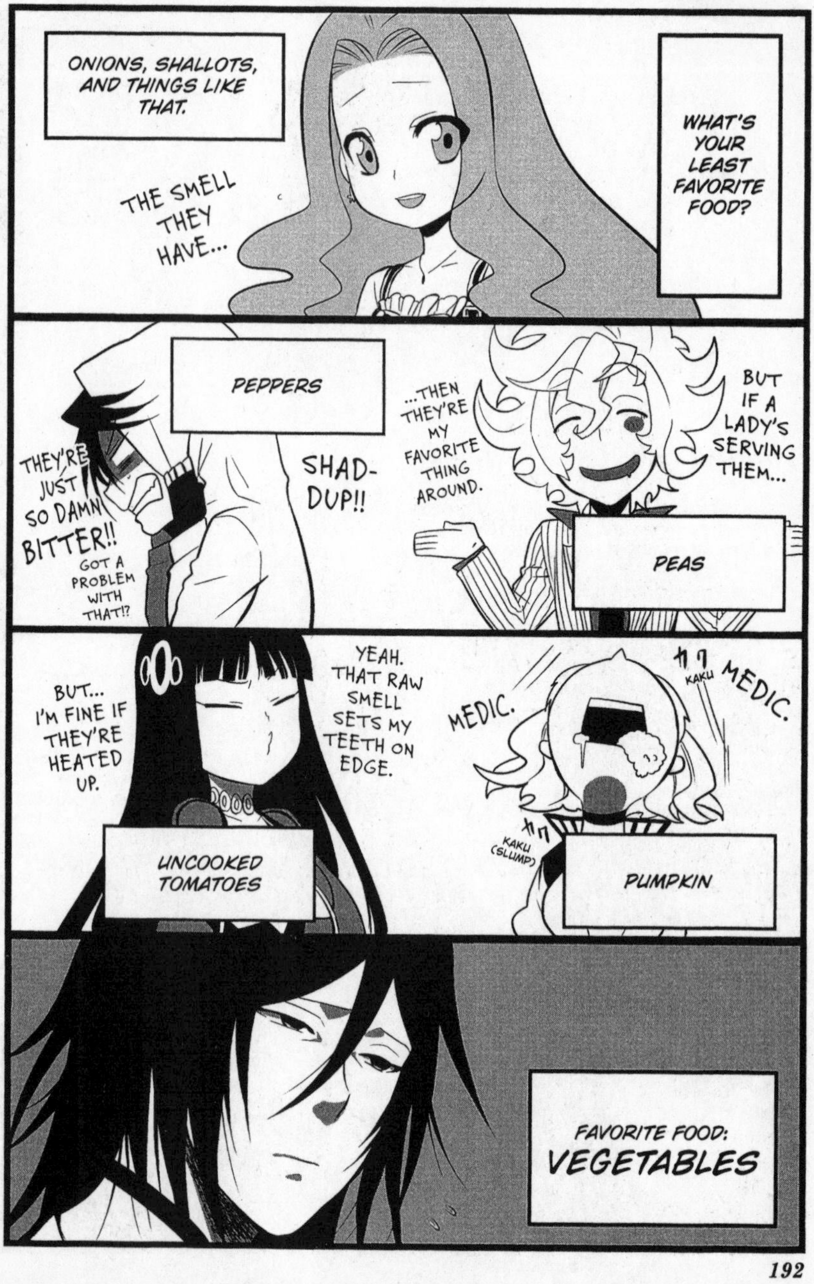
WHAT'S YOUR LEAST FAVORITE FOOD?
ONIONS, SHALLOTS, AND THINGS LIKE THAT.
THE SMELL THEY HAVE...
BUT IF A LADY'S SERVING THEM...
...THEN THEY'RE MY FAVORITE THING AROUND.
PEAS
SHAD-DUP!!
PEPPERS
THEY'RE JUST SO DAMN BITTER!!
GOT A PROBLEM WITH THAT!?
MEDIC.
カク KAKU
MEDIC.
カク KAKU (SLUMP)
PUMPKIN
YEAH. THAT RAW SMELL SETS MY TEETH ON EDGE.
BUT... I'M FINE IF THEY'RE HEATED UP.
UNCOOKED TOMATOES
FAVORITE FOOD:
VEGETABLES

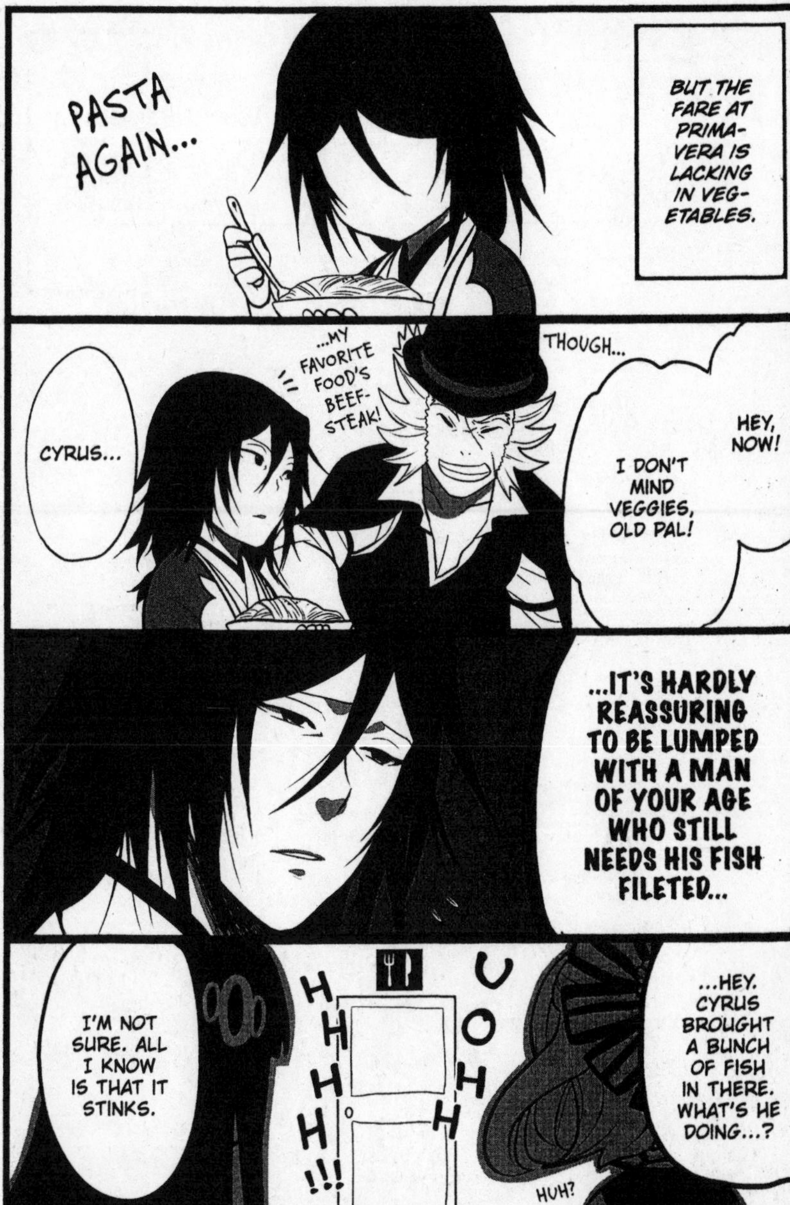

BUT THE FARE AT PRIMAVERA IS LACKING IN VEGETABLES.
PASTA AGAIN...
HEY, NOW!
I DON'T MIND VEGGIES, OLD PAL!
...MY FAVORITE FOOD'S BEEFSTEAK!
CYRUS...
THOUGH...
...IT'S HARDLY REASSURING TO BE LUMPED WITH A MAN OF YOUR AGE WHO STILL NEEDS HIS FISH FILETED...
...HEY. CYRUS BROUGHT A BUNCH OF FISH IN THERE. WHAT'S HE DOING...?
HUH?
UOHHHHHHH!!!
I'M NOT SURE. ALL I KNOW IS THAT IT STINKS.

ROSE GUNS DAYS SEASON 1 ②

RYUKISHI07
SOICHIRO

Translation: Caleb D. Cook • Lettering: Lys Blakeslee

ROSE GUNS DAYS Season 1 vol. 2
© RYUKISHI07 / 07th Expansion
© 2013 Soichiro / SQUARE ENIX CO., LTD.
First published in Japan in 2013 by SQUARE ENIX CO., LTD.
English translation rights arranged with SQUARE ENIX CO., LTD.
and Hachette Book Group through Tuttle-Mori Agency, Inc.

Translation © 2015 by SQUARE ENIX CO., LTD.

Yen Press
Hachette Book Group
1290 Avenue of the Americas
New York, NY 10104

www.hachettebookgroup.com
www.yenpress.com

Yen Press is an imprint of Hachette Book Group, Inc.
The Yen Press name and logo are trademarks of Hachette Book Group, Inc.

The publisher is not responsible for websites (or their content)
that are not owned by the publisher.

First Yen Press Edition: December 2015

ISBN: 978-0-316-35136-2

10 9 8 7 6 5 4 3 2 1

BVG

Printed in the United States of America